When Ideas Matter

How do ideas shape government decision-making? Comparativist scholarship conventionally gives unbridled primacy to external, material interests—chiefly votes and rents—as proximately shaping political behavior. These logics tend to explicate elite decision-making around elections and pork barrel politics but fall short in explaining political conduct during credibility crises, such as democratic governments facing anti-corruption movements. In these instances, Baloch shows, elite ideas, for example concepts of the nation or technical diagnoses of socioeconomic development, dominate policymaking. Scholars leverage these arguments in the fields of international relations, American politics, and the political economy of development. But an account of ideas activating or constraining executive action in developing democracies, where material pressures are high, is found wanting. Resting on fresh archival research and over 120 original elite interviews, *When Ideas Matter* traces where ideas come from, how they are chosen, and when they are most salient for explaining political behavior in India and similar contexts.

Bilal A. Baloch is a political scientist and visiting scholar at the Center for the Advanced Study of India (CASI), University of Pennsylvania, where he taught at the Lauder Institute, Wharton School of Business. His research interests cover the political economy of government decision-making and intellectual history with a focus on South Asia and the Middle East and North Africa. He studied at the London School of Economics, The Fletcher School, and the University of Oxford, where he received his doctorate in politics. Bilal is also co-founder of GlobalWonks, a software company that uses artificial intelligence to deliver expert insights to organizations worldwide. A London native, he now lives in Washington, D.C.

SOUTH ASIA IN THE SOCIAL SCIENCES

South Asia has become a laboratory for devising new institutions and practices of modern social life. Forms of capitalist enterprise, providing welfare and social services, the public role of religion, the management of ethnic conflict, popular culture and mass democracy in the countries of the region have shown a marked divergence from known patterns in other parts of the world. South Asia is now being studied for its relevance to the general theoretical understanding of modernity itself.

South Asia in the Social Sciences will feature books that offer innovative research on contemporary South Asia. It will focus on the place of the region in the various global disciplines of the social sciences and highlight research that uses unconventional sources of information and novel research methods. While recognising that most current research is focused on the larger countries, the series will attempt to showcase research on the smaller countries of the region.

General Editor
Partha Chatterjee
Columbia University

Editorial Board
Pranab Bardhan
University of California at Berkeley

Stuart Corbridge
Durham University

Satish Deshpande
University of Delhi

Christophe Jaffrelot
Centre d'etudes et de recherches internationales, Paris

Nivedita Menon
Jawaharlal Nehru University

Other books in the series:

Government as Practice: Democratic Left in a Transforming India
Dwaipayan Bhattacharyya

Courting the People: Public Interest Litigation in Post-Emergency India
Anuj Bhuwania

Development after Statism: Industrial Firms and the Political Economy of South Asia
Adnan Naseemullah

When Ideas Matter

Democracy and Corruption in India

Bilal A. Baloch

CAMBRIDGE
UNIVERSITY PRESS

CAMBRIDGE
UNIVERSITY PRESS

University Printing House, Cambridge CB2 8BS, United Kingdom

One Liberty Plaza, 20th Floor, New York, NY 10006, USA

477 Williamstown Road, Port Melbourne, VIC 3207, Australia

314–321, 3rd Floor, Plot 3, Splendor Forum, Jasola District Centre, New Delhi–110025, India

103 Penang Road, #05–06/07, Visioncrest Commercial, Singapore 238467

Cambridge University Press is part of the University of Cambridge.

It furthers the University's mission by disseminating knowledge in the pursuit of
education, learning and research at the highest international levels of excellence.

www.cambridge.org
Information on this title: www.cambridge.org/9781316519837

First published 2021
Reprint 2022

Printed in India by Thomson Press India Ltd.

A catalogue record for this publication is available from the British Library

ISBN 978-1-316-51983-7 Hardback

For my untiring parents,
Hassina Baloch and Mohammed Bux Baloch

Contents

Tables

Preface

How do ideas shape government decision-making? Comparativist scholarship conventionally gives unbridled primacy to external, material interests—chiefly votes and rents—as proximately shaping political behavior. These logics tend to explicate elite decision-making around elections and pork barrel politics but fall short in explaining political conduct during credibility crises, such as democratic governments facing anti-corruption movements. In these instances of high political uncertainty, I argue in this book, elite ideas, for example concepts of the nation or technical diagnoses of socioeconomic development, dominate policymaking. Scholars leverage these arguments in the fields of international relations, American politics, and the political economy of development. But an account of ideas activating or constraining executive action in developing democracies, where material pressures are high, is found wanting. The purpose of this book is to trace where ideas come from, how they are chosen, and when they are most salient for explaining political behavior in India and similar contexts including Brazil, Turkey, and Indonesia.

The empirical analysis in this book delves into government response to two movements from contemporary Indian history in order to examine political behavior during the broader credibility crisis. The suppressive response of decision-makers in the Congress Party government to the Jayaprakash Narayan, or JP, protests that brought to a crescendo a credibility crisis in 1975; and the negotiated concessions of elites in the Congress-led United Progressive Alliance coalition to the India Against Corruption (IAC) protests that illustrated the credibility crisis faced by that government in 2012.

The contemporary case relies on over 120 elite interviews from the period including Prime Minister Manmohan Singh, cabinet ministers, party leaders, and senior bureaucrats. The historical case is rooted in deep archival research into over 4,000 documents of official government records and memos, meeting minutes, and private diaries and letters across three national archives (India, US, and UK). I have also conducted a forensic study of daily newspaper reports covering both periods. The project utilizes fresh process-tracing methods and "thick" description to tell a narrative causal story.

Acknowledgments

Writing this book has been an intense process of intellectual and personal growth. The journey has been unwaveringly supported, stimulated, and patiently assisted by many people and places.

My greatest intellectual debt is owed to Vali Nasr. Since my graduate studies began at the Fletcher School of Law and Diplomacy, Tufts University, and onto my doctorate at the University of Oxford, Vali has deftly guided me through the mechanics of policymaking as both teacher and colleague. His enthusiasm for intellectual history and the transnational diffusion of ideas has left a lasting effect on me and can be seen throughout the pages of this book. Vali also provided me an opportunity to join him in a senior advisory capacity at the Johns Hopkins School of Advanced International Studies (SAIS). Here, invigorating discussions with leading academics and policymakers from around the world gave me unique insights into the workings of international politics. Vali and his family's friendship have helped me grow in more ways than he is aware, and I am grateful for his unwavering confidence in me.

I am also fortunate to have studied South Asia, a deeply composite part of our world, at the altar of two of its leading thinkers. Ayesha Jalal was my co-advisor at Fletcher, and it is in her classroom where my interest in the study of the region thrived. Ayesha's broad and exquisite brushstrokes of the subcontinent's history, society, and politics first presented me with its mosaics that I went on to explore during graduate work. As her student and teaching assistant I developed the tools needed to conduct research on contemporary South Asia as well as the pedagogy of the subject. My doctoral dissertation was turned into a book manuscript during my time as a postdoctoral fellow at the Center for the Advanced Study of India (CASI) at the University of Pennsylvania, where I had the privilege of working with Devesh Kapur. Devesh has picked up the moniker *guru-ji* from a globally spread community of students, academics, and policymakers. True to this nickname, he has been a formidable intellectual guide, going far beyond India and always nudging the utilization of a wider world of referencing in research. I am thankful to Devesh for bringing me to CASI and for peeling back layers in the study of decision-making in India that I otherwise would not have discovered.

ACKNOWLEDGMENTS

My regional interest has strengthened during the writing of this book due to my exposure to leading debates and methods in comparative politics, for which I must thank the inimitable Nancy Bermeo. From encouraging me to undertake my doctoral studies at Oxford to being a constant source of academic inspiration, scholarly creativity, and, above all, perspective on work–life balance, I could not have wished for a more ideal dissertation supervisor. Her focus on theory, piercing analysis, as well as prompt reading and parsimonious edits have taught me a lot about advanced research and, for that, I am tremendously appreciative. Relatedly, St. Antony's College, Nuffield College, and the Department of Politics and International Relations at Oxford were the most vibrant incubators to conduct graduate studies. I am thankful to them, among other reasons, for generous research and travel grants including the Norman Chester, Andrew W. Mellon, and College awards.

I would also like to recognize the terrific readers and examiners of my doctoral work and subsequent book manuscript drafts, including Milan Vaishnav, Christophe Jaffrelot, Laurence Whitehead, Faisal Devji, Jody Laporte, Adnan Naseemullah, Adam Auerbach, Amit Ahuja, and Michael Walton. Their patience, questions, and probing refined and deepened my analysis from perspectives that I could not have discovered alone. The manuscript was also strengthened by the diverse set of reviews received from four anonymous referees. To Qudsiya Ahmed of Cambridge University Press, I am grateful for her diligence and patience in seeing the manuscript through to the end, and to Aniruddha De for his meticulous editing and continuous support.

Fieldwork has been a critical component of this book and the most energizing. Conducting over 120 interviews and excavating libraries and national archives in three countries became testing and required bandwidth that was largely enabled by some fascinating and generous people, such as: John Lipsky, David Sloan, Nader Mousavizadeh, Pramath Raj Sinha, and Pratap Bhanu Mehta. They all gave up valuable time and energy to provide comments and feedback on my topic and played an instrumental role in helping me navigate institutions and interviewees that became the bedrock for data collection in my project. In this regard, I must give a special mention to Montek Singh Ahluwalia and the late Isher Judge Ahluwalia, both of whom gave me impartial and critical access to their own reflections, network, and time.

From Washington, Philadelphia, and New York to London, Delhi, and Mumbai, I have had the pleasure of spending time with leading journalists, scholars, activists, and businesspersons, conversations with whom significantly enhanced my understanding of government decision-making in India. This includes Vikram Mehta, Rick Rossow, Rathin Roy, Gaurav Dalmia, Rakesh

ACKNOWLEDGMENTS

Kapoor, Ashley J. Tellis, Madhav Dhar, Subir Gokarn, Reuben Abraham, Samir Saran, Yamini Aiyar, Pavan Ahluwalia, Ramachandra Guha, M. R. Madhavan, Jayati Ghosh, Rajiv Sennar, Vivek Reddy, Srinath Raghavan, Indrani Bagchi, Ajay Shah, Jonah Blank, Josy Joseph, Jagdeep Chhokar, Manu S. Pillai, Gautam Pemmaraju, Surjit Bhalla, Suyash Rai, Ashok Malik, Ajai Shukla, Shivam Vij, E. Sridharan, S. Y. Quraishi, Shamika Ravi, Shankkar Aiyar, and Zorawar Daulet Singh. While at Penn, both at CASI and as a lecturer and regional director at the Lauder Institute, Wharton School of Business, I was surrounded by a stimulating group of scholars, staff, and students working on India whose conversations have left an indelible mark on this book, especially Juliana Di Giustini, Thomas Tartaron, Sanjoy Chakravorty, Meghan Garrity, and Sumitra Badrinathan. Work on this book was made considerably easier with the help of research assistance from Suhail Shersad, Corey Ray, Taylor Leet-Otley, and Maya Camargo-Vemuri. I must also thank friends who helped me traverse not only data sources but life more generally while living in India as a grad student, including Ravi Shankar Chaturvedi, Sajit Gandhi, Aman Ahluwalia, Basharat Peer, Ananya Vajpayi, Dhruva Jaishankar, James Crabtree, and Pankaj Mehta, all of whom went above and beyond to assist. And a special thanks to John Floretta, Jyoti Dastidar, Veena and Vikas Mankar, and Ayesha Sood who facilitated living comforts during my time in the field; I will always cherish the warmth they showed me in their homes. There are many others throughout my travel to and time in India whom I may have missed or who will go unnamed, but whose contribution and impact throughout the research and writing of this book is no less valued.

In terms of the content of my arguments and assertions in this project, I have always been challenged by wonderful peers and teachers. From its inception, this book benefitted immensely from exchanges with a superb group of colleagues including Vinay Sitapati, Christopher Swift, Yelena Biberman, Christopher Clary, Niloufer Siddiqi, Simon Chauchard, Bryon Fong, Bapu Vaitla, Zack Zimbalist, Matt Herbert, Salman Younas, Alex Noyes, Sameer Lalwani, Peter Rough, Frances Brown, Amanda Kerrigan, David Knoll, Annelle Sheline, Adam Ziegfeld, Gilles Verniers, Constantino Xavier, Rahul Verma, and Emmerich Davies. Julian Gruin, Neelanjan Sircar, and Ahsan Butt provided invaluable encouragement and gave their sharp treatment to evaluating important parts of the book. Workshops at Oxford, SAIS, University of California, Berkeley, Harvard University, Tufts, Penn, and New York University and the annual meetings of the American Political Science Association (APSA) and International Studies Association (ISA) delivered prized feedback and direction. More broadly, meaningful discussions with and direction from several academics and practitioners have inspired my thinking and the concepts within this project over the last decade, tracing back to undergraduate classrooms at the London School of Economics, including: John Worrall, Amartya Sen, Sugata Bose, Bryan Hehir, David Kilcullen, Partha Chatterjee, Walter Andersen, Ainslie Embree, Riordan Roett, Emirhan Yorulmazlar, Foad Dizadji-Bahmani, Bengt Autzen, Matthew Nelson, Brett O'Brien, Emma Sky, Jean-Louis Tiernan, Rahul Mukherji, Maya Tudor, Ashutosh Varshney, Francisco Gonzalez, and Vipin Narang. At Fletcher, Richard Shultz served as a perpetual source of advice, as did Andrew Hess and the late Stephen Bosworth. I remain in their debt. And finally, as sentimental as it may read, my high school history teacher, Nicholas Clarke, who first instilled in me a passion for learning and this book is in large part a culmination of the academic and life lessons he taught me several years ago.

Of course, my deep appreciation extends to dear friends who unconditionally offer counsel, comfort, and have always been models of progress. Most of all, they have provided good humor during the toughest moments of this book project and its preamble, especially Mikesh Vora, Nick Strutt, Thomas Granado, Torbjorn Larssen, Kartik Misra, Brooke Smith, Tayyeb Shah, Shamila Chaudhry, Meshal Lakhani, Min Ma, Jennifer Nanni, Fatema Dada, Katie Neff, Dhiraj Mangal, Aditya Gokal, Seeta Haria, Richa Bhalla, Alex Dresner, Siddharth Kapoor, Azhar Yaqub-Khan, Jake Brockman, Julian Ciampa, Cenk Sidar, Noor Shah, Anne Wingate, Matt McNabb, Sasha Kapadia, Ida Norheim Hagtun, Alex Leipziger, Ezra Steinhart, Amir Saleem, Rabeh Ghadban, Anna Levine, and Jo Murkens. They, and many other friends, have smoothed my journey to the conclusion of this project and I hope I can now be a more present friend to them all.

Finally, a special thanks to my family. They have always ensured the emotional and moral backing I need for any pursuit—even if it has come under their own constraints. I am grateful to the support of my parents, Hassina Baloch and Mohammad Bux Baloch, to whom I dedicate this book, as well as that of my sisters, Mahreen Rashdi and Shahzeen Shah, their respective spouses, Irfan Rashdi and Faisal Shah, and my sister-in-law Hayfa Matar. And my niece, Zuleika, and nephews, Aaryan, Zaviyar, Hamza, Ziyad, and Zacharia, for their wit and wisdom. My gratitude extends to the family I have gained through marriage, Kevin Kingfield, Patricia Lopiano, and Michael Kingfield, who have, true to form, offered encouragement, curiosity, and attentiveness throughout this project. My daughter, Zahara Hassina Kingfield-Baloch, who has enriched my life in more ways than she will ever know, was born during the final stretch of writing and has been the ultimate source of happiness throughout it. I must, however, pause here to mention my older brother, Tariq Baloch.

In ninth grade, my final English exam asked students to write about an inspirational figure. While friends plucked footballers, musicians, and world leaders from their imagination, I wrote about my brother. This episode has since been a point of humor and awkwardness for us both in its re-telling. However, there is no doubt he hacked down the jungle in order to clear my path through it, and has been my head cheerleader ever since I can remember. I hope this book goes some way to repaying his endless faith in me.

Finally, and above all, I want to thank my wife, Jacqueline Kingfield. Without her, I would not have embarked on doctoral work and certainly would not have had the stamina to finish this book. Her work as a diplomat has allowed me to enjoy the many splendors of our world, warts and all, while researching and writing from San Juan, Costa Rica, along the Rio Grande Valley on the US–Mexico border, the high altitudes of Quito, Ecuador, the familiar corridors of Washington, all the way to Hyderabad, India, and, most recently, Abu Dhabi, UAE. She has supported me with her indefatigable optimism, deep intellectual input into innumerable drafts, and love throughout and, it is to her, that my greatest debt is owed. Many people have helped me get to this point, countless others no doubt missed. They will never walk alone. All errors, invariably, remain my own.

Washington, D.C.
October 1, 2020

Abbreviations

AAP	Aam Aadmi Party
ABVP	Akhil Bharatiya Vidyarthi Parishad
AIADMK	All India Anna Dravida Munnetra Kazhagam
AICC	All India Congress Committee
FBL	All India Forward Bloc
AIMIM	All India Majlis-e-Ittehadul Muslimeen
TMC	All India Trinamool Congress
ADR	Association for Democratic Reforms
BSP	Bahujan Samaj Party
BJS	Bharatiya Jana Sangh
BJP	Bharatiya Janata Party
BLD	Bharatiya Lok Dal
BJD	Biju Janata Dal
CBI	Central Bureau of Investigation
CIC	Central Information Commission
CVC	Central Vigilance Commission
CPA	Centre for Policy Alternatives
CEC	Chief Election Commissioner
CMP	Common Minimum Programme
CWG	Commonwealth Games
CPI	Communist Party of India
CPI(M)	Communist Party of India (Marxist)
CAG	Comptroller and Auditor General
CII	Confederation of Indian Industry
CSP	Congress Socialist Party
CWC	Congress Working Committee
CID	Crime Investigation Department
DTC	Delhi Transport Corporation
DIG	Deputy Inspector General
DMK	Dravida Munnetra Kazhagam
DSE	Delhi School of Economics

ABBREVIATIONS

FICCI	Federation of Indian Chambers of Commerce and Industry
FIR	first information report
GOM	Group of Ministers
IAC	India Against Corruption
IAS	Indian Administrative Service
INC	Indian National Congress
IUML	Indian Union Muslim League
IB	Intelligence Bureau
IMF	International Monetary Fund
JKNC	Jammu and Kashmir National Conference
JD(S)	Janata Dal (Secular)
JNU	Jawaharlal Nehru University
JPM	Jayaprakash Narayan Movement
JMM	Jharkhand Mukti Morcha
JVM	Jharkhand Vikas Morcha
MISA	Maintenance of Internal Security Act
MKSS	Mazdoor Kisan Shakti Sangathan
MRTP	Monopolies and Restrictive Trade Practices Act
NAC	National Advisory Council
NCPRI	National Campaign for People's Right to Information
NCC	National Coordination Committee
NDA	National Democratic Alliance
NIC	National Innovation Council
NREGA	National Rural Employment Guarantee Act
NCP	Nationalist Congress Party
NMML	Nehru Memorial Museum and Library
ORF	Observer Research Foundation
PCC	Pradesh Congress Committee
PSP	Praja Socialist Party
PMEAC	Prime Minister's Economic Advisory Council
PMH	Prime Minister's House
PMO	Prime Minister's Office
PPP	public–private partnership
RJD	Rashtriya Janata Dal
RSS	Rashtriya Swayamsevak Sangh
RBI	Reserve Bank of India
RSP	Revolutionary Socialist Party
RTE	Right to Education

ABBREVIATIONS

RTI	Right to Information
SP	Samajwadi Party
SCR	*Shah Commission Report*
TMC	Trinamool Congress
TRS	Telangana Rashtra Samithi
TRAI	Telecom Regulatory Authority of India
UN	United Nations
UPA	United Progressive Alliance

1

Introduction

Prologue

A phone rang around 9 p.m. in New York City's Upper East Side neighborhood.

"Namaste, is guru-ji there?" enquired a quiet, measured voice.

"Father, I believe India's next Prime Minister is on the line for you," came the instinctive reply. There had been rumors, after all.

"I have been expecting your call, Manmohan." The elderly voice of a teacher or guru, a fellow technocrat who had dependably served Mrs. Indira Gandhi 30 years earlier, came calmingly through the phone in Delhi.

"What is your counsel, guru-ji? This game is not for me. We are not supposed to be politicians. I'm an economist."

There was a pause. And then a response. "The first thing you must do, Manmohan, is sit down and write your resignation letter. Place it in your pocket and take it into work every single day. You have no idea the compromises you will have to make and the battles you will have to fight."

May 13, 2004, was a momentous day for the Indian National Congress. Against the predictions of pollsters, the party rose to power at the federal level, or center, in a coalition government. It was the return of India's "Grand Old Party" after eight years of political exile on the opposition benches. Just a week later, a different coalition was born, this time unprecedented in the history of Indian politics. On May 22, 2004, India's technocrat prime minister, Dr. Manmohan Singh, walked into Parliament's Ashoka Hall for his swearing-in ceremony. After taking his oath, he approached Mrs. Sonia Gandhi and gave a slight bow of respect. Although Mrs. Gandhi's ability to build a left-leaning coalition, premised on constructing a government for the "common man" (*aam aadmi*), had won Congress the highest office in India, it would be the former finance minister and chief architect of the 1991 neoliberal reforms, Dr. Singh, who had been anointed by the Gandhi family to sit in that most coveted seat.

Bringing Ideas Back In

How do ideas shape government decision-making? Comparativist scholarship conventionally gives unbridled primacy to external, material interests—such as votes and rents—as proximately shaping political behavior.[1] These logics tend to explicate elite decision-making around elections and pork barrel politics but fall short in explaining political conduct during credibility crises, such as democratic governments facing anti-corruption movements. In these instances of high political uncertainty, I argue in this book, elite ideas, for example concepts of the nation or technical diagnoses of socioeconomic development, dominate policymaking. Scholars leverage these arguments in the fields of international relations, American politics, and the political economy of development. But an account of ideas activating or constraining executive action in developing democracies, where material pressures are high, is found wanting.[2] The purpose of this book is to trace where ideas come from, how they are chosen, and, above all, when they can be the most salient for political behavior in developing democracies. The study focuses on India, with similar settings, including Brazil, Turkey, and Indonesia, among others, explored in the concluding section.

In most developing democracies, state institutions are not neutral arenas, but rather reflect government decision-makers' preferences and power. Rather than consider Indian politics as a contest among competing figures with clear and stable interests who develop strategies to pursue those objective interests, this book develops a vision of Indian politics as a struggle for power and control among decision-making elites who are motivated by a myriad of ideas. Fundamentally, this requires us to understand decision-making elites, and the subset of political leaders specifically, and how they develop and deploy their preferences to structure institutions. Therefore, we will consider the questions explored in this book through a constructivist approach in which advances in historical institutionalist studies allow theorization of the interactions between ideas, human agents, and political and state structures. After all, when actors interpret their interests and preferences using an ideational framework, they are also deeply conscious of power. Elites in this book are denoted as decision-makers within the executive arena, chiefly the prime minister, and include the cabinet and other offices, party officials, and institutions that interact regularly with the executive and maintain key political economy powers. The specific set of ideas identified and reduced in this book revolve around concepts of the nation as well as technical ideas around social and economic development.

Research Puzzle

The puzzle animating this book began to take shape in the summer of 2012. That July, I witnessed thousands of citizens from across India take to the streets in her capital, New Delhi. The Congress-led United Progressive Alliance (UPA) coalition government of Prime Minister Manmohan Singh faced its biggest civic challenge in an anti-corruption movement led by supporters of the activist Anna Hazare, a veteran social justice campaigner who had undertaken a hunger strike in New Delhi. The India Against Corruption (IAC) movement reached a crescendo due to deteriorating economic conditions and a sequence of high-profile corruption scandals that implicated senior officials all the way up to the prime minister. The government found itself in the midst of a credibility crisis. Fast forward to the smoldering summer months of 2013, when the cries of citizens across developing world democracies—from Chile, Brazil, and Mexico to Turkey and Indonesia—raised the global volume of movements calling for better central governance through the eradication of corruption, which would reverberate throughout that decade. Each government faced mounting pressure, and several closed in on re-election campaigns. Some, such as in Turkey, arbitrarily crushed the anti-corruption groundswell, while others, such as Brazil, were compelled into negotiated concessions. These fascinating trends piqued my interest in these movements, the credibility crisis environment in which they swelled, and, more intriguingly, *the determinants of government responses to anti-corruption movements*—the motivating empirical question explored in this book.

A nationwide anti-corruption movement creates a credibility crisis environment where political uncertainty obfuscates state elites' understanding of predictable interests, such as votes and rents. The full range of alternative strategies and their relative costs become narrowed. Such situations are hardly uncommon in matters of political interest, and are especially frequent in the messy political realities of India and plausibly other developing country contexts. Given the volatility of uncertain political situations, decision-makers are unsure about what their objective interests are, let alone how to maximize the utility of these interests. This book argues that in such distinctive moments, or critical junctures that disrupt the existing social, political, and economic balance, the waters of statistical prediction are muddied. *Instead, decision-makers seek to reconstitute interests, and establish narratives regarding the causation behind the crisis and functions of the respective anti-corruption movements.* In this scenario, ideas serve as "weapons" between decision-making elites in the struggle to diagnose the overall crisis, and re-establish credibility to reduce uncertainty.[3]

Corrupt State Narrative and Credibility Crisis

The empirical research in this book examines the determinants of government behavior during a credibility crisis in India as denoted by the rise of a nationwide anti-corruption movement. In the cases I look at, corruption implicating ministers all the way up to and including the highest levels of government has been exposed in the context of deteriorating economic conditions. Government credibility has plummeted, and uncertainty engulfs the political arena as social movements narrating the crisis using the language of anti-corruption come to the fore to challenge the national government—the *corrupt state narrative*. It is more important today than ever before that social scientists, policymakers, and businesspersons study these movements, and responses to them, for theoretical and empirical reasons.

First, national-level collective action in developing as well as developed democracies has recently amplified and is bound to be a fixture of future citizen contestation, given the global penetration of technology as a mobilization tool and the enlargement of political society in distinct countries that demand increased legitimation of the state.[4] Second, such movements are an essential part of democratic politics, specifically the evolution of modern political institutions. In late-nineteenth-century United States, for example, anti-corruption movements allowed the passage of important legislation such as the Pendleton Act of 1883, which established the principle of merit-based recruitment into the federal bureaucracy.[5] Contemporary developing democracies such as India are at a similar critical juncture in their social and economic development, and issues such as government corruption and malfeasance are no longer an acceptable norm to an increasingly middle-class citizenry.[6]

Such movements coalesce around the language of anti-corruption but are not, in their organizational form, a monolith. Upon inspection, they can often appear as a set of contradictions due to the diverse motivations and groupings within them as well as the fluid tactics espoused by their activists and leaders. In both cases I consider, the movement simultaneously denotes a group of civic activists and reformers who represent the vanguard of the corrupt state narrative and many mobilizers who use the collective action to further their own social and political ideals. For example, the inclusion of a semi-loyal opposition together with the mobilizational depth and zeal of the religious nationalist Rashtriya Swayamsevak Sangh (RSS) in both the Jayaprakash Narayan (JP) and the IAC movements delegitimized the entire collective action in the eyes of some decision-makers. This tension can be reconciled by envisioning anti-corruption agitation not as a singular, unified movement, but rather as a series of shifting, dynamic, loose coalitions where corruption becomes a powerful and overarching rallying call. By neglecting the real divisions among movement mobilizers, we fail to explore the mechanics of the associations they build, the reforms they seek, and the steep evolution of these movements. By focusing on these factors, we can investigate the many ways in which specific sets of government decision-makers can interface with the fluid configurations of anti-corruption movements and their causes. Of course, the bandwagoning of mutually referencing groups is a common occurrence in nationally mobilized social movements around the world.[7] This approach allows the broader applicability of my argument, given that there are several movements around the world that advance their goals through the corrupt state narrative, especially in contexts such as India, where there are plausibly very distinct ideas about what constitutes good governance and the corrupt elite. I look at some of these cases in the concluding chapter. However, as fascinating as these movements are on their own, this project focuses squarely on the government's response to the movement within the larger contours of a credibility crisis.

The empirical analysis in this book delves into government response to two movements from contemporary Indian history. Both movements' aims are defined through the language of anti-corruption and have been key to India's contemporary political development: the Jayaprakash Narayan movement (JPM) in 1975 and the IAC movement in 2012. The corrupt state narrative, publicly salient in recent years, is one that emerged in India leading to the 1975 Emergency and soared during it. It has been fueled by both the reality and the perception of an Indian state beholden to corrupt deals with businesses and corporates, which has, in turn, frequently shaped the behavior of state actors, the electorate, and civil society. However, the aforementioned movements and those coalitions similar to them around the world and across much of history cannot be examined in isolation. They represent the culmination of a series of domestic and international pressures that, together with the crescendo of collective action on the street, represent a credibility crisis for the incumbent political elites. So, the entire crisis must be interrogated if we are to understand political actors' response.

Cases and Unit of Analysis

This research project gives primacy to causal process tracing and the use of case studies. The focus here is on providing intensive analysis of two cases, compared across time, at the national level in India. While the project primarily remains a comparative study of two governments in one country, its central concepts resonate with government responses to anti-corruption movements in other parts of the world. Hence, the concluding chapter illustrates contingent generalizability of the core argument cross-nationally in several other developing democracies.[8]

Case selection employs a most-similar, different-outcome logic. The political episodes encompass the Congress Party government's institutionalization of an internal Emergency in the face of the JPM (1974–75) and the Congress-led UPA government's negotiated response in the face of the IAC (2011–12). Although this case selection allows control for partisanship, it is important to note that the cases follow sequentially. In this context, the use of the internal Emergency policy mechanism, as instituted under Prime Minister Indira Gandhi, was less likely under Prime Minister Manmohan Singh in 2012. The Emergency period (1975–77) left an indelible mark on the country's post-Independence history as an aberration on her democratic development. Some have even called it a dictatorship.[9] As we will see in Chapter 3, freedom of the press, political opposition, and assembly, among other civil liberties, were crushed during this period using Emergency laws. Congress governments since this time have, at least publicly, remained highly selective and often revisionist in their reflections of government suppression under Gandhi.[10] Nevertheless, and starkly given this historical backdrop, many other forms of, and justifications for, government suppression have continued to take shape in India at the center and state-levels since the early 1970s and, as the evidence in the empirical chapters show, were strongly considered and in a few instances carried out by some decision-makers in the UPA in 2011–12.[11] I analytically evaluate and reconcile these factors of continuity and change—which are core to any ideational argument—in the next chapter, as well as offering a detailed empirical study of the cases.

The first chapter of each case deploys case-specific knowledge of the formal and informal institutional structures within each government. Most notably the balancing of executive power and political competition, the broader economic and social conditions and challenges, and the substantive issues (government corruption, the emergence of national collective action against it, and the government's tactical response) at hand. Given the causal interaction between structure and agency in my argument, I supplement this approach with a fresh ideational process-tracing method.[12]

The second part of my analysis seeks to measure, illustrate, and trace decision-makers' ideas. The amorphous characteristics of ideational mechanisms make them especially difficult to study compared to materially driven causal processes that dominate rival explanations. In this study, decision-making elites analyze the anti-corruption movements and form responses through their cognitive frames around social and economic development as well as their concepts of the nation. Here, I follow three steps when examining data pertaining to these ideas in the second chapter of each case:

1. Identify the decision-makers' ideational commitments.
2. Establish that the relevant ideas were applied to the choice being explained.
3. Locate an ideational source external to the situation being explained.

This approach begins by expanding the empirical scope of the study in terms of its temporal range to trace the ancestry of ideas. The key here is to establish where cognitive frameworks come from. I therefore take seriously decision-making elites' statements and behaviors at critical moments as directly related to the outcomes I trace; that is, their response at the time of and around the anti-corruption movement. I also consider several sequences of indirectly related events and the movement of decision-makers, or idea carriers, across institutional settings over an extended period, including prior to entering authoritative positions in government. Beyond establishing the exogeneity of ideas and their subsequent diffusion, I look to reduce their multicollinearity against objective, material interests to illustrate causal weight and divergent preferences. This is where proxy measures, for example election results and specific policies that align with the interests of large capital domestically and/or international pressures, examined against decision-makers' ideas can temper material incentives alone. Over time, traced patterns of ideas help to undermine the sufficiency of purely instrumental causal narratives, and to locate and scrutinize the availability of the relevant ideas that are necessary for the outcome to take shape. Of course, the aforementioned methodological and data-gathering tools come with both advantages and disadvantages.[13] Ultimately, however, I examine diverse, complex, and sometimes conflicting claims, and have judged the credibility, plausibility, and trustworthiness of these claims according to the best practices of empirical verification. The test lies in producing a tightly specified theory with thickly detailed causal observations that substantially enhances the discriminating power of my argument.

The contemporary case utilizes over 120 original elite interviews from the period of study, including Prime Minister Manmohan Singh, senior members of the party, cabinet ministers, senior bureaucrats, and other senior officials in apex institutions of policymaking power, such as the Planning Commission and the National Advisory Council (NAC), in addition to the Election Commission, the Comptroller Auditor General's (CAG) office, the judiciary, and opposition groups, as well as a close study of daily newspaper reportage.[14] In addition, I use assessments garnered from seven focus groups conducted with members from a cross-section of civil society, businesses, and the bureaucracy. The historical case rests on over 4,000 documents encompassing a broad set of decision-makers' private letters, correspondence, and speeches collected from three national archives (India, the United States [US], and the United Kingdom [UK]) that are yet to be examined collectively in the context of the subject of this book, as well as a forensic study of newspaper reports, party manifestos, memoirs, and autobiographies. Given that the evidence presented here relies heavily on the private and public statements, accounts, and decisions of state elites, and how they develop and deploy their preferences to structure institutions, the analysis focusses on individual leaders and their networks.

I denote government response as the behavior of decision-makers within the executive arena, which encompasses the cabinet and other offices under the control of the governing parties. Where I rest on evidence from the parliamentary or extra-parliamentary (for example, civil society actors or consultants in government) arena, I do so in terms of their interaction with the executive. In the main, this is because the executive branch has important agenda-setting powers in parliamentary democracies, and India is no exception. These powers privilege the cabinet vis-à-vis parliament, and they render parliamentary control of cabinet members onerous. Executive power over parliament is plausibly strengthened during a credibility crisis when there is less space for deliberation and decision-making requires urgency. Moreover, and as we see across democracies today, executive overreach is a hallmark of populist regimes. The political executive and parliament both consisted of a Congress majority under Prime Minister Indira Gandhi in 1975. In the case of the UPA in 2012, more than two distinct parties comprised the political executive and parliament as part of the coalition government. I measure government response in terms of the number of imprisonments, the physical harm imposed on movement participants, leaders, and sympathizers such as the press or academics, and the death count. For example, in its suppressive response to the JPM, the Congress government instituted Emergency rule in June 1975, under which 110,806 citizens were arrested and a black-out of selected newspapers was introduced, among other mechanisms of suspending civil liberties.[15] JPM activists, leaders, and supporters were the first and most prominent dissenters to be targeted. In contrast, under the UPA's response in 2012, a small number of IAC demonstrators were temporarily detained, while the government was embroiled in negotiating with movement leaders. My argument reconciles this variation within cases and between controlled comparisons.

Argument

In this book, I outline two ways in which ideas play a role in Indian politics. The first is through activating government populism and the second is through an ideational checks and balances mechanism. Below, I detail specific dynamics in the causal interaction between power and ideas in each case.

The Congress Party won a landslide election in 1971 on a populist wave, which gave it a two-thirds majority in the national assembly and complete control of the cabinet and executive. State elites—chief among them Prime Minister Indira Gandhi—harnessed state power to reshape society, a process that began by centralizing executive power to monopolize decision-making within a majority government. This political and institutional setting serviced the structural conditions that allowed the executive to proclaim an Emergency and to act strongly against the JPM. On the other hand, the UPA government, led by the Congress since coming to power in 2004 and then again in 2009, was made up of a coalition of parties—a system firmly entrenched since the fragmentation of Indian politics from 1989. Furthermore, and more proximately to the structural drivers of the narrative in this book, UPA state elites orbited a division of policymaking power at the executive level between Prime Minister Manmohan Singh and the Congress Party president, Sonia Gandhi. Indeed, both dominant and subordinate decision-makers share a set of *rules of the game* that specify, often tacitly, the precise forms of struggle that are legitimate in each government.

In the Congress government led by Indira Gandhi, contestation among decision-makers was low and cooperation high, and this government often displayed autonomous and arbitrary policy action. In contrast, in the UPA, there was high contestation among decision-makers and often low cooperation on public policy action, thus resulting in constrained action within a polycentric executive arena. This intensified fissures between decision-makers, meaning that the government could not act arbitrarily in dealing with the IAC movement at the cost of inviting further pressure upon a precarious government. Additionally, unlike the Congress government in the lead-up to the 1975 suppression of the JPM, the UPA coalition in 2012 included decision-making elites, chiefly technocrats, with divergent ideas dispersed in authoritative positions of power.

In the majority Congress government, Prime Minister Indira Gandhi held de facto presidential powers and was the main custodian of the national interest, which she proclaimed was incumbent upon her and the Congress to define. The government's perspectives, led mainly by Gandhi, were enshrined within her Congress (R) faction's populism that had been concretizing in the lead-up to, and after, the unified Congress's split in 1969. This populism interlaced around the Congress's concepts of the nation—anchored in secularism, with a preference during this period for socialism and focus on minority rights. The prime minister, along with her close advisers, viewed the JPM as mobilized through right-wing religious nationalist groups such as the RSS and backed by opposition parties. The Gandhi-led Congress Party's unchecked, homogenous ideology cognitively locked the executive into building solidarity within the government—especially in a crisis environment where government credibility was low and had to therefore be re-established—and suppress ideological "others" within the JPM and its sympathizers. Hence, Prime Minister Gandhi could take unitary action to suppress the anti-corruption movement, wherein 110,806 citizens were detained and civil liberties crushed.

In contrast, no such unified cognitive lock emerged in the UPA government. Here, not only party politicians as in the historical case, but bureaucrats, activists, and technocrats also occupied authoritative positions of power and between them held different ideational frameworks that led them to view the IAC collective action, and the sources of government corruption, divergently. Decision-makers possess separate incentive structures and preferences based on their distinct professional and personal backgrounds. Proponents of how to approach policy challenges in the UPA included: pro-liberalization technocrats (market liberals) who entered government in the 1980s and 1990s and then took up authoritative positions of power during the UPA government as part of Manmohan Singh's Prime Minister's Office (PMO), cabinet, and Planning Commission; and the pro-redistribution technocrats and activists (social reformists) of the rights-based movements of the 1990s and early 2000s who also took up authoritative positions of power during the UPA principally as part of the de facto parallel cabinet under Sonia Gandhi, the NAC. In the main, market liberal and social reformist elites contested for influence over policy design, and in particular the state's role in Indian social and economic life, that for the UPA's tenure in government resulted in a Polanyian double transformation to take shape concurrently.[16] These perspectives, together with those of secular nationalists within the Congress Party, shaped the government's diagnosis of, and strategy toward, the IAC: on one end of the scale, some were more sympathetic toward the IAC and, on the other end, some were more hostile. The interaction between a polycentric executive environment and divergent ideologies among decision-making elites produced an ideas-based checks and balances mechanism upon the arbitrary power of the UPA in the face of anti-corruption collective action, which made the subsequent negotiated response more likely.

How the Book Proceeds

This book is structured as follows. In Chapter 2, I develop my theoretical argument, outlining why the dominant determinants of government decision-making in India, advanced by both scholars and policymakers, do not hold under credibility crisis conditions such as during episodes of nationwide anti-corruption movements. I begin by describing the broad, constructivist analytic framework of my argument. I then explicate and evaluate the primary strands of literature that provide alternative hypotheses for my outcome of interest. These accounts relate decision-making drivers around elections, the predictable politics of budgets and policy formulations, and underspecified regime mechanisms. I then carefully build out my theoretical argument, drawing on a range of insights from political theory as well as social psychology and neuroscience, wherein I illustrate the precise details of how, and under which conditions, ideas shape government response to credibility crises in India.

Chapters 3 and 4 focus on the historical case of the Congress Party government's (1971–75) suppressive response toward the JPM (1974–75). Chapter 3 traces the events that led to the Emergency, specifically the rise of the JPM and credibility crisis faced by the government, and the steps taken by Gandhi and her close advisors to suppress the movement. Chapter 4 focuses on the elite decision-makers' perspectives as they diagnosed the anti-corruption movement. These ideas gave content and shape to Gandhi's populism, substantiated by the Congress's secular nationalism. The party's dominant ideology (that had been concretizing in party conferences, manifestos, meetings, and other media since the 1969 Congress Party split) created a cognitive lock on decision-makers' actions throughout the government's tenure, and ultimately led elites to optimize on building party solidarity during a crisis in which government credibility was low and needed to be re-established—even through suppression.

Chapters 5 and 6 focus on the contemporary case of the Congress-led UPA government's (2004–14) negotiated response toward the IAC (2011–12). Chapter 5 details the specific polycentric institutional environment, alongside the large number of ruling parties in the coalition, which placed structural constraints on the behavior of the executive branch, and traces the episodic engagement between the government and movement. Chapter 6 focuses on decision-makers' divergent perspectives in diagnosing the anti-corruption movement. These distinct ideas are linked to state elites' specific professional and sociological backgrounds, from which three main cognitive frameworks emerge around social and economic development (market liberal/social reformist) and nationalism (secular nationalist). These decision-makers—party politicians, technocrats, and activists—contested for influence over policymaking throughout the UPA and jostled to shape the government's strategy toward the IAC. The ensuing checks and balances among elites produced a negotiated government response.

Chapter 7 presents a summary of the study's findings within which I take a look at India today, and what the mechanisms in my argument tell us about the incumbent Narendra Modi–led Bharatiya Janata Party (BJP) government (2014–present). I then turn to a comparative assessment with other plausible cases where my argument resonates. I specifically consider contexts like India, namely low- to middle-income, stable multi-party developing democracies that have faced nationwide anti-corruption movements in recent years, such as Turkey, Brazil, Indonesia, and Malaysia, among others. I conclude by considering some theoretical and empirical implications of my argument, specifically pertaining to the politics of ideas and the power of leadership in our understanding of democratic Indian politics.

When Ideas Matter makes a fresh contribution to the study of Indian politics by placing the contemporary arc of elite political behavior in much deeper historical, psychological, and sociological context by centralizing the role of ideas.

Notes

1. Politicians distribute electoral seats to malfeasant but wealthy and viable politicians (Milan Vaishnav, *When Crime Pays: Money and Muscle in Indian Politics* [New Haven: Yale University Press, 2017]); institute meaningful reform when threats to bribes for election financing are low (Jennifer Bussell, *Corruption and Reform in India: Public Services in the Digital Age* [New York: Cambridge University Press, 2012]); and instigate violence as a means to hold onto the spoils of office (Steven Wilkinson, *Votes and Violence: Electoral Competition and Ethnic Riots in India* [New York: Cambridge University Press, 2004]).

2. Henry Kissinger, *Diplomacy* (New York: Simon and Schuster, 1994); Doris Kearns Goodwin, *Team of Rivals: The Political Genius of Abraham Lincoln* (New York: Simon and Schuster, 2005); Ole Jacob Sending, *The Politics of Expertise: Competing for Authority in Global Governance* (Ann Arbor: University of Michigan Press, 2015).

3. My framework is significantly shaped by the seminal work of Mark Blyth (*Great Transformations: Economic Ideas and Institutional Change in the Twentieth Century* [New York: Cambridge University Press, 2002]).

4. Lina Dencik and Oliver Leistert, eds., *Critical Perspectives on Social Media and Protest: Between Control and Emancipation* (London: Rowman & Littlefield, 2015); Partha Chatterjee, *The Politics of the Governed: Reflections on Popular Politics in Most of the World* (New York; Columbia University Press, 2004).

5. Francis Fukuyama, "America in Decay," *Foreign Affairs* 93, no. 5 (September 2014): 5–26.

6. Susan Stokes, "Perverse Accountability: A Formal Model of Machine Politics with Evidence from Argentina," *The American Political Science Review* 99, no. 3 (August 2005): 315–25. On the political and economic implications

of India's growing middle class, see Devesh Kapur, Milan Vaishnav, and Neelanjan Sircar "The Importance of Being Middle Class in India," 2017, https://carnegieendowment.org/2017/11/03/importance-of-being-middle-class-in-india-pub-74615 (accessed October 1, 2020).

7. Sidney G. Tarrow, *Power in Movement*, 3rd edn (rev. and updated) (Cambridge; New York: Cambridge University Press, 2011).

8. For similar designs by comparativists working on developing country contexts, see: Melani Cammett, *Compassionate Communalism: Welfare and Sectarianism in Lebanon* (Ithaca: Cornell University Press, 2014); and Steven Wilkinson, *Votes and Violence: Electoral Competition and Ethnic Riots in India* (New York: Cambridge University Press, 2004).

9. Christophe Jaffrelot and Pratinav Anil, *India's First Dictatorship: The Emergency, 1975–77* (London: Hurst & Co., 2020).

10. In recent years, former Congress Party president Sonia Gandhi claimed that it is difficult to predict how Indira Gandhi would view the Emergency period today, but that she believed the former prime minister would not have called for elections in 1977 had she not felt "extremely uncomfortable" with the preceding two years (Rajdeep Sardesai, "Sonia Gandhi to India Today: I'm Not the Right Person to Decide on Rahul's Elevation as Congress Chief", *India Today*, November 21, 2016, http://bit.ly/2ssuzVV [accessed October 1, 2020]).

11. That an Emergency in its 1975 form is politically unviable today is true of non-Congress governments too. However, this does not mean that alternative (and subversive) methods of intolerance do not take shape, as we are witnessing under the current Bharatiya Janata Party (BJP) government in India that has been accused of carrying out or covering suppression with regard to arrests of political opponents, extra-judicial killings, blocking of judicial appointments to bring the institution in line with the government's ideological vector, press censorship, and generally suppressive policies bound up in, and sheltering vigilantes beating and killing in the name of, religious nationalism (among many articles on this subject, see Pratap Bhanu Mehta, "There Is No Emergency," *Indian Express*, November 5, 2016, http://bit.ly/2exBvIT [accessed October 1, 2020]). See the Conclusion chapter for more on the current and future resonance of the book's core arguments in India.

12. Alan Jacobs, "Process Tracing the Effects of Ideas," in *Process Tracing: From Metaphor to Analytic Tool*, ed. Andrew Bennett and Jeffrey T. Checkel, 41–73 (New York: Cambridge University Press, 2015).

13. I have triangulated all interview data with other primary and secondary sources to corroborate the collected information and, where interviews are the only source of information available, I have required at least one other independent

interview source to corroborate that piece of evidence before the claim can be viewed as reliable (P. H. J. Davies, "Spies as Informants: Triangulation and Interpretation of Elite Interview Data in the Study of Intelligence and Security Services," *Politics* 21, no. 1 [2001]: 73–80, 78). The sheer number of interviews in the contemporary case (120+) largely exceeds the number of interview observations in most comparable studies.

14. Following Oisin Tansey, I used both "reputational" as well as "positional" non-probability sampling methods, that is, respondents were based not only on their formal positions but their reputations or informal influence within a particular decision-making grouping in the UPA (Oisin Tansey, "Process Tracing and Elite Interviewing: A Case for Non-Probability Sampling," *PS: Political Science and Politics* 40, no. 4 [October 2007]: 765–72). To protect interviewees from possible negative consequences, most responses have been anonymized based on the interviewee's wishes.

15. Era Sezhiyan, ed., *Shah Commission Report: Lost and Regained* (henceforth *SCR*) (Chennai: Aazhi Publishers, 2010), Third and Final Report, Annexure to Chapter XIX.

16. For more on this discussion of a concurrent Polanyian double transformation in India, see Pratap Bhanu Mehta and Michael Walton, "Ideas, Interests and the Politics of Development Change in India: Capitalism, Inclusion and the State", 30 September 2014, ESID Working Paper No. 36, https://bit.ly/3j4Na00 (accessed October 1, 2020).

2

A Constructivist Approach to Political Behavior in India

In decisive historical moments, political capacity (which includes organization, will, and ideologies) is necessary to enforce or to change a structural situation. Intellectual evaluation of a given situation and ideas about what is to be done are crucial in politics.

—Fernando Henrique Cardoso and Enzo Faletto, 1979

It is a paradox that scholars, whose entire existence is centered on the production and understanding of ideas, should grant ideas so little significance for explaining political life.

—Kathryn Sikkink, 1991

Ideas and Institutional Politics in India

The behavior of decision-making elites during credibility crises in India and other developing democracies should be considered through a constructivist framework. Existing explanations provide inadequate answers to the questions posed by these crises. Contemporary approaches are either over-reliant on external, material interests that shape decision-making, such as the literature on corruption and political economy; or are underspecified, such that empirical correlations may prove consistent with several alternative interpretations of underlying explanatory mechanisms, such as the literature on democracy and authoritarianism. Rather than considering Indian politics as a contest among competing figures with clear and stable objective interests, who then develop strategies to pursue those interests, this chapter develops a vision of Indian politics as a struggle for power and control among decision-making elites who are motivated by myriad ideas. These ideas include elites' conceptualization of the nation and technical diagnoses of social and economic development.

We will consider the questions explored in this book through an analytical framework that incorporates advances in both historical and discursive institutionalism in political science, as well as insights ranging from economic sociology to behavioral psychology and neuroscience. This will allow for the theorization of the interactions between ideas, human agents, and political and state structures.[1] In the main, the introduction of ideas into traditional historical institutionalist approaches attends to who talks to whom, where, and when, and by charting the formal and informal institutional contexts that shape interactive patterns of discursive power, especially at the executive level.[2] This interactive framework facilitates two core propositions for the book's argument.

First, in most developing democracies, state institutions are not neutral decision-making apparatuses, but rather reflect government decision-makers' perspectives and power.[3] As such, state institutions are contestable social settings whose structural logic differs according to the specific sets of ideas competing for policymaking influence.[4] In anticipation of this struggle, decision-making elites build ideational coalitions, or epistemic communities and networks, to support their policy programs.[5] Contestation takes shape through the distribution of ideas among positions of authority across the state as well as through defining the most "legitimate" ideas. After all, ideas have to swim in viable institutional waters. It is important to note that institutions play an interactive role in such ideational contestation, including by structuring political openings for mobilization.[6] These openings provide a pathway to more directly observe individuals and leaders with specific worldviews—whom we will call "idea carriers"—across the state as well as trace their formal and informal policymaking roles and impact.[7] Which ideas "win out," therefore, is not purely about intellectual refinement as it is also about structures—political institutions such as parties, for example, constrain political behavior through the operation of rules, norms, and organizational settings and the articulation of interests.

Second, ideas render interests actionable. Much of Indian politics inherently involves a clash of interests between majorities and minorities, and the outcome hinges on access to executive power and mobilization. Here, dominant and subordinate decision-makers often share a set of "rules of the game" that specify, if tacitly, the legitimate forms of intra-government struggle.[8] At times, however, decision-makers can alter these rules, thereby subsuming both the interests vying for power and diverse perspectives on policy. Therefore, decision-makers do not always behave in direct reference to external interests such as voters or special interest groups, but may do so in reference to and in pursuit of balancing other government decision-makers. In other words, there exists a self-referencing dynamic among decision-makers in the constellation of institutional constraints and competing ideas, and this dynamic can also shape executive action.[9] This is especially the case in pressure cooker crisis environments such as under study here, in which uncertainty is salient and interests are not given, while cogent idea-based preferences are slow to change and therefore prove meaningful to decision-making.[10]

Alternative Explanations

Analyses of government corruption foreground existing approaches to the strategic behavior of decision-makers in contexts rife with a corrupt state narrative.[11] One line of inquiry holds that decision-makers often manipulate policy and provoke consumption to improve government credibility among voters directly preceding elections.[12] This provides decision-makers the opportunity to align rent and ballot interests during electoral business cycles.[13] A compelling prediction of this model that resonates with political behavior in India is that proximity to elections moderates decision-makers' actions.[14] Although this argument has some explanatory value, it does not fully account for the frequency and interrelation of national- and state-level elections and the continuous campaign environment in India, nor the role of regional parties at the center.[15] Likewise, it fails to consider that decision-makers in some governments, namely coalitions, represent diverse constituencies and face distinct policy challenges that make cohesive governing difficult. A primary assumption of these analyses is that, to remain electorally competitive, the pursuit of revenue streams through corrupt practices while in office is of paramount importance to many decision-makers.[16] This logic is widely held within, and often a derivative of, a second set of insights from the political economy of development.

The prevailing models of government behavior in developing democracies assume that "vested interests" such as elite lobbies and other rent-seeking groups have their way with public policy at the expense of citizens. In this model, governments make decisions that do not threaten their material interests.[17] This logic extends to economic considerations of societal outcomes and political systems. These studies argue that the Indian state is a non-autonomous mechanism of rent extraction that has been captured by dominant class coalitions between the state on one hand and either capital or labor on the other.[18] The 1991 liberalization reforms purportedly reinforced this relationship, such that the government–business alliance became hegemonic, and the state was captured by capital classes.[19] Whereas policy reform and the active mobilization of special interest lobbies are often linked, this relationship impedes neither decision-makers from acting against these interests nor the state from simultaneous negotiation with conflicting interests. During the early 1970s, for example, the Congress government increased its regulatory grip over industries to mixed response, and, later, some capital interests suffered while others did not during the Emergency period. Meanwhile, under the UPA (2004–14), the state experienced a kind of Polanyian "double transformation" simultaneously in which the government favored markets and managed political and social consequences by developing a welfare state.

These theories rely on two claims to explain the drivers of government decision-making. First, that elites are rent-seekers and, second, that electoral incentives perpetuate elites' rent-seeking behavior.[20] However, external interests are not the *sine qua non* of political outcomes.[21] This presumption has led to an "over-structuring" of the political game by limiting decision-making pathways in government.[22] Missing is a sufficient account of decision-making elites' ideas and an examination of their perspectives, contestation, and heterogeneity of backgrounds. After all, political actors are reflexive and are open to altering their ideas, deliberating over courses of action, and even changing their minds.[23] Ideas about interests, and therefore interests themselves, may change. Without sufficient consideration of the role of ideas, we cannot understand decision-making elites' interests, nor can we explore the diverse strategies and tools elites pursue to maximize these interests. In short, cognitive frameworks have so far been under-emphasized in studies of government behavior in India and across rational choice theory.[24]

The democratization literature also offers explanations for why we observe variation in government behavior. The most straightforward argument is that democratically elected leaders are held accountable for government outcomes in a way that non-democratic governments are not, and that they are therefore less likely to act arbitrarily in the face of nationwide anti-corruption collective action.[25] In other words, toleration defines democracy, or *polyarchy*.[26] However, scholars (and indeed practitioners and journalists during the current, new wave of democratic "backsliding") have demonstrated that the democracy–authoritarianism dichotomy is not always a clean predictor of government behavior.[27] We have seen non-democratic regimes from the United Arab Emirates to China build legislative institutions that provide space for tolerance by allowing elites to obtain access to public opinion, thus facilitating bargaining.[28] By forming such bodies, these regimes recognize that it is often better to include the public in the governing process than to risk street demonstrations.[29]

Rather than toss out this established dichotomy in its entirety, we should develop arguments sensitive to greater differentiation in democracies by examining the interaction between decision-making elites' ideas and state power.[30] Despite India's democratic framework remaining intact since her independence, it has seen a dramatic shift as the party system has fragmented from a dominant one-party (Congress) system to a multi-party system.[31] This fragmentation belongs to the broader dispersal of state power, both historically and spatially, that this book centralizes. First, given India's size, diversity, and federal structure, party system fragmentation took a regional form.[32] As regional parties grew, the coalition era announced itself in 1989 and became entrenched by 1996. Since that time, these parties have enjoyed policymaking power at the center, and have rooted their rule in crucial states. The rise of coalitions precipitated openings for new, divergent, idea-carrying decision-makers to enter government, while also often instating a gridlock on collective policymaking.[33] Second, apex state institutions such as the Election Commission of India (ECI), the Reserve Bank of India (RBI), and the Supreme Court have gained autonomy over time, and have regularly protested executive overreach. But in spite of this progress, these institutions continue to centralize power in their chiefs, who often exercise discretionary influence while staving off consistent political interference.[34] Recently, one-party dominance and executive overreach has returned to India under the premiership of Narendra Modi in echoes of Indira Gandhi (more on the scope of this parallel in the concluding chapter).[35]

A final set of scholars posit that international pressure to respond favorably to anti-corruption movements among democracies has increased and therefore directs government behavior.[36] The past two decades have seen increased attention by developing world governments to political corruption, although such arguments come with high degrees of variation in outcomes.[37] First, they assume a hierarchy among nations in the international community, such that decision-makers respond directly and proportionately to the demands of outside powers when they bring to the world's attention a matter of pressing domestic concern. This rationale assumes that international campaigning trickles down to the everyday work of the acting government. On the contrary, decision-makers' kowtowing to international preferences, especially during a credibility crisis, often adversely affects citizens and provides fodder for opposition parties to further discredit the incumbent government.[38] Second, this reasoning fails to sufficiently account for cross-country variation among contemporaneous democracies similarly integrated into the international community.[39]

There is no doubt that elite ideas embedded in international institutions influence and shape government actors whose professional and personal lives straddle distinct contexts.[40] Technocrats, in particular, tend to build epistemic communities or advocacy coalitions through international and domestic networks to influence policy programs.[41] For example, economists who have been trained in free-market ideas in American graduate programs or have spent a significant part of their professional lives in multilateral institutions often move into authoritative positions of power in their home governments.[42] These pathways have often led to the spread of ideas across developing nations, and go on to have an observable impact on patterns of social and economic policy as well as on democratization.[43] India is no exception.[44]

The Politics of Ideas and Crisis

This study defines "ideas" as a coherent and relatively stable set of causal beliefs or values.[45] The dynamic study of ideas in political science has come to be known as the constructivist research program.[46] Constructivists present ideas as norms, frames, and narratives that establish how actors conceptualize and diagnose the world, and this framing enables constructivists to draw connections between events and people, thus driving change through "structuration."[47] "Ideas" cover a range of behaviors, from the diffusion of international ideas in developing countries to partisan conceptualization of the nation.[48] By considering the role of ideas in political behavior, constructivist scholars consider the experiences of specific decision-makers, and how their distinct cognitive frames, for example, can explain government responses to anti-corruption movements.[49]

At the heart of this book is the logic that ideas are distinct from, and causally prior to, interests. How we evaluate social and political states, and how we judge whether they advance our "interests," depends crucially on how we define ourselves.[50] We may see ourselves as members of an ethnic community, a nation, a social class, an academic association, or a mosaic of these groups.[51] In this way, constructivists argue that interests are historically, socially, and politically constructed, and move beyond the deployment of objective, material factors in situations in which political behavior is negotiated by decision-makers.[52] In existing accounts of government action in India, decision-makers with structurally fixed preferences react to self-apparent political situations and external interests. These interests derive from the electoral or rent-seeking motivations of political elites. Such a static framework underestimates the critical role of ideas. Ideas provide decision-makers with the interpretive framework with which they diagnose and approach political phenomena, especially infrequent challenges such as credibility crises. As such, ideas do not have a zero-sum relationship with interests, but are causally prior to interests. Before interests can be established, ideas provide a cognitive guide. As no interests are *given*, interests are simply *one form of idea*, and specifying these interests is less about structural determinism than about the construction of *wants* as mediated by *beliefs* or *ideas*.[53] This causality enables dynamic means by which decision-makers evaluate the relative merits of contending courses of action.

The distinction between ideas and interests is not only semantic, but has important conceptual implications—chiefly that political action is agency-centered. For rational choice theorists, decision-makers' interests evolve as changes in their material circumstances change their situations. An ideational logic, however, is predicated on the assumption that interests change as decision-makers change their understanding of the world and recalculate their priorities.[54] This may well represent a strategic assessment of what would most benefit that individual (or their group), but it may also necessitate a fundamental reinterpretation of priorities and identities.[55] For example, economic liberalization has been both actively rejected and welcomed by political and bureaucratic elites at different moments in India's history. At times when liberalization has been popular, it has not been so because liberalization served these elites' interests, but because liberalization was *perceived* to serve their interests. Ideas, in other words, give form to interests, and new ideas can profoundly change an agent's interests. This fundamentally alters the nature of the question that has been posed: How and why do decision-making elites come to conceive of their interests in such terms? The answer, in part, is that perceptions and interpretations cannot be derived from context alone.[56] To argue otherwise is to assume that similarly located decision-makers, armed with complete information, would conceive of their interests in an identical fashion and, if rational, would be motivated by such interests to behave identically. Such a state would empty our world not only of ideas, but also of power and politics. If choices were endogenous to institutions, then we would have to argue, for example, that Manmohan Singh would have approached the 2016 demonetization policy and the 2019 revocation of Article 370 of the Indian Constitution in Kashmir in the same manner as incumbent prime minister, Narendra Modi. Leaders are not analytically substitutable, just as their preferences cannot simply be derived from the institutional or purely material setting in which they exist. Human cognition has an independent force, and ideas communicate with other ideas to adjudicate the merits of contending courses of action.

The analytic currency of ideas as dynamic rather than fixed, in this way, is important to outline not least as a means of avoiding essentialism. Ideas change over time in an *evolutionary* manner as their frameworks, or "research programs," are subject to intellectual as well as political debate.[57] For instance, the political, social, and economic debates between the left and right have altered over the years concerning the logic of market competitiveness, which have become especially stark this past decade.[58] In step with these changes, their respective research programs have evolved, but, critically, the "hard core" ideas—in a Lakatosian sense—have not been easily discarded by those who employ them.[59] Certainly, economic liberals in India are not as bullish regarding trickle-down economics as their American counterparts, but both seek to reduce the ambition of the state in favor of market mechanisms in development. This is especially true among technocrats whose expertise was garnered in the non-electoral realm, and who are therefore subject to less ideational volatility than party politicians. Even among politicians, however, the conceptualization of the nation, for example, may evolve without losing its "hard core," or anchoring.[60] Consider the preference for socialism bound up with the Indira Gandhi–led Congress government's secular nationalism. This preference belonged not so much to an intellectual commitment on Gandhi's part as one component of the Congress Party's ancestry and many domestic economist and bureaucrats' zeitgeist for developing nations at the time.[61] As research demonstrated that the poor were as responsive to price incentives as the rich, Congress policies began to grow market-oriented in the mid-1980s, and this trend was integrated as an "auxiliary hypothesis" into existing concepts of the nation after 1991.[62] In other words, this development did not alter the "hard core" of Congress's nationalism, namely its secularist position—and it is this ideological core that placed a cognitive "lock" on the behavior of some decision-makers in both of the cases under study, such that they could not diagnose beyond the mobilization of religious nationalist groups within the anti-corruption movements.[63]

Indeed, decision-makers consider some ideas as more plausible, or strategic, avenues of policy prescription. Hence, it is important to emphasize the plausibility of the configurations, and even ambivalence, of values and ideas that decision-makers possess in order to clearly identify the anchoring of a particular worldview.[64] Political change through ideas, in this sense, is agency-centered. An important implication here is that ideational conflict is a constant in politics, which can enhance our understanding of power and decision-making. And when ideational conflicts occur, "true" or even normatively desirable ideas do not always win out.[65] Such struggle opens space for further political contestation, as decision-makers seek to make policy decisions reflect a set of ideas as well as ensure their political, often popular, palatability. This is especially (and most extremely) the case among populist actors and parties, who seek to institutionalize their ideational repertoires to actively and strategically participate in the definition and reproduction of group boundaries and inequalities.[66] Such efforts may legitimize the suppression or demonization of certain populations, for example, immigrants, refugees, Jews, Muslims, and others in much of Europe and the US under right-wing populist governments over the past decade.[67] While left-wing populists, less in vogue today but rampant certainly across Latin America and parts of Asia over the last 50 years, are alert to the threats of unregulated globalization, unfettered trade, American imperialism, and so on. When events can be credibly connected to such political rhetoric, combined with an established set of core ideas that coincide with decision-makers' beliefs, then populist interpretations of crises emerge.[68]

Under Indira Gandhi's premiership, the Indian state and political institutions were actively brought under the umbrella of the dominant conceptions of the nation—with secularism as its "hard core," and a preference for socialism and focus on minority rights—enshrined in the Congress Party that serviced Gandhi's populism.[69] It had grown concrete during and after the unified Congress's split in 1969 and played a constitutive role in the nation's political realignment, as moral boundaries were drawn between *us* and *them*.[70] The executive, leaning on secular nationalism, justified its focus on solidarity in the government and the suppression of ideological *others* within the JPM. As normatively desirable as secular conceptions of nationhood may be to the typical reader (and indeed the author) of this book, it can also undercut democracy in its populist form. Institutionally embedded ideas and the conflicts they incite among decision-makers can demonstrate the reproduction of inequalities and asymmetrical power relations through populism. Ideas that fill and shape such populist strategies are not always consciously articulated like traditional ideologies, but coexist with them. They operate much more like a discursive frame that are "activated" through and during a particular context by decision-makers. In this sense, it is important to consider the sentient actors themselves—the decision-making elites.[71]

When we ask how state elites make decisions, we step into an immensely consequential and challenging field of study. In this sense, decision-making and leadership are intuitively related—most people consider "leaders" as those who make decisions that affect other people, and the term evokes single names such as Lincoln and Roosevelt, Churchill and Thatcher, or Nehru and Gandhi. Invariably, decision-making is difficult to study in a rigorous and controlled way, as there is a momentous difference between the lab and the war room. The same is true of leaders' worldviews. For example, charisma has been intimately tied to our understanding of populism, yet these personal characteristics and traits prove tricky to interrogate, not least because leaders can often go through multiple iterations of the style and substance of political projection—from the time she rose to office to her assassination, we perhaps saw three distinct models of Indira Gandhi's leadership.[72] There have, however, been a multitude of approaches to such study. Where cognitive, social, and organizational psychologists once worked in methodological silos, advances in surveying, neuroimaging, and statistical modeling have led to the emergence of an interdisciplinary approach. By drawing on insights from across these disciplines and by fusing these insights with political theory, we can better understand decision-makers' attempts to move from a highly uncertain world to a less uncertain world in a credibility crisis, which operationalizes ideas.

Power and Decision-Making

Insights from behavioral psychology demonstrate that decision-making is rarely, if ever, rational. People give money with no expectation of recompense, punish others even at a cost to themselves, chronically misestimate probabilities, and prioritize information that is irrelevant to the task at hand. We tend to minimize and squander utility as often as we maximize it. Behavioral psychologists Daniel Kahneman and Amos Tversky systematized this approach to decision-making. They argue that people make decisions heuristically in ways that minimize constructs such as risk and uncertainty, and that decisions are driven by cognitive processes such as attention, learning, and emotion. Kahneman and Tversky later characterized two discrete cognitive systems of attention and learning that govern decision-making: A "fast" system that produces intuitive, automatic judgments driven by exogenous stimuli, and a "slow" system suited to complex, effortful judgment driven by internal cognitive processes. These systems co-exist and each have distinct value in contexts such as elite decision-making.[73] According to this reasoning, under uncertainty and high-pressure conditions such as those brought about by a credibility crisis, decision-makers tend to shift towards heuristics—or frameworks—of less complexity at the cost of greater ambiguity, while simultaneously exhibiting heightened risk-seeking behavior.[74]

While the brain may not always evaluate utility rationally, it tracks subjective values and beliefs in a systematic way.[75] In his seminal work on ideas and institutions, political economist Mark Blyth has argued that most political phenomena should be explained in terms of Knightian uncertainty, as they belong to a world that is not directly observable.[76] Such contexts are typical of developing countries such as India that are characterized by constant political disequilibria. Here, subjective beliefs and ideas guide actionable understandings of causal relationships in uncertain times such as crises.[77] Both the Congress government in the lead-up to the JPM and the UPA government in the lead-up to the IAC movement faced international and domestic pressures that diminished their credibility. Economic conditions deteriorated, international oil prices grew volatile, and, most pertinently, both governments saw sitting ministers, including the prime minister, accused of corruption. Each government's crisis of credibility came to a crescendo with nationwide anti-corruption demonstrations. Such an environment is common across contexts in which corrupt state narratives become nationally salient. The movements heighten a sense of insecurity and threat perception among government leaders and lower their credibility in the eyes of the public.[78] Importantly, the re-establishment of credibility is a motivating factor in decision-makers' response to anti-corruption movements. In an environment of Knightian uncertainty, decision-making elites seek to reconstitute interests and establish *their* narratives of the crisis and the respective movements.[79] Here, ideas serve as "weapons" mobilized by leaders in the struggle to contest with such movements.[80]

In addition to evaluating the social world and monitoring their own cognition to narrate a crisis, decision-makers must "mentalize"—that is, map the mental states of—other political actors and incorporate social information into their own models. While group decision-making leverages many of the same neural and cognitive systems as does individual decision-making, the added complexity of tracking others' cognition, attending to complex stimuli such as status and power, adapting to colleagues' decisions, and allocating resources create policymaking challenges. Perceptions of power, specifically, are instructive to understand government behavior. Power can be understood either perceptually or materially. From a perceptual perspective, it consists of individual evaluations of differences between oneself and others.[81] While power is a function of individual characteristics, it is enacted through social and relational behaviors.[82] Adam Galinksy presents a unified approach to power's influence on perception and behavior. Galinsky has demonstrated that those in power tend to be overconfident in their decisions, less able to mentalize others' perspectives, less able to accurately determine the knowledge of others, and less likely to register their emotions.[83] Furthermore, that these effects disappear or are greatly diminished when individuals are made to feel *subjectively* less powerful, even when their *objective* power in material terms remains constant.[84] A parliamentary, multi-ethnic, and federalist system such as India's may see dramatic variation in the distribution and salience of power among decision-makers. This is certainly evidenced in my study.

For example, decision-making power in India is held not only at the executive level by the prime minister and the heads of parties and apex state institutions, but also by a variety of actors such as chief ministers, powerful dynasts, religious gurus, and opposition parties. Adding intricacy, these roles can often be combined in the same individual or faction. In the UPA, for instance, Sonia Gandhi served as the chairperson of the coalition and the NAC, as well as president of the Congress Party and a dynast. This gave the Gandhi family unfettered access to the executive branch, which steeply diminished the subjective power of Prime Minister Manmohan Singh. In contrast, in the lead-up to the Emergency in 1975, the Congress Party president, as well as cabinet ministers, were all affiliated with the majority Congress government, and, crucially, all owed their political capital and station to Prime Minister Indira Gandhi's patronage—which emboldened her authority and centralization of executive power. Furthermore, while state leadership positions in the UPA were held by decision-makers from minority communities, such as Roman

Catholic Sonia Gandhi and Sikh Manmohan Singh, in the 1970s Congress, Indira Gandhi and her close advisors were mostly upper-caste Hindus. These factors may well nod toward why Gandhi viewed herself as the maternal embodiment of the Indian nation, and therefore incorruptible. As such, she perceived those that would rally behind her government's corruption, purported or proved, as doing so because they were antagonistic toward the nation itself. The technocrat Manmohan Singh, meanwhile, knew intimately that leaders and governments can be corrupted, but believed he was not guilty of corruption based on record not an exceptionalism.

Although power remains something of a "black box" for scholars of political science, its effect on decision-making behaviors through positional, demographic, introspective, and other differentials is potent. Perhaps the most relevant decision-making behaviors are known in social psychology as *pro-social* and *anti-social* behaviors. Economic theories of utility often struggle to explain altruistic behaviors such as charitable giving, as well as threatening behaviors such as mutually assured destruction. Why would a leader give material aid with no return, or commit to a war in which one's own death should preclude any utility gained from retributive violence? While these behaviors are irrational from a utilitarian, short-term perspective, they can be beneficial from an evolutionary, future-oriented perspective. State elites' legacies, particularly in India, are often defined by patterns of pro-social behavior. At their most basic, pro-social behaviors contravene the decision-maker's material interests from a purely utilitarian perspective, either by rewarding others in ways that do not immediately benefit the decision-maker, or by punishing others in ways that also harm the decision-maker.[85] Meanwhile, anti-social behaviors, though ethically complicated for testing, tend to be self-focused and threat-sensitive with the use of tactics such as bullying and intimidating subordinates to even injuring or killing competitors.

While these behaviors are not widely considered in cognitive or neuroscience research, such extremes are relevant to political phenomena. For example, people tend to make fewer risky decisions and tend to favor pro-social decisions when they are aware of the presence of third-party observers, or when making decisions democratically in groups.[86] This tendency can be observed in different ways throughout the UPA government, which, in addition to having a polycentric power structure between Congress Party president Sonia Gandhi and Prime Minister Manmohan Singh, was a multi-party coalition. Though this environment brought about group compromise and consensus early on, by the second UPA administration (2009–14), when the IAC was in its pomp and the government under crisis, the larger number of "third party observers" in decision-making positions made it challenging to assign the adjustment costs of policy choices to a particular group, as other parties and partners in the government often vetoed the potential options.[87] Each coalition partner, for instance, was incentivized to protect the programs that benefited their constituency. In the lead-up to the IAC movement, partner parties thwarted some of the government's proposed policy approaches to the agitation, especially those focused on improving the investment climate as a mechanism to stabilize the economic environment. Although coalition partners do not always interfere in policy matters, they are likely to interject in a credibility crisis of the type faced by the UPA, in which the government falls under suspicion of corruption and in which partners' influence and political benefits are compromised. [88] The result, nevertheless, is a non-radical policy outcome.[89]

In contrast, decision-makers evidence more risk-seeking behaviors when making decisions dictatorially.[90] This is a well-established assumption in the literature on authoritarianism in political science. As evidenced in our consideration of Prime Minister Gandhi's institutionalization of the Emergency, state elites' sense of power may drastically shift group behaviors and outcomes in situations that are characterized by uncertainty. A pertinent insight here is that decision-makers who are prone to risk-seeking behaviors and to preserving control over and even bullying subordinates tend to (somewhat counterintuitively) elicit greater cooperation from group members.[91] This behavior can profoundly affect decision-making in group settings, which is often psychologically gratifying to leaders. In other words, groups are often more willing to cooperate with or obey leaders who demonstrate willingness to take strategic risks in situations marked by uncertainty.[92] One political arena where we may observe these discursive processes directly is in cabinet meetings and parliamentary or executive committees, in which decision-makers transform individual thoughts and ideas into discourse and collective action.[93] No mechanism for this deliberation took shape in the Congress government under Indira Gandhi during the public unrest of the JPM. In fact, Gandhi's support among members of her government was such that she was able to subsume all collective institutions and committees, chiefly her own cabinet, to institute the suppressive Emergency decree. In contrast, the UPA government saw a proliferation of committees and cabinet meetings, especially during the

IAC movement. Consequently, although the concept of polyarchy encourages us to consider how democracy deepens as the cost of suppression rises and the cost of toleration declines, it is essential that we systematically analyze how and under which conditions specific state elites calculate these costs.[94]

It is therefore essential to build an account of elite decision-making that is sensitive not only to external sources of power such as votes and rents, but also to the behaviors of specific leaders and decision-makers, and the distribution of (and consciousness around) policymaking power internally. In this regard, one notable shortfall in the comparativist literature on elite decision-making behavior in India is the insufficient differentiation between the socialization of state elites such as politicians and technocrats and others in government. Indeed, not all decision-makers are subject to the same motivations.[95] Some decision-makers are elected officials who must accrue rents to fund elections; others are bureaucrats; yet others are technocrats or civic activists, who need rents for different incentives than do elected officials, if they need rents at all.[96] Identifying and studying these differences enriches our approach to political institutions, and moves away from a simplistic model in which a single, median policymaker responds to a single, median voter or interest group. [97]

The Congress government of the early 1970s, for example, saw primarily Congress Party politicians in key decision-making positions.[98] Party politicians were more likely to engage in defining and defending a particular conceptualization of the nation than were technocrats.[99] The Congress government, led by populist Prime Minister Gandhi, narratively framed the JPM in terms of inclusion and exclusion, as she and her colleagues viewed the movement as a threat to the government's concepts of the secular Indian nation. In the Gandhi-led Congress government's narrative, therefore, the suppression of this movement given its mobilization with right-wing religious nationalists was necessary to India's political—ironically democratic—survival and development. Motives in the political realm are more complex than in the economic realm, and cannot be reduced to economic ends, as perhaps it might be for technocrats.[100] As today's populist politics and movements remind us, humans are willing to undercut institutions and even suppress or kill others for causes couched in concepts of the nation.

By contrast, in the UPA, not only party politicians, but also technocrats and civic activists held important policymaking roles in India's social and economic development.[101] Technocrats, specifically, proved a valuable state-building resource.[102] For example, marketist technocrats entered the Indian government in the late 1980s and 1990s when the nation's primary economic architecture was being restructured through liberalization reforms. These decision-makers took up authoritative positions of power in the UPA as members of the cabinet, the PMO, and the senior bureaucracy.[103] In addition, reformist technocrats and activists who became the vanguard for renewed nationwide civic activism in the rights-based movements of the 1990s and early 2000s held authoritative positions of power during the UPA government as part of Congress Party president Sonia Gandhi's de facto parallel cabinet, the NAC.[104] These decision-makers—party politicians, technocrats, and activists—contested for influence over policymaking within the UPA government that resulted in a Polanyian double transformation to take shape concurrently. It is important to identify these idea carriers, which are not only clearer to trace among technocrats, but, additionally, their presence in executive decision-making illustrates the influence of specific preferences, collective action, and epistemic communities in government.[105] In sum, decision-makers evidence a variety of incentive structures and priorities that are rooted in their diverse perspectives and grow from their distinct professional and personal backgrounds.

Visions of Credibility: Concepts of the Nation and Social and Economic Development

Political party ideology is distinct from technocratic policy prescription, although both represent a subset of ideas. Party ideology is predicated on the creation of a political community or an organization that would not exist in its absence.[106] By contrast, technocratic policy prescriptions are formed through a disparate set of cultural, social, or economic assumptions that overwhelmingly dominate public discourse at a given moment in time—a zeitgeist.[107] Ideas, therefore, may range from specific programmatic ideas to more general ideas typical of ideologies such as liberalism. Party ideology here focuses primarily on dueling nationalisms (secular/religious), while technocratic ideas focus on social and economic development (market liberal/social reformist). Of course, real policy choices feature mixed strategies that are not quite so reductive. Nevertheless, this framing device adequately illustrates the ideational anchoring of decision-makers in the cases under study here, and the variation therein, and plausibly resonate with contexts similar to India.

The state remains central to the above interface between politicians, technocrats, civic activists, and other groups, from Nehruvian grand designs and distrust of the bureaucracy to citizen demands to redress corruption. And the performance of the Indian state varies greatly—the government successfully manages many large-scale tasks in times of crisis while performing poorly on seemingly basic tasks. This performance has led one scholar to describe the country as a "flailing state" tied to a nexus of both deals and rules.[108] These deals and rules are the result of a substantive and cognitive coalition between special interest groups, activists, bureaucrats, and politicians, which breeds divergent and dissonant elite perspectives on the state and its capacity for social and economic development.

In the UPA coalition government, for example, party politicians, technocrats, bureaucrats, and even activists utilized a framework of rights-based social reform as well as economic liberalization to diagnose the credibility crisis. Both groups constellated their ideas around the role of state institutions in economic and social development. Technocrats who promoted economic liberalization accorded primacy to deficit reduction, which they hoped would control the economic deterioration and inflation that they considered to be the proximate cause of public discontent. These decision-makers sought to signal a credible government commitment to stabilizing the nation's economic environment, thereby improving conditions for investment and minimizing the ire of citizens. Although these decision-makers maintained a role for the state in the distribution of the economic benefits of growth, they believed that the rights-based ideas of some state elites distorted government priorities and bureaucratic behaviors. Meanwhile, state elites who promoted social reformist ideas pushed for expansionary fiscal stimuli by strengthening state-led social welfare programs, as they believed that the absence (or certainly insufficiency) of these programs was the proximate cause of public discontent. These elites aimed to restore credibility through short-term growth by increasing economic demand, and maintained that the Indian capitalist project was an excuse for rent extraction and deal-making between businesses and politicians. The Indian state, they argued, must be a citizen-oriented social welfare state rooted in the rights of citizens. Overall, market liberal technocrats sought limited government engagement with the anti-corruption movement, and social reformists pursued full engagement with the movement. A third group in the Congress Party, the secular nationalists, aimed to disengage the movement while assertively disparaging the social and political forces behind the collective action. These decision-makers argued that the movement emerged as an extension of the religious nationalist right, which opposed state and national interests and thus delegitimized the credibility of the movement. Interacting with the polycentric institutional environment in the UPA, these diverse frameworks not only varied in their approaches to social and economic stability and growth, producing a simultaneous Polanyian double movement from 2004 to 2014, but also acted as a checks and balances mechanism on arbitrary government behavior in response to the IAC movement, thus making negotiated concessions more likely.

The state is also central to Indian partisan politics, which has historically (and incorrectly) been considered non-ideological, in part because partisan ideology does not follow the left–right spectrum traditional of European politics.[109] This continuum is not applicable in many multi-ethnic, postcolonial states, argue Pradeep Chhibber and Rahul Verma in their pathbreaking book which outlines that, in India, party ideology implies "having a distinct and defining vision regarding the politics of statism and the politics of recognition."[110] That is, one's ideology defines the extent to which one believes that the state should dominate society, regulate social norms, and redistribute private property, as well as whether and how the state should accommodate the needs of various marginalized groups and protect minority rights.[111] These factors function as essential parts of the two dominant conceptualizations of the nation in India—secular and religious. Critically, this debate has led to ideological turf wars, in the political and non-political realms, regarding the conceptualization of the Indian nation since Independence. Specifically, the Congress Party from 1969, composed entirely of party politicians, doubled down on that party's concepts of the nation as rooted in secularism, with a preference for socialism and focus on minority rights—which gave shape and content to Indira Gandhi's populism. After its first tangle with leadership, electoral, and regional challenges in the 1960s, the Congress under Gandhi sought a more active role for the state to achieve its objectives. In many respects, this political period is epitomized by the conflict regarding the role and organization of the state, which contributed to both the party split and the emergent ideological factions in the party system. The ideology of Gandhi's faction of the Congress dangerously clashed with her government's diagnosis of the JPM as a movement mobilized by and for right-wing religious nationalists in India. The government's populist interpretation of the credibility crisis played a constitutive role in political realignments in which moral boundaries were drawn between *us* and *them*. This populism, interacting with centralized power, facilitated Gandhi's focus on building solidarity in the government and suppressing ideological *others* in the JPM to re-establish credibility.

In these cases, as in others, cognitive frameworks make it possible for decision-makers to diagnose anti-corruption movements by espousing interpretive frameworks that narrate the political, economic, and social world by defining its central elements and their causal interrelations. Hence, by deploying ideas, decision-makers shape government action during a credibility crisis.

Notes

1. The framework presented here departs from theories of institutional behavior that propose the supremacy of endogenous over exogenous variables, and structure over agency. Such arguments do not give sufficient explanatory weight to ideas and, instead, consider ideas simply as auxiliary hypotheses (Vivien Schmidt, "Taking Ideas and Discourse Seriously: Explaining Change Through Discursive Institutionalism as the Fourth 'New Institutionalism'," *European Political Science Review* 2, no. 1 [2010]: 1–25).

2. Clifford Geertz, "Thick Description: Toward an Interpretive Theory of Culture," in *The Interpretation of Cultures: Selected Essays* (New York: Basic Books, 1973), 3–30.

3. James Mahoney and Kathleen Thelen, eds., *Explaining Institutional Change: Ambiguity, Agency, and Power* (Cambridge: Cambridge University Press, 2010).

4. Consider here the widely-cited theory of the "third dimension" of power: "The capacity to secure compliance to domination through the shaping of *beliefs* and *desires*, by *imposing internal constraints* under historically changing circumstances" (Steven Lukes, *Power: A Radical View* [Basingstoke: Palgrave, 2005], 143–44). However, rather than focus on "domination," let us consider power as a function of collective action, which involves coordinated efforts to affect others' preferences to shape specific political outcomes (Daniel Beland, "The Idea of Power and the Role of Ideas," *Political Studies Review* 8 [2010]: 145–54). In this sense, power is less about *domination* than about *influence*.

5. "Elites" are decision-makers in the executive arena, chiefly the Prime Minister. This includes the cabinet and other offices, party officials, and institutions that interact with the executive branch and maintain key political and economic powers. This is not inconsistent with the usual understanding of elites as a small dominant group that enjoys privileged social status.

6. Irfan Nooruddin, *Coalition Politics and Economic Development: Credibility and the Strength of Weak Governments* (New York: Cambridge University Press, 2011); Evan Lieberman, *Race and Regionalism in the Politics of Taxation in Brazil and South Africa* (Cambridge: Cambridge University Press, 2003).

7. It is important to note that decision-makers can engage in ideational contestation without "carrying" the idea. By "institution," I mean the formal structures, organizations, and processes that order and define national decision-making authority (see Karen Oren and Stephen Skowronek, *The Search for American Political Development* [Cambridge: Cambridge University Press, 2004]). Considered with ideas in a common framework, the claim for the analytical fusion of ideas and institutions emerges all the stronger.

8. Pierre Bourdieu, *Pascalian Meditations*, trans. Richard Nice (Stanford: Stanford University Press, 2000); Douglass C. North, *Institutions, Institutional Change, and Economic Performance* (Cambridge: Cambridge University Press, 1990). In India, for example, the government—whether single party majority or multi-party coalition—develops its own norms and rules, which are learned through experience. For example, in coalition governments, we observe the emergence of "coalition dharma"—a set of norms that necessitate compromise solutions among decision-makers. Often, during periods of high uncertainty and crisis, these norms collapse (for more on this point, see Nooruddin, *Coalition Politics*).

9. Mark Blyth (*Great Transformations*) views ideas as "weapons" with which decision-makers contest the very essence and establishment of institutions.

10. As Mark Blyth argues: "In moments of uncertainty, crisis-defining ideas not only tell agents 'what has gone wrong' but also 'what is to be done'" (Mark Blyth, "Powering, Puzzling, or Persuading? The Mechanisms of Building Institutional Orders," *International Studies Quarterly* 51, no. 4 [December 2007]: 761–77, 762).

11. Ben Olken and Rohini Pande, "Corruption in Developing Countries," *Annual Review of Economics* 4, no. 1 (2012): 479–509; Abhijit Banerjee, Rema Hanna, and Sendhil Mullainathan, "Corruption," in *Handbook of Organizational Economics*, ed. Robert Gibbons and Johns Roberts, 1109–47 (Princeton: Princeton University Press, 2013). Corruption has once again struck the imagination of citizens and scholars in recent years. The phenomenon subverts the functioning of elections, state mechanisms of representation and accountability; and undermines public trust in state institutions, thus leading to public unrest. Extant scholarship has reflected these issues and more. India, specifically, has become fertile ground for the study of corruption ranging from the link between lobbying practices and political corruption and the divergent reform practices of governments reliant on petty versus grand corruption to the very selection of corrupt candidates in high office. Elsewhere, experimental studies in India (particularly at the sub-national level) have burgeoned, which tend to focus on the effects of corruption on economic development and growth. All of these works build on a long-standing

tradition in political science investigating the relationship between politics and corruption at varying levels of analysis (Vineeta Yadav, *Political Parties, Business Groups, and Corruption in Developing Countries* [New York: Oxford University Press, 2011]; Jennifer, *Corruption and Reform in India*; Vaishnav, *When Crime Pays*; A. V. Banerjee, Donald P. Green, Jeffery McManus, and Rohini Pande, "Are Poor Voters Indifferent to Whether Elected Leaders Are Criminal or Corrupt? A Vignette Experiment in Rural India," *Political Communication* 31, no. 3 [July–September 2014]: 391–407; Olken and Pande, "Corruption in Developing Countries").

12. A related set of studies claim that decision-makers are compelled by favoritism along ethnic, religious, or other communitarian lines (F. Caselli and W. J. Coleman, "On the Theory of Ethnic Conflict," *Journal of the European Economic Association* 11, no. 1 [2013]: 161–92; R. Franck and I. Rainer, "Does the Leader's Ethnicity Matter? Ethnic Favoritism, Education, and Health in Sub-Saharan Africa," *American Political Science Review* 106, no. 2 [2012]: 294–325). The dynamics of identity politics in government behavior have been well documented recently (Francis Fukuyama, *Identity: The Demand for Dignity and Politics of Resentment* [New York: Farrar, Straus and Giroux, 2018]) and has a long tradition in the India case (Kanchan Chandra, *Why Ethnic Parties Succeed: Patronage and Ethnic Head Counts in India* [New York: Cambridge University Press, 2004]; Ashutosh Varshney, *Ethnic Conflict and Civic Life: Hindus and Muslims in India* [Connecticut: Yale University Press, 2003]). However, these biases are conditioned on a range of contingent factors that are highly heterogeneous in nationwide, socially cross-cutting, anti-corruption movements. The relevance of these studies is that they propose ethnic and identity bias as ideology.

13. Adi Brender and Allan Drazen, "Political Budget Cycles in New versus Established Democracies," *Journal of Monetary Economics* 52, no. 7 (October 2005): 1271–95; Kaushik Chaudhri and Sugato Dasgupta, "The Political Determinants of Central Governments' Economic Policies in India: An Empirical Investigation," *Journal of International Development* 17, no. 7 (2005): 957–78; Shawn A. Cole, "Fixing Market Failures or Fixing Elections? Elections, Banks, and Agricultural Lending in India," *American Economic Journal: Applied Economics* 1, no. 1 (2009); S. Khemani, "Political Cycles in a Developing Economy: Effect of Elections in the Indian States," *Journal of Development Economics* 73, no. 1 (2004): 125–54.

14. The significance of electoral considerations in government responses also permeates broader comparative studies on India (Kanchan Chandra, "Counting Heads: A Theory of Voter and Elite Behavior in Patronage-Democracies," in *Patrons, Clients and Policies*, ed. Herbert Kitschelt and Steven Wilkinson,

84–109 [Cambridge: Cambridge University Press, 2007]; Wilkinson, *Votes and Violence*).

15. For example, in 1967, the Congress's hegemonic power was undercut by greater regional competition. By 1975, as state and national elections had taken place on independent political calendars since 1971, campaigning became more frequent and the election cycles more aggressive (Vaishnav, *When Crime Pays*, 127–30). These trends have become even more prominent since 1989 with the rise of the coalition era and a greater number of parties. The number of political parties contesting elections jumped from 38 in 1984 to 117 in 1989. Moreover, by 2009, the average margin of victory in a parliamentary contest registered at 9.7 percent—the narrowest margin since Independence (ibid., 127–29). See also E. Sridharan, ed., *Coalition Politics in India: Selected Issues at the Centre and the States* (New Delhi: Academic Foundation, 2014). This trend came to a staggering halt with the 2014 and 2019 general election results. We have yet to see if this marks a structural shift in the Indian party system (Adam Ziegfeld, "A New Dominant Party in India? Putting the 2019 BJP Victory into Comparative and Historical Perspective," *India Review* 19, no. 2 [2020]: 136–52).

16. Across developed and developing democracies alike, contesting elections has become a costly undertaking. However, one key difference between advanced and developing democracies is the role played by illicit election funds in the latter (Michael Pinto-Duschinsky, "Financing Politics: A Global View," *Journal of Democracy* 13, no. 4 [2002]: 69–86; Naseem Faraz and Marc Rockmore, "Election Cycles in Public Credit: Credit Provision and Default Rates in Pakistan," *Journal of Development Economics* 147 [2020]). Political office is widely perceived as a highly lucrative proposition in India. More than two decades after the 1991 economic reforms, politicians retain significant discretionary power to influence resource allocations, contracts, licenses, and other government-provided benefits. The regulatory intensity of the state remains extremely high in several key growth sectors of the economy, which, in turn, gives politicians and the bureaucrats who serve them abundant opportunity to engage in rent-seeking behaviors (Trolochan Sastry, "Towards Decriminalisation of Elections and Politics," *Economic and Political Weekly* 49, no. 1 [2014]: 34–41, 38).

17. Daron Acemoglu and James Robinson, *Why Nations Fail: Power, Prosperity and Poverty* (New York: Crown, 2012).

18. Pranab Bardhan, *The Political Economy of Development in India* (Oxford: Blackwell, 1984); Atul Kohli, *State-Directed Development: Political Power and Industrialization in the Global Periphery* (Cambridge: Cambridge University Press, 2004).

19. Dani Rodrik and Arvind Subramanian, "From 'Hindu Growth' to Productivity Surge: The Mystery of the Indian Growth Transition," *IMF Staff Papers* 52, no. 2 (2005): 193–228; Atul Kohli, *Democracy and Development in India: From Socialism to Pro-Business* (New Delhi: Oxford University Press, 2010). Atul Kohli has stated that India's liberalization reforms were not pro-market, but pro-business. This assumes that the reforms were static and did not have second- and third-order effects that were endogenous to the reform program, as rooted in the market liberal ideas of the technocrats who oversaw it. For example, foreign capital and competition arrived in sectors where they had not existed before. Consequently, companies, especially in the Indian information technology (IT) sector, such as Infosys, Wipro, and most recently Ola and Flipkart, which are not traditional "big businesses," were not captured by state regulation in the way presumed by the literature. The 1991 reforms are therefore better understood as an ideational disruption to the previous equilibrium (Rahul Mukherji, *Globalization and Deregulation: Ideas, Interests, and Institutional Change in India* [New Delhi: Oxford University Press, 2014]). Overall, the point here is that the story is not so clear-cut as a captured versus a non-captured state, and that we must afford agency to decision-makers within the government and therefore go beyond this binary to understand government behavior.

20. It is worth noting that vote maximization is analytically different from rent maximization; one is not necessarily a derivative of the other. For example, regional parties in India, such as the Samajwadi Party, often aim to protect their communities. Decision-makers can serve their communities through reservations, targeted benefits, or even revivalism. In any given political situation, revivalism rather than rent may be the goal of a decision-maker. Each is important, but the two are not necessarily interchangeable.

21. If India was a patronage democracy alone, then there would not be as many vacancies in public sector jobs (a primary handout mechanism) as we see, especially in states such as Uttar Pradesh where patronage politics is deemed most vibrant (see Atul Thakur, "Central and State Governments Sit over 24 Lakh Vacancies amid Debate over Job Drought," *Times of India*, 5 August 2018, https://bit.ly/2rTJZ6f [accessed October 1, 2020]). Though not a case for ideas, per se, this data nods to a puzzle that brings into question the patronage democracy and clientelism literature that has long dominated the study of Indian politics. It is now being challenged by, among others, Jennifer Bussell, *Clients and Constituents: Political Responsiveness in Patronage Democracies* (New York: Oxford University Press, 2019). Moreover, and relatedly, we are witnessing the slow emergence of an ideational research program vis-à-vis the study of Indian politics: Pradeep Chhibber and Rahul Verma, *Ideology and*

Identity: The Changing Party Systems of India (New York: Oxford University Press, 2018); Mukherji, *Globalization and Deregulation*. This will only grow with a landmark new database built by the New York University scholar Rahul Sagar that indexes 255 English-language pre-Independence magazines from India (see the "Ideas of India" database, https://bit.ly/2YcZHFM [accessed October 1, 2020]).

22. Dani Rodrik, "When Ideas Trump Interests: Preferences, Worldviews, and Policy Innovations," *Journal of Economic Perspectives* 28, no. 1 (Winter 2014): 189–208, 194.

23. P. Petit, "Why and How Philosophy Matters to Politics," in *Oxford Handbook of Contextual Political Studies*, ed. R. E. Goodin and C. Tilly, 35–57 (Oxford: Oxford University Press, 2006).

24. As Dani Rodrik argues:

   Failure to recognize the role of ideas in shaping interests (and their pursuit) has especially serious implications in political economy. Taking ideas into account allows us to provide a more convincing account of both stasis and change in political-economic life. It provides a way of bridging the sharp divide between policy analysis (what should be done) with political economy (what actually happens). (Rodrik, "When Ideas Trump Interests," 190)

25. Adam Przeworski, Michael E. Alvarez, Jose Antonio Cheibub, and Fernando Limongi, *Democracy and Development: Political Institutions and Well-Being in the World, 1950–1990* (New York: Cambridge University Press, 2000).

26. Robert Dahl, *Polyarchy: Participation and Opposition* (New Haven: Yale University Press, 1971); Robert Dahl, *Democracy and Its Critics* (New Haven: Yale University Press, 1989). Dahl outlines seven attributes of inclusion, participation, and civil and political rights that secure polyarchy. In short, polyarchy is defined primarily as a system that ensures citizens free and fair access to determining who holds access to power. Dahl's procedural minimalist definition of democracy is perhaps most widely used in comparative studies.

27. On the global democratic "recession" or "backsliding" debate, see David Waldner and Ellen Lust, "Unwelcome Change: Coming to Terms with Democratic Backsliding," *Annual Review of Political Science* 21 (2018): 93–113; Adam Przeworski, *Crises of Democracy* (Cambridge: Cambridge University Press, 2019); Daniel Ziblatt and Steven Levitsky, *How Democracies Die: What History Reveals About our Future* (New York: Crown Press, 2018).

28. Joseph Wright, "Do Authoritarian Institutions Constrain? How Legislatures Affect Economic Growth and Investment," *American Journal of Political Science* 52, no. 2 (2008): 322–43; Jennifer Gandhi, *Political Institutions under Dictatorship* (New York: Cambridge University Press, 2008). A somewhat related study in international relations on when and why militaries side with

protestors reveals that military officers (in Tunisia) care not just about their material interests, but also about their political power—in this case, their policy influence (Sharan Grewal, "Military Defection during Localized Protests: The Case of Tataouine," *International Studies Quarterly* 63, no. 2 [2019]: 259–69).

29. Scott Gehlbach and Philip Keefer, "Investment without Democracy: Ruling-Party Institutionalization and Credible Commitment in Autocracies," *Journal of Comparative Economics* 39, no. 2 (2011): 123–39. Recently, developed and developing democratic regimes globally have illustrated a low tolerance for dissent.

30. Thomas Carothers, "The End of the Transition Paradigm," *Journal of Democracy* 13, no. 1 (January 2002): 5–21, 12.

31. Yogendra Yadav, Suhas Palshikar, and K. C. Suri, eds., *Party Competition in Indian States: Electoral Politics in Post-Congress Polity* (New Delhi: Oxford University Press, 2014).

32. Adam Ziegfeld, "Coalition Government and Party System Change: Explaining the Rise of Regional Political Parties in India," *Comparative Politics* 45, no. 1 (2012): 69–87, 70.

33. Nooruddin, *Coalition Politics and Economic Development*.

34. Milan Vaishnav, "India's Elite Institutions Are Facing a Credibility Crisis," *Livemint,* February 20, 2018, https://bit.ly/2rL2PN9 (accessed October 1, 2020).

35. For an insightful discussion on whether or not India is returning to a dominant party system (this time through the BJP), see Ziegfeld, "A New Dominant Party in India?"

36. Anna Persson, Bo Rothstein, and Jan Teorell, "A Failure of Anti-Corruption Policies: A Theoretical Mischaracterization of the Problem," The Quality of Government Paper Series, Gothenburg: University of Gothenburg, June 2010; Mark Bevir, "Governance and Interpretation: What Are the Implications of Postfoundationalism?" *Public Administration* 82, no. 3 (2004): 605–25; Sarah Chayes, *Thieves of State: Why Corruption Threatens Global Security* (New York: W. W. Norton and Company, 2015). Since the fall of the Berlin Wall and the subsequent breakup of the Soviet Union, India has reoriented itself toward liberal-capitalist nations, and has sought to engage more concretely with international institutions such as the United Nations (UN), the International Monetary Fund (IMF), and the World Bank, as well as become part of political and economic fora related to the G20 (Group of 20), BRICS (Brazil, Russia, India, China, and South Africa), and regional organizations such as the Asian Development Bank (ADB).

37. Alina Mungiu-Pippidi, Masa Loncaric, Bianca Vaz Mundo, Ana Carolina Braga, Michael Weinhardt, Angelica Solares, et al., "Contextual Choices for

Results in Fighting Corruption," commissioned by NORAD, Hertie School of Government, Berlin, 2011; Melchior Powell, Dina Wafa, and Tim A. Mau, eds., *Corruption in a Global Context: Restoring Public Trust, Integrity, and Accountability* (London: Routledge, 2019). Since a landmark 1996 speech on corruption by former World Bank president James Wolfensohn, many scholars and policymakers have emphasized the role of the global crackdown on corruption, its influence on government corruption, and its ill-effects on social and economic prosperity (Kenneth W. Abbott and Duncan Snidal, "International 'Standards' and International Governance," *Journal of European Public Policy* 8, no. 3 [2001]: 345–70; Wayne Sandholtz and Mark M. Gray, "International Integration and National Corruption," *International Organization* 57, no. 4 [2003]: 761–800).

38. For example, during the IAC agitation, the US urged the Indian government to exercise democratic restraint, which angered ministers in the Indian government across party lines (*Indian Express*, "US Remark on Exercising Democratic Restraint Angers India," 13 August 2011, http://bit.ly/2onHBSY [accessed October 1, 2020]). Such aversion to outside pressures in its current form dates to the Cold War era, particularly at the height of Indira Gandhi's Congress rule, when suspicions of Central Intelligence Agency (CIA) operatives meddling in Indian politics became central to the "foreign hand" arguments referenced in parliamentary debates (Khushwant Singh, *Indira Gandhi Returns* [New Delhi: Vision Books, 1979]).

39. After all, facing anti-corruption movements under comparable macroeconomic conditions and credibility crises, the Adalet ve Kalkınma Partisi (AKP) government in Turkey suppressed the anti-corruption movements it faced, while India under the UPA and elsewhere in Brazil under the Partido dos Trabalhadores (PT) government were more tolerant. All three democracies have increasingly become part of the international system over the past two decades, yet have behaved at variance with this embeddedness.

40. Clean left–right ideational frames do not always explain political cleavages in non-Western contexts. See Christophe Jaffrelot, "Refining the Moderation Thesis: Two Religious Parties and Indian Democracy—The Jana Sangh and the BJP between Hindutva Radicalism and Coalition Politics," *Democratization* 20, no. 5 (2013): 876–94. In comparativist work on developed (primarily Western) contexts, the notion of ideology is quite narrow. It tends to be defined exclusively in terms of the economic left and right (Seymour M. Lipset and Stein Rokkan, *Party Systems and Voter Alignments: Cross-National Perspectives* [New York: Free Press, 1967]). The intellectual ancestry of this spectrum is in the idiosyncrasies of state formation itself, which differs between societies (Chhibber and Verma, *Ideology and Identity*).

41. Chalmers Johnson, *MITI and the Japanese Miracle: The Growth of Industrial Policy, 1925–1975* (Stanford: Stanford University Press, 1982); Miguel Angel Centeno, *Democracy without Reason: Technocratic Revolution in Mexico* (University Park: Pennsylvania State University Press, 1994); Anne-Marie Slaughter, *A New World Order* (Princeton: Princeton University Press, 2005).

42. The socializing role of education has long been recognized in bodies of literature across the social sciences, as education crafts individual value systems. It is hardly controversial, for example, to argue that anthropologists and economists place different weight on similar issues, or even that economists trained in varying frameworks diverge on policy prescriptions. See, among others, Sarah L. Babb, *Managing Mexico: Economists from Nationalism to Neoliberalism* (Princeton: Princeton University Press, 2001); Juan Gabriel Valdés, *Pinochet's Economists: The Chicago School of Economics in Chile* (New York: Cambridge University Press, 1995). Idea carriers' belief systems can often be inferred by reference to their *sociological context*—such as their embeddedness in a professional network or the site of their training or education—or from *past verbal communication*. Thus, the most useful idea carriers for examination are technocrats, those that have a prior track record of activity outside of politics—an intellectual or professional setting in which incentives for strategic misrepresentation or beliefs are limited (Jacobs, "Process Tracing the Effects of Ideas," 68; on tracing of programmatic ideas, see Sheri Berman, *The Social Democratic Moment: Ideas and Politics in the Making of Interwar Europe* [Cambridge, MA: Harvard University Press, 1998]). Distinct conceptual frameworks can lead actors to prioritize separate goals, attend to distinct pieces of information, or employ particular causal logics.

43. Devesh Kapur, *Diaspora, Development, and Democracy: The Domestic Impact of International Migration from India* (Princeton: Princeton University Press, 2010), 2; Wayne Leighton and Edward Lopez, *Madmen, Intellectuals, and Academic Scribblers: The Economic Engine of Political Change* (Stanford: Stanford University Press, 2012), 49–79; Wendy Larner and Nina Laurie, "Travelling Technocrats, Embodied Knowledges: Globalising Privatisation in Telecoms and Water," *Geoforum* 41, no. 2 (March 2010), 218–26. Mitchell Orenstein argues that transnational actors, particularly at the World Bank, have the capacity to directly influence national policymakers—largely by shaping their perception of what is "good" for them (*Privatizing Pensions: The Transnational Campaign for Social Security Reform* [Princeton: Princeton University Press, 2008]). However, Orenstein recognizes the constraining power of domestic institutions, such that actors cannot exert unlimited ideational influence on less-developed countries due to domestic veto players who are in a strong position to shape national legislative and political outcomes (ibid., 55–57).

This is perhaps most salient in today's populist and global retrenchment moment.

44. In the UPA government, technocrats who worked and interacted with the IMF, World Bank, UN, and other institutions, and who held liberal ideas of social and economic development, held authoritative positions of power during the 2012 credibility crisis.

45. I rest on Kathleen Knight's definition for ideas: *a coherent and relatively stable set of beliefs or values*. To this "core" definition, Knight adds supplemental terms of *contrast* (parties, groups, and "isms" such as nationalism that juxtapose one abstract group, and its beliefs, with another) and *spatial conceptualization* (location on a left–right or liberal–conservative continuum) (Kathleen Knight, "Transformations of the Concept of Ideology in the Twentieth Century," *American Political Science Review* 100, no. 4 [2006]: 619–26, 625). Elsewhere, as per Douglass North, Sheri Berman, and Mark Blyth, among others, I use "ideas," "ideational," and "ideology" interchangeably (North, *Institutions, Institutional Change, and Economic Performance*; Berman, *The Social Democratic Moment*; Blyth, *Great Transformations*). These terms get a sense of ideas that fit together to give individuals guidance on how to make sense of causal relationships in the world and act within it.

46. The last decade has seen some excellent work in comparative politics using the constructivist research program, but the program remains under-utilized. See, among others, N. Jabko, *Playing the Market: Political Strategy for Uniting Europe, 1985–2005* (Ithaca: Cornell University Press, 2007); Alan Jacobs, *Governing for the Long Term: Democracy and the Politics of Investment* (New York: Cambridge University Press, 2011); Chhibber and Verma, *Ideology and Identity*.

47. Alexander Wendt, "The Agent-Structure Problem in International Relations Theory," *International Organization* 41, no. 3 (1987): 359–60; T. Fossen, "Constructivism and the Logic of Political Representation," *American Political Science Review* 113, no. 3 (2019): 824–37.

48. John Campbell, "Ideas, Politics, and Public Policy," *Annual Review of Sociology* 28 (2002): 21–38.

49. Political actors, after all, often aggregate social and political demands, and sometimes act against these demands (Theda Skocpol, *Protecting Soldiers and Mothers: The Political Origins of Social Policy in the United States* [Cambridge, MA: The Belknap Press of HUP, 1992]).

50. Rodrik, "When Ideas Trump Interests," 192.

51. Amartya Sen, *Identity and Violence* (New York: Norton & Co., 2006).

52. Blyth, *Great Transformations*. In her influential constructivist study of democratization, Sheri Berman argues that the differential trajectories of

Germany and Sweden in the 1930s, into fascism and social democracy respectively, are best explained by the ideas held by key academics, labor unions, and political actors (Berman, *The Social Democratic Moment*).

53. Blyth, *Great Transformations*, 29; Daniel Béland and Robert Henry Cox, eds., *Ideas and Politics in Social Science Research* (New York: Oxford University Press, 2010), 10. An *a priori* assumption in much of the literature on Indian politics is that ideas are derivatives of material gains alone. In contrast, my theory rests on the claim that ideas are sequentially placed prior to the generation of interests.

54. The notion that ideas are "cluster concepts," as outlined by Mark Blyth (*Great Transformations*), helps us understand this theory. As clusters, ideas embrace thoughts, emotions, and desires as well as interests, all in a delicate and fluid balance.

55. For materialists, cognitive processes have little significance than to lead one to the *discovery* of their interests. For ideationalists, by contrast, cognition is a process of interpreting the world, not simply discovering it.

56. Lukes, *Power*, 81.

57. P. Kjaer and O. Pedersen, "Translating Liberalization: Neoliberalism in the Danish Negotiated Economy," in *The Rise of Neoliberalism and Institutional Analysis*, ed. J. L. Campbell and O. Pedersen, 219–48 (Princeton: Princeton University Press, 2001). For a similar approach to the "evolution" of nationalism, see Nadav G. Shelef, *Evolving Nationalism: Homeland, Identity, and Religion in Israel, 1925–2005* (Ithaca: Cornell University Press, 2010).

58. Peter Hall, "The Economics and Politics of the Euro Crisis," *German Politics* 21, no. 4 (2012): 355–71; Nicholas Wapshott, *Keynes, Hayek: The Clash That Defined Modern Economics* (London and New York: W. W. Norton & Co., 2012).

59. In his seminal interpretation, Peter Hall, leaning on Thomas Kuhn, sees ideas as part of *paradigms* (Peter Hall, "Policy Paradigms, Social Learning, and the State: The Case for Economic Policymaking in Britain," *Comparative Politics* 25, no. 3 [1993]: 275–96). When challenges or failures sufficiently accumulate in a set of ideas, social learning occurs, and paradigms are replaced and tossed out. Unlike Hall, I lean on Kuhn's contemporary Imre Lakatos in viewing ideas as part of a research program. In a Lakatosian approach, a central hypothesis, or "hard core," is protected by auxiliary hypotheses that protect and refine the core's central claims. In this way, when a set of ideas are challenged, adherents do not pin the blame on their "hard core" assumption, but direct criticism at their "protective belt" of auxiliary hypotheses, which are modified to deal with the challenge. In this way, ideas remain robust to new information and are not easily cast off. Overall, the longitudinal pattern of ideas is based strongly on

the conditions under which ideas change or continue. This approach allows us to move away from essentialist charges against the treatment of ideas (Lakatos, "The Methodology of Scientific Research Programmes").

60. Politicians often make political compromises or indulge in tactical measures that should be adjudicated against the longitudinal continuity and changes in ideas. For example, when Indira Gandhi returned to power in 1980, she appropriated elements of Hindu politics at her convenience (especially in Punjab), and more recently we also saw with her grandson and Congress heir, Rahul Gandhi, in his campaign toward the 2019 general election. However, this does not necessarily indicate fundamental, or core, ideological change.

61. P. B. Mehta and M. Walton, "India's Political Settlement and Development Path," mimeo, Centre for Policy Research and Harvard Kennedy School, 2012, 17–18.

62. Anne O. Krueger, "Trade Policy and Economic Development: How We Learn," *The American Economic Review* 87, no. 1 (1997): 1–22. See note 59.

63. On cases of cognitive locking, see Berman, *The Social Democratic Moment*. Recall from earlier, which ideas win out, therefore, is not purely about intellectual refinement as it is also about structures—political institutions such as parties constrain political behavior through the operation of rules, norms, and organizational settings as well as by structuring political openings for group mobilization and the articulation of interests. Interactively, and in turn, we have long known that ideology can serve as a cohesion mechanism within parties (Maurice Duverger, *Political Parties, Their Organization and Activity in the Modern State*, trans. Barbara and Robert North [New York: John Wiley & Sons, Inc., 1954]). In a recent study on how party ideology (especially via populism) has an observable effect on the political economy of development, see David Blakeslee, "Politics and Public Goods in Developing Countries: Evidence from the Assassination of Rajiv Gandhi," *Journal of Public Economics* 163 (July 2018): 1–19.

64. Blyth, *Great Transformations*.

65. For related arguments, see Matthias Matthijs, *Ideas and Economic Crises in Britain from Attlee to Blair (1945–2005)* (London: Routledge, 2011); Kathleen McNamara and Matthias Matthijs, "The Euro Crisis' Theory Effect: Northern Saints, Southern Sinners, and the Demise of the Eurobond," *Journal of European Integration* 37, no. 2 (2015): 229–45; Mark Blyth, *Austerity: The History of a Dangerous Idea* (New York: Oxford University Press, 2013).

66. In line with the recent discursive turn in the study of populism (see, among others, Rogers Brubaker, "Why Populism?" *Theory and Society* 46, no. 5 [2017]: 357–85) I view populism as having heterogenous, often ambivalent, ideological commitments and programmatic goals, which begs a more thorough, empirical

exploration into populist politics to identify its ideational content—as I have done in the case chapters of this book.

67. The most significant examples of populist politics include an exclusionary nationalist rejection of ethnic and multicultural diversity (for example parties in Europe such as the French National Front or Freedom Party of Austria).

68. Kirk Hawkins, Madeleine Read, and Teun Pauwels, "Populism and Its Causes," in *The Oxford Handbook of Populism*, ed. C. R. Kaltwasser, Paul Taggart, Cristóbal Rovira Kaltwasser, Paul Taggart, Paulina Ochoa Espejo, and Pierre Ostiguy, 267–86 (Oxford: Oxford University Press, 2017).

69. Populism and nationalism are distinct though closely articulated discourses. Many instances of populist politics have been nationalist, and nationalist movements often have a populist component. For the purposes of the present discussion, populist actors and parties are typically organized at the level of the nation-state, and therefore their claims and ideas are defined using concepts of the nation. As such, populism can align itself with political projects and ideas of the left or right. Some populist parties celebrate social and cultural liberalism or attack it; they may be secular or religious. For a discussion on the conceptual distinctions and overlap between populism and nationalism, see Benjamin De Cleen, "Populism and Nationalism," in *The Oxford Handbook of Populism*, ed. C. R. Kaltwasser, Paul Taggart, Cristóbal Rovira Kaltwasser, Paul Taggart, Paulina Ochoa Espejo, and Pierre Ostiguy, 341–62 (Oxford: Oxford University Press, 2017).

70. Stefano Fella and Carlo Ruzza, "Populism and the Fall of the Centre-Right in Italy: The End of the Berlusconi Model or a New Beginning?" *Journal of Contemporary European Studies* 21, no, 1 (2013): 38–52. This study considers populism as a "thin-centered" ideology, as per Cas Mudde's influential and widely cited definition: "[Populism is] a thin-centered ideology that considers society to be ultimately separated into two homogenous and antagonistic groups, 'the pure people' versus 'the corrupt elite,' and which argues that politics should be an expression of the *volonté générale* [general will] of the people" (Cas Mudde, "The Populist Zeitgeist," *Government and Opposition* 39, no. 4 [2004]: 542–63, 543).

71. On "actor-centered constructivism," see Sabine Saurugger, "Constructivism and Public Policy Approaches in the EU: From Ideas to Power Games," *Journal of European Public Policy* 20, no. 6 (2013): 888–906.

72. The study of Indian politics has become replete with experimental methods, filled with assumptions at the individual level that do not always match up to social and political realities. Hence, we see the concretization of assumptions such as "rent-seeking politicians" which act as covering laws in several extant works on political behavior in India. In the present study, it would be

unrealistic and too expensive to separate treatment and control groups with regard to complex government procedures such as cabinet decision-making. Such topics require a high degree of differentiation and thick description.

73. The fast system tends toward simple heuristics, and is prone to error when faced with the complex inputs that characterize leadership. Leaders can make better decisions by "slowing" their thinking and deliberately attending to information (Daniel Kahneman and Amos Tversky, *Thinking Fast and Slow* [New York: Farrar, Straus and Giroux, 2011]).

74. L. Spiliopoulos, A. Ortmann, and L. Zhang, "Complexity, Attention, and Choice in Games under Time Constraints: A Process Analysis," *Journal of Experimental Psychology: Learning, Memory, and Cognition* 44, no. 10 [2018]: 1609–40.

75. Psychologists have characterized three forms of cognitive "utility": experienced utility, which is "hedonic" and "associated with a good or bad event"; anticipated utility, or how we *think* we will feel after making a decision; and decision utility, which is anhedonic and is inferred through the weighing of potential outcomes (E. Fehr and C.F. Camerer, "Social Neuroeconomics: The Neural Circuitry of Social Preferences," *Trends in Cognitive Sciences* 11, no. 10 [2007]: 419–27). This is borne out on a neurological level, as patterns of activation in the prefrontal cortex (PFC), ventral striatum (VS), and cingulate cortex (CC) have been shown to track these discrete aspects of value, and separate sub-regions evaluate prospective outcomes versus actualized outcomes (J. A. Clithero and A. Rangel, "Informatic Parcellation of the Network Involved in the Computation of Subjective Value," *Social Cognitive and Affective Neuroscience* 9, no. 9 [2014]: 1289–302). These features explain literally (if tautologically) why leaders want what they want, and they collectively explain behaviors such as risk tolerance and uncertainty that are characteristic of certain styles of leadership.

76. Blyth, *Great Transformations*. See also Frank Knight, *Risk, Uncertainty, and Profit* (Eastford: Martino Fine Books, 2014 [1921]).

77. Beland, "The Idea of Power and the Role of Ideas." If interests are a function of beliefs and desires, and if decision-makers are confused about their desires in situations of uncertainty (as during a nationwide anti-corruption movement), it follows that decision-makers' interests must be unstable too. Ideas are therefore causally prior to interests (Blyth, *Great Transformations*). Decision-makers in such environments know that they act on the basis of imperfect information, but their cognition guides their diagnoses with this *negative capability* in mind (cf. John Keats, *The Letters of John Keats*, ed. H. E. Rollins [Cambridge: Cambridge University Press, 1958 (1817)], 193–94).

78. There is consensus in the literature that incumbent politicians involved in scandals suffer at the polls as their trust among citizens plummets (Rodrigo

Praino, Daniel Stockemer, and Vincent G. Moscardelli, "The Lingering Effect of Scandals in Congressional Elections: Incumbents, Challengers, and Voters," *Social Science Quarterly* 94, no. 4 [2013]: 1045–61; Philip Cowley, *Revolts and Rebellions: Parliamentary Voting under Blair* [London: Politico, 2002]).

79. Crisis environments "upset routine calculations of interest, invalidating rational short cuts and injecting a large dose of uncertainty" (Andrew Polsky, "When Business Speaks: Political Entrepreneurship, Discourse, and Mobilization in American Partisan Regimes," *Journal of Theoretical Politics* 12, no. 4 [2000]: 455–76, 466). Furthermore, Knightian uncertainty is arguably heightened in a coalition government setting, in which bargaining between partner parties further obscures the relationship between policy instruments and political outcomes (Kaare Strøm, Wolfgang C. Müller, and Daniel Markham Smith, "Parliamentary Control of Coalition Governments," *Annual Review of Political Science* 13, no. 1 (2010): 517–35).

80. As Blyth argues: "In moments of uncertainty, crisis-defining ideas not only tell agents 'what has gone wrong' but also 'what is to be done'" (Blyth, "Powering, Puzzling, or Persuading?" 762).

81. This entails introspection (perceiving one's own mental state), mentalizing (attributing and interpreting the mental states of others), and attending to stimuli that are salient to power, which can be behavioral (verbal and body language), demographic (age, gender, and ethnicity), or contextual (explicit markers of status such as accent and clothing).

82. Gender and body language are both particularly salient methods to evaluate others' power. In one study, individuals were quicker to process words related to power and authority after viewing images of men or people in power poses than women or people in submissive poses (April H. Bailey and Spencer D. Kelly, "Body Posture and Gender Impact Neural Processing of Power-Related Words," *The Journal of Social Psychology* 157, no. 4 [2017]: 474–84).

83. Adam D. Galinsky, Joe C. Magee, M. Ena Inesi, and Deborah H. Gruenfeld, "Power and Perspectives Not Taken," *Psychological Science* 17, no. 12 (2006): 1068–74.

84. Adam Galinsky and J. Magee, "Social Hierarchy: The Self-Reinforcing Nature of Power and Status," *The Academy of Management Annals* 2, no. 1 (2008): 351–98.

85. A framework has emerged in recent years at the intersection of social psychology and economics called social value orientation (SVO), which characterizes various archetypical pro-social behaviors. In the SVO framework, people are characterized by their pro-social behaviors: those who give without expectation of revenue are "martyrs," those who maximize collective payoffs are "pro-social," those who maximize their own payoffs are

"competitive," and those who are willing to minimize collective payoffs to prove a point are "sadomasochists" (R. O. Murphy and K. A. Ackermann, "Social Value Orientation: Theoretical and Measurement Issues in the Study of Social Preferences," *Personality and Social Psychology Review* 18, no. 1 [2014]: 13–41).

86. R. Yokoyama, Takayuki Nozawa, Motoaki Sugiura, Yukihito Yomogida, Hikaru Takeuchi, Yoritaka Akimoto, et al., "The Neural Bases Underlying Social Risk Perception in Purchase Decisions," *NeuroImage* 91 (2014): 120–28; S. C. Rom and P. Conway, "The Strategic Moral Self: Self-Presentation Shapes Moral Dilemma Judgments," *Journal of Experimental Social Psychology* 74 (2018), 24–37; S. Bougheas, J. Nieboer, and M. Sefton, "Risk Taking and Information Aggregation in Groups," *Journal of Economic Psychology* 51 (2015) 34–47. See also classic experiments such as the Asch conformity paradigm (S. E. Asch, "Effects of Group Pressure upon the Modification and Distortion of Judgments," in *Groups, Leadership and Men: Research in Human Relations*, ed. H. Guetzkow, 177–90 [Pittsburg: Carnegie Press, 1951]).

87. J. Tavares, "Does Right or Left Matter? Cabinets, Credibility, and Fiscal Adjustments," *Journal of Public Economics* 88, no. 12 (2004): 2447–68; Scott Gehlbach and Edmund Malesky, "The Contribution of Veto Players to Economic Reform," *The Journal of Politics* 72, no. 4 (2010): 957–75.

88. Strøm, Müller, and Smith, "Parliamentary Control of Coalition Governments," 524.

89. Nooruddin, *Coalition Politics*; George Tsebelis, *Veto Players: How Political Institutions Work* (Princeton: Princeton University Press, 2002); R. W. Price, "The Political Economy of Fiscal Consolidation," OECD Economics Department Working Papers No. 776, 2010. Nooruddin's influential *Coalition Politics* is the single monograph-length academic study of Indian politics that rigorously examines coalition politics as an independent variable to explain government behavior. His "credible constraints" framework argues that the diffusion of policymaking authority across different parties with separate accountabilities instates a system of checks and balances on the executive's ability to arbitrarily change economic policy.

90. G .E. Bolton, A. Ockenfels, and J. Stauf, "Social Responsibility Promotes Conservative Risk Behavior," *European Economic Review* 74, no. C (2015): 109–27.

91. H. Qiu, Y. Zhang, G. Hou, and Z. Wang, "The Integrative Effects of Leading by Example and Follower Traits in Public Goods Game: A Multilevel Study," *Frontiers in Psychology* 9 (2018): 1687; Xiangyi Zhang, Xiyou Chen, Yue Gao, Yingjie Liu, and Yongfang Liu, "Self-Promotion Hypothesis: The Impact of Self-esteem on Self-other Discrepancies in Decision Making Under Risk,"

Personality and Individual Differences 127 (2018): 26–30. Power may emerge from individual differences in value control over outcomes. Research has shown that some people are willing to sacrifice objective outcome measures such as earnings to maintain control over others' decisions (Ernst Fehr, Holger Herz, and Tom Wilkening, "The Lure of Authority: Motivation and Incentive Effects of Power," *American Economic Review* 103, no. 4 [2013]: 1325–59). Conversely, many are deeply averse to control by others, and are willing to suffer consequences to avoid having their outcomes dictated by others' decisions (Sarah Rudorf, Katrin Schmelz, Thomas Baumgartner, Roland Wiest, Urs Fischbacher, and Daria Knoch, "Neural Mechanisms Underlying Individual Differences in Control-averse Behavior," *The Journal of Neuroscience* 38, no. 22 [2018]: 5196–208).

92. Qiu, et al., "The Integrative Effects of Leading by Example and Follower Traits in Public Goods Game."

93. Vivien Schmidt, *Democracy in Europe* (Oxford: Oxford University Press, 2006); Jacobs, *Governing for the Long Term.*

94. Nancy Bermeo, "Myths of Moderation: Confrontation and Conflict during Democratic Transitions," *Comparative Politics*, Transitions to Democracy: A Special Issue in Memory of Dankwart A. Rustow, 29, no. 3 (1997): 305–22, 315.

95. Leighton and Lopez, *Madmen, Intellectuals, and Academic Scribblers*, 178.

96. See Tables A4.1–A4.3 in Appendices. When decision-makers extract rents, they do so not purely for pecuniary gain, but rather to enhance their hold on policymaking power (Francine Frankel, *India's Political Economy, 1947–2004* [New York: Oxford University Press, 2005]).

97. Jacobs, "Process Tracing the Effects of Ideas," 68. These idea carriers enter institutions at different moments, depending on when the institutions open and close. The key is that these idea carriers often remain in government, even in positions of authority (see Hall, "Policy Paradigms"). In order for new ideas to overcome vested interests, policy "entrepreneurs notice and exploit those loose spots in the structure of ideas, institutions, and incentives" (Leighton and Lopez, *Madmen, Intellectuals, and Academic*, 134).

98. As much as comparativist scholarship on government behavior focuses on parties, the preferences of specific decision-making elites in authoritative positions of power are not widely considered. These are not analytic equivalents. Parties are bound in their preferences by elections and constituents, whereas interrogation into specific decision-makers, from politicians to technocrats and activists, reveals distinct and diverse sets of ideas and incentive structures. A focus on decision-makers over parties also creates pathways to examine cases of ideological diversity (R. Lavigne, "The Political and Institutional

Determinants of Fiscal Adjustment: Entering and Exiting Fiscal Distress," *European Journal of Political Economy* 27, no. 1 [2011]: 17–31).

99. This could be specific to India, given its freedom struggle, but we see it in other countries as well, such as Turkey and Malaysia. It is most likely a function of later postcolonial societies. See Jon Elster, "Rational Choice History: A Case of Excessive Ambition," *American Political Science Review* 94, no. 3 (2000): 685–95.

100. Rodrik, "When Ideas Trump Interests," 191.

101. A technocrat is any decision-maker who possesses non-partisan political expertise that is directly relevant to his or her government role. NB: Although I present a neat split between technocrats, party politicians, bureaucrats, activists, and others, these professional backgrounds are not sufficient conditions to determine ideas. This is particularly the case in the formal and informal networks that lead to the exchange of ideas and discourse between each of these decision-makers. Thus, some social learning takes place in which politicians may adopt the ideas of technocrats, for example. These backgrounds should be seen as a framing device, and the focus should remain on the ideas in the government.

102. Technocrats play the part of puzzling and persuading by framing ideas in a legitimate context. This extends beyond technical knowledge on a specific policy matter, but also to how things should be—a kind of moral authority (Gil Eyal, "For a Sociology of Expertise: The Social Origins of the Autism Epidemic," *American Journal of Sociology* 118, no. 4 [January 2013]: 863–907; Sending, *The Politics of Expertise*).

103. This is true not only among policymakers with diverse backgrounds, but also among coalition partners with diverse incentive structures. The communist parties, such as the Communist Party of India (Marxist) (CPI[M]), maintain separate preferences from those of the All India Anna Dravida Munnetra Kazhagam (AIDMK), which represents communal interests.

104. When experts enter government in a strategic context, their ideas are not epiphenomenal. After all, these idea carriers hold longer-term influence after their initial political masters have departed the scene, and may hold key positions of policymaking power.

105. In Duncan McDonnell and Marco Valbruzzi's framing, the Congress government in the early 1970s was a "party government" and the UPA coalition government was a hybrid "party-technocratic government" (Duncan McDonnell and Marco Valbruzzi, "Defining and Classifying Technocrat-Led and Technocrat Governments," *European Journal of Political Research* 53, no. 4 [2014]: 654–71). In a fully "technocratic government", (*a*) all major government decisions are not made by elected party officials, (*b*) policy is not decided

within parties, which then act cohesively to enact it, and (c) the highest officials (such as ministers and prime ministers) are not recruited through the party. This definition is derived from mirror image classic ideal-type definitions of a "party government" (ibid.).

106. Sheri Berman, "Ideology, History, and Politics," in *Ideas and Politics in Social Science Research*, ed. Daniel Béland and Robert Henry Cox, 105–26 (New York: Oxford University Press, 2010), 105.

107. Jai Mehta, "The Varied Roles of Ideas in Politics," in *Ideas and Politics in Social Science Research*, ed. Daniel Béland and Robert Henry Cox, 23–46 (New York: Oxford University Press, 2010), 40.

108. Lant Pritchett, "Is India a Flailing State? Detours on the Four Lane Highway to Modernization," Working Paper Series RWP09-013, John F. Kennedy School of Government, Harvard University, Cambridge, MA, 2009; Lant Pritchett, Kunal Sen, and Eric Werker, eds., *Deals and Development: The Political Dynamics of Growth Episodes* (Oxford: Oxford University Press, 2018).

109. Rajni Kothari, "The Congress 'System' in India," *Asian Survey* 4, no. 12 (1964): 1161–73.

110. Chhibber and Verma, *Ideology and Identity*, 7.

111. Consider, for instance, the diverse approaches to and recent debates around how historically marginalized groups such as Dalits and Muslims should be incorporated into the Indian state.

3

The Emergency and the Jayaprakash Narayan Movement

Jayaprakash [Narayan] has never taken me seriously. He does not understand that for action to be potent, time is of the essence…. One has to be really ruthless if the need arises. I am ruthless for what I think right.

—Prime Minister Indira Gandhi to Pupul Jayakar, 1971

Indira is India, India is Indira.

—D. K. Barooah, CPP meeting, 1975

Congress Party and Indira Gandhi

Indira Gandhi declared an internal Emergency throughout India on the night of June 25, 1975, thereby formally suppressing the anti-corruption JPM. As one historian of the period has remarked: "While the functioning of the Emergency may be seen in isolation, any analysis of its causes, its historical significance, as well as its consequences, has to be in the context of the JP movement."[1] The Emergency continued for 21 months, during which India witnessed the abuse of state powers to undercut institutions and the suppression of civil liberties and freedom of the press. This period in India's history (1975–77) has been insufficiently considered by scholars and historians.[2] The primary reason is the dearth of primary evidence and the simplistically dichotomous, or perhaps partisan, historiography of first-hand accounts.[3] This chapter will consider the way in which state elites—chief among them Prime Minister Indira Gandhi— harnessed state power to reshape society, a process that began by centralizing executive power to monopolize decision-making. Conditions underscoring this political and institutional setting provided the structural pathways that allowed the government to proclaim an Emergency and crush the JPM.

Prime Minister Indira Gandhi, who rose to office on a populist platform, enjoyed almost absolute political power in India—in large part due to the political strength of the Congress Party. During Gandhi's tenure, several highly publicized corruption scandals damaged government credibility, and the public outcry over these scandals came to a crescendo immediately before the government proclamation of a national internal Emergency. The centralizing state power in the hands of the populist prime minister, coupled with the force of a majority Congress, provided fertile conditions for Gandhi to supersede state institutions and declare a national Emergency. This chapter considers the Indian government's response to the JPM, and traces both the events that led to the Emergency and the steps taken by Gandhi and her close advisors to suppress the movement.

Indira Gandhi became the undisputed leader of her government in 1971.[4] That year, the Congress swept the national polls and won a two-thirds majority in the Lok Sabha (Lower House). The 1971 India–Pakistan War propelled Gandhi's prestige, as India defeated a regional foe while asserting its national interests. By March 1972, upon the swing of favorable state assembly election results, the Congress established its power across India. Gandhi revived the party's dominance, which had faded since the demise of its founding prime minister and her father, Jawaharlal Nehru, the 1967 elections, and the party split of 1969 (see Table 3.1).[5]

Table 3.1   Congress Party's General Election Performance, 1951–71

Election Year	Total Seats in Lok Sabha	Seats Contested by Congress Party	Seats Won by Congress Party	Congress Share of Seats in Lok Sabha (%)
1952	489	479	364	74
1957	494	490	371	75
1962	494	488	361	73
1967	520	516	283	54
1971	518	441	350	68

Source: www.elections.in.

Indira Gandhi's Rise to Power

Indira Gandhi entered high office after the untimely demise of the incumbent prime minister, Lal Bahadur Shastri, in January 1966. A leadership struggle ensued that resulted in Gandhi's victory over the veteran politician Morarji Desai. With this victory, the seeds of an internal battle of power and ideology were planted. In 1969, the Congress split along ideological lines, resulting in two factions: The "organization" faction (O) under the leadership of the party's senior right-of-center politicians, and the "requisitionist" faction (R) under the leadership of Gandhi and her left-of-center loyalists. Congress (R) dominated the 1971 elections in light of the success of the populist platform promoted by Gandhi. The new Congress cut across traditional electoral divisions, and swept the 1971 polls under Gandhi's leadership, winning 68 percent of the Lok Sabha seats (see Table 3.2).[6]

Table 3.2   General Election Results and Lok Sabha Seats, 1971

Party	Seats in Lok Sabha at Dissolution in 1970	Seats in Lok Sabha after 1971 General Election	Change in Seat Share
Congress (R)	229	350	+121
Communist Party of India (Marxist)	19	25	+6
Communist Party of India (CPI)	24	23	-1
Dravida Munnetra Kazhagam (DMK)	24	23	-1
Jana Sangh	23	22	-1
Congress (O)	65	16	-49
Swatantra Party	35	8	-27
Sanyukta Socialist Party (SSP)	17	3	-14
Praja Socialist Party (PSP)	15	2	-13
Bharatiya Kranti Dal (BKD)	10	1	-9
Other/Independent	52	48	-4

Source: www.elections.in.

Gandhi's populist platform emphasized ideas of secularism, socialism, and the representation of minorities.[7] Before 1971, many observers did not believe that any one party would gain a majority in the election. Just over 55 percent of the electorate voted, as opposed to the 61 percent who voted in the previous election.[8] Gandhi's Congress garnered nearly four million more votes than had the undivided Congress in 1967. Consequential to this victory were the votes that Congress (R) received from minorities—the poor, Scheduled Castes,

Sikhs, Muslims, and women.[9] As the election approached, the Congress aimed to "link the top and bottom layers of agrarian society by buttressing the waning political clout of high caste, old landed elites" and to champion "the common interests of subordinate castes and classes which transcended local and regional arenas."[10] Congress elites decided in a strategy session held before the election that their party must commit itself fully to a leftist program that emphasized social emancipation and, in turn, must unite around Indira Gandhi to maximize party aims.[11]

This populist strategy exacerbated Gandhi's authoritarian tendencies, and those that already bedeviled state structures. Decision-makers, chief among them Prime Minister Gandhi, used the state to reshape society, and began to centralize executive power while subordinating apex state institutions such as the Supreme Court and pressing civil, policy, and military institutions more broadly in the service of the ruling Congress Party. Holding the notion of a strong center as the "concomitant of Indian unity and national weal ingrained in her political philosophy," Gandhi concentrated power in her hands throughout her rise and sought to consolidate it thereafter.[12]

The 1971 victory shored up Gandhi's role as the leader of her government, which subsumed the Congress Party and its homogenizing ideological vector.[13] Between 1971 and 1975, the Congress (R) became less federal in structure, and power became centralized in the executive branch under Prime Minister Gandhi.[14] Historically, the inverse was standard. Gandhi also replaced Congress chief ministers and other state-level leaders who had independent political bases.[15] Those who remained or who were instated by Gandhi were ideologically and politically committed to, and even shaped, her Congress faction for many years thereafter.[16] Indeed, a group of powerful Congressmen who had been members of Gandhi's "kitchen cabinet" or inner circle since she rose to office in 1966 were appointed to powerful positions in the new government—they occupied critical cabinet posts, became president of the Congress Party, chief ministers of battle-ground states, and even included the president of India at the time, Fakhruddin Ali Ahmed.[17] Some, namely P. N. Haksar and Mohan Kumaramangalam, had a deep influence on the ideational direction of the Congress Party and government. These decision-makers shared in the Congress's concepts of the nation, anchored in secularism, which gave shape and content to Gandhi's populism, and fully cooperated in the decision-making process that led to the suppression of the JPM.

Emergence of the Corrupt State and Credibility Crisis

By the end of 1972, the government's credibility began to wane in the wake of poor economic growth, an international financial crisis, a sense of unfulfilled campaign promises, and the exposure of corruption scandals at the center. It is against the background of this broad socio-economic crisis and these scandals that the JPM rose to prominence. The Jayaprakash Narayan Movement (JPM), which captivated India between 1974 and 1975, was symbolized by the Gandhian activist Jayaprakash Narayan (JP). JP, a one-time member of the Congress Socialist Party (CSP), was active in the 1942 Quit India movement, and led the Indian anti-corruption wave of the early 1970s. After the CSP broke away from the Congress in 1948, JP renounced official party politics and became involved in social activism.[18] The famine in Bihar (1966–67) was a turning point for JP's intellectual and political evolution, as it signaled a breakdown of society around him, and would fuel the impending call of "total revolution" that JP would make in the 1970s through the anti-corruption movement. JP emphasized an activist approach to civic engagement, which resulted in the JPM tactics of marches, sit-ins, and fasts-unto-death. The movement aimed to cleanse the Indian government of corruption and to bring about "a moral regeneration of its politics."[19] JP reflected that, during his time in the Sarvodaya movement for self-determination and social equality, corruption had been the primary source of poor governance, poverty, and other ailments in India, as it "ate into the very vitals of [the] nation."[20]

From January 1974 to June 1975, India underwent a turbulent period of demonstrations against government corruption. These demonstrations, which were led by JP and his allies, began at the state level in Gujarat and Bihar, and quickly escalated to the national level. The protests consumed a cross-section of society, with up to 500,000 people demonstrating against governmental corruption at the movement's peak.[21] In early April 1974, JP declared: "I cannot remain a silent spectator to misgovernment, corruption and the rest.... It is not for this that I at least had fought for freedom [India's independence]."[22] Two months later, JP repeated: "The problem of corruption has become more intolerable to me personally and I have come out personally to wage a fight against it."[23] Later, while in prison, JP reflected in his diary, "Corruption has been the central point of the movement, particularly corruption in the government and administration."[24]

Scandals and the Corrupt State

The exposure of government corruption scandals was widespread in India in the late 1960s and early 1970s, and at their peak, these scandals even implicated the prime minister. State investigations began to ratchet up into increasing allegations of corruption. The Santhanam Committee, for example, was appointed by Lal Bahadur Shastri in 1962 to "review the existing instruments of checking corruption in the Central Services" and to provide advice on the "practical steps that should be taken to make anti-corruption measures more effective."[25] The committee submitted its report in 1964. The report indicated that specific allegations of political corruption against any government minister should be promptly investigated by "an agency whose findings would command respect." In March 1970, the Direct Taxes Enquiry Committee was appointed by the president of India under the chairmanship of former chief justice of India K. N. Wanchoo to investigate the emerging issues of, among other things, black money and tax evasion and avoidance. These conditions precipitated the narrative of the corrupt state and the national relevance and rise of the JPM. For example, in mid-1971, Indira Gandhi's son and informal advisor Sanjay Gandhi was dubiously chosen from eighteen applicants by the Ministry of Industries to receive a trade license to produce 50,000 cars annually. This car, called Maruti, was to be a small and affordable vehicle produced entirely in India. The Congress chief minister of Haryana, Bansi Lal, acquired 290 acres of land for the Maruti factory near Gurgaon, just southwest of Delhi, at far below the market price. The prospective location of the factory violated the federal regulation that no factory should be built within 1,000 meters of a defense installation (in this case, a munition dump). Meanwhile, as Sanjay Gandhi raised significant capital investments from businessmen, the remaining capital was acquired through unsecured loans from nationalized banks. Accusations of nepotism and corruption hounded Gandhi's venture.[26]

During this time, and after the Congress re-election of 1971, governmental corruption became weekly headline news. From the alleged bribery of politicians to the sale of trade licenses for private favors, senior government officials and cabinet ministers became mired in highly publicized scandals. The most prominent case implicated L. N. Mishra, the cabinet minister of railways and Congress Party fundraiser, in what was deemed the "Pondicherry License Scam." Congress minister Tulmohan Ram, who allegedly acted under the instruction of Mishra, was indicted for forging the signatures of twenty-one MPs to seek licenses from the Ministry of Commerce and Industry for several Pondicherry businessmen in exchange for financial contributions to the Congress Party. Mishra escaped punishment, but the parliamentary opposition pounced on the scandal and sought a federal investigation into the affair. Gandhi attempted to prevent the investigation, and refused to remove Mishra from her cabinet. The Kapoor Commission concluded that there had been no proper accounting of the funds, a conclusion also reached by B. N. Tandon and D. P. Dhar, two key advisers to the prime minister who assiduously reviewed the audit reports.[27] P. N. Dhar, Gandhi's Principal Secretary at the time, believed that the government's handling of the Mishra case had been flawed, and urged the prime minister to initiate an enquiry into Mishra to re-establish the government's credibility.[28] However, S. S. Ray, Congress chief minister of West Bengal and close advisor to the prime minister, counselled against this, arguing that the motion to hold an enquiry would be defeated in parliament, but could easily be completed without the parliamentary hearing.[29] Gandhi followed Ray's counsel—not for the first time—and protected Mishra. The opposition, in turn, put the government on the defensive, and continued its call for action against Mishra. This call came to a halt, however, with the minister's sudden and suspicious demise during a bombing in Bihar in early January 1975.[30]

As the allegations detailed above engulfed her government, Gandhi consistently took a defensive posture regarding the corruption of the center.[31] The center's credibility eroded not only due to mounting charges of corruption among ministers, but also due to the strong sense that Gandhi had not marked eliminating corruption as a high priority in her policy agenda, and that she had actively protected corrupt members of her government.[32] In a diary entry from the period, B. N. Tandon, a Joint Secretary to Gandhi, noted that the prime minister was "very angry and upset" about the Pondicherry License Scam, but that she had no intent to take action against Mishra. According to Tandon, Gandhi thought that her father, Jawaharlal Nehru, had "made a big mistake by removing T.T. Krishnamachari [1958] and Krishna Menon [1962] from the cabinet," and did not plan to repeat Nehru's mistake.[33] In another diary entry of May 21, 1975, Tandon noted that Gandhi viewed government corruption "purely from a political standpoint":

> So many cases of corruption against Congress Chief Ministers and Ministers have been placed before the PM, but not a single file has been returned. Om Mehta [Minister of State for Home Affairs] is a close confidante of the PM and he also follows the same policy. I told him that if the central government

orders a judicial enquiry even in one or two cases, the people will begin to regain their confidence in the government. *But he replied that the circumstances were very difficult and that it was essential to view all such matters from a Party viewpoint.* He said that the PM also was of this view. (My emphasis here, and elsewhere, in italics unless stated otherwise)[34]

At an address to the Indian Political Science Conference in Calcutta on December 27, 1972, the prime minister provided clear insight into her stance on government corruption:

> When people speak of corruption, there is a tendency to imagine that bribery was unknown in British times.... I admit that there were administrators of high rectitude then as there are now. But the entire old system, whether it was colonial rule or princely rule, was thoroughly corrupt.... *Merely by running down the present, we shall not be able to generate the will to correct and improve.*[35]

The impression that corruption emanated from and was absolved at the highest levels of the central government was exacerbated when the prime minister herself was implicated in the abuse of her office.[36] On June 12, 1975, Justice Jagmohanlal Sinha of the Allahabad High Court dealt a blow to the credibility of Gandhi and her government by implicating the prime minister in a case of corrupt campaign practices while in office.[37] As he judged the election petition filed by Raj Narain, the candidate who Gandhi had defeated in the 1971 Lok Sabha election, Sinha made recourse to two offenses. The primary offense was the illegally proffered services of the prime minister's close aide, Yashpal Kapoor, during the 1971 campaign. Kapoor had resigned from government service, but his resignation had not yet been accepted by the president, nor had it been properly gazetted. The second offense was the construction of a dais by police and the provision of electricity by the state electricity department, which flouted regulations regarding the use of government mechanisms during political campaigns. Gandhi's star suddenly crashed, as this conviction meant that she could not seek election to parliament or hold public office for a period of six years, and that she could not legitimately continue as prime minister.[38] This scandal galvanized the efforts of the JPM.

Credibility Crisis and Rise of the JPM

The JPM captured citizens' anger at government corruption that emerged against a backdrop of deteriorating economic conditions, and culminated in a credibility crisis for Indira Gandhi's government. Although from 1967 to 1972 the national economic and political mood was confident due to positive gross domestic product (GDP) growth and the successful liberation of Bangladesh, the period from 1972 to 1975 marked a deterioration in this atmosphere that resulted from domestic and international economic crises.[39] An economic recession, growing unemployment, and rampant inflation created a sense of crisis in the country, which was now beset by emergent strikes and protests. This downturn hit the Gandhi government hard due to the prevailing political economy, which was organized around deeply penetrative social policies and the state-mediated provision of agricultural inputs such as seeds, fertilizer, water, and guaranteed markets. Acute shortages in household items gave unscrupulous traders and manufacturers the opportunity to indulge in hoarding and black-market practices.[40] The broadening exposure of the corrupt state narrative heightened with increased citizen awareness and politicization during this period of rural poverty, as well as with deficits in education and healthcare. These factors combined to erode citizens' support for the ruling Congress government.[41]

Beginning in January 1974, JP began to lead major demonstrations against corruption, which sprouted across India and put the government under tremendous strain.[42] These demonstrations were instigated by students on university campuses, most prominently in the states of Gujarat and Bihar, and subsequently spread across the country and consumed a cross-section of Indian society.[43] Upon taking formal leadership of these loosely organized agitations in early 1974, JP declared, "I have decided to fight corruption and misgovernment.... This is not meant as a threat, but as a friendly warning. That shall be the beginning. The rest will follow."[44] At one of the first public meetings of the JPM in Patna on April 9, 1974, JP noted: "For 27 years I have watched [corrupt] events unfold, but I can stand on the sidelines no longer. I have vowed not to allow this state of things to continue."[45]

At first, JP repeatedly emphasized that India was ripe for revolution, and that his anti-corruption movement was its vanguard.[46] Thereafter, JPM rallies became national phenomena that drew large crowds, especially in the political capital of New Delhi.[47] From March to November 1974, when it clashed with state security forces, the movement spread across the nation to states such as Uttar Pradesh (UP), Orissa, West Bengal, Punjab, and Rajasthan, among others.[48] Despite its lack of a full-fledged program, the movement presented a Charter of Demands to parliament at its most prominent demonstration in

March 1975. This charter called for the implementation of the Santhanam Committee findings to combat corruption, including the institutionalization of an anti-corruption ombudsman (Lokpal) to investigate cases of political corruption against ministers at the center.[49] As the movement evolved, the JPM became focused on the purported sources of corruption within the ruling Congress government, principally targeting the prime minister.[50] As such, the movement vowed to support non-corrupt and non-Congress candidates in state elections. In the aftermath of the Allahabad High Court judgment, which charged Prime Minister Gandhi with corrupt campaign practices, the movement turned squarely toward displacing the incumbent Congress government.

As the JPM expanded, the movement grew to include many students, citizens across classes and across the rural–urban divide, business elites, politicians, and social activists.[51] Supporters of the movement viewed the confrontation between the JPM and the government as an expression of the "people's power" that emerged in the mass movement against the "state power" vested in the corrupt system of politics.[52]

JPM Support and Composition

As the movement gained momentum, the JPM gained external backing from opposition political parties such as the Jana Sangh, Anand Marg, Congress (O), Bharatiya Lok Dal (BLD), DMK, Akali Dal, and SSP.[53] Despite this support, JP consistently maintained that he led a "people's movement" rather than a partisan political movement.[54] In fact, he continued to express frustration at claims to the contrary.[55] K. S. Radhakrishna, JP's confidante and a prominent activist in the JPM, repeated up until the Allahabad judgment that "the movement has never sought the removal of this or that person. If throwing out a chief minister or prime minister were all that there was to the movement then it would be in no way different from the earlier attempts at the political level [by opposition parties]."[56] In November 1974, at a meeting of all non-communist Indian political parties, JP reiterated that the purpose of the JPM was to purify the government of corruption rather than to replace one political party with another.[57] He declared that he would do all in his power to "bring opposition parties together on the national level, [but] again in the context of the people's movement [JPM]," and continued to urge that parties should eschew their "party mentality" if participating in the movement.[58] The opposition parties' support for the JPM intensified in June 1975 against the backdrop of a key assembly election in Gujarat and the Allahabad judgment, and as combating corruption became synonymous with removing the prime minister from office.[59] Most critically, suppression of the JPM began months before the emergence of deepening support for the movement among semi-loyal opposition parties.

The most instructive crackdown on the JPM in 1974 occurred that November with the increasing visibility of its mobilization of the religious nationalist Rashtriya Swayamsevak Sangh (RSS) in the JPM.[60] Unlike the more sporadic and verbal support from opposition parties, which increased in action as the movement came to national prominence, tens of thousands of members and workers of the RSS were involved earlier as a mobilization force.[61] Although he was a vocal critic of the RSS and its political arm, the Jana Sangh, and although for many years he referred to the religious nationalist group as the "enemies" of Hinduism and India, JP eventually softened his opposition to RSS involvement in the JPM to encourage the anti-corruption movement to realize its goals.[62] The JPM and RSS did not share an ideology, per se, and many JPM activists were concerned about the RSS presence. However, the two groups shared several overlapping interests.[63] The JPM, for example, shared with the RSS a concern for political decentralization. In this way, both groups were to differing degrees ideologically opposed to the Nehruvian state and its modernization championed by Indira Gandhi's Congress Party.[64] One major difference between the JPM and the RSS, however, was that the former valued welfare-maximizing efforts such as the removal of corruption on humanitarian grounds, whereas the RSS argued that such policies served the ultimate aim of endowing Hindu society with a new ideology.[65] Overall, where the JPM relied on the RSS as a mobilization vehicle, the RSS found in the JPM a vessel to integrate itself into a more legitimate form of political engagement.

A close reading of JP's own political evolution suggests that the above-described "paradoxical positionality" was not unique to this political episode.[66] JP did not officially represent or speak for a specific group or entity, and "therefore he could address the issue of imperial fragments—unruly peripheries of empire that postcolonial states saw the need to forcibly absorb and directly rule."[67] It is clear from fresh archival material and biographies—heavily footnoted in these pages—that JP was a complicated and often elusive man. He believed that a binary understanding of social and political concepts obscured the potential for malleability, negotiation, and reconciliation. This made him ideal to lead movements that combined different political philosophies.[68] We may be tempted to side with JP sympathizer Bhola Chatterjee, who argues that the RSS were welcomed into the JPM due to their mobilizational strength, and that JP, in turn, felt it necessary to placate the RSS to achieve the movement's goals.[69] Indeed, in 1966, JP wrote a letter to Indira Gandhi—with whom he had a productive relationship at this time and who utilized him akin to an emissary on specific matters of policy concern—on a host of issues that concerned him, including religious nationalism: "We profess secularism, but let Hindu nationalism stampede us into trying to establish it by repression." He closed his letter with a reminder of his own personal connection with the Indian people: "There is no one in your government who is as constantly and widely in touch with the people as I." JP, of course, remained outside Gandhi's government. In light of later events, an implicit threat hung heavily behind these words. And though Gandhi's position at this time was as a fresh, newly installed leader, she turned against JP when he threatened her power and his previously disavowed links to the RSS surfaced visibly under the umbrella of the JPM.[70]

Government Action and the Emergency

Confrontations between JPM and the Government

It is crucial to the purposes of the current case study to understand that the RSS–JPM relationship became visible to the government whose ideological vector was forcefully oppositional to this make-up. When the JPM emerged, Indira Gandhi worried a great deal about the unrest that such a mass movement could cause to her government against India's backdrop of international uncertainty and internal socioeconomic difficulty.[71] She sought to disparage the movement as ineffective and misleading: "We all know that this kind of peaceful movement is never successful. Their intention has nothing to do with the results of this kind of movement [anti-corruption]."[72] On November 1, 1974, several months after the movement's inception, Gandhi and JP held their only meeting during the period of demonstrations in Delhi.[73] The prime minister offered a compromise—she was willing to dismiss the government in JP's home state of Bihar, where the movement had begun, provided that the JPM campaign ended nationally. Gandhi sensed a growing tide in the movement. JP declined, sensing that the center sought to dilute the anti-corruption agitation and its emerging national appeal, and he continued to organize demonstrations across India.

Days later, on November 4, Gandhi instructed the Bihar government and the state security forces stationed there to crush the JPM demonstrations planned for the next day.[74] Despite the government's attempts to prevent demonstrators from travelling to Patna for the march by cancelling trains and capturing boats, at least 20,000 people still took part in the demonstration.[75] A police clampdown ensued, and security forces used tear gas and batons (*lathi*s) to suppress the demonstrators. JP and others, such as prominent RSS leader Nanaji Deshmukh who took the heavy *lathi* blows, were injured during the police clampdown, and nearly 3,000 people were arrested.[76] Nevertheless, the movement remained undeterred and was emboldened by this explicit act of government suppression. JP claimed that the "rumble" of the movement's "chariot" would now be heard in Delhi as the movement sought to recover.[77] As anti-corruption fervor rose, small sections of Gandhi's government favored dialogue with the JPM.

A minority of ministers continued to push for dialogue, but Gandhi ignored their call, as a quorum failed to emerge.[78] Chandra Shekhar, for example, a Congress politician who would be imprisoned by the government during the Emergency for his alleged close relationship with JP, later recorded that he "pleaded with Mrs. Gandhi time and again" to meet with JP and to resolve their differences. He argued that "with the political power Mrs. Gandhi enjoyed and the moral power Jayaprakash possessed, both should unite to lift the country out of the morass."[79] Shekhar's statement is corroborated in the memoirs of Gandhi's Principal Secretary at the time, the technocrat P. N. Dhar, who wrote that he attempted to reach across the aisle to create dialogue with JP.[80] Instead, when the corruption-mired cabinet minister L. N. Mishra died under suspicious circumstances in Bihar, a stronghold of the JPM, the prime minister sensed a direct attack on her government, and was so taken aback that she considered preventatively arresting JP.[81] At this point, negotiations between the government and the JPM were completely off the table. At the All-India Congress Committee (AICC) meeting in late 1974, Gandhi said of the proposal to negotiate with the JPM: "I do not understand what 'negotiations' mean. What do you negotiate about? How to destroy democracy? Is this negotiable?"[82]

After denouncing the JPM as an attempt to alter the government by unconstitutional means, Gandhi, in classic populist zeal of privileging popular will, requested that the movement legally test the legitimacy of the government by contesting her candidacy in the general elections held in February and March of 1976.[83] Gandhi claimed that this was the most appropriate mechanism by which to measure the sense of the Indian people.[84] JP, in turn, agreed to take the movement's agitation to the polls—not as a party, but as a movement to rally the populace against corruption and to support non-corrupt candidates from opposition parties. On November 18, 1974, at a large rally at the Gandhi Maidan in Patna, Bihar, JP declared:

> I have accepted the challenge and we shall wait till the next elections for the people's verdict. Since the Prime Minister has dragged the conflict into the electoral arena, I shall take my position in the battlefield, not as a candidate, but as a leader. The contest will be only between those who support the struggle and those who oppose it.[85]

JP led a twenty-member National Coordination Committee (NCC) at a conference of fifty political parties and groups in Delhi. The role of the committee was to direct anti-corruption agitation across the country, especially in the capital at the parliament. The committee even planned to undermine All-India Radio while waiting for the elections to be held.

On March 6, 1975, JP led a procession of half a million citizens to the Indian parliament.[86] The government tried to prevent protestors from joining the demonstrations by cancelling bus permits and other methods of transportation to the capital. Nevertheless, members of the RSS as well as students, citizens from across classes and the rural–urban divide, business elites, politicians, and Sarvodaya members mobilized together to peacefully demonstrate.[87] No party flags or slogans were raised, as all individual parties met under the JPM umbrella to present parliament with a Charter of Demands to implement, among other matters, the Santhanam Committee findings.[88] In turn, Gandhi's government sought to undermine the JPM agitation. Congress leader Jagjivan Ram called the march "an insult to the Constitution,"[89] while D. K. Barooah, the Congress president, called it a "flop."[90] One national newspaper, *The Hindu*, commented that the RSS presence in the JPM had "infuriated Mrs. Gandhi to the point of ruling out the possibility of any talks with him [JP] in the near future."[91] Within three months, the movement and its supporters had been crushed by the institutionalization of an internal Emergency.

The events that immediately led to this suppression began in mid-June 1975. On June 12, the Allahabad High Court judgment that implicated the prime minister in corrupt campaign practices damaged the government's credibility. At 10 o'clock that morning, the Allahabad High Court judgment reached the PMO. Within thirty minutes, Minister of Law and Justice H. R. Gokhale, S. S. Ray, legal counsel N. Palkhivala, Additional Private Secretary to the Prime Minister R. K. Dhawan, and Gandhi's son Sanjay had gathered at the Prime Minister's House (PMH) to strategize with her.[92] There was intense discussion, and confusion, about whether the prime minister should resign.[93] Her advisors agreed unanimously that she should not.[94] That evening, another blow hit the credibility of the government, as the state election results from Gujarat showed that the Congress's political capital had diminished. Despite Gandhi's active campaigning in Gujarat during the previous two months, the Janata Front, a right-of-center alliance of parties led by Morarji Desai and backed by the JPM, had won 87 seats against the Congress's 75 seats in a House of 182 seats.[95]

The Allahabad High Court judgment and the Gujarat election results energized the JPM, and more intensely aligned both the movement and the rightist coalition in their call to oust the prime minister. Whereas the coalition of opposition parties had long called for a change in government, as detailed earlier, the JPM now held a greater common cause with these parties, as Gandhi had been exposed as corruptly occupying the highest office in the country. The leaders and supporters of the movement called for the prime minister to resign immediately, fearing that a dubious appeal would be pursued by the government. Demonstrations erupted in Delhi, outside parliament as well as the president's house on June 13, 1975. Newspapers also joined the chorus of dissenters and called for the prime minister to uphold democracy and to step down from the high office that she had illegitimately gained.

Gandhi refused to concede her office, and found allies among her cabinet and advisors. They viewed Justice Sinha's judgment as insufficient cause to invalidate her election. Gandhi was widely advised that the evidence against her was not strong enough to withstand a Supreme Court inquiry, and that she should therefore appeal the decision. Moreover, as P. N. Dhar notes in his memoirs, the prime minister worried "about the consequences of her exit to the governance of the country," and "the opposition [parties] coming to power ... was a specter that haunted her because she believed it would be a disaster for the country."[96] Dhar, who despite heading Gandhi's secretariat we will later see was sidelined in the decision-making process that preceded the Emergency, privately held reservations about the prime minister's counsel—namely that these decision-makers would prescribe "gimmicky" populist measures to please Gandhi, and that these steps would not revitalize the government's credibility. In contrast, Dhar hoped to implement the following policies: "First, to keep the prices of items of common, everyday consumption under control; second, to implement land reforms; and third, a strong effort to raise production in industry and agriculture. He thought that ... gimmicky measures would only damage the economy, not benefit it."[97] Dhar, one of the few technocrats among Gandhi's close advisors during these days, believed that policy solutions lay at the core of the angst that fueled the JPM. Ultimately, however, Dhar was "helpless to do anything since the PM was surrounded by people who were giving her all kinds of foolish advice [that she wanted to hear]."[98]

Government decision-makers met in parliament on June 18, 1975, to reiterate their "fullest faith and confidence" in Gandhi's leadership. Ministers unanimously signed a loyalty pledge that stated: "Mrs. Indira Gandhi continues to be our Prime Minister. It is our firm and considered view that for the integrity, stability, and progress of the country, her dynamic leadership is indispensable."[99] The resolution was enacted by Jagjivan Ram and Y. B. Chavan, two leaders with significant political followings. It was at this meeting that the now-notorious phrase was first uttered by the Congress Party president, D. K. Barooah—"Indira is India, India is Indira"—in a distasteful hearkening to the language used by Deputy Fuhrer Rudolf Hess to conflate Adolf Hitler and Germany.[100] Subsequently, in line with Dhar's prediction of "gimmicky" politics, beginning on June 20, pro-government demonstrations were staged in Delhi by the prime minister's close advisors led by her son Sanjay Gandhi to counter the ongoing rallies of the JPM.[101] While the government attempted to recover from the scandal, the JPM agitation was emboldened.

Although the Supreme Court was set to hear the prime minister's appeal against the Allahabad High Court judgment on July 14, Justice V. R. Krishna Iyer, the vacation judge of the Supreme Court, offered both sides a pyrrhic victory on June 24 with the pronouncement of a *conditional* stay in office for Gandhi. While Gandhi's appeal had asked for an *absolute* stay, Justice Iyer, while holding that Gandhi had not been convicted of "any of the graver electoral vices," gave her only a conditional stay, as the High Court ruling, until upset, held good, however weak it might ultimately prove. Iyer concluded that, until the appeal could be heard by the full bench of the Supreme Court, her electoral disqualification stood "eclipsed" and she should continue as prime minister. He ruled that she could not, however, vote or draw a salary as an MP. With this ruling, both the government and the JPM drew confidence. For the latter, the conditional stay was a snub to Gandhi's credibility, while for the government, the order virtually exonerated the prime minister.

Buoyed by the conditional stay decision, JP led a major rally at Delhi's Ramlila Maidan on June 25. At the rally, he affirmed that Gandhi continued to corruptly hold office, and had therefore lost the moral right to rule.[102] He urged citizens to refuse to listen to or take orders from a "disqualified head of a discredited government."[103] He urged the crowd to refuse to allow Gandhi to continue to corrupt the nation's top post, and to compel her to resign through week-long rallies, demonstrations, and civil disobedience. The campaign would be organized by a new body, the Lok Sangharsh Samiti (People's Struggle Committee), which was instituted that very day by JP in conjunction with a wide range of opposition parties and groups.[104] These demonstrations would seek to "bring everything to a standstill."[105] What followed was completely unanticipated by the JPM and its supporters.[106] After the rally, JP returned to the Gandhi Peace Foundation and retired to bed. In the early hours of the next morning, the police knocked on his door with a warrant for his detention under the Maintenance of Internal Security Act (MISA), and informed him that a state of Emergency had been proclaimed across India.

Prime Minister Indira Gandhi instituted an internal Emergency under Article 352 of the Indian Constitution in the early hours of June 26 to suppress the JPM. The order led to the arrest of JPM leaders and activists, including many university students, as well as a ban on the right-wing parties and organizations that had helped to mobilize the JPM. The fundamental architecture of the Indian Constitution was suspended, such as civil liberties, such as the freedoms of speech, the press, and assembly, including the holding of meetings, processions, and demonstrations guaranteed under Article 19.

Partisans Proclaim the Emergency

To underscore the primacy of Gandhi's centralized executive power to monopolize decision-making, it is necessary to trace the steps that led to the Emergency proclamation. Around midnight on June 25, 1975, President Fakhruddin Ali Ahmed, acting on the advice of Prime Minister Gandhi, signed a proclamation that would come into effect the next morning, and which declared a state of internal Emergency in India that crushed the JPM. The proclamation was signed on the grounds that "a grave emergency exists whereby the security of India is threatened by internal disturbances."[107] This security threat alluded, of course, to the JPM. The prime minister's cabinet remained uninformed of the proclamation and the decisions that led to it, and became aware of it only when summoned for a meeting the following morning. Their ideological alignment and deference to Gandhi, which had only days before been reinforced, meant that she faced no compulsion to consult her cabinet on the issue. Overnight, a select few decision-makers absorbed immense powers into the executive branch.

In the twenty-one months that followed the declaration of Emergency, 110,806 citizens were arrested under the draconian MISA and other laws. JPM activists, leaders, and supporters were the first to be imprisoned, and thirty MPs from opposition parties that had supported the movement, along with some dissidents from the Congress who had expressed sympathy for the movement, were detained.[108] In a strong illustration of the ideas that activated the government's populism, twenty-six communal groups and organizations, primarily those that had formed the locus of the JPM, such as the RSS, were banned, and their workers and members were arrested.

This framework, which aligned with the government's suppressive response toward the JPM, had been visible months before, and preceded the Allahabad High Court judgment and coming together of the movement and opposition parties. In her recent account of the Emergency, journalist Coomi Kapoor reproduces a previously unseen handwritten note given by S. S. Ray to Indira Gandhi that clearly illustrates that the West Bengal chief minister, along with H. R. Gokhale, D. K. Barooah, and Bombay Pradesh Congress Committee (PCC) leader Rajni Patel, floated the idea of an internal Emergency as early as January 8, 1975.[109] In the letter, Ray writes that "some people do not realize the seriousness of the situation in the country," and that a secret message should be sent to every Congress chief minister "directing him to prepare a list of all prominent Anand Marg and RSS members in his state" who mobilized against the government.[110] These leaders formulated this plan at the very moment that Gandhi had been rattled by L. N. Mishra's sudden and acrimonious demise during an explosion in Bihar, which Gandhi blamed on the JPM's demonstrations in the state.[111] Although that January the prime minister eventually eased on the suppression of her detractors upon the advice of P. N. Dhar, the events of the Emergency on June 25 were a near copy of those outlined in the letter Gandhi received from Ray.[112]

On June 25, Prime Minister Gandhi took into confidence a select group of advisors, who were all members of the ruling Congress Party or close confidantes such as her son and personal secretary, regarding the government's plans to suppress the JPM. Congress chief ministers of several states were instructed by R. K. Dhawan and Om Mehta, the Minister of State for Home Affairs, to expect important orders from the PMH that evening.[113] S. S. Ray had been summoned to the PMH earlier that morning.[114] Upon sitting down to talk, Gandhi informed her long-time friend Ray, who was her former cabinet minister and then Congress chief minister of West Bengal, that "the country was in great difficulty and that, in view of all round indiscipline and lawlessness, she wanted something to be done."[115] She read from a report that purportedly gave advance information about what JP would say at his rally that day in Delhi, and that predicted that he would make an effective call for continued, massive protests within two to three days.[116] This movement, Gandhi concluded, threatened lawlessness in many parts of northern India. The prime minister wanted to act, and she needed a trusted, audacious figure who understood the constitutional parameters to move forward. Ray, a barrister presiding over a troubled state, fit the bill.[117]

Ray, tasked with finding constitutional justification for what appeared to be an impending crackdown, asked for time to consult the relevant laws, and left the PMH. He returned around 5 o'clock that evening, and suggested that the prime minister use Article 352 of the Constitution to impose an internal Emergency. Gandhi immediately asked Ray to accompany her to see President Fakhruddin Ali Ahmed. Ahmed was close to Gandhi and had served in her informal "kitchen cabinet" when the Congress began to fray into separate ideological factions in the mid- and late-1960s, and would later sit in her formal cabinet after the 1971 election victory before becoming president of India. At the mere twenty-five-minute meeting, Gandhi informed the president of the planned demonstrations, and asked Ray to provide constitutional justification to him for the possible pathways to action against the JPM. The president asked Gandhi to make her recommendation by that evening. On their return to the PMH, Gandhi posed three questions that clearly indicate her desire for swift decision-making in response to the JPM: (*a*) Could she make a decision without the approval of the cabinet? (*b*) How should she word her letter to the president? (*c*) What should the Emergency proclamation say? Upon considering the pathways made possible by the Business Rules of the Constitution, the prime minister decided that she would send a letter to the president that evening asserting that an internal Emergency must be instituted immediately, and that she would call a meeting with her cabinet the following morning.

Indeed, in recent weeks Gandhi's cabinet and senior party officials had committed their unwavering support for her, and she confidently presumed their cooperation, acting without concern for internal sanction. Together with Ray and D. K. Barooah, the prime minister crafted her letter to President Ahmed, who would ratify the decision. The process took roughly three hours.[118] Only a select group of advisors took part in this decision-making process, which included the primary patrons of the Congress Party and the government. In addition to Ray and Barooah, there was Sanjay Gandhi, as well as Mehta and Dhawan. These men unanimously supported the prime minister's decision.[119] Home Minister Brahmananda Reddy was summoned to PMH at 10:15 that evening, and was informed that due to the "deteriorating law and order situation," an internal Emergency would be announced that night. In his deposition to the Shah Commission years later, Reddy noted that he replied to the prime minister at the time that she should undertake whatever action she believed best.[120] His deference reflected Gandhi's centralized power over both the government and the Congress. Reddy then signed the letter to the president.[121]

At 11:20, Akhtar Alam, Special Assistant to the President, received R. K. Dhawan, who brought documents from the prime minister which stressed that Gandhi wanted to act expeditiously, as she felt confident in the support of her government.[122] Secretary to the President K. Balachandran presented these documents to the president, which included a letter that referenced the discussion that had taken place between Gandhi and the president earlier that day. Balachandran's deposition confirms that the prime minister made explicit in this letter that she had not consulted her cabinet due to the "shortage of time," and that the urgency of the matter permitted a departure from the Transaction of Business Rules that regulated the exercise of her powers under Rule 12. This course of action had been advised by Ray earlier that day.[123] The draft proclamation, dated June 25 and addressed to the president with a "Top Secret" letterhead, underlined that "there is an imminent danger to the security of India being threatened by internal disturbance" and that "a requisite Proclamation under Article 352(1) has become necessary."[124] The president concurred, and signed the proclamation of Emergency close to midnight. The Emergency execution, which led to the first period of despotic rule in India's post-Independence history thus far, and which would suppress several hundred thousand Indian citizens, took just over six hours. Indira Gandhi stood squarely atop this decision-making chain, and acted with minimal constraints and the full cooperation of decision-makers in her government.

Cabinet Secretary B. D. Pande received a phone call from the PMH at around 4:30 in the morning on June 26, and was told that a cabinet meeting would be scheduled to take place at 6 o'clock that morning. The mere hour and a half between the inception and session of the meeting illustrated its simple formality.[125] According to Pande, neither the need for the declaration of Emergency nor the conditions that warranted such a move had figured in any prior cabinet meetings. Thus, Gandhi had received no intimation that she would face any obstruction from her cabinet colleagues, as, on the contrary, they had recently fully established their support.[126] Unsurprisingly, the only decision-maker known to have disagreed with the measure at the time, Principal Secretary P. N. Dhar, was only called to the PMH at 11:30 the night before the meeting, when he and the Prime Minister's information advisor H. Y. Sharada Prasad were asked to peruse a draft of the speech that Gandhi would make over the radio.[127] Gandhi's presumption that her cabinet and staff would support her decision further underscores her unrestrained power to act unilaterally and arbitrarily.

Prime Minister Gandhi could formally suppress the JPM by instituting the Emergency—and by mobilizing the despotic powers this decision afforded her—in part because no political constraints compelled her to act otherwise. Gandhi's decision was buttressed by cooperative advisors who shared her diagnosis of the JPM. The prime minister told the president, who had served in her cabinet and was a former Congress politician who revered Gandhi, that she would inform her cabinet of the decision the next day as mere formality. With this gesture, Gandhi illustrated the strength and power of her executive. However, the structural drivers of this narrative do not sufficiently explain the dynamics of intolerance shown by Gandhi's government to its critics. To better understand this dynamic, we must consider these decision-makers' worldviews, and why they chose to undermine the JPM. The government's suppression of the JPM was an attempt to build solidarity within the Congress Party by crushing ideological others within the anti-corruption movement. The interaction between the government's populism, anchored in the Congress' secular nationalism, in the next chapter and the structural conditions presented in this chapter illustrate a fuller picture of the government's suppressive response to the movement.

Notes

1. Bipan Chandra, *In the Name of Democracy: JP Movement and the Emergency* (New Delhi: Penguin Books, 2003), 1.
2. There have been limitations in my exploration of this case, given the restricted access the Government of India provides to researchers of this period. Many official documents have been destroyed, while Indira Gandhi's private papers and government records are not open to scholars. Even P. N. Dhar, whose memoirs are perhaps one of the most widely referenced of any primary writing on the Emergency, did not have access to official records (P. N. Dhar, *Indira Gandhi, the "Emergency," and Indian Democracy* [New Delhi: Oxford University Press, 2000]). The official, legal investigation into the decision to institute an Emergency and its effects—the Shah Commission Report—was released in August 1978. However, when Gandhi returned to power in January 1980, she had all known copies withdrawn and destroyed. A couple of libraries in the UK and Australia maintained the report and a resurrected copy of the report was published in 2010 by former Indian member of parliament (MP) Era Sezhian (Sezhiyan, *Shah Commission Report*). Despite the political wrangling around the report (most recently former president of India P. Mukherjee's memoirs (Pranab Mukherjee, *The Dramatic Decade: The Indira Gandhi Years* [New Delhi: Rupa Publications, 2015]), .leading legal experts in India today believe the commission report to be reliable and the only official enquiry into the causes and events of the Emergency. Meanwhile, Jayaprakash Narayan's (JP's) papers at the Nehru Memorial Museum and Library (NMML) are private in name only, as they consist almost entirely of articles and speeches that can be found available open-sourced. Evidence that is unavailable often lowers the upper limit of the probability one can attach to the explanation. One way I have overcome this is through triangulating the evidence, including excavating private correspondence from related archives that includes the actors under study. For example, uncovering diplomatic cables from the US and UK where I found first-hand observations and interviews with Congress Party leaders and other decision-makers from the period. A look at diplomatic cables for purely domestic political analysis is seldom employed, and has not been utilized in other studies of the Emergency in the explicit context of the JPM. The evidence that follows in the empirical chapters is as much about corroborating evidence as it is about uncovering primary material from India and elsewhere. In tracing the causal steps leading up to the decision to institute the Emergency, I have concerned myself with what is written, but also with how it is written and what has been excluded.

3. Emma Tarlo attentively articulates the historiography of the Emergency period, dividing accounts of the period into two camps: first, writings that welcome the Emergency, which were generally published between 1975 and 1976, and, second, those which deride it, which were generally published between 1977 and 1978. This dichotomy continues to provide the vector of analysis for this period (B. Chandra, *In the Name of Democracy* in the former case; Coomi Kapoor, *The Emergency: A Personal History* [New Delhi: Penguin Books, 2015] in the latter, for example). It is with this bifurcation in mind that many of the secondary sources considered in these chapters must be measured. Those that welcome the Emergency consider the step as a constitutional necessity that gave Prime Minister Gandhi and her government the required tools to deal harshly with disruptive elements and to set the nation back on the path to economic and social progress. Those writings that deride it argue that the Emergency was instituted under the corrupt and tyrannical proclivities of Prime Minister Gandhi and her government of sycophants. Notably, the latter is the dominant contemporary narrative. For excellent coverage of this historiography, see the second chapter of Emma Tarlo's *Unsettling Memories: Narratives of the Emergency in Delhi* (Berkeley: University of California Press, 2003). A long-term study on the history and politics of the Emergency period from Christopher Jaffrelot and Pratinav Anil will no doubt deepen our understanding, which I have read early drafts from: Jaffrelot and Anil, *India's First Dictatorship*.

4. Raj Thaper, once a close friend of Indira Gandhi, wrote in her 1991 memoirs prior to the Emergency: "Power seems to flow from a single source—Indira Gandhi.... It is clear that she will stop at nothing. Let all institutions be subverted to her own ends" (Raj Thaper, *All These Years: A Memoir* [New Delhi: Penguin Books, 1991], 401).

5. The 1967 election planted the seeds of *non-Congressism* in Indian politics. That is, new state governments elected regional parties and non-Congress coalitions. Although most of these governments fell before 1970, the rise of regional parties had begun (Christophe Jaffrelot, "The First Reign of Indira Gandhi: Socialism, Populism, and Authoritarianism," in *India since 1950: Society, Politics, Economy and Culture*, ed. Christophe Jaffrelot, 24–40 [New Delhi: Yatra Books, 2012], 26).

6. To outside observers—particularly those in the Soviet Union, which was widely considered the chief international patron of the Indian Congress—the election victory was not welcome news. Although Moscow openly expressed its preference for Indira Gandhi, Russian leaders had privately estimated that, if she were to obtain even a mere majority, she would creep closer to the ideological center. The Soviet Embassy in Delhi was reportedly "appalled"

at Gandhi's landslide victory (General Records of the Department of State [DOS] [Central Foreign Policy Files], 1970–1973, Political and Defense, POL 14, National Archives and Records Administration College Park [NACP], College Park, Maryland, USA).

7. The next chapter provides extensive detail regarding the Congress's manifesto and platform, and traces the exogeneity of state elites' dominant ideas. This ideology was anchored in the Congress' core idea of secularism with a preference for socialism and a focus on minority rights, which underpinned the government's narrative of the JPM and its supporters, who were viewed in hostile terms as mobilized by religious nationalists anchored in ideas of religious majoritarianism and who sidelined minority rights. As we shall see, this framework interacted with the structural conditions evaluated in the present chapter to produce a suppressive response to the JPM.

8. DOS (Central Foreign Policy Files), 1970–1973, POL 14, NACP.

9. Ibid.; Foreign and Commonwealth Office (FCO) Records (South Asia), FCO 37, 812, General Elections in India, 1971, The National Archives (TNA), Kew, Richmond, UK. There was also support from CPI and DMK.

10. Ayesha Jalal, *Democracy and Authoritarianism in South Asia: Comparative and Historical Perspective* (Cambridge University Press, 1995), 72.

11. Two key illustrative personnel moves in this regard are worth noting. (*a*) Jagjivan Ram, a Dalit, was selected as Congress president and was appointed to the working committee in January 1970, thus reiterating the party's goal of turning the organization into an effective tool of social transformation. Special advisory committees and cells were created within the Congress to monitor the problems facing minorities, "backward" castes and classes, and industrial labor. (*b*) Mohan Kumaramangalam, a former communist, became Gandhi's key political and economic strategist alongside the socialist P. N. Haksar before the 1971 election (Jalal, *Democracy and Authoritarianism in South Asia*, 73–75).

12. Ibid., 75. Interestingly, Gandhi refrained from completely subsuming the state under her power during the Emergency, despite the protestations of her advisors and ministers. This approach, advanced vociferously by Bansi Lal and B. K. Nehru, among others, sought to provide her with presidential-style powers akin to those held by the leaders of the US and France. As historian Srinath Raghavan notes, "Ironically, the enthusiasm of her advisors gave Indira Gandhi pause. Standing at the cusp of almost absolute power apparently made her more sensitive to both its potential and its dangers" (Srinath Raghavan, "How Emergency Provided the Template for the Mobilisation of Hindutva Forces," *Hindustan Times*, March 29, 2017, https://bit.ly/2VVDFWt (accessed October 1, 2020]).

13. This is corroborated in an interview that Gandhi gave to *Socialist India*, a Congress weekly, for its 1975 Independence Day issue:

    The Centre should at all times have the power to hold the country together and deal with basic national challenges.... A vast country like India can remain strong and united only by making adequate provision for the expression of regional loyalties. I do not envisage any change in this concept. (Indira Gandhi, *Democracy and Discipline: Speeches of Shrimati Indira Gandhi* [New Delhi: Indraprashta Press, 1975], 101, emphasis mine)

14. Inder Malhotra, *Indira Gandhi: A Personal and Political Biography* (London: Coronet Books, 1991), 147. This centralization is reflected in that the PMO was given 60 percent of the Home Ministry's portfolio, including the intelligence services and the central administration. Eventually, Indira Gandhi would take over the ministry herself (Jaffrelot, "The First Reign of Indira Gandhi," 30). NB: The Prime Minister's Office (PMO) was called the Prime Minister's Secretariat before 1977. I use PMO to maintain continuity with subsequent chapters.

15. Elections to state Congress committees and their offices, especially the position of president, were superseded through direct appointments by the all-India Congress president.

16. In a fascinating meeting on May 14, 1968, with the British High Commissioner, Morarji Desai confided that Gandhi had ceased to be useful to the party's high command because she had surrounded herself with left-wing "flatterers" (FCO, 37, 41, 1968, TNA).

17. Throughout her rise to power, chiefly when she came to office in 1966, Gandhi always had a "kitchen cabinet" of advisors whom she trusted. These advisors did her bidding, spread rumors that helped Gandhi's cause, and strategized against her opponents. In March 1968, for example, these elites combined with the left wing of the Congress, the Congress Forum for Socialist Action (CFSA), to support S. N. Mishra's demand that an Emergency meeting of the All-India Congress Committee (AICC) should be held to consider the state of the organization and to debate the "deteriorating political situation" in the country and within the party. This intra-party agitation would go on to contribute to the party split along ideological lines in November 1969, which will be discussed further in Chapter 4. Gandhi's "kitchen cabinet" included Fakhruddin Ali Ahmed, Dinesh Singh, S. S. Ray, Mohan Kumaramangalam, P. N. Haksar, H. R. Gokhale, and I. K. Gujral, among others, who took up key posts in later years, notably from 1971 to 1975. Some of these leaders had been cultivated by Gandhi during her time as president of the Congress Party (1959–60), when Gandhi had made herself the spokesperson for the younger leftist forces that sought to infuse new dynamism into the party.

18. It is plausible that JP's confrontation with the prime minister stemmed from her government's working relationship with the CPI, which had sought to undermine the CSP when JP was in the party. However, after 1971, despite continuing electoral pacts at the state level, CPI influence in the Congress began to wane.

19. Jayaprakash Narayan, "Total Revolution," in *Towards Total Revolution*, 4 vols (Bombay: Popular Prakashan, 1978), vol. 4, 31, 110. Much like the IAC movement (considered in Chapters 5 and 6), the JPM was grounded in the view that democracy had "to be built from below," and had to be based on *"gram raj* (village self-government)" or "people's committees" that embodied the will of the people at the local level, and that would significantly undercut the corruption of the center (Jayaprakash Narayan, "Inaugural Address to All-India Radical Humanist Association Conference," Calcutta, December 29–30, 1974, *Everyman's Weekly*, January 12, 1974, 7). NB: At the end of 1972, JP persuaded a conclave of Sarvodaya workers to launch a new journal devoted to political commentary. The journal, which appointed JP as chairman of the editorial board, made its appearance in July 1973 as *Everyman's Weekly*, which is widely referenced as a source in this book.

20. Narayan, "Total Revolution."

21. Geoffrey Ostergaard, *Nonviolent Revolution in India* (New Delhi: Gandhi Peace Foundation, 1985), 163.

22. Jayaprakash Narayan, *Towards Total Revolution*, 4 vols (Bombay: Popular Prakashan, 1978), vol. 4, 57.

23. *Everyman's Weekly*, June 22, 1974, 8.

24. Jayaprakash Narayan, *Prison Diary 1975*, ed. Amritlal Shah (Seattle: University of Washington Press, 1979), 104.

25. Quoted in L. Palmier, *The Control of Bureaucratic Corruption: Case Studies in Asia* (New Delhi: Allied Publishers, 1985), 14

26. Kapoor, *The Emergency*, 9, 216–17.

27. D. P. Dhar was a close confidante of Gandhi at this time. He was also considered the most dynamic of the trio comprised of a small band of close advisors that were collectively referred to as the "Kashmiri Mafia," the other two being P. N. Haksar and P. N. Dhar. For all three, secularism, modernization, and a scientific spirit went hand in glove, and were the prerequisites for a modern India (for more, see Pulin B. Nayak, "Planning and Social Transformation: Remembering D.P. Dhar as a Social Planner," *Indian Economic Review*, New Series, 50, no. 2 [July–December 2015]: 317–34).

28. B. N. Tandon, *PMO Diary-I: Prelude to the Emergency* (New Delhi: Konark Publishers, 2003), 65, 93.

29. Ibid., 12. Dhar, in turn, could not understand why so much effort and risk was taken to save Mishra.
30. Ibid., 72–74. After L. N. Mishra's death in Bihar, Gandhi intimated that the JPM, whose base was located in that state, had helped to create the disruptive conditions of violence that caused Mishra's demise (Ostergaard, *Nonviolent Revolution in India*, 152). This will be considered in more detail later on in the chapter.
31. Gandhi's defensive position on governmental corruption is corroborated by her subsequent remarks at informal meetings and talks: "People have talked about corruption. There is no country in the world where there is no corruption. Those who are accusing us of being corrupt are those who have been proven corrupt in their own states" (I. Gandhi, *Democracy and Discipline*, 173–74).
32. Tandon, *PMO Diary-I*, 72–76.
33. Ibid., 53, see also 43.
34. Ibid., 347. Tandon most likely saw these corruption-laden charge sheets first-hand, given his role and the proximity of his office in the PMO.
35. Indira Gandhi, *Speeches and Writings* (New York: Harper & Row, 1975), 189.
36. Minocheher Masani, *Is JP the Answer?* (Delhi: Macmillan Co. of India, 1975).
37. Justice Sinha dismissed several more serious charges, including bribery, lavish election expenditure, the illegal solicitation of votes, and the use of religious symbols in the campaign. Even a sharp critic of Gandhi, the journalist Kuldip Nayar, who was jailed by the government during the Emergency, wrote that the two offences of which Gandhi was convicted were "too thin to justify unseating a Prime Minister." Making recourse to a *Guardian* newspaper report, Nayar continued, "It was almost like unseating the Prime Minister for a traffic offence" (Kuldip Nayar, *The Judgment: Inside Story of the Emergency in India* [New Delhi: Vikas Publishing House, 1977], 4).
38. Tandon, *PMO Diary-I*, 382–85. The threat from the courts was less potent than that posed by the JPM, as judges soon granted a conditional stay that allowed Gandhi to remain in office. This will be explored in greater depth later.
39. The price increased more than 17 percent from FY73 to FY74 (DOS [Briefing Books], 1958–1976, Box 92, NACP). In FY75, *two* budgets were presented in the Lok Sabha—such was the deterioration of the economic outlook. Another shock arrived with the 1973 global oil crisis, in which oil-producing countries cut back crude oil production and the world price of crude oil increased more than four-fold within a year, which led to a massive increase in the price of petroleum and key food-producing inputs for India, such as fertilizers. This worsened India's already precarious economic state, and sent further shocks into the economy.

40. B. Chandra, *In the Name of Democracy*, 34–36, 55.
41. Ibid., 18.
42. Ostergaard, *Nonviolent Revolution in India*, 90, 128.
43. Bhola Chatterji, *Conflict in JP's Politics* (New Delhi: Ankur Publishing House, 1984); Narayan, *Towards Total Revolution*, 98–99; Narayan, *Prison Diary 1975*, 46. Economic and social conditions had deteriorated the most severely in Gujarat and Bihar, where corruption was rampant. Prior to the demonstrations in Gujarat and Bihar, JP and his Sarvodaya colleagues considered a revised strategy that focused on movement activism and compelling the central government to reform. The group welcomed the popular mood against corruption (Ostergaard, *Nonviolent Revolution in India*, 71).
44. Narayan, *Towards Total Revolution*, 57.
45. Allan Scarfe and Wendy Scarfe, *JP: His Biography* (New Delhi: Orient Blackswan, 2014 [1975]), 422.
46. *Everyman's Weekly*, February 23, 1974, 1; Narayan, *Towards Total Revolution*, 97.
47. *Everyman's Weekly*, September 21, 1974, 2.
48. Ostergaard, *Nonviolent Revolution in India*, 115, 167. The JPM became a national movement quickly after the Bihar demonstrations. Because this state was "ground zero" for the movement and was JP's home state, the JPM is also often called the "Bihar Movement."
49. Upon the conclusion of the first Administrative Reforms Commission in 1970, and in consideration of prevailing debates in parliament since 1963, the recommended agency for combating political corruption was the institution of the Lokpal (Department of Administrative Reforms and Public Grievances, darpg.gov.in [accessed October 1, 2020]). Later chapters will further consider the Lokpal, both during the JPM agitation and, more prominently, during the later IAC agitation.
50. Ostergaard, *Nonviolent Revolution in India*, 131, 170; *Everyman's Weekly*, December 1, 1974; Narayan, *Towards Total Revolution*, 141–42.
51. Ostergaard, *Nonviolent Revolution in India*, 69, 92, 167; Kapoor, *The Emergency*; Ghanshyam Shah, *Protest Movements in Two Indian States: A Study of the Gujarat and Bihar Movements* (New Delhi: Ajanta Publications, 1977), 133–34. This is the only first-hand study of the JPM.
52. Ostergaard, *Nonviolent Revolution in India*, 95.
53. The JPM failed to garner support among prominent left-wing parties. Whereas the CPI explicitly backed the prime minister, the CPI(M) initially took a neutral position, and eventually decided to distance itself from any semblance of support for the JPM once the right-wing Jana Sangh and Anand Marg increased their support. However, the CPI(M) still backed the call for the

prime minister's resignation in light of the Allahabad High Court judgment (B. Chandra, *In the Name of Democracy*, 55; David Lockwood, *The Communist Party of India and the Indian Emergency* [New Delhi: SAGE Publications, 2016], 94–95, 98).

54. Ostergaard, *Nonviolent Revolution in India*, 74, 125, 167, 169, 191, 193, 202. Despite that a coalition of opposition parties joined to support the JPM, they did not form a cohesive bloc until May 1975, when they came together to form the Janata Front for the Gujarat elections in June 1975. This occurred separately from, and in the final two months of, the JPM. Moreover, despite this coalition, the ruling Congress remained extremely powerful, and these parties did not represent the type of opposition threat at the polls that subsequent governments, including the one considered in Chapters 5 and 6, would face (ibid., 212–13; Masani, *Is JP the Answer?* 103; Christophe Jaffrelot, *The Hindu Nationalist Movement in India* [New York: Columbia University Press, 1998], 265).

55. Ostergaard, *Nonviolent Revolution in India*, 196.

56. *Everyman's Weekly*, 15 June 1975.

57. Ostergaard, *Nonviolent Revolution in India*, 134. He also said at the time: "It is not political parties with which we are identifying ourselves but with the people struggling against a corrupt, oppressive and incompetent regime and an iniquitous social order." Thus, the JPM, according to JP, was "a vast upsurge of the people in which the parties merge and lose their identity like rivers in the sea" (Narayan, *Towards Total Revolution*, 132). JP would later reflect in his prison diaries that the involvement of political parties was crucial to the movement's organizational zeal. He wrote: "If the movement had been confined to the Sarvodaya workers alone and its principle was to keep away all political parties (*including the ruling party*), it would have been impossible to keep them away. But, then, there would have been no people's movement" (Narayan, *Prison Diary*, 56).

58. *Everyman's Weekly*, December 1, 1974. The JPM and these political parties did not agree on some key matters—they fundamentally disagreed on the selection of "people's candidates," not party politicians, by constituency councils composed of representatives from citizen action committees (Ostergaard, *Nonviolent Revolution in India*, 115). In this regard, as we will see in Chapters 5 and 6, the IAC took a similar approach to that taken by the JPM.

59. Ibid., 210–11. For JP, this conditional stay illustrated that Gandhi's "credibility stands destroyed" (quoted in ibid., 214).

60. This religious nationalism is also called Hindutva. As a Hindu nationalist sect, the RSS considers itself a non-political social organization. The organization is linked to networks of educational and welfare institutions in India, and draws

upon the commitment of an extensive volunteer cadre of *pracharak*s (Jaffrelot, *The Hindu Nationalist Movement in India*, 35). The RSS's participation in the JPM would give the organization the legitimacy it lacked, as well as a template for the populist Hindutva mobilizations of the late 1980s and early 1990s. To this day, the RSS exhibits a self-mythologizing sense of heroic adventure and a conflation of natural and militaristic metaphors that saturates national dialogue. This will be discussed in greater depth in the next chapter.

61. The RSS student wing, the Akhil Bharatiya Vidyarthi Prasad (ABVP), provided support throughout the Gujarat and Bihar movements. Trained along paramilitary lines, these RSS cadres were weaned on a communal ideology.

62. Jayaprakash Narayan, *Nation Building in India* (Ulan Press, 2012 [1975]), 132–33. The primary founders and architects of the Jana Sangh were former members of the Congress Party who rejected the party's secular policy preferences (Paul Brass, *Factional Politics in an Indian State: The Congress Party in Uttar Pradesh* [Berkeley: University of California, 1965]).

63. Anand Patwardhan, part of the JPM and ardent follower of JP, wrote two months before the Emergency:

> When old political enemies like the RSS or old individual politicians of dubious virtue have come out in his support, JP has almost invariably welcomed them as prodigal sons who have undergone a change of heart. [JP must overcome this] naiveté or otherwise [this] strange myopia [will make it difficult for his] credibility as a champion of a clean social order to be maintained. (Anand Patwardhan, "Is JP's Movement at the Crossroads?" *Everyman's Weekly*, April 20, 1975)

64. Jaffrelot, *The Hindu Nationalist Movement in India*, 255, 263–64, 280. In contrast to Gandhi, JP did not align state and nation in his conception of Indian sovereignty (more on this in the next chapter), and, in this regard, claimed Mahatma Gandhi's, not Jawaharlal Nehru's, lineage for his thinking: "While the rest of the national leaders relied solely on the power of the state to accomplish their task of nation-building, Gandhiji was clear in his mind that the state could never be the sole instrument for creating the India of his dream" (quoted in Ajit Bhattacharjea, *Jayaprakash Narayan: A Political Biography* [New Delhi: Vikas Publishing House, 1978]).

65. Jaffrelot, *The Hindu Nationalist Movement in India*, 262.

66. JP functioned both inside and outside Indian politics, an advocate for both political justice and national liberation, an Indian patriot and internationalist cosmopolitan. He was a vocal critic of state sovereignty, but this emanated from a non-statesman who did not have constituents or held elected or appointed office, who did not hold power, but who was deeply concerned and informed about the relation between and within states (Lydia Walker, "Jayaprakash

Narayan and the Politics of Reconciliation for the Postcolonial State and Its Imperial Fragments," *The Indian Economic and Social History Review* 56, no. 2 [2019]: 147–69, 149).

67. Ibid., 150.

68. The organizations that originated from the JPM are today completely antagonistic in thought and action. This contradiction is because the movement brought together citizens and organizations on issues of corruption, inflation, landlessness, and untouchability. The JPM, and many other instances in his political career, underlines how JP was able to bridge the gap and be considered the ideal figurehead of movements that combined different political philosophies.

69. Chatterji, *Conflict in JP's Politics*, 191–92. The fact that JP later renewed his criticism of the RSS lends credence to this view. An information advisor and aide in the PMO to Indira Gandhi (1966–78) wrote in one of his autobiographical articles of JP: "A man who had deep reservations about communal politics had become instrumental in sanitizing the Jan Sangh and giving it a share in power." This was in reference to the rise of the Janata Party, which merged the right-wing Sangh among other parties to form government in 1977 (H. Y. Sharada Prasad, *The Book I Won't Be Writing and Other Essay* [New Delhi: Chronicle Books, 2003], 61).

70. Narayan to Indraji, 23 June 1966, Subject File 12, JP Papers, Nehru Memorial Museum and Library (NMML), New Delhi.

71. During a *Meet the Press* interview on August 20, 1975, two months after the Emergency, Gandhi reflected: "Earlier they [the JPM] tried to paralyse the government of these two states which I mentioned, Gujarat and Bihar. It is obvious that if it happened on a nationwide scale—and this is what was announced—there would have been wide-scale violence. In a period of international uncertainty and internal economic difficulty, I think there was grave internal danger to the country" (I. Gandhi, *Democracy and Discipline*, 117, see also 102).

72. Quoted in Ostergaard, *Nonviolent Revolution in India*, 77.

73. The pair met prior to the emergence of the JPM in early 1974 to discuss the deteriorating macroeconomic conditions of the country. Gandhi had periodically met and exchanged letters with JP in the past, given his stature in Indian social and political life. Not long after this meeting, the JPM emerged as a political movement, and Gandhi argued that, despite his call against corruption, JP himself had received funds from highly dubious sources (ibid., 75). Years later, during the IAC, Congress Party spokesperson Manish Tewari would similarly accuse movement leader Anna Hazare of corrupt financing.

74. Ibid., 159.

75. B. Chandra, *In the Name of Democracy*, 47; Ostergaard, *Nonviolent Revolution in India*, 128.

76. Ibid., 129; Ananth Krishna, *India since Independence: Making Sense of Indian Politics* (New Delhi: Pearson, 2011), 126.

77. *Everyman's Weekly*, November 23, 1974.

78. These politicians were few. Congress leader K. D. Malaviya prepared a note regarding the government's offensive against the JPM, which stated: "The entire democratic system hangs in the balance. The basic question is whether the process of social and economic change will take place within the matrix of democratic institutions or whether the vested interests [of the right] would succeed in thwarting the process through extra-constitutional methods" (quoted in Ostergaard, *Nonviolent Revolution in India*, 132).

79. Quoted in Bhola Chatterji, *Conflict in JP's Politics*, 3.

80. Dhar, *Indira Gandhi*, 255.

81. Tandon, *PMO Diary-I*, 139.

82. Interview with *Blitz* newspaper, December 1974, in Rustom Karanjia, *Indira–JP Confrontation: The Great Debate* (New Delhi: Chetana Publications, 1975), 38. NB: *Blitz* was a news magazine run by Karanjia, who was a friend of Indira Gandhi (Mukherjee, *The Dramatic Decade*, 113).

83. Gandhi developed the impression that the JPM had always aimed to undermine her government at the center rather than to root out corruption. In an interview in December 1974, she stated: "From the very beginning we have known that his movement [the JPM] was aimed at the central government and me" (quoted in Karanjia, *Indira–JP Confrontation*, 43).

84. B. Chandra, *In the Name of Democracy*, 60.

85. *Everyman's Weekly*, November 23, 1974, 10.

86. Ostergaard, *Nonviolent Revolution in India*, 163.

87. Ibid., 69, 92, 163, and 167; G. Shah, *Protest Movements in Two Indian States*, 133–34.

88. Ostergaard, *Nonviolent Revolution in India*, 164; *Times of India*, March 7, 1975. An investigation into the diaries of B. N. Tandon reveal that he considered the institutionalization of the Lokpal as a mechanism to combat corruption and to respond to the JPM, as did Principal Secretary P. N. Dhar (Tandon, *PMO Diary-I*, 140–41). Indeed, as the march approached, the government proposed to introduce a Lokpal bill to combat corruption in that parliamentary session (Ostergaard, *Nonviolent Revolution in India*, 163).

89. *Times of India*, March 8, 1975.

90. Ibid., March 9, 1975.

91. *The Hindu*, March 11, 1975.

92. Tandon, *PMO Diary-I*, 383–85.

93. In a diary entry written on June 15, 1975, three days after the Allahabad judgment, B. N. Tandon strongly intimated that corrupt practices had taken place during the campaign:

> The truth is that [Yashpal] Kapoor had submitted his resignation only on 25 January [1971] but he backdated it to 13 January. Action was taken on it on the 25. The official noting makes it clear that there was nothing to suggest that its acceptance had been mooted before the 25. The noting is followed by the signatures of two officials and then [P. N.] Haksar's. He accepted the noting and if the resignation had been accepted on the 13 or 14 he would have written so on the file. But he wrote no such thing and signed the file. Later, [N. K.] Seshan conveyed the PMs [sic] approval. In the light of these notings and signatures, there can be no doubt left in anyone's mind that *Kapoor's resignation had not been accepted before the 25 [January]*. (Ibid., 389)

94. Ibid., 385.
95. Ibid., 382–85.
96. Dhar, *Indira Gandhi*, 259–60.
97. Tandon, *PMO Diary-I*, 406.
98. Ibid.
99. Quoted in the *Indian Express*, June 19, 1975.
100. Tandon, *PMO Diary-I*, 397
101. Gandhi's advisors manufactured a circus of rallies and popular demonstrations to illustrate that the prime minister maintained popular support (SCR, ch. 5; Mukherjee, *The Dramatic Decade*, 72; Tandon, *PMO Diary-I*, 382–85).
102. Kapoor, *The Emergency*, x.
103. *Times of India*, June 26, 1975.
104. Kapoor, *The Emergency*, 128; Ostergaard, *Nonviolent Revolution in India*, 163, 214.
105. Nayar, *The Judgment*, 31–32.
106. The JPM and its supporters did not expect this sudden suppression by the prime minister. In an interview on the evening of June 25, Morarji Desai stated that he did not believe that the prime minister would suppress the movement. He continued: "I prefer to believe that before committing such a monstrosity Mrs. Gandhi would commit suicide" (Oriana Fallaci, "Mrs. Gandhi's Opposition: Morarji Desai," *New Republic*, August 1975, 13–18).
107. "Proclamation of the Emergency by President of India, Fakhruddin Ali Ahmed" (reproduced in Kapoor, *The Emergency*, 23). This justification of "grave emergency" was later rejected by several relevant actors, most notably the Intelligence Bureau, the institution in charge of briefing the prime minister on such disturbances (*SCR*, 5.57).

108. *SCR*, especially Annexure to Chapter XIX.

109. Kapoor, *The Emergency*, 5–6.

110. We can now corroborate this letter with two other pieces of evidence. First, Ray stated to the Shah Commission that Gandhi had, on two previous occasions, made references to the internal security of the nation, and sought "some sort of emergent power or drastic power" to deal with the upsurge of agitations. Second, in an interview with German television three months after the Emergency, in response to a question about her unilateral decision-making power, Gandhi said:

> One very big lie that is propagated is that the whole Emergency and so on is run by some small group including my son, which is absolutely false. The decision was taken by the Chief Ministers of this country *and they were wanting me to take some action for quite some time before*, because they are the ones who have to manage the states.... So they were saying: "If you allow these movements [such as the JPM], while it is confined to one state or another, it is all right, but if it's going to spread, it will be very difficult for us to manage the states." So the decision was taken by the Chief Ministers....
> (I. Gandhi, *Democracy and Discipline*, 166)

111. Tandon, *PMO Diary-I*, 130–41.

112. It is important to note that this letter illustrates that it is Ray who urged Gandhi to take strong action against the right-wing religious nationalist groups and parties who mobilized with the JPM. By contrast, in his Shah Commission testimony, Ray claimed that the prime minister drove all decision-making on June 25 (*SCR*, 5.47). Indeed, Pranab Mukherjee writes in his memoirs that "Indira Gandhi told me that she was not even aware of the constitutional provisions allowing for the declaration of a state of Emergency on grounds of internal disturbance, particularly since [an external] state of Emergency had already been proclaimed as a consequence of the Indo-Pak conflict 1971" (Mukherjee, *The Dramatic Decade*, 45). This reasoning is taken on by H. Y. Sharada Prasad in his memoir-themed essays, where he writes:

> She [Indira Gandhi] might have been able to avoid the Emergency if her knowledge of constitutional law had been more intimate. With her handicap, she had to rely on advisors and lawyer colleagues [a clear reference to Ray] who, in turn, *ministered to her yen for action in preference to caution*. (Prasad, *The Book I Won't Be Writing*, 114)

On balance, and on triangulation of available material, both Gandhi and Ray had been aware of the possibility of declaring an internal Emergency at least since January 1975. However, the specific constitutional provisions were most likely investigated and framed to Gandhi by Ray.

113. *SCR*, 5.46; Kapoor, *The Emergency*, 5. Dhawan was a powerful mouthpiece at this time for the prime minister, and was listed among the chief instigators of suppressive tactics in the Shah Commission report (*SCR*, 24.14). In an interview with Coomi Kapoor, Dhawan said: "I never did anything on my own. If I called someone to give orders I did not say the PM [Prime Minister] desires it. It was understood I was following her orders" (Kapoor, *The Emergency*, 14). The PMH, led mainly by Dhawan and Sanjay Gandhi, had become an alternative, informal power source to supplement the cabinet, and was very much in line with the party's ideology and deference to Gandhi.

114. Ray and Prime Minister Gandhi had been close allies for a long time, and studied together in the UK (Kapoor, *The Emergency*, 6). Pranab Mukherjee corroborates Ray's significant impact on Gandhi's decision-making during this period, especially since the Congress split in 1969, in his memoirs. As a member of the Congress Working Committee (CWC) and the Central Parliamentary Board, Ray had "considerable influence" over the decision-making process of the organization and administration. His voice was also prominent in the meetings of the National Development Council and at the conferences of chief ministers (Mukherjee, *The Dramatic Decade*, 46–47). Indeed, Ray was often called a "Delhi-based" chief minister, given his proximity to the PMO (ibid., 107).

115. *SCR*, 5.47.

116. Ibid., 5.33–5.34; see also the deposition of Sushil Kumar, District Magistrate, Delhi (ibid., 11.1–11.5; 11.7).

117. During this period, Ray counselled Gandhi on the L. N. Mishra case, the Kapoor Commission, parliament's stand-off with the judiciary, the Naxalite insurgency in West Bengal, her election petition, and her election strategy at the national and at the state levels (Tandon, *PMO Diary-I*, 8–10, 13, 41). These were among the biggest challenges faced by that government.

118. *SCR*, 5.47.

119. Sanjay Gandhi, Indira Gandhi's youngest son, played a key, though informal, role in government decision-making. This is corroborated by evidence in personal diaries and accounts of officials in the PMO and the government (Tandon, *PMO Diary-I*; Dhar, *Indira Gandhi*; B. K. Nehru, *Nice Guys Finish Second: Memoirs* [New Delhi: Viking, 1997]). Nehru, who was very close with the prime minister and was her High Commissioner to Britain, would later comment that the prime minister was "absolutely blind as far as that boy [Sanjay Gandhi] was concerned" (Nehru, *Nice Guys Finish Second*, 564). Sanjay Gandhi's role in decision-making increased during the Emergency; for a vivid and harrowing account of the slum demolitions, sterilizations, and related policies pursued under the direction of Sanjay Gandhi, see Emma Tarlo's

Unsettling Memories. Sanjay Gandhi is a shadowy figure, and his relationship with the prime minister is too psychologically complex to fully investigate with the current dearth of primary evidence.

120. *SCR*, 5.49. Reddy was also a Gandhi loyalist. He was removed at a stroke as chief minister of Andhra Pradesh by Gandhi so that the government could avoid electoral weakening through the mooted secession of that state.

121. Mukherjee, *The Dramatic Decade*, 47; *SCR*, 5.68.

122. *SCR*, 5.50.

123. Ibid., 5.52.

124. Ibid.

125. Ibid., 5.55.

126. Senior ministers such as K. D. Malaviya and H. R. Gokhale, who claimed that they only found out about the Emergency after it had been instituted, were long-time proponents of strong action against the JPM (ibid., 5.58, 5.59, 5.60).

127. Ibid., 5.54; see also Tandon, *PMO Diary-I*, 414.

4

India under Gandhi

Populism and Partisans

Whenever you take a step forward, you are bound to disturb something. You disturb the air as you go forward, you disturb the dust, the ground. You trample upon things. When a whole society moves forward this trampling is on a much bigger scale and each thing that you disturb, each vested interest which you want to remove, stands as an obstacle.... You have to have moral courage then to stick to that—no matter what comes in your way, no matter what the obstacle and the opposition.

—Prime Minister Indira Gandhi, speech at Madras University, 1967

Populism is a thin-centered ideology that considers society to be ultimately separated into two homogenous and antagonistic groups.

—Cas Mudde, 2004

Populism and Concepts of the Nation

This chapter will present evidence for the role of ideology in the case of the Emergency. We will consider the perspectives through which decision-makers in the Congress government, chiefly Prime Minister Indira Gandhi, viewed and diagnosed the anti-corruption Jayaprakash Narayan Movement (JPM) to re-establish government credibility. Analysis of these perspectives will illustrate how Gandhi's populism, or "thin" ideology, stemmed from the Congress Party's "hard core" of secular nationalism—which placed a cognitive lock on decision-makers' actions in a crisis environment. Decision-makers viewed the JPM and its supporters as nationalists anchored in religious majoritarianism who sidelined minority rights. The Congress's concepts of the nation allowed the executive to build solidarity within the government and to suppress the ideological "others" within the JPM. Through thickly detailed process-tracing, this chapter will demonstrate that the ideas that filled Gandhi's populism were exogenous to the crisis instigated by the JPM—that is, the events that shaped the dominant Congress Party before but specifically after its split along ideological lines in 1969—and not simply applied at the time to inflate the JPM threat.

Indira Gandhi rose to power in 1971 on a populist platform.[1] After the party split of 1969, Gandhi and her Congress (R) swept political power on a *garibi hatao* (remove poverty) platform that advanced secularism, socialism, and minority rights.[2] Gandhi's populism was bound up in these concepts of the nation as enshrined in the Congress Party:

> The unity of India is in many ways due to the unity and strength of the Congress. If the Congress had not been so dominant, perhaps the country would have split up into several states when the British Empire ended. *The role of the Congress continues as long as the social revolution in India remains uncompleted, and we are very conscious of this role.*[3]

Her information advisor at the time, H. Y. Sharada Prasad, wrote in his memoir, echoing P. N. Haksar, close aide to the prime minister: "Our very existence depended on a widespread acceptance of the secular ethic which was far wider than mere tolerance or *sarvadharma samabhava* [equal respect or peaceful co-existence for all religions]."[4] These ideas not only gave content to Gandhi's populism but also played a constitutive role in political realignments after the unified Congress Party split in 1969, a period in which moral boundaries between groups were confrontationally redrawn and categories of "us" and "them" emerged.[5] Secular nationalism—the "hard core" of Congress's ideology—placed a cognitive lock on the behavior of its decision-makers, which was activated under crisis conditions.[6]

Secular nationalism came to define India's post-1947 state through the vehicle of the Congress Party. Indian secularism denotes not a strict separation between church and state, as in the European tradition, but rather a "principled distance" between religion and the state.[7] Despite the early political dominance of secular nationalism, the rising social and cultural (and recently political) tide has persisted with religious, or specifically Hindu, nationalism in India.[8] Ironically, the response to the JPM and excesses of the Emergency arguably propelled the nationalist right in India from the late-1970s onward. For Hindu nationalists in the main (as recent research shows fault lines within the tradition too) the foundation of the Indian nation is the Hindu faith.[9] The nation is therefore the exclusive domain of the majority Hindu people, and other groups and minorities must assimilate in such a way that honors Hindu cultural customs to the detriment and, eventually, dissolution of their own traditions.[10] According to political scientist Milan Vaishnav,

> A critical milestone [for Hindu nationalism] occurred in 1925 when Keshav Baliram Hedgewar formed the RSS.... Hedgewar formed the RSS as a cultural, rather than political, body with the sole purpose of strengthening Hindu society by building civic character, unifying Hindus divided by caste, and enhancing their physical strength through training and exercises. In short, the RSS was established as a bottom-up vehicle for fortifying Hindu society.[11]

These dueling nationalisms, secular and religious, as advanced by the institutions of the Congress Party and the RSS (and later parties such as the Jana Sangh and BJP) respectively, foreground the proceeding analysis.

The JPM became the target of Congress "otherizing" under Prime Minister Gandhi. With its explosive growth and its inclusion of religious nationalist groups and organizations, as well as its later alliance with a coalition of right-of-center parties, the JPM became an object of suppression among Congress decision-makers. Weaponized with a dominant ideology in her majority government, Gandhi focused on the movement only as a function of a religious nationalism that threatened her party's concepts of the nation and her policymaking power.

Unified Backgrounds and Dominant Ideology

To examine the ideological drivers of the government's suppressive response to the JPM, let us consider the Congress Party ideology under Prime Minister Indira Gandhi.[12] It is important to note here that not only were all decision-makers part of one party, the Congress, but also that there was no significant quorum of technocrats in positions of authority before the Emergency. Nearly all leaders in positions of authority were party politicians.[13] Therefore, it was unlikely that technical or alternative ideas would diagnose the JPM differently than the Congress. Government decision-makers shared a vision that was anchored in secularism, with a preference for socialism and focus on minority rights. Indeed, and as discussed in Chapter 2, in the political realm, what is to be maximized is far less evident than in the economic realm and cannot be reduced to economic ends, as perhaps it might be for technocrats. Certainly, party politicians are more likely engaged in the struggle to define and defend particular concepts of the nation than technocrats.

Prime Minister Gandhi shortsightedly believed that the JPM solely sought power at the center. In an interview with her biographer Pupul Jayakar in 1975, Gandhi asked, "Why does he [JP] refuse to accept that he has never ceased to be a politician and desires to be Prime Minister?"[14] B. N. Tandon, Joint Secretary to the Prime Minister, confirmed this sentiment in a diary entry from the period, in which he notes that Gandhi "believed JP is a frustrated man and he wants power now."[15] More discerningly, Principal Secretary P. N. Dhar argued in his memoirs that JP did desire policymaking influence, but did not want a political role, such as that of prime minister, for himself. Sugata Dasgupta, the director of the Gandhian Institute of Studies in Varanasi, and one of the intermediaries through which Dhar reached out to JP, told him that all JP wanted from the prime minister was some reverence.[16] In other words, JP wanted a relationship with Gandhi analogous to that which Mahatma Gandhi shared with Jawaharlal Nehru—the relationship of moral conscience with political voice.[17] Indira Gandhi and her colleagues were unable to make this distinction.

Pranab Mukherjee, Minister of State for Finance until 1974, noted in his memoirs that he believed that the JPM had tried to unlawfully push the prime minister out of office. Corruption scandals such as Gandhi's alleged abuse of state mechanisms during her 1971 campaign were overblown, according to Mukherjee. The JPM and its supporters, in turn, revealed their political motivations by failing to wait for the Supreme Court decision. JP, Mukherjee argues, was "without a doubt … spearheading the strategy of the opposition." He dismissed the movement as "directionless" and, in a nod to the RSS, "contradictory in that it was a movement fighting against corruption yet composed of people and parties whose integrity was not above board."[18] Mukherjee argues that the JPM sought to undermine an elected government, and that no democracy would have allowed democracy to be undermined.[19] H. Y. Sharada Prasad echoes Mukherjee's perspective on the JPM. Although he agreed with his PMO colleague P. N. Dhar that the Emergency was "an evil" and painful period in India's history, Prasad was nevertheless convinced that "if Indira Gandhi had thrown in the towel at that point of time, it would have greatly weakened the Indian state. Yes, the Emergency did damage our democratic roots badly, but the state had been saved from a grave challenge."[20]

Gandhi and her close advisors had reason to believe that the harmony of the government was threatened by the JPM.[21] Like most social movements and agitations, the JPM sought institutional sympathizers in the government to advance its cause.[22] In early 1975, JP repeatedly appealed to senior politicians and Congress leaders such as Jagjivan Ram and Y. B. Chavan to join the movement.[23] JP saw little success in this venture, given the intense deference shown by government members to the party and to Gandhi. However, there were a handful of exceptions. Congress politicians who attempted to bring JP and Gandhi together, such as Chandra Shekhar and Mohan Dharia, became explicit in their support of the JPM near the end of the movement, and suffered the consequences, as they were imprisoned and removed from office. It is plausible that such attempts to attract institutional sympathizers led Gandhi to fear that her ministers and cabinet members were courting the JPM.[24] After all, she was proud to say in later years that the unity of Congress was strengthened after the declaration of the Emergency.[25]

The government largely viewed the JPM in hostile terms, which is unsurprising, given the alignment between decision-makers under the Congress banner. There was a distinct absence of those in Gandhi's circle who could diagnose the JPM alternatively, especially from a policy standpoint. During one cabinet meeting on April 1, 1975, B. N. Tandon recounted that Gandhi was not interested in listening to dissenting voices, especially those that did not optimize party considerations:

> I want to mention especially something about today's [cabinet] meeting. Depending on the circumstances, the PM goes through her other papers during cabinet meetings and its committees. She also sends slips to ministers and officials. But today, after a while, she started off a separate meeting with Swaran Singh and Jagjivan Ram. She is interested in economic issues only to the extent of the inherent politics in them. When [P. N.] Haksar and others were speaking, she interrupted them once to say that these questions needed to be viewed from a political angle as well. Then she got busy with her own work.[26]

A notable exception to this rule was P. N. Dhar. In both his memoirs and in Tandon's diary, Dhar often appears frustrated that the prime minister privileged populist measures. This angst is instructive as to how Dhar, Tandon, and others in the PMO came to view Gandhi's decision-making style. On one occasion in April 1975, Dhar gave a note to the prime minister advising that she organize an informal committee of lawyers and academics to suggest anti-corruption and other reforms—a suggestion that, incidentally, directly mirrored the JPM's demands. Upon seeing the note, Tandon argued that government officials would not take seriously the recommendations of such a "lightweight group," and Dhar replied that, while he personally agreed, the prime minister "had got after him" to provide the list. Tandon notes that he "could not prevent blurting out" that while the prime minister claimed to seek expert opinion, in truth she "want[ed] only such experts who will toe the government line."[27] In short, Gandhi and many of her advisers maintained the perspectives of Congress politicians who gave primacy to the party's ideological contours in their diagnosis of the JPM. In an interview with the *Observer* on July 13, 1975, Gandhi claimed:

> At a time of global financial crisis there was a determined effort [by JPM] to sabotage our efforts to keep our economy going, by frequent strikes and calls for complete disruption of national activity. The law and order situation was becoming volatile. All this was a tremendous burden on a country at our stage of development. *Any government worth its name had to checkmate these designs.*[28]

It is important to understand the content of these concerns, which will allow us to more fully grasp why the government diagnosed the JPM as an ideological "other" detrimental to the narrative of the Indian nation enshrined in the majority Congress government under Gandhi's populist leadership.

Congress' Concepts of the Nation

Proclaiming the Emergency

The Gandhi-led Congress government advanced concepts of the nation anchored in secularism, with a preference for socialism and minority rights. As discussed earlier, one of the two proposed "master narratives" of Indian nationalism since the turn of the twentieth century is secularism (the other is religious nationalism). Indian secularism—which denotes religious equidistance rather than religious non-involvement by the state—was principally represented by the Congress Party during and after the Indian independence movement.[29] A pertinent and actionable illustration of this ideology is the effort made in the early years of the republic by Congress leaders, especially Jawaharlal Nehru, to refuse to grant religion any special state access or privileges despite the protestations of the RSS.[30] Nehru believed that powerful national leaders, especially in the Congress Party, would ensure the dominance of the secularist vector.[31] His daughter Indira Gandhi's populism was rooted in this secularism, which was most prominently espoused by Nehru, and, according to Gandhi, even figures such as M. K. (Mahatma) Gandhi (no relation). In a July 1957 article, "My Reminiscences of 'Bapu'," Indira Gandhi outlines her comprehension of a secular order:

> Another of his [M. K. 'Mahatma' Gandhi's] glorious legacies is the secularism for which he gave his life. *Secularism means neither irreligion nor indifference to religion, but equal respect for all religions – not mere tolerance, but positive respect. Secularism demands constant self-examination and unceasing exertion.* That great truth is inscribed on rocks by Asoka, that no man reverences his own religion unless he reverences others' religion also. *India has been great and has risen to high places in those periods when the truth was acknowledged and practiced by her rulers.* In our times Gandhiji and Jawaharlal Nehru made it [secularism] a living reality for us. *Without it there is no future for our nation....* Jawaharlal Nehru integrated our ideals into our national life laying the *firm foundation of a secular democracy directed towards socialism.*[32]

Despite the inspiration she drew from her father, Indira Gandhi and Nehru were quite distinct in the evolution of their ideas as well as their leadership style. While Nehru can be considered a nationalist, Gandhi was fundamentally a populist. Whereas the latter distrusted non-elected institutions and actively sought to supersede them, the former refrained from attacking apex institutions, such as the judiciary, even when his fundamental policy goals were thwarted.[33]

The prime justification for the Emergency and the suppression of the JPM emerged from the Gandhi-led Congress government's populism that activated its secular conception of the Indian nation.[34] Throughout the JPM, its suppression, and the years after the Emergency, Prime Minister Gandhi and Congress leaders referenced the movement synonymously with right-wing and religious nationalist groups and parties, underlining the government's "otherizing" of the anti-corruption movement. All of Gandhi's available speeches, letters, and notes, which are heavily footnoted in this book, confirm this outlook. She variously referenced the JPM as an opposition "group,"[35] "front,"[36] "morcha,"[37] "combined opposition,"[38] and "alliance."[39] When making recourse to the "opposition," she often referred to movement activities of the JPM, and vice versa.[40] In an interview with a UK newspaper, she made this synonymy explicit when she described the JPM as "divided into many groups pulling in different directions."[41] That Gandhi saw the JPM as oppositional underlines the oratorical "otherizing" that accompanied the government's actions to implement the Emergency.

Despite some salient ideological and political differences between these entities, and despite that the suppression of the JPM began far earlier than the movement's support by opposition parties, it is crucial to note that the Congress government observed and advanced the narrative of a religious nationalist mobilizational core in the JPM, namely through the RSS, which Gandhi understood to even undermine Indian democracy.[42] Gandhi and the Congress's conceptualization of the Indian nation was for them bound up in the very system of Indian democracy, and so their perspective of the nation, and specifically what threatens the meaning of the nation, necessitated the stance that the JPM threatened democracy.[43] According to the governmental white paper "Why Emergency?" which was presented to parliament on July 21, 1975, the Emergency was intended "to withstand the calculated onslaught on the country's political institutions and economic progress."[44] Furthermore, the government claimed that the Emergency was an important step as the JPM and the RSS "had combined with a set of frustrated politicians to challenge the very basis of democratic functioning and to destroy the country's self-confidence."[45] In a speech to the Lok Sabha less than four weeks after enacting the Emergency, without acknowledging the irony of her own strangling of democratic institutions, Gandhi argued:

> *Democracy has not been endangered by what government has done* [the Emergency] but democracy was being weakened, was being endangered and would have been destroyed had the opposition front [JPM] been allowed to launch direct action and its *plan of sabotage under RSS guidance* and to go ahead with its campaign to create dissatisfaction in the army, the police, and amongst industrial workers [in reference to JP's speech in Delhi on June 25].[46]

For the prime minister and her advisors, the religious nationalist and right-wing RSS, which formed a key mobilization vehicle for the JPM, provided the primary threat to democracy against which her government needed to safeguard. In a television interview on August 1, 1975, she argued that Indian democracy would be threatened by the heightened power of either the "extreme Right or extreme Left," and that democracy was "weakened by those who, claiming to be non-violent and democratic [JP], give respectability to and ally themselves with fanatic religious organizations [RSS] and with parties wedded in terrorism [Jana Sangh]."[47]

Gandhi argued that religious nationalism mobilized under the JPM threatened Indian democracy, and should therefore be crushed using the might of the state.[48] The RSS activists of the JPM, she argued, were a "fanatical organization based on the doctrine of Hindu superiority" who preached "hatred of Muslims and Christian minorities" and who stood against both "rational and scientific thinking" and India's "economic and foreign policies." Gandhi, with populist fervor, noted that although "sane and secular elements have long demanded th[e] banning" of these groups, the "permissiveness of the law in India" barred such a suppressive act.[49] According to Gandhi, the RSS and its political arm, the Jana Sangh, were communal and anti-minority, and their "secret" constitution was logically in line with the dominant traits of fascist movements of the early- and mid-twentieth century.[50] In the aforementioned July 22 Lok Sabha speech, justifying the conditions under which the Emergency was instituted, Gandhi stated:

> I deplore the type of training they [RSS] give to our younger people in the *sakhas*, the violence they preach. But their real weapon is something else—it is the whispering campaign they indulge in. Yesterday another member of the opposition [parties] wanted to know what fascism was. Fascism does not mean merely repression; it does not mean merely that the police use excessive force or that people are imprisoned. Fascism is the use of falsehood. Over and above everything, it is the propagation of the big lie. *It is the rise of whispering campaigns, the search for scapegoats. This has been the major weapon of the Jana Sangh and the RSS.*[51]

Gandhi repeatedly linked the RSS to fascism, often focusing on the religious nationalists' penetration of the JPM as distinct from the support the movement received from opposition parties. The anti-corruption agenda of the JPM was superseded by this exclusionary framing. In an interview with a German reporter three months after the Emergency was proclaimed, Gandhi argued that although the RSS did not "consider itself a political group," it followed the "text-book techniques of fascism, that is, *believing in the superiority of one race, having a sort of private army; even propagating the big lie day in day out so that people start thinking [it].*"[52] This fascism, argued Gandhi, was projected by the JPM, which threatened the survival of the Indian nation just as Europe had been threatened decades earlier. In an interview with a foreign journalist on July 24, 1975, she outlined her position:

> *Our party—and my father and I especially—realized the danger of Fascism and Nazism at a time when very few people, even in Europe, had an understanding of the situation.* That is why we were and we are so committed to democracy. Fascism means that a small group—a minority—tries to take power somehow and destroys democracy, or works for the interests of only one section of the people.... Yet a small section of the opposition [the JPM] was making it impossible for Government to function. *People [JP] were inciting our armed forces to revolt, they were inciting the police and the industrial workers. They were encouraging students to leave the schools and colleges and indulge in violent acts.*[53]

For some government decision-makers, religious nationalists were not ideologically coextensive with JP. Ultimately, however, this did not absolve the JPM. As we saw in Chapter 3, JP claimed that the RSS, which had mobilized as part of the anti-corruption movement, had tempered its previous worldview enough to join the JPM. P. N. Dhar recounts warning JP that the prime minister worried that the RSS had taken advantage of him, and reminding JP that "the RSS had trained cadres and a well-defined ideology from which they were not going to be swayed." JP replied, Dhar writes, that he "knew some people thought they had made a fool of him, but the fact was *'they have met me, including the Poona group [the RSS leadership] and surrendered to me' [sic]*."[54] Gandhi claimed that by allowing these groups into the movement, the JPM abdicated its moral authority to champion against corruption. In her reply to American activist Benjamin Spock, who implored Gandhi to restore democratic liberties after the proclamation of the Emergency, she wrote:

> I know that you are deeply committed to pacifist causes. But I am not sure that you have been properly informed of what has been happening here. Mr. Jayaprakash Narayan has for a long time carried on a campaign against the government and against me personally, but we did not do anything to curb his movements or his free speech. *More recently he aligned himself with the RSS [Rashtriya Swayamsevak Sangh], the organization which instigated Mahatma Gandhi's murder and which is fanatically Hindu, preaching discrimination against Moslem and Christian minorities.* At the same time he encouraged the extreme Left [Naxalites]. Neither of these groups has ever claimed belief in democracy. *In his extreme anger and frustration at the lack of support, he called upon the Army and the police to disobey orders.* This is what compelled me to

take the unpleasant decision. *Democratic liberty is not jeopardized by the action that has been taken [the Emergency], but it would have been if we had permitted the country to drift.*[55]

By allowing the RSS and its affiliates to penetrate the movement, the JPM became a threat to India's very identity "and survival as a nation," Gandhi told the Rajya Sabha (Upper House). She accused the JPM of sheltering parties that "did not interpret unity or integrity in the manner that we had done all these years, as the founders of this democracy had envisaged." The question this posed to her government, she argued, "was whether we should allow this deterioration to go on or put a stop to it. It is very difficult to measure how drastic a step is or should be."[56] In the same speech, she pointed out that, despite JP's hopeful approach to the organization, the RSS had not tempered its ideology or approach, and, in fact, foreshadowed the anti-corruption approach of the JPM:

> We have known the history of RSS. This organization came into being when all of us—I think there may be a few young members who were not here, but the rest of us—were very much here. We saw how it [RSS] grew. *We saw how it spread hatred. We saw how the atmosphere of hatred resulted in the assassination of the greatest Indian [referring to Mahatma Gandhi's killing by Hindu nationalist Nathuram Godse]. Can we believe that that organization has suddenly changed?... They do not believe in democracy, whatever they may say about it today.* These were the groups that were taken in this wide sweep [the JPM] *that was going to eradicate corruption, that was going to clean up society, that was going to bring total revolution!*[57]

These themes coalesced in a speech inaugurating the first All-India Conference of Educators for Secularism, Socialism, and Democracy in New Delhi on September 19, 1975, in which Gandhi argued that she did not take issue with the JPM's collective action per se, but with the specific ground that it ceded to the RSS. The government, she argued, was not against "satyagraha [non-violent demonstration] as such; we are not against criticism as such; we are not against opposition; *what we are against is when a small minority [RSS] tries to gag the vast majority of our country.*"[58] Gandhi then foregrounded the threat of the religious nationalism sheltered by the JPM to India's secular nationalist order, arguing that parties such as the Jana Sangh stood against the concept of social change as Gandhi defined it—that is, "*bringing in a more real secularism, not just in action, but, I would say, in thought,* because while you are thinking that somebody is different or he is not part of the country, that is what leads to action."[59] This stance is corroborated in an interview that Gandhi gave on August 14, 1975:

> Our complaint against Mr. Jayaprakash Narayan and some of the other senior leaders is not just about what they said, but that they gave shelter and respectability to such groups [RSS] and that the control of this coming agitation [JPM] was put in the hands of the leader of another very chauvinistic party called the Jana Sangh.[60]

Fundamentally, in Gandhi's view, the JPM and its leaders "had no qualms about handing over the management of their campaign to the RSS in spite of the known record of the RSS in fomenting communal riots and communal hatred."[61] As Gandhi widely declared in her proclamations, her government would never permit the spread of communalism or allow organizations representing such views as the RSS to influence Indian politics.[62] In an interview with M. Shamim of the *Times of India* in New Delhi on July 3, 1975, Gandhi stated that "the government can be opposed, *but not national interests.*"[63]

Lastly, and perhaps most directly, the prime minister's written statements to the Shah Commission corroborate the more immediate and public assertions and utterances above, revealing Gandhi's populist vector that showcases dueling nationalisms in the government's suppressive response to the JPM. Although Gandhi did not give evidence under oath, she wrote letters to the commission explaining the events that led to the proclamation of Emergency.[64] In her first letter, dated November 21, 1977, she defensively criticized the political procedures of the commission and argued that in the years preceding the Emergency, India was "in the grip of a grave crisis" caused by economic deterioration and "internal and international causes beyond our control." Groups such as the RSS, she argued, "wished deliberately to aggravate the situation for their own gain," and abused the rights of "*freedom of speech and expression [to] spread hatred and parochial regional sentiments.*"[65] In another letter written two years after the Emergency declaration, on December 2, 1977, Gandhi discussed in detail the collaboration between the religious nationalist coalition that met under the umbrella of the JPM, and which attempted to undercut her government's view of national interest. This collaboration determined her decision to call an Emergency:

The political opposition had been using this strategy [barbs against the prime minister] *to weaken the central government and subvert its socialist and progressive programmes for quite some years.* It was a question of change versus status quo. *Secular, democratic socialism on the one hand and retrograde, communal and capitalistic forces on the other had been struggling against each other to gain the upper hand.* The split in the Congress in 1969 gave an edge to this confrontation. The nationalization of banks and other measures which disturbed entrenched privileges and vested interests, and offered opportunity and help to the poor and weaker sections of our society, created such tremendous popular upsurge that communal and capitalistic elements probably lost all hope of being able to successfully fight on an ideological plane. *Hence they changed their methods [by joining the JPM].* Similar such political phenomena were not peculiar to India.[66]

It is interesting to note that, in this same letter, Gandhi references the US presidential system and notes that such a system provides better protections for the executive as they defend national interests—which she believed her government was doing.

The mobilization of the RSS within the opposition blurred the lines between the two groups, thus allegedly making them appear mutually threatening to the Congress government.[67] Decision-makers widely considered the aim of the JPM to "paralyze the government and indeed all national activity and walk to power over the body of the nation."[68] Therefore, for Gandhi, the imposition of the Emergency was a logical step to protect the nation from paralysis. The prime minister believed that only she could counter the nationalist threat posed by the RSS and the JPM. She mused to biographer Dom Moraes in 1978:

> After my judgement in 1975, what could I have done except stay? You know the state the country was in. What would have happened if there had been nobody to lead it? I was the only person that could, you know. It was my duty to the country to stay, though I didn't want to.[69]

This sentiment is corroborated in Gandhi's 1978 interview with another biographer, Mary Carras, as she maternalistically argued that in her absence at the helm of the government "there would have been utter political and economic chaos and nobody to fill the vacuum."[70] Gandhi believed that the JPM could not be constrained by the law, and that "some rights had to suffer" in "the cause of strengthening and survival of our country. It is only when we have a country that we have a democracy," as she told the Rajya Sabha.[71] The despotic actions taken by Gandhi and her government against the JPM and its supporters immediately after the imposition of the Emergency provide further evidence of the Congress government's ideological frame, wherein the legal and security architecture of the state justified the suppression of the JPM, its leaders, and its sympathizers.[72]

Immediate Aftermath of the Emergency

The 42nd constitutional amendment, introduced as the 44th amendment bill, aimed to strengthen the executive's powers regarding anti-national dissent. This amendment included several articles. Cosmetically, it altered the description of India in the preamble of the Constitution, wherein the words "Sovereign Democratic Republic" were substituted with "Sovereign *Socialist Secular* Democratic Republic." The amendment's explanatory Statement of Objects and Reasons stated this move was designed to clarify the high ideals of socialism, secularism, and the integrity of the nation.[73] Substantively, one of the more regressive clauses enabled the government to pass legislation banning "anti-national activities and associations" without the need to justify such bans, which would be beyond judicial review. Anti-national activities were broadly defined, and included advocacy for secession from the union, questioning the sovereignty and integrity of India, creating internal disturbances, threatening or questioning the security of the state, and intending to disrupt public services and public harmony. Incidentally, each of these activities was cited by the government to justify suppression of the JPM.

The most clear-cut evidence that the Congress's ideological opposition to the JPM was a core driver of its suppression is the number and nature of arrests that took place during the Emergency.[74] After the Emergency proclamation, the Maintenance of Internal Security Act (MISA), which had been in place since the 1971 India–Pakistan War, was amended on January 29, 1975, and July 15, 1975. These amendments introduced Sections 16A and 18, which aimed to speed up arrests by shifting powers to state security forces and underscoring that detainees arrested under the MISA would not have "right to personal liberty by virtue of natural law or common law, if any."[75] As Gandhi believed the JPM to have mobilized with religious nationalists, this represented a clear mobilization of MISA against right-wing organizations, chiefly the RSS. No major action was taken against the secular or leftist opposition parties or groups.

The nature of the crackdown on religious nationalist organizations that mobilized for and supported the JPM emphasize the brutal nature of the government's actions, and is likely graver than is widely acknowledged.[76] The highest number of arrests corresponds proportionally with states in which the JPM had a stronghold, such as UP, Bihar, Gujarat, Maharashtra, and Delhi.[77] Indeed, 43 percent of the arrests in Delhi, where the center wields power over security forces and the JPM reached national relevance, were of RSS members and their affiliates.[78] In the country as a whole, this figure is reported in some studies as high as 33 percent.[79] Symbolically, the first person to be arrested in Delhi after JP was K. R. Malkani, the editor of the RSS-controlled *Motherland* newspaper.[80] These numbers and the Shah Commission testimonies also illustrate that state governments and security forces were actively instructed by the center to prioritize detaining citizens belonging to right-wing organizations that supported the JPM.[81] State governments acted in a "frenzy" to detain these individuals, often without mentioning the specific activity for which the detainee had been arrested.[82] Again, this was particularly the case in JPM strongholds.[83] Relatedly, those individuals who were released from prison during the Emergency were those who had "genuinely" severed their relations with right-wing groups and parties, and who had openly declared support for the prime minister's ambivalent, populist Twenty-Point Program.[84] The political conversion process at play here underscores the ideological battle in which Gandhi and her government were engaged with the JPM and its supporters even during the Emergency.

Perhaps most crudely indicative of the government's targeting of religious nationalist groups is an exchange between then *New York Times* journalist Anthony Lukas and Minister of State in the Home Ministry Om Mehta. The government claimed that the police had been warned of secret hordes of arms and ammunitions with the discovery of weapons in the offices of right-wing organizations.[85] Lukas, in an official interview with Mehta regarding photos published in Indian newspapers of wooden swords and staves found in RSS headquarters, recounted:

> I asked Om Mehta, Minister of State in the Home Ministry, about this, and he replied vaguely, "there were some metal swords too." Even with some metal swords, I asked, how could boys with staves pose much of a threat to a superbly equipped army of about one million men, the Border Security Force of about 85,000, the Central Reserve of Police of about 57,000, and some 755,000 state policemen? "Well," Mehta said, "there were undoubtedly some rifles too." "Did

you seize any?" I asked. "No," he said, "but they probably kept them at home. Don't underestimate these people's [RSS members'] capacity for mischief."[86]

It is clear from this vignette, and from the data cited, that the government's justification for its suppression of the JPM and its subsequent suppression of the right-wing groups that mobilized with the JPM are intimately related. However, this raises important questions around the preceding analysis: Were the populist steps through which the government diagnosed and suppressed the JPM—given content and shaped by the Congress's secular nationalism—strategically applied at that time to either inflate the threat of the JPM or conveniently crush any and all opposition? Or did these ideas have a source exogenous to the events immediately leading to the Emergency which cognitively locked the Congress government into the suppression of the movement under crisis conditions? The next section lends credence to the latter, where I trace the genesis and evolution of the Congress Party's ideology under Prime Minister Indira Gandhi's leadership.

Exogeneity

To illustrate the causal weight of the narration of the Gandhi-led Congress government's populism, let us now trace its exogenous development through this vector's constituent parts: secularism, in the main, as well as a preference for socialism and focus on minority rights. It is a more challenging task when mapping the ideas of party politicians who dominated the Congress government under Gandhi than when tracing the exogeneity of the ideas of technocrats who tend to have established professional associations and writings, and who are rarely subject to the same incentives as political actors. Populism often comes with heterogenous, even ambivalent, ideological commitments and programmatic goals. This only makes textured process-tracing alongside an empirical exploration into populist politics valuable. We will, therefore, consider a very rich amount—and to my knowledge unique gathering—of data, stemming from over 4,000 documents across three national archives, that covers the period leading to the Emergency (1966–75), as well as some data outside this phase, to thickly illustrate the government's populism. Given the executive power Gandhi wielded, and the penetration of her personality through her party, much of this evidence pertains to the prime minister.[87]

Indira Gandhi's Populism

The Party Split and Rise of Congress (R) Ideology

The Congress split in November 1969 precipitated an ideological definition along a more distinct spectrum in the party system that was until then inchoate in India. This split gave birth to two rival Congress factions: the right-of-center Congress ("O" for "organization") under the leadership of Morarji Desai and the Syndicate, and the left-of-center Congress ("R" for "requisitionist") under the leadership of Prime Minister Gandhi and dominated by the party's Young Turks.[88]

From the beginning of her tenure in high office, Indira Gandhi openly emphasized and articulated her perspective of the Congress's ideological outlook, rooted in secularism with a preference for socialism and focus on minority rights.[89] For example, in a 1965 interview given one year before her ascent as prime minister, Gandhi argued that India had "swerved from the right path" after Jawaharlal Nehru's death, and that socialism had largely been forgotten.[90] On assuming high office on January 19, 1966, she stated: "I must say I was worried at the thought of Mr. Morarji Desai [who would go on to lead the right-of-center faction after the Congress split] becoming Prime Minister, because his policies were so diametrically opposed to what we stood for and I feared that India would immediately change direction."[91] The direction in which Gandhi wanted the Congress to move became explicit in her first broadcast to the nation on January 26. She argued that in 1947 the pledge of Indian independence was fulfilled, and "[t]he world knew that a new *progressive force*, based on *democracy and secularism*, had emerged. In the seventeen years that Jawaharlal Nehru was Prime Minister, the unity of this country with its *diversity of religion, community, and language* became a reality, democracy was born and grew roots."[92] During a Lok Sabha address in the winter of 1967, Gandhi reinforced these concepts of the nation as well as of those that stood opposed to it:

> *Secularism and democracy are twin pillars of our state, the very foundations of our society.* From time immemorial, *the vast majority of our people are wedded to concepts of secularism, religious tolerance, peace and humanity....* India has the privilege of being the world's largest composite society, and the home of many great and ancient faiths. *Communalism is an evil which divides man and fragments society; it goes against our [India's] very genius and cultural heritage.* It holds a threat to the unity and integrity of our country which must be our foremost concern.[93]

After she became prime minister in 1966, Gandhi immediately sought to stamp her leadership over the Congress government's policymaking power and autonomy. For example, upon rising to office, Gandhi inherited the Congress government's early attempts to reorient economic policy toward liberalization, which was in step with emergent global trends at the time and deteriorating conditions at home.[94] The policy began with the support of Prime Minister Lal Bahadur Shastri, but found lukewarm support among Gandhi and her advisors.[95] It is important to note here that although Gandhi had a strong understanding of socialism as a political tool for governing in India, unlike her advisors at this time and throughout her premiership leading to the Emergency, she was not as intellectually committed to it. Liberalization policies were met with opposition by the party, and when the Congress performed poorly in the February 1967 elections and its seat share was reduced from 361 to 283, Gandhi and her close colleagues viewed the results as a further rejection of a pro-trade economic orientation and sought to re-establish the party's socialist roots.[96] A note from P. N. Dhar to Principal Secretary P. N. Haksar reveals the ideological thread in this move:

> *We all but lost our independence in that period* [attempts at liberalization in the mid-60s]. *A Plan holiday was imposed on us in the name of consolidation of the economy.* Our world image as a *progressive* non-aligned country suffered.... During the same unfortunate period, the World Bank forced upon us a devaluation of the rupee.... The economy, instead of improving, plunged into deeper crisis.[97]

Dhar notes in his memoir that Haksar, one of Gandhi's key intellectual voices and later de facto head of the Planning Commission in the Emergency when Dhar became Principal Secretary, believed that the government should not only return but also double down on ideas from its recent Nehruvian (*dirigiste*) past.[98] These ideas originated both from abroad and from home. Internationally, there was Soviet inspiration for rapid, state-led industrialization, with rural areas a source of food, workers, and manufactory surplus. At home, the ideas of statistician and technocrat P. C. Mahalanobis had historically provided an intellectual rationale for the Nehruvian development path.[99] This Nehru–Mahalanobis conceptualization was not always strictly socialist, but it certainly relied on an expanded, autonomous, and strong state sector associated with (*a*) building industrial capability in strategic areas across the public sector, (*b*) working with large businesses in the state-managed license regulation system behind high trade barriers, (c) supporting the very small-scale and informal cottage industry sector, and (d) export pessimism. Gandhi and her advisors inherited these ideas, and the prime minister gave them a populist intensity. The take-away here is that the above factors formed the government's justification for a strongly modernizing industrialization strategy in which the state played a leading role in the economy. The legitimization of the state, therefore, was built upon its role as leader of the modernization drive and its power to address historical inequalities and provide inclusion to minority groups.

When Gandhi and her leftist colleagues in the Congress sought to galvanize the party by pushing forward the Ten-Point Program, which advanced the nationalization of the major banks and general insurance industry, curbing of monopolies, instigating rapid implementation of land reform, and abolishing the princes' remaining privileges, among other steps, the rightist Syndicate faction in the Congress reacted furiously.[100] Syndicate stalwart Morarji Desai, the deputy prime minister and finance minister, was particularly displeased at what he considered the rampaging socialism of some Congress politicians under Gandhi's leadership.[101] Meanwhile, in her speech at the October 1967 AICC session in Jabalpur, Gandhi doubled down on her group's approach and assured members of the party that the government believed in socialism with "no ifs and buts."[102]

By mid-1968, Morarji Desai had made explicit that the Syndicate was determined to overthrow Gandhi and her leftist supporters.[103] Subsequently, the right-of-center asserted itself at the 72nd Congress session in late April 1969. Congress president and Syndicate leader S. Nijalingappa criticized the public sector and the state's control over industry, the so-called license raj, as fomenting corruption: "Where there are control and licensing ... there is always corruption and the sooner we do away with licensing and controls the better it [will] be."[104]

Prime Minister Gandhi and her colleagues were undeterred by the Syndicate's determination, and coalesced their leftward shift. A note from P. N. Haksar to the prime minister in July 1969 underlines that this strategy was not only about political turf and power, but also necessitated an ideological narrative. Addressing Gandhi as a "fellow believer," Haksar urged that the prime minister "should reiterate her faith in a socialist society alone being able to solve the problems of our country.... The problem is to convert our system of class banking into banking for the masses." To do this, the influence and capture of industrialists and capitalists needed to be "reduced and finally eliminated." The public sector needed to be made more efficient, and business reforms should be accompanied by "a vast educational programme in favor of socialism."[105] There is little evidence to suggest that Gandhi was an intellectually committed socialist. In fact, P. N. Dhar explicitly recounts in his memoirs that Gandhi "had no ideological fixations in economic matters."[106] However, in at least two of her closest advisors, Haksar and Mohan Kumaramangalam, she had a set of intellectually dedicated (though certainly pragmatic) proponents of strengthening the public sector, with a focus on the "need for expanding public investment in industry [and] on the need for industrial licensing for the private sector"—which had all come under attack from Nijalingappa at the April 1969 AICC session.[107] By the summer of 1969, both leftist and rightist factions came to a boiling point over the nationalization program proposed by the Gandhi faction, among other issues.[108]

At the AICC meeting in Bangalore on July 12, 1969, Gandhi proposed a clear agenda calling for a stronger state sector and a focus on secularism. With this proposal, the worldview of Gandhi's faction became clearly vocalized:[109]

> Today there is a very great need for the AICC to reiterate *our basic ideas and our basic policies.* Where do we want to go? We want to eradicate poverty. The capitalist system says it wants to eradicate poverty, and the communist system also says it wants to eradicate poverty. But we have not adopted any of these systems because we find that they have not worked in their own country, and they have had to pay a tremendous price. That is why we chose another way....
> *The basic principle and policies are commitment and deep involvement with socialist policy, and commitment and deep involvement with the policy of secularism.*[110]

As tensions heightened, Gandhi dropped Morarji Desai from the cabinet, and nationalized fourteen commercial banks—which constituted 83 percent of the total banking system—on July 19, 1969.[111] In her broadcast to the nation, she argued that state control of the economy was necessary, "particularly in a poor country where it is extremely difficult to mobilize adequate resources for development, and *to reduce the inequalities between different groups and regions,*" and that the banking system, as it impacts the "lives of millions," must be "*inspired by [a] larger social purpose and has to serve national priorities and objectives.*"[112] In response, on November 12, Nijalingappa expelled Prime Minister Gandhi from office. In her letter of November 18, 1969, to members of the Congress Party after her expulsion, she argued that two distinct ideological outlooks had come to a crescendo and could no longer coexist in the government. Gandhi's populism was beginning to reify:

> There is a crisis in the Congress and in the nation.... *It is a conflict between two outlooks and attitudes in regard to the objectives of the Congress and the methods by which the Congress itself should function.* It is a conflict between those who are for socialism, for change and for the fullest internal democracy and debate in the organization on the one hand, and those who are for the status quo, for conformism and for less than full discussion inside the Congress.... I want unity which is unity on principles and on methods of work. *To speak of socialism and secularism, to vote for them in meetings, but to have a public image of association with those who are opposed to secularism and socialism is not service to the Congress ... there is a tendency to be influenced by the forces of [right–wing] reaction, revivalism, and vested interests.*[113]

Two meetings of the AICC ensued, which gave birth to two ideologically separate parties—the Congress (O) and the Congress (R).[114] Now allied with total power in her party as well as with an ideologically homogenous faction, Gandhi and her colleagues could map out the governance platform that would lead to her electoral sweep in the 1971 elections.

Congress Ideology: Secularism, Socialism, and Minority Rights

Indira Gandhi's faction, Congress (R), held its first plenary session in Bombay from December 25 to 29, 1969. They defined the party's ideological stance by shifting explicitly to the left and by committing to a secular platform that focused on socialism and minority rights. At the AICC session in Delhi that took place from June 13 to 15, 1970, the party set out two priorities: first, that Congress (R) must unite around Gandhi and, second, that the party's commitment to a leftist program would demonstrate that (R) was a favorable alternative to the extremes of the left and the right.[115] While the socialist Young Turks fast imposed their role as the "conscience" of the party, Gandhi, in turn, continued to provide the group with her support based on Haksar's counsel.[116] This session proved to be the main strategy session prior to the 1971 elections, and set the ideological tone for the administration.

The session was dominated by a discussion of communalism, and emphasized that communal groups were anathema to the party. Party workers and Congress politicians explicitly attacked the Jana Sangh and Hindu nationalist groups such as the RSS. One Congressman noted that rapid economic progress could not be made while the country was victim to communal violence, and the session produced a "strong body of opinion ... in favor of banning the RSS" and other communal organizations.[117] An amendment was incorporated into the session's resolution that directed political leaders across the country to consider whether communal organizations should be allowed "to continuously poison society with communal hatred and violence." In addition, the CWC accepted another amendment to a resolution that condemned a recent statement made by RSS chief M. S. Golwalkar that Muslims in India were not in the mainstream of society.[118] For Congress (R) officials, groups such as the RSS "blemish the All India vision and give a fragmented view of the national problem." In her speech at the session, Gandhi compared right-wing parties and groups to Nazis, and undermined their religious nationalism to enthusiastic applause.[119]

In light of her newly indisputable power in the Congress (R) and homogenizing party program, on December 27, 1970, Gandhi dissolved the National Assembly and called for general elections in 1971.[120] In keeping with the narrative built at the AICC session in Delhi, the prime minister argued that "economic difficulties and the growing impatience of the people" had been "exploited by political elements," and that right-wing and religious nationalist groups sought to divide the Indian people through "communal passions and violent activities." The challenges posed by these divisions, she argued, could be met "only by the proper and effective implementation of our secular socialist policies and programmes through democratic processes."[121] This statement would set the ideological tone for Gandhi's 1971 campaign and was proximately tied to the AICC session outcomes from 1969–70. At the Delhi session, a political resolution was passed which stated that, "in the great task of reconstructing and restructuring our society, the Congress seeks the co-operation of all those who believe in democracy, *socialism, and secularism.*"[122] In March 1971, Gandhi and the Congress (R) won the general election in a landslide against the predictions of outside observers and the press, as well as the electoral trends at the center over the previous two elections.

Any assessment of the ideological foundations of the Congress's victory requires a close look at the party's manifesto and the proclamations that were made before the election. After all, it is this faction's majority government that would suppress the JPM in 1975. The chief issue of the divergence between the right parties and manifestos of the Congress (R) concerned the power of the judiciary over parliament on constitutional amendments, particularly the

Fundamental Rights section, which would allow the Congress to implement its statist economic program. Gandhi and her Congress faction wanted to undertake "progressive" changes to the Constitution so that their policy program could be implemented and "to overcome the impediments in the path of social justice."[123] Since the *Golak Nath* case of February 1967, parliament had effectively been denied this right.[124] The judiciary–parliament stand-off became foregrounded as an area of contention due to the Supreme Court's striking down in 1970 of the ordinances on bank nationalization that had been championed by Gandhi and her allies.[125] Serial challenges by the court on this front led Gandhi to propose an even stronger set of constitutional amendments during the Emergency that would place an enormous concentration of power in the prime minister's hands, in prototypical populist fashion.[126]

Compared with the 1967 unified Congress manifesto, the 1971 Congress (R) manifesto paid markedly more attention to detailed concessions to minorities, particularly Scheduled Castes and Muslims, as well as enhanced state control of the economy.[127] The manifesto made specific recourse to the reduction of glaring disparities in income and opportunity, making every effort to prevent discrimination against minorities in recruitment and employment, and reducing communal forces of violence and disorder, among other factors in line with its nationalist narrative.[128] It is important to note that this was the first election in Indian history in which two genuinely ideologically distinct manifestos were presented to the electorate, and in which the decision-makers who presided over and shaped the content of these documents observed and believed in the importance of the ideological distinctions between their parties and policy programs. Where the opposition campaigned on a platform of *Indira hatao* (remove Indira), Gandhi's faction campaigned on the populist platform of *garibi hatao"* (remove poverty). Congress (R) won a landslide victory in the 1971 general election.

Congress Government under Indira Gandhi

At its first AICC session since sweeping the 1971 election, from April 3 to 4, 1971, Congress (R) politicians presented their victory as a verdict against the right and against the marginalization of minorities. Weaker sections of society, Congress leaders argued, had been brought into the mainstream by their faction, and they strongly felt that these minorities, cutting across caste, religion, and region, supported their secularist and socialist ideology.[129]

Subsequently, three main talking points emerged at the session: first, a "Pledge to People"; second, underscoring "Harijan" (Scheduled Caste) welfare; and third, "Tasks Before the Organization." The party pledge at this session is worth highlighting here as an indication of the ideational content of the populism that would spearhead policymaking during the government's tenure:

> Congress has to now work as an organizer, mobilizer, and defender of the *weaker sections of the society in their struggle for social transformation of India.* To achieve this task, the Congress has to involve this new consciousness of the people in the direction of national reconstruction, without which rapid social and economic changes are not possible.[130]

In other words, the government unapologetically promoted its populism that privileged and claimed to represent minority rights to achieve political and economic ends.

Likewise, the AICC decided to instruct all party units in Congress governments throughout the country to heighten activities against organizations and parties that promoted religious nationalism. Committees and members of Congress were commanded to "involve themselves in the fight against social discrimination and administrative indifference [against minorities]" for an overall program of "social emancipation." The Congress Party was also instructed to "stand by Harijans [Scheduled Castes], minorities, and others who are being harassed by the vested interests [of the right wing] because of their support of the Congress [R] in the last elections [1971]." The pledge argued that prior to the elections, the country had experienced "fissiparous tendencies, religious fanaticism and intolerance," and that "serious doubts were engendered regarding the future of democracy and the unity of the country," but that "all these doubts and uncertainties have now been dispelled [after the 1971 election victory]."[131] At the end of the session, twelve "Tasks Before the Organization" were announced that further revealed this Congress government's populist fervor, as they sought to

> [d]efend secularism and safeguard interests of minorities and the weaker sections of the community, particularly the scheduled castes, scheduled tribes, and other backward sections so that they may attain equality of status and opportunity and fraternity assuring the dignity of individuals.... Put down forces of violence and disorder so that all our citizens can live in peace and harmony.... Continue the advance to socialism through democratic process and devise an administrative system capable of speeding implementation.[132]

These proposed tasks, among other statements that were made at the session, can be seen as the ideational content of a populism that, taken to its logical conclusion, led to the suppression of the JPM, which was considered to be mobilized by religious nationalists.

It is important to note that the substance of the party manifestos and meetings highlighted earlier have some measurable impact on policy outcomes and did not just function at the level of rhetoric. Consider, for instance, the Congress's pledge to combat what they saw as the conservatism of the judiciary. By July 24, 1971, a few months into the Congress (R) administration, two constitutional bills backed by cabinet ministers Mohan Kumaramangalam and H. R. Gokhale were circulated in parliament that would become law and would reflect a match between the Congress's manifesto strategy and policy implementation.[133] The first of these bills was the 24th Amendment. This amendment would restore the parliament's power to amend any portion of the Constitution, including Part III, which relates to Fundamental Rights, by restructuring Article 368 of the Constitution. The second of these bills was the 25th Amendment. The bill substituted a new clause (2) in Article 31 that replaced the word "compensation" with the word "amount," and which made the amount and mode of payment for the takeover of property by the government for public purposes (that is, nationalization) non-justiciable.[134] This represented a strategic route to implement the party's ideological objectives through policy—in this case, enhancing state control of the economy.[135]

In addition to policy generation, the appointments within and among Gandhi's advisers and cabinet officials also remained in keeping with the party's ideological objectives (and homogeneity) wherein key decision-makers were also party politicians.[136] Chief among them were Haksar and long-time confidante of Gandhi, Mohan Kumaramangalam, who until 1966 was a member of the Communist Party. Kumaramangalam was appointed to the important Ministry of Steel and Heavy Engineering. He was a staunch advocate of the bureaucracy and judiciary being ideologically consistent with the government such that the state might enact progressive policies. Haksar was in full alignment with this view.[137] Joining them as policy advisers were H. R. Gokhale, Minister for Law and Justice, and S. S. Ray, Minister for Education.[138] There was no significant quorum of technocrats among Gandhi's close advisors, although the new head of her secretariat, P. N. Dhar, came from an academic background. Under Dhar, in the first 100 days of the administration, a policy group was established that consulted experts inside and outside of India, chiefly the

British leftist economist Lord Thomas Balogh. Balogh, an academic and former British cabinet minister, believed that the state should be heavily committed to a policy of fast growth sustained by strong income policy and supported by state intervention in industry.[139] Upon the rise of her government, Gandhi said: "The [new] Congress is committed to enlarge the economic base, until every man gets his full needs and we have a truly free India—free from economic, social, and political exploitation."[140] The government's ideological direction was displayed fully among Gandhi's advisors and cabinet choices.

The link between party ideology and government decision-making is illustrated through several policy measures in which the direction of Gandhi's populism is on show. This provides us with further evidence that government decision-making was not bound simply by strategic concerns. For example, the government undertook several measures to strengthen the regulatory powers of the state. In August 1972, general insurance was nationalized, as was the coal mining industry soon thereafter. The Foreign Exchange Regulation Act (FERA) was passed in 1973, which placed further restrictions on foreign investments and on the functioning of foreign corporate entities in India, while the Monopoly and Restrictive Trade Practices (MRTP) commission was appointed in 1971 to implement the Act, which aimed to check the concentration of industrial enterprises to only a few entities. Despite the government decision-makers' aims, in practice, however, the MRTP Act proved a blunt instrument to investigate companies.[141]

The government also implemented many anti-poverty programs, in line with its party manifesto. These programs included schemes to create employment in rural areas, and compelled nationalized banks to open branches in areas with few banking facilities, particularly rural and low-income areas, to make credit available to small industries and farmers. Naturally, not all of Gandhi's party promises came to fruition. In some cases in which other pro-poor schemes went unimplemented, namely lowering the land ceiling to 10–54 acres per household contingent on land quality and annual crop cycles, the government failed to make local stakeholders (workers, landed elites, and political operators) sufficiently enthused about the socialist cause to institute the reforms.[142] Nevertheless, at the policy level, Gandhi strengthened the industrialization planning mechanisms of the Planning Commission and appointed the trusted Haksar to lead that institution.

From the 1971 victory onwards, the government continued to push the party's programmatic commitment to a state-controlled economy and protection of minority rights while Gandhi's power in the ruling Congress government further centralized. For example, the prime minister made the PCCs, an elected body of party members that directs the Congress at the state level, more leftist and loyal. This was the case in Punjab, West Bengal, Bihar, Rajasthan, Madhya Pradesh, and Orissa. Many PCCs were dissolved and replaced with ad hoc committees that invariably contained loyalists and politicians ideologically aligned with the Gandhi government.[143] Cabinet minister Chandrajit Yadav was tasked with organizing these committees. Gandhi used the PCCs to ensure that her power extended to the grassroots of the party, and acted against the choices of her fellow members of the Parliamentary Affairs Committee—chiefly Swaran Singh, Jagjivan Ram, and Y. B. Chavan—as she reoriented the PCCs. These conditions allowed the Congress to rout the communists from their stronghold in West Bengal—while installing Ray as chief minister—a major coup and signifier that the Congress government was an effective competitor to the ideological left in Indian state politics. Her extensive state-level reach allowed Gandhi to control both her party's policy agenda and to cultivate faithful leaders within the party.[144] P. V. Narasimha Rao, the future prime minister of India whom Gandhi selected as chief minister of the potentially secessionist state of Andhra Pradesh, remarked upon his ascension as head of that state: "Whatever she [Indira Gandhi] says I will meticulously, implicitly, and expeditiously implement."[145] In step with Gandhi's centralized policymaking power, the Congress's secular nationalism continued to fuel populist rhetoric and form a cognitive lock on decision-making in the government. The prime minister wrote in an October 1972 article for *Foreign Affairs*, on the 25-year anniversary of Indian independence and at the height of her power:

> Under Mahatma Gandhi's inspiration, Prime Minister Jawaharlal Nehru and the Congress movement formulated a set of principles which have served as our guidelines and which are still valid for us. *These are democracy, socialism, and secularism as far as our internal affairs are concerned*, and non-alignment in our external relations.... *What holds people together [in India] is not religion, not race, not language, not even commitment to an economic system*. It is the shared experience and involvement in the conscious and continuous effort at resolving internal differences through political means. *It is a sense of "Indianness" which unites our people despite ethnic, linguistic and religious diversity. Most conflicts and tensions in the world originate in the failure to take note of the importance of nationalism*.[146]

In 1973, however, the Congress's star began to fade, which led to the rise of the JPM. The party was defeated in several state by-elections, and the country's economy plummeted as populist policies revealed their vacuity.[147] In 1974 alone, around 40 million work days were lost by industry due to strikes and lockouts, compared to only 6.5 million lost work days in 1965, which culminated in several public and private sector strikes, most prominently from Indian Railways workers organized by the firebrand union leader George Fernandes.[148] The government's response was to use state forces to crush these demonstrations and, for the sluggish economy, to further centralize the state and capture it via trade nationalization, which was a weak solution for problems stemming from droughts and growing inequality.[149] But even its swift response with the explosion of a nuclear device in 1974 could not boost the government's credibility and national morale. Many began to see *garibi hatao* as a populist slogan rather than an effective policy program. Gandhi, increasingly on the defensive, argued that "if anybody tries to say that poverty can go in my lifetime or during my tenure as Prime Minister, it just cannot. It has deep roots."[150] She was right, but the populism she espoused had roused expectations that were beginning to burst open. Throughout this period, the government's alleged corruption scandals came to the fore, and, as a result, agitations began that precipitated the rise of the JPM and the *bhrashtachar hatao* (remove corruption) movement.

The End of the Emergency

The end of the Emergency and the subsequent announcement of national elections in January 1977 remains a complex puzzle for many scholars of Indian politics.[151] Conjecture ranges from the excesses of the Emergency period weighing heavily on the prime minister to mounting international pressures and even Gandhi missing the thrill of the campaign trail.[152] Although this question is far larger than the scope of this book, and for the present study would venture into a post hoc fallacy, the implications of my argument—successfully crushing ideological foes and maintaining power—in the decision-making process cannot be discounted and proves instructive to our query.

In a top-secret memo to the prime minister delivered in late 1976, P. N. Haksar appraised Gandhi of the general national mood regarding the Emergency. Haksar, whose family had gone through considerable personal humiliation during the Emergency, frankly noted that the national opinion of the government was not ideal, and made explicit that opposition parties and banned groups such as the RSS had diminished their activities and appeared to be on the wane.[153] Gandhi was clearly interested in the activities of the RSS, references to which Haksar emphasized in the document by underlining names, especially the release of RSS leader Krishna Ballabh Prasad Narayan Singh (also known as Babuaji), in bold black ink.[154] Moreover, Haksar noted that BLD chairman Charan Singh had claimed that the RSS and Jana Sangh were in favor of withdrawing their support for the JPM.[155] Singh, whose party supported the JPM in the latter stages of his career, noted that he and the top leaders of the RSS agreed that the struggle against the government was wrong.[156] In a letter to Singh that Haksar also references in his note, JP states if he had known the political upheaval that the JPM would cause, he "would have certainly tried to lead the movement with much more thought and given more attention to finding another way."[157] Indeed, Singh likely viewed the movement as a mistake. Whether his words indicated genuine reflection or strategic proclamations, it is clear in this note that Haksar deliberately stressed to the prime minister that her political and ideological opposition was, at that point, fractured. More specifically, he emphasized that the RSS was aware that their involvement in the JPM and the protest tactics that the group had used had shaped the government response to the anti-corruption movement. This clearly appeased Gandhi, for on January 18, 1977, the prime minister called for elections, thus ending the Emergency.

Notes

1. Recall from Chapter 2 that I consider populism, as many other discursive approaches to the phenomena, as a "thin-centered" ideology "that considers society to be ultimately separated into two homogenous and antagonistic groups, 'the pure people' versus 'the corrupt elite,' and which argues that politics should be an expression of the *volonté générale* [general will] of the people" (Mudde, "The Populist Zeitgeist," 543).

2. Shankar Dayal Sharma, who would later become president of the AICC in 1972 and, later, president of India, wrote in a letter to Congressman Henry Austin, General Secretary of the AICC at the time, on July 23, 1971, that the Congress's ideology could be summed up as "democracy, socialism, and secularism as the content of our national polity" (S. D. Sharma, Letter to Dr. Henry Austin, July 3rd 1971, Dr. Henry Austin Papers, Correspondence with

Shankar Dayal Sharma, Nehru Memorial Museum and Library [NMML], New Delhi). For Indira Gandhi, secularism meant the equality of all religions rather than a rejection of religion itself. She even argued that there cannot be any socialism—her government's primary social and economic development framework—if there is no secularism (I. Gandhi, *Democracy and Discipline*, 139).

3. Ibid., 59. These themes featured prominently throughout her time in office, especially 1971–75. During her "Democracy in India" address to the Royal Institute of International Affairs at Chatham House in October 1971, she stated: "Our democracy is dedicated to planned economic development, the peaceful transformation of an old social order and the uplifting of millions of people from conditions of social, economic, and technological underdevelopment." She continued:

> There are forces in our society as in others which pull in opposite directions [the right wing]. The competitiveness of democracy and of contemporary living seems superficially sometimes to have strengthened the hold of caste, religion, and region, for these are now exploited for social and economic gain. *But this is a passing phase and these differences cannot weaken India's fundamental unity nor the basic sense of Indianness which is a powerful binding factor.* (I. Gandhi, *Speeches and Writings*, 182)

"Indianness" for Gandhi was

> not confined to the legal interpretation of being born within a geographical area or the constitutional imperative of accepting the equality of all citizens. To me Indianness implies a positive duty to understand and honor other points of view in consonance with the injunction that the ways to Truth are many…. *Thus freedom from [religious] fanaticism and a capacity for acceptance and assimilation have been the genius of the Indian people.* (Talk at the Indo-French Colloquium, December 13, 1969, quoted in I. Gandhi, *Speeches and Writings*, 91)

Finally, in her first Independence Day address after the declaration of the Emergency, Gandhi stated: "Real democracy will come when socialism and secularism are fully established" (I. Gandhi, *Democracy and Discipline*, 89).

4. Prasad, *The Book I Won't Be Writing*, 86

5. Gandhi often said of the RSS that they had "no faith in secularism, socialism or non-alignment [the Congress foreign policy framework]" (ibid., 102). Furthermore, she believed that calling the RSS a nationalist organization was a "contradiction in terms" (ibid., 39). For a theoretical treatment of populist "otherizing," see Fella and Ruzza, "Populism and the Fall of the Centre-Right in Italy."

6. See the section titled "Change and Continuity" in Chapter 2 for my book's Lakatosian approach to the evolution of ideas and the concept of the "hard core" in an ideological frame. On cases of cognitive locking, see Berman, *The Social Democratic Moment*. Which ideas win out, therefore, is not purely about intellectual refinement as it is also about structures—political institutions such as parties constrain political behavior through the operation of rules, norms, and organizational settings, as well as by structuring political openings for group mobilization and the articulation of interests. Interactively, and in turn, we have long known that ideology can serve as a cohesion mechanism within parties (Duverger, *Political Parties, Their Organization and Activity in the Modern State*).

7. Rajeev Bhargava, "What Is Indian Secularism and What Is It For?" *India Review* 1, no. 1 (January, 2002): 2. As Bhargava points out, the commitment to "principled distance" is not the same as "equal distance." This goes beyond semantics. The state can take measures to tackle illiberal social aspects of one religion (for example, the caste system in Hinduism) without necessarily taking corresponding steps to address some other illiberal practice in minority religions, Islam or Christianity.

8. According to Ashutosh Varshney, three competing themes have fought for political dominance since the emergence of the Indian national movement. There is the *territorial notion*, which emphasizes the fact that the land between the Indus River to the west, the Himalayas to the north, and the seas to the south and east comprise India's sacred geography. A second notion, the *cultural notion*, is the idea that Indian society is defined by the values of tolerance, pluralism, and syncretism. The final notion is a *religious notion*, which is that the land known as India is originally the homeland of the Hindu community. In line with this reasoning, while different religious communities may call India home, India fundamentally belongs to the Hindu majority. While both nationalisms are committed to India's sovereign territorial boundaries, they diverge thereafter. Secular nationalism combines a commitment to territorial integrity with the cultural notion of political pluralism, while Hindu nationalism blends territorial unity with Hindutva, or the belief that India is fundamentally a polity by, for, and of the majority Hindu community (Ashutosh Varshney, "Contested Meanings: India's National Identity, Hindu Nationalism, and the Politics of Anxiety," *Daedalus* 122, no. 3 [Summer 1993]: 227–61).

9. Kanchan Chandra, "The Triumph of Hindu Majoritarianism," *Foreign Affairs*, November 23, 2018, https://fam.ag/2XFVeLy (accessed October 1, 2020).

10. Varshney, "Contested Meanings," 231.

11. Milan Vaishnav, ed., *The BJP in Power: Indian Democracy and Religious Nationalism* (Washington, D.C.: Carnegie Endowment for International Peace, 2019), 10

12. For a similar approach, see Berman, *The Social Democratic Moment.*

13. See Table A4.1 in Appendices.

14. Pupul Jayakar, *Indira Gandhi: A Biography* (New Delhi: Penguin Books, 1992), 285–86, 391. JP had resigned several years earlier from elected office as he had come to believe in a party-less democracy. He was mooted as candidate for prime minister after the demise of Jawaharlal Nehru, and Gandhi was convinced that he sought to unseat her from office (Scarfe and Scarfe, *JP: His Biography*).

15. Tandon, *PMO Diary-I*, 7.

16. Dhar, *Indira Gandhi*, 255.

17. Ibid. Dasgupta said: "Frankly speaking, these policy questions are secondary matters. My advice to you is, *un ko kuch maan deejiye* (he should be shown some reverence)" (quoted in ibid., 255). This point is corroborated by JP's perspective in Masani, *Is JP the Answer?* 133.

18. Mukherjee, *The Dramatic Decade*, 79–80. It is important to note that Mukherjee did not question the integrity of JP, whom he describes as desiring to "truly restore moral values in Indian politics," but questions the groups and parties supportive of the JPM.

19. Ibid., 78. Mukherjee's possibly partisan position is reflected more objectively in historian Lydia Walker's research, who has recently noted,

    JP's political thought was fundamentally undemocratic in that it aspired to universal participation not universal franchise. JP did not see elections—formal participation in national politics—as the route toward political and economic reform. This view articulated a sharp critique of the state-as-vehicle for a people's independence or self-rule, but it did not provide an alternative other than volunteerism and reconciliation. (Walker, "Jayaprakash Narayan and the Politics of Reconciliation for the Postcolonial State and Its Imperial Fragments," 152)

20. H. Y. Sharada Prasad, "Can There Be a Repeat of the Emergency?" *Asian Age*, June 28, 2000.

21. It was revealed in the *SCR* that the prime minister had ordered surveillance of her own ministers and colleagues in the party, namely senior minister Jagjivan Ram, especially at the time of the Allahabad High Court decision (*SCR*, 5.27–5.28).

22. Social movement theories posit that, within democratic structures, existing sympathizers who enjoy some degree of influence can positively impact the prospects of social movement aims, as they aid more favorable conditions for movement activists such as enhanced power, repertoires, and legitimacy

to political movements (M. Giugni, D. McAdam, and C. Tilly, eds., *How Movements Matter: Theoretical and Comparative Studies in the Consequences of Social Movements* [Minneapolis: University of Minnesota Press, 1999]; S. Tarrow, *Power in Movement: Social Movements and Contentious Politics* [New York: Cambridge University Press, 1998]). For example, the Presidential Commission on the Status of Women during the Kennedy administration in the US brought feminist activists into the state, which led to the creation of the National Organization of Women (NOW) in 1966. Such government elites are known as "institutional sympathizers."

23. Narayan, *Towards Total Revolution*, 149.

24. On March 1, 1975, five days before a JPM march on parliament, Mohan Dharia, Minister of State for Works and Housing, called for talks between JP and Gandhi at a public lecture. The following day, he strongly condemned the brutal police treatment of young JPM demonstrators in Bihar, and condemned the CPI for trying to weaken the Congress and to make it dependent on the communist party (*Times of India*, March 2 and 3, 1975). The prime minister immediately stripped Dharia of his ministerial position, asserting that his views did not conform with the perspective of the Congress, and were incompatible with his position as a member of the council of ministers (*Times of India*, March 3, 1975).

25. I. Gandhi, *Democracy and Discipline*, 20.

26. Tandon, *PMO Diary-I*, 260.

27. Ibid., 265.

28. I. Gandhi, *Democracy and Discipline*, 22, see also 158.

29. Varshney, *Ethnic Conflict and Civic Life*, 56.

30. Although there were some dissenting voices, the dominant voice of Nehru resounded across the Congress, who refused to "give institutional shape to what he saw as a vestige of tradition destined to obliteration through the operation of the inexorable laws of history" (Subrata K. Mitra, "Desecularising the State: Religion and Politics in India after Independence," *Comparative Studies in Society and History* 33, no. 4 [October 1991]: 755–77, 756).

31. See Chhibber and Verma, *Ideology and Identity*.

32. I. Gandhi, *Speeches and Writings*, 29–34, see also 63. This is corroborated elsewhere in many of her private letters with Dorothy Norman, as well as in Nayantra Sahgal's biography of Indira Gandhi (Indira Gandhi and Dorothy Norman, *Indira Gandhi: Letters to an American Friend, 1950–1984* [San Diego: Harcourt Brace Jovanovich Publishers, 1985]; Nayantara Sahgal, *Indira Gandhi: Tryst with Power* [New Delhi: Penguin Books, 2012]). NB: Sahgal is Prime Minister Gandhi's first cousin, but did not share positive relations with her.

33. As discussed in Chapter 2, populism and nationalism are distinct though closely articulated discourses. Many instances of populist politics have been nationalist, and nationalist movements often have a populist component. For the purposes of the present discussion, populist actors and parties are typically organized at the level of the nation-state, and therefore their claims and ideas are defined using concepts of the nation. As such, populism can align itself with political projects and ideas of the left or right. Some populist parties celebrate social and cultural liberalism or attack it; they may be secular or religious. For a discussion on the conceptual distinctions and overlap between populism and nationalism, see Cleen, "Populism and Nationalism."

34. At the May 1967 CWC session, Gandhi identified religious nationalism in the form of the RSS-front Jana Sangh as oppositional to her concepts of the nation (Foreign and Commonwealth Office [FCO] Records (South Asia), FCO 37, 40, 1967, The National Archives [TNA], Kew, Richmond, UK).

35. I. Gandhi, *Democracy and Discipline*, 3.

36. Ibid., 11, 13, 114, 175.

37. Ibid., 31.

38. Ibid., 79.

39. Ibid., 125.

40. Ibid., 24, 37, 116, 168. All of Gandhi's examples of the "internal disturbance" that made the Emergency more urgent reference the JPM's activities in Bihar and Gujarat (ibid., 10, 15, 19, 23, 31, 36, 37, 41).

41. Ibid., 23.

42. Ibid., 16.

43. Ibid., 31.

44. Official summary of White Paper reproduced in Balraj Puri, *Revolution, Counter-Revolution* (New Delhi: Newman Group of Publishers, 1978), Appendix I, 130–136.

45. Ibid.

46. I. Gandhi, *Democracy and Discipline*, 31–33.

47. Ibid., 63.

48. Indira Gandhi's own historical experience provides a possibly ambivalent signal with regard to government intolerance. Her inspirational father, Nehru, had set a precedence in 1949 for banning and arresting ideological others in the RSS who were considered enemies of the Indian nation and its secular order, but she, along with many others in government, had been imprisoned and suppressed by state security forces under British rule as part of the Indian independence struggle prior to 1947. This ambivalence may well belong to complex human characteristics, but I believe further centralize the role of Gandhi's boundedness to Congress's secular nationalism.

49. I. Gandhi, *Democracy and Discipline,* 19.
50. Ibid., 11–19, 32–40, 79–80, 173–75. The RSS-front Jana Sangh was not a party of social minorities: 35 percent of its voters lived in white collar, middle-class towns, as compared to less than 22 percent of the Congress, whose base was primarily rural, low-income workers. Despite some efforts, the RSS proved unable to be more inclusionary with regard to Scheduled Castes and Tribes because of their reliance on the landed and princely elites, industrialists, and other notables (Jaffrelot, *The Hindu Nationalist Movement in India,* 243–48). Moreover, the RSS and Jana Sangh generally maintained an aggressive attitude toward minorities. They toned down, but did not discard, this attribute of their exclusionary nationalism as part of the JPM. Though JP felt at the time, and indeed years later, that taking part in the JPM or in government would temper their ideology, the RSS did not open the door to non-Hindu members (ibid.).
51. I. Gandhi, *Democracy and Discipline,* 27–28.
52. Ibid., 161.
53. Ibid., 53.
54. Dhar, *Indira Gandhi,* 316.
55. I. Gandhi, *Democracy and Discipline,* 174.
56. Ibid., 38, see also 105.
57. Ibid., 40.
58. Ibid., 141.
59. Ibid., 147.
60. Ibid., 79–80.
61. Ibid., 32. In the late 1960s and early 1970s, the central government adopted a tougher attitude toward Hindu nationalists as a result of increased communal violence, year-on-year, over the previous decade. A Ministry of Home Affairs report revealed that the RSS had become the largest association of volunteers in the country (Jaffrelot, *The Hindu Nationalist Movement in India,* 238). Congress decision-makers close to Gandhi enthusiastically adopted this renewed anti-communalist zeal (ibid.).
62. I. Gandhi, *Democracy and Discipline,* 1, 94, 145; Indira Gandhi, *Selected Speeches and Writings of Indira Gandhi,* vol. 3 (September 1972–March 1977) (New Delhi: Publications Division, Ministry of Information and Broadcasting, Government of India, 1984), 289, 299.
63. I. Gandhi, *Democracy and Discipline,* 13.
64. All those in her cabinet and office who did give testimony did so under oath, and their accounts have been widely referenced in this study.
65. *SCR,* 5.61.
66. *SCR,* 5.62.8.

67. I. Gandhi, *Democracy and Discipline*, 11, 85, 105, 162–75; I. Gandhi, *Selected Speeches*, 224, 241–63.

68. *Times of India*, July 4, 1975 .

69. Dom Moraes, *Mrs. Gandhi* (London: Jonathan Cape, 1980), 220. As historian Ram Guha writes, Indira Gandhi

> thought she knew better than any other Indian what was good and best for India. Hence, her lack of interest in Parliament, and her barely concealed contempt for the opposition (this was manifest well before she jailed her opponents during the Emergency). Hence, also, her destruction of the culture of inner-party democracy within the Congress, so that her party, and her cabinet, became entirely subordinated to her will, and whim. (Ram Guha, "Indira Gandhi to Modi," *Indian Express*, November 18, 2017, https://bit.ly/34jgdpS [accessed October 1, 2020])

70. Mary Carras, *Indira Gandhi: In the Crucible of Leadership* (Boston: Beacon Press, 1979), 232.

71. Ibid., 144; I. Gandhi, *Selected Speeches*, 296.

72. It is noteworthy that the international community condemned Gandhi's steps, but that this did not prevent the Emergency from being instituted or continuing for twenty-one months. Indeed, on August 15, 1975 (India's Independence Day), 700 prominent intellectuals, writers, artists, and politicians around the world signed an appeal protesting the Emergency (Kapoor, *The Emergency*, 99). This is corroborated in Dorothy Norman's letters, which she exchanged privately with Gandhi over three decades. Upon the declaration of the Emergency, Norman brought together individuals, notably writers and intellectuals in New York City, to appeal the decision, claiming distress at "the loss of fundamental human rights in India ... [which] shows that when human rights are suppressed anywhere they are threatened everywhere" (Gandhi and Norman, *Indira Gandhi*, 148).

73. Granville Austin, *The Indian Constitution: Cornerstone of a Nation* (New Delhi: Oxford University Press, 1999), 308.

74. Table A1.1.

75. *SCR*, 19.4.

76. In many Emergency arrest cases, warrants were not scrutinized, or suffered from major legal flaws, including failure to record necessary documentation. There were also several recorded instances in which state authorities did not confirm the order of detention passed by the detaining authority (*SCR*, 11.34–11.37; 19.12–19.14).

77. In addition to the arrests of Gandhi's ideological foes, other arrests included criminals and anti-social and economic (gambling, bootlegging, and so on)

offenders, going back five to ten years in offences committed. It is important to note that there are a finite number of banned groups and a much larger pool of other criminals, meaning that the force and numbers in which religious nationalist organizations were suppressed is significant.

78. *SCR*, 19.399, see Annexure to Chapter 19.
79. P. G. Sahasrabuddhe and M. C. Vajpayee, *The People versus Emergency: A Saga of Struggle* (New Delhi: Suruchi Prakashan, 1991), 212–17. Although these numbers have been questioned for their bias and inflation.
80. Kapoor, *The Emergency*, 30.
81. *SCR*, 19.22–19.23. Not only activists, but also students associated with the Jana Sangh or RSS were among the primary subjects detained (ibid., 19.28).
82. This much is corroborated in journalist Coomi Kapoor's personal experience (Kapoor, *The Emergency*, 73–74, 104–05). NB: Kapoor's husband, journalist Virendra Kapoor, was arrested and imprisoned during the Emergency, and her brother-in-law, Jana Sangh MP Subramanian Swamy, was on the run during the clampdown. Writing in a 2,000 piece, Subramanian Swamy notes the deep involvement of the RSS in the JP movement, many of whom he claims "egged" JP on during the agitation (Subramanian Swamy, "Unlearnt lessons of the Emergency," *The Hindu*, June 13, 2000, https://bit.ly/2La96J3 [accessed October 1, 2020]).
83. *SCR*, 19.23. Kapoor (*The Emergency*, 111) also argues that RSS–Jana Sangh prisoners were disproportionately detained. She also notes that RSS and Jana Sangh activists remained in prison even when many opposition leaders had been released (ibid., 299; see also L. K. Advani, *A Prisoner's Scrap-Book* [New Delhi: Prabhat Prakashan, 2016 [1978]).
84. This was launched in 1975 to frame the government's policy goals during the Emergency. It promised, among other things, the application of land ceilings, increases to agricultural wages, sufficient land grants to landless peasants, the elimination of peasants' debts, the eradication of forced labor, controlling inflation, and the creation of jobs (Jaffrelot, "The First Reign of Indira Gandhi," 37). Unlike for previous plans, this time ideas has come from a broad array of sources, including old advisors such as P. N. Haksar and parties such as the CPI (Ramesh, *Intertwined Lives*, 361). Resultantly, the plan was doctrinally incoherent.
85. Sahgal, *Indira Gandhi*, 229.
86. Anthony Lukas, "India Is as Indira Does," *New York Times*, April 4, 1976 (quoted in ibid., 229).
87. Much investigative work has gone into analyzing the personal life of Indira Gandhi. That is not my goal here; unfortunately, there is simply not enough

primary data. One set of insights about the prime minister's life emerged from the private correspondence between Dorothy Norman and Indira Gandhi, which spanned three decades (Gandhi and Norman, *Indira Gandhi*). Gandhi's letters reveal her personal and political development, and reveal a well-travelled, cosmopolitan woman who was inspired by Joan of Arc, but who became increasingly insular and distrustful when she gained office. This evolution is corroborated in the private diary of Joint Secretary to the Prime Minister B. N. Tandon (Tandon, *PMO Diary-I*) and Principal Secretary P. N. Dhar's memoirs (Dhar, *Indira Gandhi*). Gandhi wanted to emulate her father, whom she shadowed while he was prime minister, and whose secular, and to some extent socialist, leanings meaningfully influenced her policies as prime minister. Although Gandhi appeared to seek out ideological centrism whenever possible with regard to policy problems, she was far more instinctual regarding social issues and nationalist articulation than intellectual. There is a noticeable impression of a figure seeking to be a unifier between or perhaps a controller of between communities. During and immediately after Partition, for example, Gandhi, at the behest of M. K. "Mahatma" Gandhi, visited conflict-ridden Hindu and Muslim communities in Delhi ghettos to prevent violence and to provide social benefits. Her observations as a thirty-year-old are instructive of the emergent components of her worldview:

> I asked Muslims which Hindus were "good" and asked Hindus about Muslims. Then I held separate meetings of the 'good' from each group, ignoring bad elements.... We went into Muslim communities and, in spite of the danger of contracting cholera, drank from cups offered to us. To refuse would have been considered anti-Muslim. It took days to inspire trust. Finally, we persuaded as many as twenty workers to help bring harmony between the opposing factions. (Gandhi and Norman, *Indira Gandhi*, 18)

88. The Congress Forum for Socialist Action (CFSA) was founded in 1962 and formed the leftist wing of the unified Congress Party. The CFSA championed the nationalization agenda, and their leaders and loyalists were called the Young Turks. The CFSA disbanded in April 1973.

89. Prior to her ascent as prime minister, Gandhi occupied the office of president of the Congress Party for just under a year (this is traditionally a two-year term). One major initiative that Gandhi undertook during this time gives insight into her nationalist vision. Gandhi urged the central government to intervene in Kerala, where the communist government formed in 1957 had been locked in a confrontation with the Roman Catholic and Nair communities over the issue of state control of schools and colleges. Presidential rule was established in Kerala, and fresh elections were held in 1960, when an alliance of parties led by the Congress won a majority. In this decision, Gandhi displayed her

anti-communist position, which appealed to the proclivities in her nationalism. Interestingly, and illustrative of her desire for centralized policymaking power, when reflecting on why she left her position as Congress Party president one year earlier than expected, she told Nayantra Sahgal: "They wouldn't let me do what I wanted to do" (Sahgal, *Indira Gandhi*, 371).

90. Quoted in ibid., 11.
91. Indira Gandhi, *My Truth* (New Delhi: Orient Paperbacks, 2013 [1980]), 107–08.
92. I. Gandhi, *Speeches and Writings*, 51.
93. Ibid., 78.
94. India was highly dependent on Western donors for food grains and foreign exchange by mid-1966 (Mukherji, *Globalization and Deregulation*, 41; General Records of the Department of State [DOS] [Visit Files], 1966–1970, Box 1, National Archives and Records Administration College Park [NACP], College Park, Maryland, USA).
95. Gandhi hesitantly devalued the rupee in June 1966 under pressure from international institutions and the US, but was not entirely happy with this move, and quickly reversed the decision (ibid., 41; Lockwood, *The Communist Party of India*, 49–64).
96. Thus emerged the left-ward turn over the course of the next decade, until the return to considering liberalization in the mid-1970s (Mukherji, *Globalization and Deregulation*; Ramachandra Guha, *India After Gandhi: The History of the World's Largest Democracy* [New York: Harper Perennial, 2008], 435–36).
97. P. N. Dhar, "A Note on Economic Situation and Remedies to Correct the Economic Difficulties," P. N. Haksar Papers, Installment Two, Subject File 248, 1973, NMML.
98. Dhar, *Indira Gandhi*, 143. Interestingly, the business community was not aware of the direction of government thinking, and believed that the push for liberal reform would continue under Indira Gandhi's leadership (G. D. Birla, speaking on January 2, 1967, quoted in Frankel, *India's Political Economy*, 306). This is to say that the change in direction from Gandhi and her advisors was not driven simply by external pressures, thus further centralizing the role of ideology in her government.
99. Mahalanobis, a former professor of physics at Cambridge University, returned to India on Nehru's encouragement. He went on to set up the Planning Commission and became one of modern India's most influential economists.
100. Frankel, *India's Political Economy*, 397–99. Congress Party veterans, who came to be known as the "Syndicate," rose to prominence after the death of Jawaharlal Nehru and during Lal Bahadur Shastri's tenure. The Syndicate included S. K. Patil of Maharashtra, Atulya Ghosh of West Bengal, Morarji

Desai of Gujarat, Biju Patnaik of Orissa, Neelam Sanjiva Reddy of Andhra Pradesh, and K. Kamaraj of Tamil Nadu, among others. These individuals formed an informal group with the aim of pressuring Prime Minister Gandhi to act on their advice. Many of these figures and their supporters would be defeated in the regional elections of 1967, or would defect or create their own parties, and most would become vanguards of the right-of-center breakaway Congress (O) faction. In a series of private meetings between the British High Commissioner and Syndicate leaders in 1967 and early 1968, namely Morarji Desai, S. K. Patil, and C. B. Gupta, it was revealed that these individuals stood against nationalization and against the leftist faction led by Gandhi. By virtue of pushing for such policies, they claimed, Gandhi illustrated that she and her loyalists were incongruent with the party, and argued that her policy prescriptions could damage the Congress. Patil claimed that Gandhi held her office "on sufferance," adding that the "Left" faction of the party hardened and wrongfully attacked business elites (FCO 37, 40, 1967, TNA; FCO 37, 41, 1968, TNA).

101. Dom Moraes, one of Gandhi's early biographers, speaks to the recognition of this influence within the prime minister's advisory circle too, where P. N. Haksar "then Mrs. Gandhi's Private Secretary and the best advisor she has ever had, kept the young Turks from exercising too positive an influence on her" (Moraes, *Mrs. Gandhi*, 159). But even Haksar, as well as a committed socialist but ever the pragmatist, would advise that Gandhi "show a sensitive understanding of the feelings, emotions, and anxieties and thinking behind the economic programme elaborated [in July 1969 as the Congress came up to its eventual split] by the so-called Young Turks" (quoted in Ramesh, *Intertwined Lives*, 138).

102. FCO 37, 40, 1967, TNA.

103. FCO 37, 41, 1968, TNA. This was revealed in a fascinating private meeting with the British High Commissioner.

104. Carras, *Indira Gandhi*, 137–38.

105. P. N. Haksar, Note to Prime Minister, 9 and 25 July 1969, P. N. Haksar Papers, Installment One, Subject File 42, July 1969, NMML; corroborated by Dhar, *Indira Gandhi*, 143. This education should start with the Congress itself: "The Congress Party has been so long in power that it has forgotten the most elementary principles of politics, *namely to help the people in fighting injustice*" (P. N. Haksar, Note to Prime Minister, 14 December 1970, P. N. Haksar Papers, Installment One, Subject File 213, 1970–71, NMML). According to MP Madhu Dandavate, a vocal opponent of Indira Gandhi, Haksar was a major influence on the prime minister regarding bank nationalization (Oral History Project, Madhu Dandavate, 2000, NMML, 221–22). This is echoed by

her information advisor at the time, H. Y. Sharada Prasad (Prasad, *The Book I Won't Be Writing*, 85) as well as through several of Haksar's own private letters to the prime minister as quoted in Ramesh, *Intertwined Lives*, 132–86. Indira Gandhi trusted Haksar implicitly, and considered him to have "extraordinary common sense and competence," qualities which she rarely praised in others (letter from Gandhi to her son, Sanjay; quoted in Kapoor, *The Emergency*, 179). Haksar was an alum of the London School of Economics, which, at the time of his attendance, was firmly within the grasp of its Fabian origins.

106. Dhar, *Indira Gandhi*, 14
107. Ramesh, *Intertwined Lives*, 133, 321–22.
108. The need to elect a new president of India after the unexpected demise of Dr. Zakir Husain in May 1969 became another occasion for confrontation between the two Congress factions beyond the nationalization debate. Gandhi fought the Syndicate's choice "tooth and nail," fearing that the candidate might hamper her power as a prime minister, as well as her desired policy program (Mukherjee, *The Dramatic Decade*, 57). After a complicated and repeated vote, the prime minister's candidate, V. V. Giri, won the election. This stand-off is illustrative of Gandhi's repetition of the ideas and tactics of her father, Jawaharlal Nehru. When the 1951 election for Congress Party president was contested between P. Tandon and the more secular candidate, J. B. Kripalani, Tandon was elected, but Nehru, who had supported Kripalani, forced him to resign from the presidency. Nehru's action sought to ensure the dominance of the secularist position in the Congress Party (Chhibber and Verma, *Ideology and Identity*, 34).
109. Mukherji, *Globalization and Deregulation*, 10; Frankel, *India's Political Economy*, 403–04.
110. I. Gandhi, *Speeches and Writings*, 98–100. Gandhi is also reported to have said that beyond steps such as bank nationalization, "[i]t was important to ensure that persons who managed these institutions [banks and industries] had a commitment to our ideologies and policies" (Moin Zaidi, ed., *The Encyclopedia of the Indian National Congress*, vol. 20: *1968–69: Facing the City Bosses* [New Delhi: Chand and Company Ltd., 1983], 363).
111. Mukherjee, *The Dramatic Decade*, 57.
112. Indira Gandhi, "Broadcast on Bank Nationalization," July 19, 1969, quoted in Zaidi, *Encyclopedia of the Indian National Congress*, vol. 20.
113. I. Gandhi, *Speeches and Writings*, 111–14.
114. Guha, *India After Gandhi*, 439. Right-wing Jana Sangh president Atal Bihari Vajpayee stated at the 16th Annual Session in Patna, held from December 28 to 30, 1969, that the formal Congress split had "precipitated [a] radically new situation in Indian politics" that created two genuine political blocs (FCO 37, 594, 1970, Congress Party in India, TNA).

115. At this session, Young Turks such as Chandra Shekhar were appointed to the working committee.

116. Ex-communist Young Turks had a closer relationship with Gandhi than did the ex-Praja Socialist Party (PSP) Young Turks, such as Mohan Dharia, Chandra Shekhar, Krishan Kant, and Y. B. Chavan (FCO 37, 594, 1970, Congress Party in India, TNA). Also see note 101.

117. FCO 37, 594, 1970, Congress Party in India, TNA.

118. Even though there was criticism of both left and right extremes in the party system, Congress politicians especially attacked the RSS (FCO 37, 594, 1970, Congress Party in India, TNA). Indeed, in the late 1960s, the Muslim vote swung in favor of the Congress in the critical state of UP when Muslims and other minorities were alarmed by the growing strength of the Jana Sangh, and began to turn actively toward the Congress.

119. FCO 37, 594, 1970, Congress Party in India, TNA.

120. With the rise of opposition and regional parties from the previous election, and considering Gandhi's goal to strengthen her faction's power at the center, the calling of an early national election in 1971 primarily allowed for state-level election cycles to be separated from national elections, thus favoring Congress (R) at the ballot (Lloyd I. Rudolph and Susanne Hoeber Rudolph, *In Pursuit of Lakshmi: The Political Economy of the Indian State* [Chicago: University of Chicago Press, 1987], 135).

121. Indira Gandhi, *Selected Speeches and Writings of Indira Gandhi*, vol. 2 (August 1969–August 1972) (New Delhi: Publications Division, Ministry of Information and Broadcasting, Government of India, 1975).

122. However, it should be noted that at the AICC session in Patna on October 12–14, 1970 (two months before dissolving the Lok Sabha), Gandhi rejected a proposal to explicitly build a front with leftist parties, keeping the central-left space occupied. Gandhi wanted the Congress to remain maneuverable, and here, once again, her politics show full interplay with her faction's ideology (FCO 37, 594, 1970, Congress Party in India, TNA).

123. FCO 37, 812, 1970, General Elections in India, TNA.

124. *I. C. Golaknath & Ors v. State of Punjab & Anr* 1967 AIR 1643.

125. The opposition, meanwhile, championed the independence of the judiciary, and refused to tamper with the Constitution.

126. The Supreme Court was so weakened by Indira Gandhi's rule during this time that it would continue to capitulate during the Emergency period, notably in the *habeas corpus* case of 1976, in which it put its seal on the Gandhi government's vast powers of preventive detention and denied citizens recourse to these powers, and the 42nd Amendment's abolition of judicial review. Since the Emergency, as we will see in the contemporary case study, the Supreme

Court, among other apex institutions in India, came to reassert its role in checking executive power during the UPA (although not always constructively).

127. FCO 37, 812, 1970, General Elections in India, TNA.

128. The platform also outlined: ending anachronistic privileges such as privy purses; enlarging the role of the public sector (and improving its performance) by (a) taking over general insurance, (b) increasing state participation in the import–export trade, (c) providing the state a greater role in industries in which substantial public funds have been invested, and (d) expanding the activities of the Food Corporation of India; giving scope to the private sector to play its proper role in the economy while curbing the concentration of economic power and wealth; state control of prices; discussing a National Works Program (which would go on to form the basis of the NREGA [see Chapters 5 and 6]); and a large-scale state-run housing program.

129. This greater emphasis on tackling historically entrenched social inequalities is rooted in the ideas that led to a largely "social" Constitution at the founding of the republic, and were shaped in particular by B. R. Ambedkar. The Directive Principles in the Constitution were intended to guide democratic decisions over central societal aspirations, as resources allowed.

130. FCO 37, 815, 1971, TNA.

131. Ibid.

132. Ibid.

133. In a letter of December 18, 1971, to the chief justice, who had written to the prime minister expressing concern regarding the 24th Amendment, Gandhi replied:

> I personally have no doubt whatsoever that as our nation moves forward and our society gains inner cohesion and sense of direction all our great institutions, Parliament, Judiciary, Executive, will reflect the organic unity of our society…. We have all to guard against the danger of substituting those inarticulate major premises of social and economic thinking of which we as individuals might happen to approve for a given time for the will of the people as reflected in Parliament. (Mukherjee, *The Dramatic Decade*, 68)

For Gandhi and her advisors, the homogenization of ideology to undergird state institutions was key. This was explicitly the counsel of close advisor and cabinet minister Mohan Kumaramangalam; see note 137. The primacy of parliament, and therefore of her government, was key in this regard. See also Sahgal, *Indira Gandhi*, 116.

134. In two previous judgments of 1951 and 1965, the Supreme Court had upheld parliament's right to amend the fundamental right to property to make legislation in this regard non-justiciable. However, in 1967, Chief

Justice Koka Subba Rao of the Supreme Court in the *L.C. Golak Nath v. State of Punjab* case reversed the earlier decision to uphold the parliament's supremacy to amend fundamental rights to property (voted 6–5). This sowed the seeds of confrontation between the government and the judiciary, and resulted in the sidelining of the Congress's flagship policy goals regarding bank nationalization and the abolition of privy purses. The 24th and 25th Amendments sought to undercut the Supreme Court's apparent conservatism in this matter.

135. Some weeks prior to the introduction of the constitutional amendments discussed here, a presentation was given to Prime Minister Gandhi wherein 210 Congress (R) MPs demanded that the government should, in that parliament session, set about implementing the "progressive socialist policies" laid down in the party's 1971 general election manifesto. Perhaps, most interestingly, in terms of measuring the weight of ideological considerations against more pressing, strategic policy concerns, politicians believed it necessary to push the party pledge to the prime minister while the government was in the full throes of war with Pakistan (FCO 37, 815, 1971, TNA).

136. See Table A4.1.

137. P. N. Haksar, *Premonitions* (Bombay: Interpress, 1979), 200–09; Sahgal, *Indira Gandhi*, 88; Kapoor, *The Emergency*, 179.

138. Kumaramangalam and Ray would prove critical in the government's turf battle with the judiciary (the other being H. R. Gokhale), and we have seen in Chapter 3 the role that Ray played in the Emergency decision (Mukherjee, *The Dramatic Decade*, 63–66). Kumaramangalam, meanwhile, in 1973 led the lobbying of Prime Minister Gandhi to supersede three Supreme Court judges, J. M. Shelat, K. S. Hegde, and A. N. Grover, with junior judge A. N. Ray as chief justice. Significantly, all three senior judges had ruled against the government in the landmark *Kesavananda Bharati v. State of Kerala* case, wherein the Supreme Court decreed that the Constitution could not be changed, even by an enactment of parliament.

139. Philip Arestis and Malcolm Sawyer, *A Biographical Dictionary of Dissenting Economists* (Cheltenham: Edward Elgar Publications, 2001), 29.

140. FCO 37, 812, 1970, General Elections in India, TNA.

141. Stanley Kochanek, "Briefcase Politics in India: The Congress Party and the Business Elite," *Far Eastern Survey* 27, no. 12 (1987): 1278–301.

142. Jaffrelot, "The First Reign of Indira Gandhi," 33; P. S. Appu, *Land Reforms in India: A Survey of Policy, Legislation, and Implementation* (New Delhi: Vikas Publishing House, 1996), 158–73.

143. DOS, Briefing Books, 1958–76, Box 92, NACP.

144. Defections were a hallmark of political maneuvering through the intra-party struggle in the Congress from the mid-1960s onwards. From 1957 to 1967, 540 defections took place, while from 1967 to December 1970, 1,400 defections took place from among approximately 4,000 legislators in the country. Until 1967, Congress had been a net gainer of defections, whereas from 1967 (when the intra-party struggle began in earnest) to the Congress split in November 1969, the party was a net loser of defections. After the split, and immediately before the 1971 elections, the Congress (R) was the biggest gainer of defections. These trends refocused the emergent polarization of the party system and made Gandhi focus on consolidating her government and preventing disloyalty to the policy program (FCO 37, 812, 1970, General Elections in India, TNA).

145. FCO 37, 815, 1971, TNA.

146. I. Gandhi, *Speeches and Writings*, 203–04.

147. Despite importing 5 million tons of food grains in 1974, there remained a significant shortage, which fuelled food prices and negatively impacted the fiscal deficit. Moreover, due to India's dependence on imports of petroleum and petroleum products, its import bill rose significantly. This produced an even larger gap between import and export volumes, and drained India's foreign exchange reserves, further increasing the budget deficit. The government, much to its chagrin, had to appeal to the World Bank and IMF for emergency aid, and, in turn, accepted harsh conditions on these loans while displaying an effort toward economic reforms.

148. B. Chandra, *In the Name of Democracy*, 18; Rudolph and Rudolph, *In Pursuit of Lakshmi*, 227. Indicatively, workers of Indian Railways, as one of the largest employers in India, formed independent trade unions and went on a series of strikes in 1974 across the country. The preceding year's economic downturn had precipitated existing anger from the railwaymen around wages and contractual job protections or the lack thereof. They were crushed by the Gandhi government that May. For a deeper look into these strikes which added to the overall sense of credibility crisis that the government faced, see Ranabir Samaddar, *Crisis of 1974: Railway Strike and the Rank and File* (New Delhi: Primus Books, 2017).

149. In his memoirs, Congress politician Pranab Mukherjee claims that during this time, while nationalization in sectors such as coal mining created confidence in the minds of the working class, these measures extracted their own "pound of flesh" from the Indian economy, while measures such as the MRTP deterred private investment (Mukherjee, *The Dramatic Decade*, 50). Moreover, the move to take over wheat distribution in 1973–74, which was opposed to by P. N. Haksar, led to acute shortages in that staple and was duly discarded.

150. Quoted in Tariq Ali, *The Nehrus and the Gandhis: An Indian Dynasty* (London: Picador, 2005 [1985]), 177.
151. Rudra Chaudhuri presents the results of a survey of hundreds of archival documents and demonstrates a connection between international media pressure, *not* international government pressure, and Indira Gandhi's decision to call for elections (Rudra Chaudhuri, "Re-reading the Indian Emergency: Britain, the United States and India's Constitutional Autocracy, 1975–1977," *Diplomacy and Statecraft* 29, no. 3 [2018], 477–98).
152. On recent studies of the Emergency period itself and its implications, see, among others, Gyan Prakash, *Emergency Chronicles: Indira Gandhi and Democracy's Turning Point* (Princeton: Princeton University Press, 2019).
153. For more on the treatment of P. N. Haksar and his family during the Emergency and the subsequent estrangement between him and Gandhi, see Ramesh, *Intertwined Lives*, 363–421
154. P. N. Haksar, Untitled Top Secret Memo to the Prime Minister, P. N. Haksar Papers, Subject File: 57, 1977, NMML. Incidentally, Babuaji would be imprisoned again in 1992 under the Congress government for joining protests against the ban on the RSS after the organization's role in the Babri mosque demolition.
155. Subramanian Swamy claims that the RSS had by this time also "finalised the document of surrender to be signed" at the end of January 1977, the news of which must have at the very least made its way to Gandhi through the intelligence agencies she deeply relied on and who acted on her command (Swamy, "Unlearnt Lessons of the Emergency").
156. Ibid.
157. Ibid.

5

Checks and Balances and the India Against Corruption Movement

Where there is a consciousness of unjust or dishonorable purposes, communication is always checked by distrust in proportion to the number whose concurrence is necessary.

—James Madison, 1788

I think we [the UPA] were a double coalition. The Congress Party itself was a coalition. There were people in the party that did not believe in policies that myself and those close to me put forward. But, superimposed on this was that we were a coalition government – the communists, regional partners, and others. Their commitment to our party and our government was never watertight.

—Manmohan Singh, author interview, 2015

Polycentric Power Center

Between 2011 and 2012, the United Progressive Alliance (UPA) coalition government engaged in a series of negotiations with the India Against Corruption (IAC) movement. These negotiations were less a result of decision-makers' collective desire to actively engage with the movement. Rather, state elites, as part of a division of policymaking power at the executive level between Prime Minister Manmohan Singh and the Congress Party president Sonia Gandhi, established divergent diagnoses in response to the movement. Some leaders urged full negotiation, while others urged counteraction. Several distinct decision-makers were tasked with crafting a response to the anti-corruption agitation, namely within the PMO, the cabinet, senior politicians in the Congress Party, and the NAC, and played an important role in this polycentric environment.[1]

Prime Minister Singh effectively shared executive-level authority over policymaking during UPA rule with the Congress chief, Sonia Gandhi. Whereas the prime minister maintained objective power by leading the cabinet and the PMO, a statutory body comprised of technocrats, civic activists, and some politicians was formed under Sonia Gandhi to offer the dynast executive-level policy input, consequently diminishing Singh's subjective power in government. This statutory body, the NAC, would be the primary vehicle to design and implement core features of the Common Minimum Program (CMP), which ensured coherence on policy matters among UPA coalition partner parties and allies.[2] Given the backgrounds of the decision-makers who comprised the de facto parallel cabinet, the NAC would interface between the government and civil society to supplement cabinet policymaking recommendations. Crucially, the decision-makers who surrounded the prime minister and the party president maintained divergent ideological approaches to social and economic development issues (as we will see in the next chapter), including the causes of the nationwide anti-corruption collective action. This polycentric institutional environment, alongside the large number of ruling parties in the coalition, placed structural constraints on the behavior of the executive branch to act arbitrarily in response to the emergence of the IAC movement in 2011. This chapter considers this response and traces both the events that led to a negotiated settlement and the decision-making steps taken by Singh, Gandhi, and their close advisors to the crisis faced.

The United Progressive Alliance (UPA) Coalition

Decision-makers in the Congress-led UPA government (2004–14) functioned within a coalition with a high degree of internal fractionalization, which made coalition management a regular feature of governance. In 2004, the UPA obtained 219 seats in the 543-member Lok Sabha—53 seats short of the 272-seat majority. To ensure the minimum number of parliamentary seats to secure a simple majority, the UPA sought pivotal outside support from the Left Front parties, who together added 61 seats.[3] The CPI(M), which held 43 seats, thus became the second-largest party in the ruling alliance. In 2009, the UPA returned stronger, holding 262 seats on its own, although its reduced outside support cut down its overall (net) seat share by 13 seats. The Congress performed well off of its first administration's record, and contributed 61 seats, but still needed to include more than eleven parties in the coalition to secure a simple majority. Between the UPA-1 (2004–09) and UPA-2 (2009–14) administrations, several coalition allies, notably the Telangana Rashtra Samithi (TRS) and the Left Front, would first threaten and then actually withdraw their support over policy disagreements with the government. Likewise, between 2009 and 2014, several UPA members, notably the All India Trinamool Congress (TMC) and the Dravida Munnetra Kazhagam (DMK), would acrimoniously leave the coalition during the IAC crisis.[4]

Decision-making among the many parties of the UPA coalition was complicated by political players who extended "outside" support, and was made more complex by the division of power in the executive branch between the prime minister and the Congress Party president. The 2004 and 2009 elections provided the UPA with the mandate to govern, but also afforded the Congress Party the opportunity to affect a stronger role in the government–party relationship. Executive-level power, which is often vested primarily in one individual in parliamentary democracies, was split in the UPA. Under this informal framework, Manmohan Singh, who held no political base of his own, became prime minister, while Sonia Gandhi, whose political base and support had allowed her to secure a successful campaign and to bring together a governing coalition, remained as Congress Party president.[5] The fact that Gandhi eschewed the role of premier created an additional power center in governance, which had historically been subsumed within, or subservient to, the prime minister.[6] This government–party dynamic was highlighted when the UPA returned to power in 2009 with a greater Congress seat-share than it had held in the previous eighteen years.[7]

Crystallization of the Corrupt State Narrative

The IAC movement captivated India between 2011 and 2012. The movement was symbolized by the Gandhian activist Anna Hazare. Before 2011, Hazare had led social movements in the state of Maharashtra to promote rural development, the right to information (RTI), and the fight against corruption. Hazare's primary tactic was the fast-unto-death. Although Hazare was certainly the symbol of the IAC, its war room was led by the savvy bureaucrat-turned-activist Arvind Kejriwal.[8] It was Kejriwal who brought Hazare to Delhi to energize and lead the nascent movement against corruption.[9] The IAC urged the institutionalization of an anti-corruption ombudsman (or Lokpal) as a necessary step to combat corruption.[10] The first public meeting of the movement that would become the IAC took place in November 2010.[11] This was a gathering of diverse civic activists who had long fought against corruption across the country.[12] These activists met each day at 6 in the evening in central Delhi to formulate early drafts of what they deemed the citizen's anti-corruption ombudsman (or Jan Lokpal) bill.[13]

From early 2011 to November 2012, the IAC led a turbulent period of demonstrations against government corruption across India. In April 2011, India was rocked by the exposure of the alleged large-scale misappropriation of public funds during preparations for the 2010 Delhi Commonwealth Games. This scandal lit the tinder from which the IAC mobilized—first in Delhi, and then across the country. In his 2012 book *Swaraj*, Kejriwal reflected: "In Delhi, in the name of CWG [Commonwealth Games 2010], the government blew up Rs. 70,000 crore [USD 15.32 billion]. Perfectly fine roads were demolished and redone. At the same time MCD [Municipal Corporation of Delhi] sweepers did not receive their salaries for three months."[14] The IAC's first public demonstrations began on April 5, 2011, at Jantar Mantar in Delhi, as demonstrators demanded the passage of the Jan Lokpal Bill. Immediately, the media and the Indian public recognized the movement. For over a year thereafter, large crowds spilled onto the streets in the hundreds, and then tens of thousands, to support the IAC.[15] This agitation was advanced through fasts-unto-death, sit-ins, and marches against the cacophony of high-profile government corruption scandals at the center.

The Comptroller and Auditor General (CAG) Reports

The tide of corruption has destroyed the credibility of many central and state governments in India, especially since the emergence of the corrupt state narrative we saw in the previous chapters. However, it was the ten-year rule of the UPA coalition that would become synonymous with corruption on a scale that surpassed the government indiscretions previously seen in the country.

The scale and exposure of the corruption scandals that plagued the UPA administration were the impetus for the IAC, and drove its mass appeal. The disclosure of these scandals occurred primarily through the reports produced by the Comptroller and Auditor General's (CAG) office.[16] Among the most noteworthy scandals was the Adarsh Housing Society Scam, which began in 2002. In this scam, land that was designated to build a welfare housing cooperative for retired defense personnel in the upmarket Colaba area of

Mumbai, Maharashtra, was allotted as apartment space for politicians, bureaucrats, military officers, and their close relatives at artificially lowered prices. Elsewhere, the notorious 2G spectrum and coal scandals were rooted in the reported exploitation of existing allocation mechanisms that distributed government contracts to private companies. These scandals implicated senior government officials and cabinet ministers all the way up to Prime Minister Manmohan Singh.

The exposure of these corruption scandals, and their subsequent investigation, stained the credibility of the UPA government, and exacerbated a crisis environment of which the IAC movement was the chief manifestation.[17] The IAC erupted not only against the backdrop of the 2G scam, but also at the very moment when the V. K. Shunglu Committee report on the CWG scam revealed that the government should have removed Congress leader Suresh Kalmadi from office a year before the Games. Kalmadi was arrested as the first wave of IAC agitations began in spring 2011. High-profile arrests of government officials further heightened the sense of crisis in the UPA and, in the case of the 2G scam, bruised the coalition.[18] Later, in April 2012, Congress politician Dalijeet Singh was arrested by the Central Bureau of Investigation (CBI) in connection with the food grains scam in UP, just as an interim draft of the CAG report on coal allocation in India had embroiled the prime minister.

The impression that corruption emanated from—and was consistently absolved by—the heights of central government was exacerbated when Prime Minister Manmohan Singh, who held the coal portfolio between 2005 and 2009, was implicated in a coal allocations scam. In March 2012, an interim draft report from Vinod Rai, the CAG, accused the government of inefficiently allocating coal blocks between 2004 and 2009, and of underpricing sales to steel, cement, and power companies by as much as USD 33 billion. In September 2012, the Supreme Court expressed its support for the CAG, and began mounting official investigations into coal block allocations.[19] The report claimed that although the government had decided to allot coal blocks through a system of competitive bidding, it actually employed an opaque, subjective allocation method.

The CAG reports on the 2G and coal scandals provided damning evidence of government corruption, and brought the executive branch squarely into the focus of the IAC.[20] Throughout these scams, the CAG reasoned that, had the government followed proper methods of contract allocation, procurement practices, and executive oversight over ministries, the national exchequer could have saved (the equivalent of) several billions of dollars. These funds, implied the CAG reports, instead padded the pockets of crony government capitalists.[21] In response to this report, some decision-makers went on the offensive, interrogating the CAG's claim of a depleted national exchequer.[22] The CAG's exposure of government corruption drove the IAC to organize and galvanize citizens across India against the corrupt state.[23] A million mutinies erupted against corruption once again, and the IAC became its vanguard.

The Credibility Crisis and Rise of the IAC

The IAC movement captured citizens' anger at corruption, and gained traction against the backdrop of deteriorating economic conditions in India. Between 2004 and 2010, the national economic and political mood was positive, as India's GDP grew at an unprecedented average of 8 percent, inflation hovered around 5 percent, and the US–India civil nuclear deal raised national morale and international recognition.[24] However, by early 2011, as the effects of the global financial crisis and rising international oil prices worsened, the government raised spending at an unsustainable rate, while private investment fell by 4 percentage points to 22 percent of GDP.[25] Additionally, the price of essential food items rose at an average of 10 percent, with inflation running twice as high in India as the emerging world average.[26] As Indian workers had come to expect higher prices, they demanded higher wages, and the RBI began to issue open warnings about the threat of a wage–price spiral.[27] A sense of crisis gripped the nation. In early 2011, this climate further deteriorated as large-scale corruption scandals that implicated senior government officials were brought to the fore of public attention, causing an erosion of support for the ruling UPA.

At the inception of the IAC movement, activist reformers furthered their anti-corruption cause through mass meetings, petitions, and fasts.[28] Central to the IAC demands was the institution of an anti-corruption ombudsman who would regulate the indiscretions of political actors at the center (Lokpal) and in the states (Lokayukta).[29] The IAC asserted that the Lokpal should hold the authority to investigate parliamentary and cabinet wrongdoings, from local bureaucrats to the prime minister. As the movement evolved, much like the JPM, its aims expanded to garner public and institutional support to reform government accountability in the face of widespread corruption. This evolution led to demonstrations against the Congress government as well as widespread support for non-Congress candidates in state elections who vocalized commitment to "patriotism" and the "country's development."[30] In the aftermath of the coal allocations scam, which many believed to have involved the prime minister, Arvind Kejriwal stated: "We will uproot the current corrupt government. Till now we have been only requesting the government to implement the Jan Lokpal bill, but now it is a larger movement. We have to throw them out of power."[31]

The IAC quickly became a national phenomenon known for its anti-corruption demonstrations across India.[32] Countless column inches, social media hits, television hours, and national magazines brought IAC actions broad exposure.[33] The movement's diffusion across India was swift.[34] As it expanded, the movement came to include many students, citizens across socioeconomic classes, especially the urban middle class, business elites, politicians, and right-wing religious nationalist groups, with peak daily crowds over consecutive days consistently surpassing 100,000 demonstrators in Delhi alone.[35]

IAC Support and Composition

The IAC developed coalitions of support from both inside and outside the government, and a broad range of citizens mobilized in its ranks. As it gathered momentum, the IAC received support in parliament and on the streets from non-Congress political parties.[36] The opposition leaders, as well as the leftist parties, launched their own demonstrations against corruption in solidarity with the IAC.[37] The IAC, in turn, often met with opposition ministers such as BJP leader L. K. Advani, CPI leader A. B. Bardhan, and CPI(M) general secretary Prakash Karat, to garner support for the movement.[38] Opposition parties partnered with the IAC on a range of issues, most notably the inclusion of the prime minister under the purview of the Lokpal.[39] However, the movement also criticized—and was criticized by—these opposition parties. For example, many regional parties moved strongly against the Lokayukta provisions in the IAC draft bill, and when the movement demonstrated outside the homes of Manmohan Singh and Sonia Gandhi over corruption scandals in the UPA, they also demonstrated outside BJP president Nitin Gadkari's house. Although IAC activist Kiran Bedi argued that the movement should not target Gadkari, given the support that the IAC had received from the BJP,

Arvind Kejriwal disagreed, and insisted that the movement emphasized that the "BJP and Congress were hand-in-glove over the coal allocation [scam]."[40] Nevertheless, the narratives of the opposition and the IAC began to align in the aftermath of the CAG interim report on the coal allocations scandal, and continued to do so until the end of the agitation, when both the BJP and IAC called for the prime minister to resign.[41] Overall, IAC support by major non-Congress parties was driven by the recognition that the movement had struck a chord with citizens on the issue of corruption. In turn, this support could prove beneficial at the ballot, as it did for the BJP in both the state elections and the 2014 general elections.

The IAC received external backing from opposition parties, and mobilizational support arose from a broad range of activist groups. There was, for example, a strong religious nationalist presence throughout the IAC, and RSS chief (*sarsanghchalak*) Mohan Bhagwat claimed that his organization shared a long-standing relationship with IAC leader Hazare.[42] This support also included the saffron-clad spiritual and political guru Baba Ramdev, who mobilized large crowds and opposition support for the IAC, and who rallied citizens behind ostensible anti-corruption measures such as demonetization.[43] Ramdev, who became a staunch supporter of the right-wing BJP government, was a founding member of the IAC, and continued his involvement as the movement grew.[44] At the beginning of the movement, there was some apprehension among IAC leaders regarding Ramdev's public appearances during anti-corruption demonstrations, especially his appearance with the RSS's Sadhvi Ritambhara.[45] However, these doubts soon dissipated in consideration of Ramdev's ability to mobilize large crowds, and IAC activist Kiran Bedi described Ramdev and the IAC as two sides of the same coin: "What you are seeing is the coming together of civil society against corruption…. If corrupt can come together, why can't the voices against corruption [*sic*]."[46] Arvind Kejriwal reinforced this sentiment, and left little room for doubt regarding the relationship between Ramdev and the IAC: "It is not a competition. Ultimately, we have to think about the country. We will have to think about the welfare of the people. [Baba] Ramdev is taking up some issues. Anna Hazare has taken up some issues, no one is outshining anyone."[47]

The RSS is an unmatched mobilizational force in India, especially in national social movements, and did penetrate the IAC. But although Hindu nationalist symbols were on full display at early IAC demonstrations, the activists who joined the IAC demonstrations were more than religious nationalists.[48] Participants notably included the All India Students' Association, the student wing of the left-wing CPI(M), ex-servicemen associations, resident welfare associations (RWAs), Bollywood celebrities, and liberal bloggers and journalists.[49] The movement also received support from prominent chief executive officers (CEOs) and businesses, including the two main chambers of commerce, the Federation of Indian Chambers of Commerce and Industry (FICCI) and the Confederation of Indian Industry (CII), as well as industrialists such as Adi Godrej, Rahul Bajaj, Meher Pudumjee, and G. K. Gopinath. Such a diverse set of supporters is common among nationally mobilized social movements, especially in India, as is the "bandwagon" mentality produced by such mutually referencing groups.

Government Paralysis and Negotiations

The First Wave of the IAC

The first wave of the IAC emphasized the significant divisions within the UPA government—namely between the PMO and the cabinet on one hand, and the Congress Party president–backed NAC on the other. These factions promoted differing approaches to engagement with the IAC, which prevented a unified initial response, and also allowed the movement to place further pressure on the government. This division culminated in the establishment of a joint committee comprised of both IAC activists and cabinet ministers who negotiated the Lokpal bill, much to the chagrin of Congress Party politicians.

Government Divisions, IAC Pressure, and the Joint Committee

By the end of 2010, corruption scandals that implicated ministers and senior officials in the UPA government had begun to emerge, and the government began to formulate policy prescriptions that would combat rampant political malfeasance. The UPA looked to the leader of the coalition, Congress Party president Sonia Gandhi, to bring the government's indiscretions into check. At the 83rd Plenary Session of the AICC that winter, Gandhi announced a four-point plan to battle government corruption.[50] A Group of Ministers (GOM) committee was formed to investigate policy solutions to corruption, wherein the Lokpal bill re-emerged as a key reform.[51] Simultaneously, Gandhi instructed her own de facto cabinet, the NAC, to propose reforms to anti-corruption measures.[52]

By the spring of 2011, sensing little progress toward anti-corruption reform in the scandal-mired government, the IAC began demonstrations designed to quicken the establishment of the Lokpal. The IAC felt that any reforms that were regulated by government officials would be weak, and leaders feared that the ombudsman would not be instituted, given the unsuccessful history of the proposed law.[53] Despite that the NAC and IAC maintained close contact, the movement's leadership lost patience with the slow progress on the bill in the cabinet and the GOM, and organized demonstrations at Jantar Mantar in Delhi on April 4, 2011.[54] The IAC called for a citizen-led ombudsman bill that covered all ministers, including the prime minister and the executive branch, and which would maintain independence similar to that enjoyed by the Supreme Court and the Election Commission.

From the outset, the IAC distrusted the government's commitment to the establishment of the Lokpal, and this distrust worried UPA officials, chiefly the prime minister.[55] Singh met with leaders of the movement to assure them that the GOM who proposed the Lokpal bill would consult the activists. However, the prime minister personally felt antagonized by the activists' refusal to engage on the government's terms, and to instead press forward their demands regarding the substance of the bill and the hard deadline of August 15 for its passage.[56] A close advisor to Singh recounted one of the earliest meetings between the prime minister and the IAC, which corroborates this assertion:

> What we failed to understand was that from day one, Anna [Hazare] and his cronies [in the IAC] were seeking confrontation. I remember four to five weeks before the agitation started, they all came to Racecourse [the official residence of the prime minister]: Anna Hazare, Kiran Bedi, Prashant Bhushan, Arvind Kejriwal, Shanti Bhushan, and a couple of others. The prime minister was there, as was [A. K.] Anthony, and myself. *The prime minister told them, "You want a Lokpal, as do we. I cannot get involved too much, but I will have some of my ministers consult you."* Kiran Bedi asked that Anthony meet with them so that promises can be kept. *The prime minister looked at Anthony, and despite his internal reservations, said "Yes, we'll make that happen."* But after they [the IAC] left, the movement immediately said they do not trust the government's intentions, and thereafter their agitation began. *They [the IAC] went out and distorted the whole story to the press and the PM [prime minister] was very irritated.*[57]

As public support for the IAC grew, so did its capacity to face off with the government. The government, meanwhile, was unable to interface with the movement in a unified, coherent manner. The aforementioned official further noted that the government "wasn't acting united or thinking united" about the IAC, and that "everyone in the government was in disarray, saying different things." Each Friday, he said, a core group of government officials met to discuss the issue, but when the group failed to "settle on what to do," they "eventually stopped having this meeting" and made "haphazard" decisions.[58] The PMO and many in the cabinet shared the prime minister's nascent antagonism toward the IAC, but this antagonism was not shared by the NAC and its supporters, which exacerbated internal government divisions.[59] Various chambers of the government prescribed disparate strategies to engage with the IAC. The NAC was sympathetic toward the IAC and remained critical of the ombudsman bill drafted by the GOM.[60] The NAC sub-group on Transparency and Accountability, led by leading rights-based activist Aruna Roy, fully engaged with the IAC at this time, met with movement activists, and declared that the government's version of the Lokpal bill was weak.[61] As such, NAC members Roy and Harsh Mander, among others, came out explicitly in defense of the IAC civic agitation, and claimed that larger consultations on the Lokpal were necessary, and should include the IAC. Under Congress Party president Sonia Gandhi's leadership, the de facto parallel cabinet had acted as a bridge between government and civil society, which many believed the PMO and the cabinet did not prioritize. A senior member of the NAC stated:

> *One of the things that happened as a result of the NAC was that the government had to consult civil society groups. It started with the NAC, as they couldn't do anything without talking to us.* So when IAC emerged, they [the government] were caught out. *But, the cabinet's only solution to the movement, and many other problems, was to set up committees. I don't even think the Prime Minister knew how many committees he was chairing.* His staff was setting this up. The number of commissions and committees they set up is incredible. *And these committees were there to appease everyone's views.*[62]

While the PMO and the cabinet argued that any drafted legislation should remain within the control of the elected government rather than be outsourced to civic activists, the NAC pushed for the executive branch to further engage with the movement.[63] The demands of the NAC could not be ignored, given the support offered to the group by the Congress president, and given its wide-ranging role in public policy design. At this time, the NAC was deeply involved in drafting legislation pertaining to food security, land acquisition, and communal violence,[64] and the PMO and the cabinet were compelled to be seen engaging with the IAC, although in truth the two groups had fallen into a stalemate.[65] A senior cabinet minister articulated the roots of the divergence between the institutional factions of the government, which served to constrain executive action at this time and beyond:

> The prime minister didn't protest too much against them [the NAC]. They were supported by Mrs. [Sonia] Gandhi, our president, who has enormous influence. NAC saw the PM as the person obstructing their brilliant ideas. She [Sonia Gandhi] was interested in the social sector very intensely, but she didn't take on the mantle of PM. If she had, she would have had to find the money for all the [social] programs herself! But she wasn't the PM, Dr. Singh was. So she remained as the visionary. And he [Manmohan Singh] tried to comply with her aspirations as much as he could, but at the end of day he couldn't say to the finance minister, "Open up the bank vaults and let everything go!" So practical compulsions of running a day-to-day government, his own ideas, and dealing with the visionary [Sonia Gandhi] came into play. So, being a practical politician [such as Manmohan Singh] and a visionary are two different things. If you can get both, great, but it is rare.[66]

He argued that, although the NAC had harmed the government's ability to act, the movement could not be circumvented. Unlike activist groups such as the NAC, who proclaim that "whichever government comes in, we will help to improve the life of the common man," those in political office must "reconcile everyone's demands." If the government "could have acted as we wanted," he argues, "we could have dealt with them [the IAC] far better."[67] One effect of this political impasse was a proliferation of committees and meetings that the government hoped would reconcile these disparate demands and reach an actionable solution. One Congress politician who participated in the negotiations with the IAC leadership recounted:

> The prime minister kept those close to him in the loop on what was happening with the movement. But then as the crisis grew, he asked others "What shall I do?" And so I took the initiative and went on my own to speak with them [the IAC]. I quickly realized it could have been sorted easily. When I went to speak to the activists, they were ready to speak. It was no problem. But I am not the

prime minister—that is who had to come out. *An experienced politician would have known what to do, but not a technocrat [the prime minister] who is isolated around a few people.* Many of us said at that time, "This movement is going to take us down." *All he could do was create a committee to negotiate with them and he put the most aloof, disconnected people on it.* I don't think anyone knew how bad things were in our party. But they [the IAC] saw it was a moment to capitalize [*sic*].[68]

After deliberations between these factions of the UPA, another subcommittee was formed under Minister of Defence A. K. Anthony, a close ally of Sonia Gandhi, to examine the issue of the Lokpal in consultation with the IAC.[69] However, movement activists wanted to go further—they noted the government factions that emerged after the NAC–PMO stand-off, and one of the founding members of the IAC explained what the movement began to observe in these early days of the agitation:

From the start we were non-ideological and instead we became problem oriented. *Also, many leaders in the government were at odds with one another.* And so we didn't appeal to the political elites. *We were able to harass them; we scared them.* We showed them that now you will be chased like dirty dogs. You cannot get away with corruption now. From Ram Lila to Jantar Mantar, everyone shouted "*sarey neta chor hain*" [all politicians are crooks]. *There was a conspiracy of silence from a divided government* and we started shouting: The king is naked![70]

Within a few days, on April 8, 2011, a settlement emerged after discussions between Minister of Human Resource Development Kapil Sibal and IAC activists Swami Agnivesh and Arvind Kejriwal. The negotiations culminated in the establishment of a ten-member joint committee that included an equal share of IAC activists and cabinet ministers, and which would investigate and draft a national Lokpal bill.[71] For some members of the Congress Party, the joint drafting of a government bill with activists was anathema. These party elites believed that, instead of engaging with the IAC, the government should have engaged directly with citizens on the issue of corruption:

Some unique things happened during those early days of the agitation—serious questions around the government and our credibility were raised. And the PM didn't know how to handle it. *It is tough to handle these things when the government has no credibility.* We completely stalled after the hot water of the

2G and CWG reports. Every policy decision we tried to take then was couched under corruption. *So we were stifled. We became disconnected with outside and so had no choice but to set it up [the ten-member joint committee].* That's where you need a proper statesman. We didn't have one in Dr. Singh. *We should have weathered the movement away, but our people had an ostrich attitude.* We thought, "Talk about the bill and it will go away." No. People wanted us to come out and talk to them—"If you are not dishonest then show you are not dishonest," they cried. Politics is about drama and we didn't show up on stage.[72]

   With the establishment of the joint committee, the first wave of IAC agitation ended at 10:30 on the morning of April 9.[73] However, between April 9 and August 15, 2011 (the IAC deadline for the Lokpal bill), the government faced further challenges, including increased support for the movement among opposition parties and the joint committee's failure to reach a broad-based resolution. These developments were exacerbated by the relationships among UPA coalition allies, which began to show signs of fracture that would continue throughout the anti-corruption agitation.

The Second Wave of the IAC

The second wave of the IAC continued to produce fissures in the UPA, primarily among decision-makers at the executive level, but also among coalition and regional party partners. Meanwhile, the continued exposure of government corruption scandals, together with the failure of the joint committee to reach a resolution, led to widespread belief that the government was experiencing "policy paralysis." In an offensive move, some decision-makers decided to arrest IAC leader Anna Hazare. In the wake of this arrest, popular support for the movement grew, as did its support among some decision-makers, chiefly in the NAC. This wave culminated in an in-principle parliamentary agreement on the movement's demands within days of a speech given by Sonia Gandhi's son, Rahul Gandhi, in support of Hazare and the Lokpal bill.

Government Fissures, Anna Hazare's Arrest, and Rahul Gandhi's Entry

After the first agitation, a narrative emerged among cabinet ministers in the joint committee that drafting legislation was the duty of parliament, and should not be dictated by outside activists or opposition parties. Finance minister and Congress veteran Pranab Mukherjee accused activist movements such as the IAC of "undermining the democratic process and constitutional authorities," and of Hazare's successful presentation of the Lokpal bill before parliament and his threatened fast-unto-death should the bill not be passed by August 15, he demanded: "How can someone from outside dictate the terms of Parliament? This is certainly an attempt to weaken the democracy [*sic*]."[74] Fellow cabinet ministers Kapil Sibal, Salman Khurshid, and P. Chidambaram further stated that the powers of the Lokpal as advanced by the IAC undermined the parliamentary process. They objected to the IAC demand to investigate the prime minister under the ombudsman. In this demand, the IAC was joined by the opposition parties, who launched their own anti-corruption demonstrations in solidarity with the IAC in June and July of that year.[75] UPA officials remained resolute, and the subsequent draft of the Lokpal bill rejected the inclusion of the prime minister under the Lokpal's investigatory powers.

As the government found no resolution with the IAC on the Lokpal, and as it faced the political opposition's support of the movement, internal fractures among coalition partners began to surface. The first coalition fracture saw Congress's relationship with ally and the third-largest party in the UPA, the DMK, plunge.[76] In July 2011, the DMK expressed its support of the IAC's demands. At this time, the southern party was displeased with the arrest of its ministers in the 2G scam, namely A. Raja and Kanimozhi, the DMK president's daughter. These relations were further strained with the resignation of DMK politician and cabinet minister Dayanidhi Maran as part of the 2G debacle.[77] Senior government leaders held divergent positions regarding how severely A. Raja should have been treated, and therefore the extent to which the coalition and its relations with the DMK should have been tested at that critical time.[78] One cabinet minister, a close ally of both Sonia Gandhi and Prime Minister Singh, observed:

The first sign of the situation [the 2G scandal] with [A.] Raja and we should have sacked him—and here I believe coalition politics played a role. Had we have sacked Raja there and then, the DMK would have withdrawn support, which the prime minister couldn't afford. Had he disregarded these coalition dynamics and said, "We will remove Raja because I don't want to spoil the integrity of my administration," the CAG reports and the subsequent ire of the people wouldn't have happened. *Instead, the constant capitulation to coalition allies led to over compromise and delayed action. And Raja ultimately left and was arrested, and the partners went on to leave the government to face these problems on their own anyway!*[79]

This remark stands in stark contrast to that of the following Congress Party politician, who was loyal to Gandhi and who served as a negotiator between the Congress and the IAC:

The prime minister was never tested until the IAC. Only time. He should have, when the 2G report began to gain momentum in 2011, come out and explained what happened and why. *Instead, why did he let [A.] Raja hang? Why didn't he talk about the auction? He should have defended it.* Why didn't he come out and say what happened? The people cared about the amount apparently lost in the auctions—but they made prices lower for the people. He should have told them that. The people would have listened.[80]

Competing interests among coalition members made it difficult for the government to formulate a coherent response to the IAC, and to government corruption in general. Many cabinet ministers and PMO officials alleged that the intransigence of regional parties in the coalition was a proximate cause of this difficulty. The divergent interests highlighted above reflect wide discontent as to the role of coalition partners, specifically regional party partners, in policymaking. After all, the number of regional parties in the central government had more than doubled in the preceding twenty years (see Table 5.1).[81] In an interview with a cabinet minister, these coalition dynamics prevented swift action against the movement:

Our government coalitions are much worse [than other democratic countries]. *Here coalitions are different.* We had one with CPM and it broke on the Nuclear Deal. Nobody is opposing the deal now. *The prime minister put his foot down, even against the preference of the party leaders including Mrs. [Sonia] Gandhi.* But he said, "I will risk my government and put my reputation at stake because this needs to be done." We broke all the barriers, and today all the issues are our own—but we get no credit for it. *But coalition issues mainly surface when there is a crisis, such as when the protests [IAC] kicked off. There isn't a camaraderie with coalition partners; it is always antagonistic.* There are some exceptions, but by-and-large *it is a marriage of convenience, especially when there is no ideological convergence. They [coalition partners] are all mainly in their states, looking at the next election. That is their priority.*[82]

Table 5.1 National and Regional Party Representation among Elected Members

Party	2009	2004	1999	1998	1984
National Parties	69.24%	67.03%	67.96%	71.27%	85.4%
Regional Parties	29.1%	32.04%	30.94%	27.62%	12.2%
Independents	1.66%	0.92%	1.1%	1.1%	2.4%
Total	100%	100%	100%	100%	100%

Source: Statistical reports on general elections, 1984–2009, Election Commission, India, https://eci.gov.in/statistical-report/statistical-reports/ (accessed October 1, 2020).

One cabinet minister was far more forthcoming about the role of regional allies as well as that of Congress ministers with primarily state-level interests, and he argued that these parties and politicians sought to extract rents from the center to benefit their specific constituencies, and therefore played an intractable role in governance.[83] However, despite this dominant perspective within the PMO and among Congress cabinet ministers, the government needed to ensure that coalition allies were not sidelined or antagonized, as their withdrawal would cripple the government's ability to function:

> *Politicians in the Congress, but especially our regional partners, turned certain ministries into a pork barrel.* Take, for instance, water resources. After I announced the accelerated irrigation program some time in 2004, I was appalled to see the number of irrigation projects that were half completed or three-quarters complete. I had laid out a plan that a certain pot of money would be made available to complete the last mile of projects. That is, projects that have reached the last phase of implementation, but they lack an extra INR 75–100 crore [USD 13–18 million]. But what happened? Successive water resources ministers lobbied the prime minister and cabinet and everyone dipped into the money to implement small water supply schemes. It became so ridiculous that the Minister of Water Resources, Harish Rawat, brought a paper to the cabinet advanced by AIPP [Asia Indigenous Peoples Pact] that had found that individual borewells should be implemented in his home state of Uttarakhand. It was shot down initially, but then the PM compromised. *He [Prime Minister Manmohan Singh] had to compromise not only with regional partners but also politicians from his own party. He had to maintain support across the government. So when you talk about action [against the IAC], you have to remember that our environment was always one of forced compromise.*[84]

Echoing this reasoning, another cabinet minister argued that the extractive behavior of some coalition partners, who made demands without a commitment to identify solutions to government challenges such as the IAC, was symptomatic of the extensive discretionary powers enjoyed by the government:

> Politicians monopolize everything they can get hold of—such politicians wouldn't do anything of substance, but purely spread patronage. *Regional partners, for example, come in, you put them on a railway advisory committee—they get to have three meetings a year and a pass to travel free on railway. That's what they want.* If we had real privatization, the minister would have no control, except in large-scale lobbying like you have in the US. *So, when things turned bad with the IAC, people in regional parties, and even in our own party, started to say it is because of people like the prime minister instead of looking at their own actions.*[85]

As the public sensed these early fractures in the ruling coalition, the rhetoric of "policy paralysis" became common parlance when referring to the UPA among the IAC, the opposition, citizens, and the media, as well as among government bureaucrats who were severely hampered by the constant threat of corruption scandal.[86] As one cabinet minister remarked to me: "The government was seen as not functioning cohesively—it was seen as mired in corruption. And this stemmed from an inability to communicate with people and [coalition] partners, which made things worse."[87] Coalition fissures, which would continue to intensify, exacerbated the polycentricism at the executive level, and therefore meant that the government could not act unilaterally against the IAC, and risked inviting greater outside pressure upon a precarious governing architecture. These cracks allowed the second IAC agitation to erupt.

Before the second IAC agitation in August 2011, the government was completely engulfed by a crisis of credibility. The CAG actively sought further UPA culprits in the 2G and CWG corruption scandals, which led to the arrest of Congress minister Suresh Kalmadi. Furthermore, the notion of a government in "paralysis" continued to grow as economic conditions worsened through rising inflation, and no agreement emerged between the IAC and the government. Hostility grew from the opposition benches, as not only the BJP but also leftist parties such as the CPM, CPI, Forward Bloc, and Revolutionary Socialist Party continued to demonstrate in support of the IAC. A senior minister in the government stated:

> The CAG reports on 2G spectrum allocation, CWG, as well as on coal blocks, that came out throughout that time [2011–12], *provided ammunition*

for civil society protests. If CAG reports hadn't been in the public domain, the movement wouldn't have picked up the way it did. Here was a constitutional body putting forward startling revelations on the extent of corruption in the central government, and doing it in a way that didn't keep it within the chambers of government but through leaks in the media. *The "loss to the exchequer" part shocked people, and the numbers stuck. The [IAC] movement was given constant fuel by them and the political parties.*[88]

A cabinet minister reiterated this position to me, wherein decision-makers in the PMO and cabinet believed that the CAG reports, which energized the IAC, failed to fully understand the government processes that drove the alleged allocation scandals:

The IAC made use of these two to three reports of the CAG with regards to the coal scam, Commonwealth Games, and 2G scam. We tried to explain to people what our reasoning was, but they [the IAC] and the CAG had no interest in knowing how government works. 2G and coal were picked up by the media and the country became even more hostile toward us. We were hamstrung, and there was a lot of hostility. We didn't have a problem with [A.] Raja in that he wanted the [allocation] process [for 2G] to be the same as that which BJP had followed before us.[89]

The shrinking credibility of the government, which was stressed daily by the IAC, even brought calls for the resignation of the prime minister. An interview with a senior member of the NAC revealed that, even within government, there was strong support for the removal of Prime Minister Singh. This NAC official expressed that Singh "should have been replaced" during the IAC crisis, as "he was not able to govern and everyone was going over him." The official proposed Finance Minister Pranab Mukherjee as Singh's replacement, as Mukherjee "knew how to manage parties and talk to the public. The PM wasn't doing it and Mrs. Gandhi was unwell."[90] A Congress minister in the Lok Sabha argued that the Prime Minister's deliberate style and allegedly failed liberal economic policies were the cause of the social conditions that gave rise to the IAC, and also proposed party loyalist Mukherjee as Singh's replacement:

The highlights of UPA were the investments we made in the social sector, in rural economy, NREGA [National Rural Employment Guarantee Act]. All of it came from Congress—*these are ideas from core Congress leaders. From Sonia Gandhi. Not from Manmohan Singh.* From the enlightened leaders of Congress. This is what people wanted and we stopped doing it because those who are technocrats like the PM and don't understand people didn't provide support. I sat in government for ten to twelve years. I know which system became better and who was responsible for it: *And it was the Prime Minister and those around him who isolated themselves when the chips were down during the [IAC] agitation. It would have been better if he would have left then and there*—there were enough leaders, good leaders, people like Pranab Mukherjee, who would have taken his place and done a better job.[91]

Meanwhile, for decision-makers in the PMO and the cabinet, the sense that members of government, of the opposition, and coalition partners had turned against Singh was quite clear. One cabinet minister saw a clear link between the prime minister's loss of support and the slowdown in the government's effective response to the IAC. He argued that the government's response to the IAC "slowed down pretty exceptionally" due to party disunity, and as the "mood in the country was against the government," the opposition parties, "as well as some of our own partners, had all turned against me and our record." In a crisis, he argued, "people are not interested in the collective."[92] A senior bureaucrat and close advisor of the prime minister, echoed this sentiment, complaining that while many in the government "were trying to keep the fiscal deficit down," the Congress

was only interested in implementing populist acts. *These are things where, on the political side, there were too many voices talking past one another.* The biggest problem is that I don't think that Dr. [Manmohan] Singh ever sat down with Mrs. [Sonia] Gandhi and educated her on what his ideas were and why they would work.[93]

As the IAC's August 15 deadline approached, a standstill emerged between the government and the IAC movement. Manmohan Singh emphasized that the office of the prime minister would not be subject to the jurisdiction of the Lokpal—a key demand of the IAC.[94] Thereafter, the government entered a stage of schizophrenic interaction with the movement. Ministers recognized the public outrage at corruption and the rising support for the IAC, but refused to be held at ransom by the IAC on a constitutional matter. Some politicians began to viciously attack the IAC, provoking those NAC members and Congress ministers who had attempted to engage with the movement to react with aversion. Anticipating further street agitation, the cabinet decided to take an offensive approach by arresting IAC leader Anna Hazare. In his August

15 Independence Day address, Prime Minister Singh stated that the power to make laws rested only with parliament. At this point, some ministers in the cabinet, together with Prime Minister Singh, agreed that Hazare, the symbol of the IAC, should be detained if he proved unwilling to undertake a time-bound fast.[95] On August 16, 2011, when negotiations on the Lokpal failed to achieve a breakthrough, and as Hazare prepared for his fast, the Delhi police arrived at his residence in Mayur Vihar at the orders of the central government and arrested him. A Congress minister who was surprised to hear of Hazare's arrest recounted his response to this news:

> Putting Anna [Hazare] in jail was the wrong move, and that was the catalyst. I went into Parliament and told my colleague who was part of the meeting the day before, "Why did you guys arrest him?" And she said, "No, we met this morning and decided he [Hazare] will not be arrested as such. He will just be picked up by the police and sent back to his home. Then he will come back and we will do the same again. Him being arrested and then sent to prison was not part of the plan." But these things are not happenchance [sic]. *The Delhi police comes under the Center's control. The directive must have come, "Take strong action," and the rest gets lost in translation. But why go there in the first place? By attacking Anna, we were seen as being on the side of the corrupt, and we lost further credibility. Something I later told Mrs. [Sonia] Gandhi and she agreed. We didn't even try to combat the movement cohesively.* If we would have tried, people would have noticed. The PM [Prime Minister] had one crisis on his hands—people wanted a Lokpal bill—and he didn't know how to handle it. It was the only time Mrs. Gandhi wasn't around—she was abroad and unwell—and this is key. Had she been around, they [the PMO and cabinet] wouldn't have taken such missteps against the movement.[96]

Coalition partners claimed that they had not been consulted regarding Hazare's arrest, while in her absence, the de facto parallel cabinet of Sonia Gandhi, the NAC, and Gandhi loyalists in the Congress claimed that they lacked the political support to counter the PMO and cabinet.[97] A senior member of the NAC recounted that, "unlike UPA-1, by UPA-2, we [the NAC] were much bigger *albeit by now many in the government had figured out how to sidestep us.*" Ultimately, he noted, "the buck stopped with Mrs. Gandhi. *She could have been stronger with the prime minister, but her health began to deteriorate during the IAC agitation, and without her there the government didn't support us in our engagement with the IAC.*"[98] A Congress Party politician further contextualized and corroborated the invaluable role of Sonia Gandhi in providing influence and direction to the NAC and her allies, which further underscored the division of power within the government between the party and the executive branch:

> Our [party] system doesn't allow debate. You have to be a mature, developed system to do that. *We don't have a party debating structure, we have a party instruction structure.* Which works quite well most of the time. It works because you find a leader that's popular, who wins elections and then that leader says— none of us is going to do this, or we are doing this. And if anyone questions it, that person will be isolated. *Without her [Sonia Gandhi], most of her followers would not know where to go or what to do.* It's a systemic issue.[99]

Before she left India for medical treatment in the US, Sonia Gandhi had set up a committee to look after the daily affairs of the Congress Party, including the issue of the IAC. This precipitated the emergence of another locus of influence during the crisis: Rahul Gandhi. The committee was composed of veteran leaders A. K. Antony, Ahmed Patel, and Janardhan Dwivedi, along with Sonia Gandhi's son, Rahul. The younger Gandhi held center stage in this committee, and was displeased with the government's decision to arrest Hazare.[100] Prominent members of the NAC such as Jean Drèze, Aruna Roy, and Harsh Mander also criticized the government's actions, and US State Department spokesperson Victoria Nuland told reporters that India must exercise democratic "restraint" in its response to the IAC. The FICCI also spoke against the arrest.[101] Demonstrations erupted across the country, and opposition parties poured into the streets to support the movement. Three days later, Hazare was released to jubilant crowds, and was taken to the Ramlila Maidan in Delhi, where the IAC continued its agitation. In the weeks that followed, the movement grew in national prominence, supported by opposition parties as well as the NAC, and the government was once again gripped by indecision. NAC decision-maker Aruna Roy had commented only a few days earlier: "Momentum should be used to lobby with MPs and political parties."[102]

Congress heir-apparent Rahul Gandhi spoke in favor of the Lokpal bill in a parliamentary debate a week after Hazare's release on August 26, 2011, resisting the narrative presented by the cabinet and the PMO.[103] Gandhi thanked Hazare for his agitation, and called for the Lokpal to be given constitutional status in a cry similar to that of the IAC: "Madam Speaker, why not elevate the debate and fortify the Lokpal by making it a constitutional body accountable to

Parliament like the Election Commission? I feel the time has come to seriously consider this idea."[104] Rahul Gandhi's emergence in the government's face-off with the IAC added another layer of complexity to the decision-making matrix of the UPA.[105] A Congress cabinet minister and member of the joint committee that negotiated with the IAC recounted of Gandhi's intervention on the Lokpal debate:

> When Rahul Gandhi spoke up for the Lokpal in parliament after Hazare's arrest, *he wasn't trying to insult the prime minister; he was acting on impulse and his passions. But he didn't have to worry about consequences for the government.* If someone said, "If you don't do X, the government goes [coalition allies leave] next week," what would he do? He didn't have that concern because his mother [Sonia Gandhi] would take care of things. Meanwhile, the prime minister is left picking up the pieces. *It [the UPA] was a real mish-mash of directives at that point.*[106]

For yet others, especially UPA elites close to Prime Minister Singh, the increasing involvement of Rahul Gandhi in government affairs was testament to the continued demotion of the prime minister's decision-making power, thus reducing his subjective power in government, which added to tensions among government factions. A senior advisor to the prime minister expressed the following viewpoint, which reflected a common theme among those close to, or within, the PMO:

> I would say that in my personal experience in the UPA government that we unleashed a lot of energies that we were not given credit for. Dr. Singh produced, over ten years, an average growth rate of 7.9 percent. *And yet the Congress party never campaigned on the performance of the Dr. Singh government. I think that's where Rahul [Gandhi] comes in. During that time [IAC agitation], those near them [the Gandhi family] said that given the importance of the Gandhi family to Congress, the best thing would be for Rahul to join the government, get a portfolio, and begin to focus with responsibility.* And Dr. Singh was happy with Rahul to join the cabinet. I think he may have even explicitly asked him to do so, but I don't recall. *But he [Rahul Gandhi] didn't, and why would he? Why do you need to join in a junior position after you can come in as a Prime Minister! If you turn up and say "My great, great grandfather was Motilal Nehru," people will vote for you. This is the truth. He is not going to go in and say, "My mother put in place a guy that gave you 9% growth, support him; back him."* It is peculiar that Dr. Singh's record was never sold.[107]

He continued:

> Look, most Congress guys [party politicians] do not believe that they actually have a message to give to the electorate. *The ones in office, at least, have been brought up to believe that the Gandhis alone can get you into office and for that you better solidly be for them, the party, and be sycophantic. And they dutifully are.* They have no loyalty beyond this, even if it concerns the prime minister. *But not all of us subscribe to this; not all of us are Congress "people."*[108]

The impasse between the government and the IAC was temporarily resolved the day after Rahul Gandhi's parliamentary speech on August 27, 2011. Many politicians credited Gandhi with the breakthrough. While some cabinet ministers, such as Kapil Sibal and the Prime Minister's Principal Secretary T. K. A. Nair, together with some coalition partners, refused to back the bill,[109] parliament passed a "Sense of the House" resolution on select IAC demands. The bill was supported by Aruna Roy and Harsh Mander of the NAC, as it established the citizens' charter—that the lower bureaucracy would fall under the jurisdiction of the Lokpal and the Lokayuktas, or state-level anti-corruption ombudsmen.[110] This resolution was unprecedented, as never before had an out-of-session parliament gathered to discuss an issue raised by a non-elected figure.

The Final Wave of the IAC

Beginning in the winter of 2011, and in the twelve months that followed, inter- and intra-governmental fractures intensified as the divergence in policy approaches to the IAC crisis intensified. By November 2012, when the IAC movement came to an end, all key coalition allies had left the government. These allies departed the coalition due to the market liberal steps that the government had taken to ease its credibility crisis. Meanwhile, the CAG's preliminary report on the coal allocations scandal incited vociferous calls from the IAC for the prime minister to be formally investigated, and for his resignation. The IAC narrative shifted its focus from the Lokpal to intense scrutiny of the government. As the movement began to wane by the autumn of 2012, in a surprise move, the leaders of the IAC created a political party that brought the movement to an end.

Policy Prescriptions, Targeting Government, and the End of the Movement

During the winter of 2011, the UPA government faced renewed resistance from coalition allies. In December, the government's Core Committee, which was comprised of Manmohan Singh, Pranab Mukherjee, P. Chidambaram, S. M. Krishna, Ahmed Patel, and, crucially, the returning Sonia Gandhi, met to discuss the IAC. The prime minister also held meetings with coalition allies after their refusal, chiefly the TMC, to back the Lokpal legislation. During the previous six months, the Indian economy had continued to wane, growing at its slowest rate in two years, and the solution proposed by Singh and his close aides was to push for further market liberal reforms that would boost the economic environment, solving the slump that the PMO strongly believed had incited the anti-corruption agitation.[111] However, the TMC and DMK opposed the prime minister's push for further reforms, and the government relented.[112]

To compound this factional dissent among the coalition parties, the NAC heightened its criticism of the PMO and the cabinet during this period. This tension had been on the rise for several months due to the NAC's outward denunciation of the government's land acquisition bill and its criticism of the Lokpal bill, which added to the general feeling that the group's recommendations were consistently diluted by the PMO, the cabinet, and the Planning Commission.[113] Then, just as the government had gained the upper hand with the IAC, the NAC opposed the cabinet's version of the Citizen's Charter and Grievance Redressal bill—a proposed anti-corruption reform that would possibly placate the movement. NAC senior member Aruna Roy argued that the bill was "seriously compromised" and would fail to provide weaker sections of society with any relief.[114] The IAC demanded that grievance redressal be included in the Lokpal, and joined the NAC in its criticism of the government version of the bill. When parliament tabled the Lokpal bill once again in late December, the exclusion of the prime minister from the investigatory powers of the ombudsman, among other factors, further alienated the IAC, which continued its agitation and drew hourly crowds of up to 15,000 demonstrators throughout the day.[115] In sum, the government failed to decisively deal with the IAC and its demands in no small part due to its internal factions.

The failure of the government and the IAC to negotiate proved the crisis point at which the movement became more closely aligned with opposition parties, as they targeted the Congress Party as the source of government corruption. For instance, the IAC welcomed all major non-Congress parties to demonstrate with the IAC in December, turning its message against the coalition-leading party.[116] IAC activists decided that they would campaign against Congress in the upcoming polls by supporting non-corrupt candidates, evoking the earlier decision of the JPM. Anna Hazare led the charge against the Congress, saying: "The Prime Minister holds the high office, but three or four others also think they are PMs. He is not able to make decisions, and no one listens to him."[117] Emboldened by the rising nationwide tide against the Congress, non-Congress parties joined together at the state level. In Manipur, for example, the Manipur People's Party, Nationalist Congress Party, Janata Dal (U), Rashtriya Janata Dal, and CPI(M) formed the Peoples' Democratic Front (PDF). Although the BJP, the chief opposition party at the center, did not become a formal member of this alliance due to ideological differences with the CPI(M), the MPP and BJP reached a seat-sharing agreement that resulted in an alliance within the alliance. This allowed the BJP to continue its strategy of extending support to non-Congress candidates throughout the country.[118] A clear trend emerged of opposition parties collectively seeking to undercut the Congress. Overall, by early 2012, there were continued calls from the IAC and opposition parties for the prime minister to resign and for fresh elections to take place amidst rising inflation and the exposure of corruption at the center.

The IAC mobilized against the Congress-led government in the wake of the interim CAG report on the coal allocations investigation. The coal portfolio was overseen by Prime Minister Manmohan Singh during the period of the alleged scam. When the IAC returned to the protest stage in March 2012, it explicitly targeted the Congress-led UPA government by demonstrating outside the prime minister's home. The movement threatened to undermine government institutions and public law and order by filling up jail cells and filing legal cases against cabinet ministers.[119] IAC activist Arvind Kejriwal named P. Chidambaram, Kapil Sibal, Praful Patel, and Vilasrao Deshmukh among fourteen allegedly malfeasant ministers. Dialogue increasingly adopted an anti-government tone, and Hazare fired at the Congress leadership: "Bring Jan Lokpal or go out of power in the 2014 general elections."[120] Turning on the prime minister, IAC leaders called for a legal investigation into Singh, who they claimed had abused his position to offer significant pecuniary benefits to private entities.[121] Meanwhile, Congress veteran and cabinet minister Ambika Soni claimed that the IAC sought to "demolish" the constitutional office by its aggressive call for a probe into Manmohan Singh.[122]

Internally, decision-makers continued to provide divergent pathways to solve the IAC crisis, which now aimed the full force of public opinion at the government.[123] The PMO, the Planning Commission, and many cabinet members sought to focus on mechanisms to generate short-term growth that they believed would serve as an antidote to the anti-corruption wave and to public discontent. Others, chiefly the Congress Party and the NAC, sought to fuel immediate investment in social services to deter political opposition and to signal the effectiveness of governance to demonstrating citizens who had observed the government as lining its own pockets to the detriment of Indian citizens.[124] As one minister stated, "Both in the country and in the party, there was a clash of ideology between the statists and free-marketeers."[125] Another minister and member of a regional party partner of the UPA coalition surmised: "The goal of the UPA was to help the laborers, the social sector, and create an inclusive society. During the time of the agitation, it seemed they were torn about that goal."[126] A non-Congress parliamentarian who had observed the government at close quarters added:

> *By the end of their time, the government was a fish market. The buck didn't stop anywhere, least of all the prime minister. Everyone would contradict everyone else.* And then our infrastructure slowed; our government expenditure increased; fiscal deficit went out of control; rising inflation. Then they [Congress Party] started harassing businesses by re-introducing the license permit raj with this [retroactive] tax. So investment dried up. Some of them tried to make calls for further FDI [foreign direct investment], but to no avail. We all thought they were falling over themselves.[127]

As the PMO and members of the cabinet sought to revitalize investment conditions to resuscitate the economy, reignite the government's credibility, and combat the IAC, finance minister and Gandhi loyalist Pranab Mukherjee introduced the General Anti-Avoidance Rule (GAAR), an anti-tax avoidance regulation, in his March 2012 budget session. A populist measure, this retroactive tax was controversial due to its provision that allowed the government to seek taxes from past foreign investment deals involving local assets, which could further deter investment.[128] One senior cabinet minister close to the prime minister noted that the premier "didn't have the courage to overrule Mr. Mukherjee" even as he was "told explicitly by some of us not to implement a retrospective tax." Had the prime minister been privy to the budget papers, this minister argued, "he would have said, 'No, sorry, you can't do this.' *Dr. Singh agreed with me it was a mess, but how many factions can you handle?*"[129]

Meanwhile, politicians in the Congress hierarchy, as well as members of the NAC, opposed the solutions proposed by the PMO. One cabinet minister reflected:

> I recall [P.] Chidambaram [finance minister] shaking his head vigorously in parliament when I said that the Bernanke boom had bust. He wanted to say that this was a Manmohan Singh-led growth story and that we should trust him. But they can't justify it. This is why I was on the opposite side! *Other countries manage growth and keep away social conflict by complete control; but these guys [decision-makers advancing market liberal reforms] did not have complete control. The IAC reflected these guys' failed policies. To them [the IAC], Congress was responsible for the change of policies that had disadvantaged them—so why would they support us?* You can't go and tell one constituency that the common man is my priority, all the while you are telling investors that you will make FDI a priority. *People on the street are not oblivious. So the movement leaders said, "The government is only interested in itself," and then of course the scandals give them proof.*[130]

He continued:

> I am a socialist, in the true tradition of the Congress. *And those of us who had this persuasion understood that in an economy like India's, state intervention is absolutely necessary for the country's development and to temper social conflict.* We had to do something actively to arrest the decline in our credibility. Unfortunately, the prime minister and others didn't understand this, and so remained aloof.[131]

Reflecting on the adversarial relationship between the factions of the UPA coalition, a senior advisor to the prime minister noted that leftist parties "occupied a tremendous, though disproportionate, amount of intellectual space in India," and that Singh was "not unaware to the ultimate goal of creating a social safety net for the country's poor." Singh did not merely "compromise with the left," this advisor argues, but "also understood their perspective. But they wanted to hack him down. He would have liked it if the left had acknowledged what he was doing for India, thus intellectually validating him."[132] One cabinet minister underscored this sentiment to me, opining that, in his view, leftists are "thinking people, right or wrong, and they do their homework when they come to Parliament and are forceful speakers. *But they also made it very difficult for us to move fast on anything we wanted to do to solve our problems during the [IAC] movement.*"[133] Another senior minister in the UPA highlighted the ideological underpinnings of these intra-government fissures, but underscored that the outcome and content of government action worked in favor of both ideological camps at different moments of policy formation:

> *The prime minister and his close allies were not leftists. The key players in the executive were people who were disillusioned with this politics, but were in a government that was anchored in a left party that was dealing with even more leftist [coalition] partners.* A celebrated example is the push for FDI in multi-brand retail to get us going. [The Congress] Party was opposed to it. PM and FM [finance minister] wanted it. Same with the nuclear deal—party was deeply unhappy that we are opening ourselves up to Americans. But the PM ultimately got his way. Free trade agreement [FTA] is another example. PM went and signed them with everyone. Mrs. [Sonia] Gandhi wrote a letter to him, I wrote a letter to him saying "don't sign so many FTAs," but he did it anyway. These are high profile examples of negating that specific people in the party prevented the PM from making decisions. He had some important wins too.[134]

Beyond these growing ideological factions among decision-makers, coalition allies also opposed the various pathways that were prescribed to stabilize the government in the face of the IAC crisis. Coalition allies were angered by a government approach that led to steep oil price hikes and a continued push for FDI, while they remained resistant to the centrally mandated Lokayukta (state-level ombudsman) in the Lokpal bill.[135] As one cabinet minister reflected:

> *There is no doubt that too many coalition parties was a problem.* Despite there being less parties in the coalition during UPA-2 than UPA-1, *the problem was that those that were there were in the coalition had key positions and were intractable at times. This came down to ideological incoherence.* Look at the history of recent coalitions. Mr. Vajpayee [prime minister, National Democratic Alliance (NDA), 1998–2004] had twenty-three partners in his coalition; we had twenty in our coalition and eleven had high level positions. With Vajpayee, regional parties attached to him were not happy with the Hindutva agenda, but on all

other factors, chiefly the economy, they had no axe to grind. So the Vajpayee government took a lot of steps on disinvestment, and others followed. So they didn't suffer from the same level of ideological challenge that we had. We couldn't change this because we couldn't afford it on electoral mathematics. There were no other parties available. Nevertheless, some things done in UPA-1, with the blessing of all partners, cannot be typecast in ideological terms—rights-based policies such as RTI, RTE [Right to Education], NREGA. Right-of-center people in the government saw these as necessary ways to shore up political acceptability of the center; and left people saw it as purely ideological ends. And the result was non-confrontational and not problematic. *But in things like FDI and disinvestment, that we had to pursue more aggressively at that time of crisis [the IAC movement], that's when ideological fissures opened up in UPA that wouldn't have been present in other coalitions such as the NDA. No one could agree at that stage.*[136]

At the root of the simmering disagreements among coalition partners was the separation between narrow state-level interests for coalition partner parties and broader national-level interests for decision-makers in the cabinet, PMO, and other government institutions. As one cabinet minister outlined:

Coalitions prevented us from acting in many situations, especially during the time of the protests. Coalition parties are all state-level—they don't look beyond their own state interest. They are not even regional interests, they are state interests—Mamata [Banerjee] is not eastern, she is Bengali; Mulayam [Singh Yadav] is not central, he is just in UP. And being state-level means they are dependent on caste and community. Lalu [Prasad Yadav] is heavily dependent on Yadavs [in Bihar] for example. Kalyan Singh was dependent on Lodhis. These are all backwards [castes]—it is the upsurge of backwards. And they used to have strength in numbers, but not enough, until they entered into coalitions at the center, especially with us [Congress Party]. The real institutional, political, and money power is with the backwards. They started with nothing and now have all this power [reservations]. If you go to UP and go to colleges, businesses, and police stations, they are all filled by Yadavs. District magistrates the same. *They [regional parties] wield enormous power in the states and ensure they get their way at the center. State parties don't want accountability and they block things that the center wants. If you are in coalition, you walk out.*[137]

Inter-coalition factions led partners to threaten to leave the coalition, notably during the IAC agitation, which heightened the already intractable decision-making environment. A senior Congress politician reflected that the

Congress Party "has always had a big tent, and we have wanted to accommodate all the views within it. If we didn't have that, and became narrow, I think we would have been less effective. However, the number of parties we had to bring along with us [in UPA] proved prohibitive."[138] For one official in the PMO, the intransigence of coalition partners such as the TMC and DMK was fundamentally rooted in these groups' conception of the center as a location of rent extraction, as well in the ideological differences between the partners:

> *In the history of Indian executives, there are formal powers and then informal powers. In the coalition era, this is even more so [the case].* Power had to be shared in order to maximize power—this meant that the PM wouldn't be so strong. The PM was very much hamstrung by coalition politics. Very much. *Not because he didn't understand how to deal with coalitions—remember he had been part of the Rao coalition—but because this time [UPA] there was no ideological convergence. If you just come together to share power without sharing ideology, then you have a reduction of your ability to conduct business of the state.* You cannot authoritatively distribute resources, assuage people's discontent [the IAC] or any other issues you face. Politicians joined the UPA thinking that they will get one or two ministries, which will lead to benefits. That's a pre-condition. Then you have to keep their access going or turn a blind eye. *So UPA had two coalitions—between parties, and then between the government and Congress, which further complicated everything when it came to dealing with our problems, as it made misunderstandings worse and everyone worked in silos.*[139]

A cabinet minister further emphasized the institutional inflexibility of coalition politics at the center, arguing,

> *In our country, we have a peculiar problem where regional parties that are at the center are primarily interested in what happens in their states. This in turn directly impacts and influences the center's ability to govern and have sway.* It cannot be helped; and it was very problematic then during the [IAC] movement, right when we wanted to attract investors to rally the economy against people's anger! But it's a reality.[140]

As the difficulties of coalition management increased during the UPA–IAC standoff in the summer of 2012, Rahul Gandhi took a more vocal and visible role in the Congress and the government.[141] Indeed, some senior members of the party called for him to lead them into the 2014 general elections—a call that they made almost two years before the elections.[142] Gandhi's increasing role in the daily affairs of the government added further complexity to an already polycentric governing environment at a time at which the UPA needed fewer disturbances. As one back-channel negotiator with the IAC confirmed:

> They [the Congress Party] called me in and said, "Let's make a meeting between Rahul [Gandhi] and Anna [Hazare], and Rahul will get the benefit electorally." Whether the PM wanted me to meet Anna [Hazare] or not didn't matter, it wasn't up to him. Just like the BJP has RSS people, Congress has its own too. And Sonia [Gandhi] held me in high regard.[143]

A non-Congress minister in the Lok Sabha likewise observed that the UPA struggled to reconcile the relationship between the IAC and Rahul Gandhi, as the latter "came out of left-field and he is not suited to be in politics."[144] This minister characterized Gandhi as "a confused person—*at any point he had the ability and authority to overrule the Prime Minister*," adding that "to play the outsider when you are the crown prince is very odd."[145] Furthermore, a senior official in the PMO argued that the salient role of Rahul Gandhi at the center of the government's actions unintentionally but severely hampered the ability of the government to act:

> *Dr. Singh's ascension post-2009 was jarring for people in the Congress hierarchy, which created dissonance. The plan among the Gandhi loyalists was, "We'll form a government and at some point Rahul will come in." They didn't expect Dr. Singh's mandate to propel him. This threatened many people in the government, and several ministers felt unease. So the way the government slits emerged during the [IAC] crisis is an example of this. Rahul's entry was the final nail in the coffin.* Encouraged by the party and many in the government who were opposed to Dr. Singh led to the narrative, "It's only a matter of time before RG [Rahul Gandhi] takes over as PM." *So instead of backing the PM during this crisis [the IAC movement], people in the government and party began to place Rahul as the de facto leader of the nation!* [146]

Beginning in June 2012, the public and political pressure that emerged from the coal scam increased as the IAC agitation recommenced. Gaining pace from earlier months, the IAC's narrative de-emphasized the Lokpal and instead emphasized the corrupt Congress-led government at the center. Meanwhile, the government focused its energy on an attempt to gain the support of coalition partners and government colleagues regarding its policies to improve the economy.

The government's final push to promote market liberal economic reforms was born from a compromise in which the government agreed to pursue certain populist measures at a later date, closer to the general elections.[147] These steps were fully in line with Finance Minister Chidambaram's recent chant of "perform or perish." However, leftist parties such as the TMC and DMK, as well as outside supporters of the UPA coalition such as the SP, JD(U), and BJD, publicly denounced the proposal to allow 51 percent FDI in multi-brand retail, among other reforms. In turn, eight non-Congress parties decided to call for a nationwide *bandh* (strike) against these measures. By September, TMC had left the UPA, while fellow coalition member DMK decided to join the opposition *bandh*, and even rejected the Congress offer of cabinet posts. Nevertheless, facing the opposition and withdrawal of coalition partners, the prime minister remained resolute, and continued to push to control subsidies and to revive investor confidence. In mid-August of 2012, Singh emphasized that his aim was to increase "the pace of the country's growth, take steps to encourage new investment in the economy, improve management of government finances and work for the livelihood and security of the common man...."[148] Singh believed economic growth to be the clearest path to combat the IAC movement.[149] Outside Singh's circle of allies, however, opposition parties and the IAC continued to accuse the government of corruption.

While the coalition fractured, the IAC focused its anti-corruption agitation squarely upon the Congress. The IAC consistently demonstrated outside the homes of Manmohan Singh and Sonia Gandhi.[150] Police detained demonstrators for vandalism and damaging government property, and, on one occasion, officers mobilized water cannons and twenty rounds of tear gas shells to quell 2,000 protestors who stormed the high-security administration offices of Delhi's South Block.[151] Much like its predecessor, the JPM, the IAC began to encourage demonstrators to defy their universities and employers to rise against corruption at Jantar Mantar.[152] By August 2, 2012, however, as the movement began to lose steam, the IAC announced its plans to enter the electoral arena to provide a political alternative to the allegedly corrupt political class—thereby directly presenting the IAC as an opposition party. The BJP welcomed the move, and one politician stated: "Their [IAC] voice will only supplement our efforts to mobilize voters against the corruption in the Congress.... Even if they do some damage to the BJP's traditional middle-class vote bank, the damage to the Congress vote bank will favour the BJP."[153] The IAC's shifting goals were now explicit: "We will uproot the current corrupt government. Till now we have been only requesting the government to implement the Jan Lokpal bill but now it is a larger movement. We have to throw them out of power," declared movement leader Arvind Kejriwal.[154] Fellow demonstrator Baba Ramdev later added: "This government should be socially and politically boycotted. People will show their anger in the Lok Sabha elections when the Congress does not get votes."[155] The drive to formally politicize the movement began with Kejriwal, not Hazare, who preferred to support anti-corruption candidates. With this shift, the dominant message of the IAC changed, and Kejriwal often roared, in an echo of Jayaprakash Narayan: "The war should be for a revolution and not just for the Lokpal Bill."[156]

On November 24, 2012, Arvind Kejriwal and others from the IAC formed the Aam Aadmi Party (AAP), thus bringing to an effective end the anti-corruption movement. Hazare retreated to his village, Ralegan Siddhi in Maharashtra, to continue his social activism there. In December 2013, the AAP formed a minority government in Delhi with Arvind Kejriwal as its chief minister. The Lokpal bill passed on December 17, 2013, six months before the general elections. Congress loyalists considered this a victory for Rahul Gandhi and for the common man (*aam aadmi*).[157]

This chapter illustrates that the separation of powers between decision-makers in institutions of authority primarily at the executive level, as well as coalition dynamics across parties in the UPA secondarily, precipitated the structural conditions that made an arbitrary response to the IAC less likely. The origin, context, and rise of the IAC; the diverse institutions and committees that crafted a response to the anti-corruption agitation; and the counterbalancing dialectic between government elites played a role in the government's negotiated response to the IAC. However, the structural conditions of this narrative do not sufficiently explain the dynamics of the government's behavior. For this, we must study the role of decision-making elites' ideology—the market liberal, social reformist, and secular nationalist perspectives—that interact with the political and power dynamics above to produce ideological checks and balances that regulate government behavior.

Notes

1. Although some recent works recount how the IAC movement emerged and trace its goals, as yet, no account considers how and why the government

pursued the strategies it chose to pursue during the two years in which the IAC was active.

2. The CMP had unraveled by UPA-2 (2009–14), when the leftist parties departed the coalition.

3. The "outside support" of leftist groups, a common feature of the coalition era in India, meant that these groups did not take on the responsibilities of governance, but exerted substantial influence on central government policies through a negotiated CMP that guided policy and governance. This will be discussed in greater detail in Chapter 6.

4. See Tables A2.1–A2.2 in Appendices.

5. Singh is the only Congress prime minister who has never won a Lok Sabha election, and who instead took the Rajya Sabha route to parliament since 1991. Preempting further acrimony around the issue of her foreign birth (Italian), Sonia Gandhi anointed Manmohan Singh as prime minister, despite herself having the support of over 300 MPs (*Times of India*, May 18, 2004).

6. At least since the time of Indira Gandhi, as we saw in Chapters 3 and 4.

7. See Table A2.2. Sonia Gandhi remains the longest-serving Congress Party president in Indian history. There is no doubt of the leverage the Nehru-Gandhi family enjoys in the Congress. Over time, and especially after the 1975 Emergency, this dynastic penetration of the party has weakened its capacity to develop internal democracy (Zoya Hasan, *Congress after Indira: Policy, Power, Political Change (1984–2009)* [New Delhi: Oxford University Press, 2012], 111–13). Paradoxically, there has risen a simultaneous political demand for this dynasty to play the role of arbiter to promote democratic norms within Congress (see Kanchan Chandra, ed., *Democratic Dynasties: State, Party, and Family in Contemporary Indian Politics* [New Delhi: Cambridge University Press, 2016]; James Manor, "The Congress Party and the Great Transformation," in *Understanding India's New Political Economy*, ed. Sanjay Ruparelia, Sanjay Reddy, John Harris, and Stuart Corbridge, 204–20 [London: Routledge Press, 2011]).

8. See Table A3.2 in Appendices for interviews: Del-2; Del-30; Del-31.

9. Ibid.

10. Arvind Kejriwal, *Swaraj* (New Delhi: Harper Collins India, 2012), 30. Although the IAC had a more structured and programmatic agenda than did the JPM, as both movements grew, they moved away from their initial aims and became more directly focused on the specific cases of corruption within the Congress-led governments they opposed.

11. Saba Naqvi, *Capital Conquest: How the AAP's Incredible Victory Has Redefined Indian Elections* (New Delhi: Hachette India, 2015), 31.

12. Ibid., 30.

13. Del-1; 2015-fgACTV.
14. Kejriwal, *Swaraj*, 13.
15. Vinay Sitapati, "What Anna Hazare and the Indian Middle-Class Say about Each Other," *Economic and Political Weekly* 46, no. 30 (2011); *Times of India*, July 28–29, August 1, 2012.
16. There was also the publication of the Niira Radia tapes in *Outlook* magazine in November 2010, which leaked her telephone conversations (tapped with legal authorization by the tax authorities) with prominent politicians, including the DMK's A. Raja, businessmen, and others which presented to the public a vivid illustration of cronyism. See *Outlook*, "The Radia Tapes," November 18, 2010, https://bit.ly/324ZIyD (accessed October 1, 2020).
17. See Table A3.3 in Appendices for focus groups: 2015-fgBURC, 2015-fgINTL; Table A3.2 for interviews with elite respondents: Del-25b, Del-68.
18. The individual arrested in the 2G case, Telecom Minister A. Raja, was a cabinet minister from coalition partner DMK.
19. In August 2014, the Supreme Court ruled that the coal blocks allocated by the government between 1993 and 2010 were illegal.
20. CAG Vinod Rai is often considered an activist due to the exposure and volume of his reports. He has widely been compared to T. N. Seshan, the former Chief Election Commissioner, whose clampdown on government malfeasance is credited with strengthening the Election Commission during the 1990s.
21. Reports here: http://bit.ly/2poFkWE (accessed October 1, 2020).
22. See Sandip Sukhtankar, "The Impact of Corruption on Consumer Markets: Evidence from the Allocation of 2G Wireless Spectrum in India," *Journal of Law and Economics* 58, no. 1 (February 2015): 75–108. Sukhtankar illustrates, with specific recourse to the 2G allocation, that this type of corruption involves illegitimate transfers from one group to another, but does not lead to lower efficiency. The author concludes that, while this offers no justification for unjustified appropriation, GDP is not affected by such transfers.
23. Table A3.3: 2015-fgPRIJ; Table A3.2: Del-36, Del-77, Del-26.
24. Biswa Swarup Misra, *Revisiting Regional Growth Dynamics in India in the Post Economic Reforms Period* (London: Palgrave Macmillan, 2013).
25. Ruchir Sharma, *The Rise and Fall of Nations: Forces of Change in the Post–Crisis World* (New York: W. W. Norton and Company, 2016), 250.
26. Ibid., 234.
27. Ibid., 251.
28. Table A3.3: 2015-fgACTV; Table A3.2: Del-31.
29. The anti-corruption ombudsman is the most widely established global institution designed to curb political corruption (Mungiu-Pippidi et al., "Contextual Choices for Results in Fighting Corruption"). The ombudsman

is "a public sector office appointed by, but separate from the legislature, [that] is given the authority to supervise the general administrative conduct of the executive branch through investigation and assessment of that conduct" (Linda Reif, *The Ombudsman, Good Governance, and the International Human Rights System* [Leidan: Martinus Nijhoff, 2004], 2).

30. *Times of India*, December 12, 2011, August 3, 2012.
31. Ibid., August 4, 2012.
32. Ashutosh Varshney, "Has Urban India Arrived?" *Indian Express*, August 25, 2011, http://bit.ly/1puByA1 (accessed October 1, 2020).
33. Table A3.2: Del-85, Del-79c. The use of technology as a tool of mobilization is obviously far more salient in the IAC than it was in the JPM. In turn, it could perhaps be argued that a government can more easily control and suppress newspapers and radio outlets, which were used to spread the JPM message, than the modern technologies of the internet and smartphones, which were used to mobilize the IAC. However, the rapid shutdown of specific social media tools such as Twitter by Turkish prime minister Recep Tayyip during the anti-corruption movements of 2013 or the instruction to the messaging app WhatsApp by the Narendra Modi government in 2019 to shut down its services in the contentious state of Kashmir to thwart collective action provides a counter-point to this claim. Overall, although both movements considered in this study took place in different contexts, their politics remain eerily similar. That movements across time share such stark similarities, both facing Congress-led governments, provides a notable opportunity for a social scientist studying India to hold constant the stimulus of the movement and focus on the government response—a lens that can also tell us much about the composition of these movements.
34. Table A3.3: 2015-fgPRIJ, 2015-fgONLJ.
35. *Times of India*, August 22, 2011
36. Ibid., August 18, 24, 2011, December 12, 27–28, 2011. This was not simply a case of *disloyal opposition*. Like the JPM, the IAC did not deny the legitimacy of the democratic system. However, the parties that extended support to both movements displayed *semi-loyal behavior*, as they were willing to encourage and justify the actions of the movements (Juan Linz and Alfred Stepan, eds., *The Breakdown of Democratic Regimes* [Baltimore: Johns Hopkins University Press, 1978], 29–32).
37. *Times of India*, June 6, 2011, August 17, 2011, December 1, 2011.
38. Ibid., June 25, 30, 2011.
39. Ibid., July 4, 2011.
40. Ibid., August 27, 2012. Indeed, Kiran Bedi would later join the BJP in 2015, and was projected as the chief ministerial candidate for the Delhi Assembly

elections against, ironically, Arvind Kejriwal and his party, the Aam Aadmi Party.

41. Ibid., March 15, 18, 24, 2012. Vinod Rai stated that it would be misleading and erroneous to infer concrete conclusions from the *interim* report. However, IAC activists and opposition parties saw the report as definitive, just as JPM activists had observed the *conditional* decision on Indira Gandhi's corrupt campaign practices as tantamount to a refusal of her appeal (ibid., June 1, 2012).

42. Ibid., November 10, 2011; Table A3.3: 2015-fgACTV.

43. *Times of India*, June 4–8, 2012, July 28, 2012, August 12 , 2012. On the role of spiritual gurus in political life in India, see Christophe Jaffrelot, "The Political Guru: The Guru as Eminence Grise," in *The Guru in South Asia: New Interdisciplinary Perspectives*, ed. Jacob Copeman and Aya Ikegame, 80–96 (New York: Routledge Press, 2012). Jayaprakash Narayan's leadership, as we saw in the previous chapters, was built on the same messianic foundations seen consistently since the freedom movement in India.

44. Naqvi, *Capital Conquest*, 12.

45. *Times of India*, June 4, 2011.

46. Ibid., April 24, 2012. She repeated a similar statement in early June (ibid., June 4, 2012), and another in August of that year during a series of tweets on Twitter (ibid., August 10, 2012). Anna Hazare also explicitly stated that the IAC and Ramdev were working together and "fighting for the country" (ibid., April 21, 2012; see also June 3, 2012).

47. Ibid., June 4, 2011.

48. The initial demonstrations at Jantar Mantar in Delhi took place onstage under an image of Bharat Mata, the national personification of India as a Hindu mother goddess, and, notably, an emblem of RSS activities, while banners used by Hindu nationalists such as the Akhil Bharatiya Hindu Mahasabha, Arya Veer, Veerangana Dal, and Arya Samaj were also prominent (ibid., June 5, 2011; Naqvi, *Capital Conquest*, 14). *Deshbhakti* (patriotic) songs resounded during the IAC fasts. However, this iconography shifted when the backdrop was changed to an image of Mahatma Gandhi (ibid., 15).

49. Table A3.3: 2015-fgONLJ, 2015-fgNGOW, 2015-fgACTV; Table A3.2: Del-30; *Times of India*, August 3, 2012; Naqvi, *Capital Conquest*, 14.

50. Table A3.2: Del-26, Del-12, Del-34.

51. The idea of an anti-corruption ombudsman (Lokpal) first emerged in 1963 during a debate regarding the demands for grants by the Ministry of Law and Justice. Accordingly, a Lokpal bill was introduced in parliament for the first time in 1968. However, the bill lapsed with the dissolution of the Lok Sabha. At that time, the first Administrative Reforms Commission recommended

that two independent authorities, one at the central and one at the state level, should be established to enquire into complaints against public functionaries, including MPs. The bill was subsequently introduced (without ratification) in the Lok Sabha eight more times after 1968, in 1971, 1977, 1985 (officially withdrawn), 1989, 1996, 1998, 1999, and 2001 (Rajani Ranjan Jha, *Lokayukta: The Indian Ombudsman* [Varanasi: Rishi Publications, 1990]; John Monteiro, *Corruption: India's Painful Crawl to Lokpal* [Houston: Strategic Book Publishing and Rights Co., 2013 [1966]; Shashi Sahai, *Lokpal Bill: Anna's Movement That Shook the World* [New Delhi: Kalpaz Publications, 2014]).

52. Table A3.2: Del-14, Del-4, Del-36b.
53. Table A3.2: Del-2, Del-31.
54. Ibid.
55. Table A3.2: Del-19, Del-21, Del-34.
56. Ibid.
57. Table A3.2: Del-19.
58. Ibid.
59. Table A3.2: Del-36, Del-34, Del-33, Del-12.
60. Table A3.2: Del-36b, Del-14.
61. Table A3.2: Del-36b
62. Table A3.2: Del-14.
63. Table A3.2: Del-26, Del-34, Del-36b, Del-2.
64. After the first two years of the UPA, and certainly after the withdrawal of the Left Front in 2008, the party–government relationship was often non-cooperative on economic and social policy matters. The Congress Party and the NAC, as led by Sonia Gandhi, pushed harder for large social welfare schemes, while the PMO, large parts of the cabinet, and the senior bureaucracy continued to push for economic growth and, more specifically, economic reforms.
65. Table A3.2: Del-26, Del-10b.
66. Table A3.2: Del-26.
67. Ibid.
68. Table A3.2: Del-7.
69. Table A3.2: Del-26, Del-10b.
70. Table A3.2: Del-1.
71. The ten-member committee would have five cabinet ministers from the government and five representatives chosen by the IAC. Representing the IAC were Anna Hazare, Santosh Hegde, Arvind Kejriwal, Shanti Bhushan, and Prashant Bhushan, and representing the government were Finance Minister Pranab Mukherjee, Home Minister P. Chidambaram, Telecom Minister Kapil Sibal, Law Minister Veerappa Moily, and Water Resources Minister Salman Khurshid.

72. Table A3.2: Del-7.
73. Meetings between activists and ministers on the joint committee began well and occurred frequently, but quickly devolved into antagonism as each side attacked the other side's credibility and ability to draft an anti-corruption bill.
74. *Times of India*, June 13, 2011.
75. Ibid., June 25, 30, 2011.
76. See Table A2.1.
77. Table A3.2: Del-33, Del-34.
78. In February 2012, the Supreme Court laid blame for the 2G embezzlement squarely on A. Raja, effectively absolving the prime minister and other key cabinet ministers questioned in the case. In 2013, the report of a thirty-member Joint Parliamentary Committee (JPC) on allocation and pricing of telecom licenses and 2G spectrum during 1998–2009 was presented to Lok Sabha Speaker Meira Kumar and made public. It categorically rejected the concept of presumptive loss, though it was not a consensus document.
79. Table A3.2: Del-12.
80. Table A3.2: Del-7.
81. Consistent bargaining is common among coalition partners in anticipation of repeated interactions at both national and state levels, given the high frequency of elections (see Chapter 2). Partners, therefore, expect positive spillover effects from cooperation elsewhere (Strøm, Müller, and Smith, "Parliamentary Control of Coalition Governments," 521). During the government's credibility crisis, coalition bargaining came undone for ideological as well as strategic reasons.
82. Table A3.2: Del-26. The US–India Civilian Nuclear Cooperation Agreement gave India a waiver from the rules of the Nuclear Suppliers Group. The act ended a thirty-four-year ban on nuclear trade with India, and marked a significant positive change in US–India relations. Prime Minister Singh led the negotiations, and was convinced that to sustain India's growth, the country needed to improve energy, economic, technological, and political ties with the US. The prime minister's approach linked his economic ideas with the government's foreign policy priorities ("The Manmohan Singh Doctrine"; see Sanjaya Baru, "India and the World: The Economics and Politics of the Manmohan Singh Doctrine in Foreign Policy," ISAS Working Paper No. 53, Institute of South Asian Studies, National University of Singapore, 14 November 2008).
83. After the resignations and arrests of DMK politicians at the center, the subsequent cabinet reshuffle left two seats vacant to accommodate DMK replacements.
84. Table A3.2: Del-33.

85. Table A3.2: Del-26.
86. Table A3.3: 2015-fgPRIJ, 2015-fgBURC; Table A3.2: Del-23.
87. Table A3.2: Del-12.
88. Ibid.
89. Table A3.2: Del-34. This will be considered further in Chapter 6.
90. Table A3.2: Del-14. Sonia Gandhi was in the US at this time receiving medical treatment. The NAC, as well as Gandhi loyalists in the Congress, claimed that they lacked sufficient political clout to fully engage in government decision-making in her absence.
91. Table A3.2: Del-7. The National Rural Employment Guarantee Act 2005 (NREGA) is a social security measure that aims to guarantee the right to work in rural areas by providing at least 100 days of guaranteed wage employment in a financial year to every household whose adult members volunteer to perform unskilled manual labor.
92. Table A3.2: Del-34.
93. Table A3.2: Del-35.
94. Singh was at first willing to allow the PMO under the jurisdiction of the Lokpal, but was convinced to oppose this position by his cabinet and advisors.
95. Table A3.2: Del-7, Del-9, Del-26, Del-33, Del-34.
96. Table A3.2: Del-7.
97. Table A3.2: Del-12, Del-15, Del-36b; *Times of India*, August 21, 2011. In January 2017, 710 NAC files were selectively released by the ruling BJP government. Despite the disclosure's political signaling, the content of these files is instructive of the accounts in this chapter regarding the power delineation between the PMO under Prime Minister Singh and the NAC under Sonia Gandhi as well as the very clear existence of distinct ideational groupings within the UPA advocating for contrasting policy prescriptions. See Yatish Yadav, "Straight from PMO Files, How Sonia Ruled as Proxy PM," *New Indian Express*, January 8, 2017, https://bit.ly/2ib2857 (accessed October 1, 2020).
98. Table A3.2: Del-14. It is important to note here that the Left Front no longer provided outside support to the UPA at this time, yet the NAC continued to engage with the group.
99. Table A3.2: Del-26.
100. Table A3.2: Del-12, Del-7, Del-26, Del-10b. Congress spokesperson Manish Tewari accused the IAC leader of corruption. Former Attorney General Soli Sorabjee's comments reflected the general mood surrounding Hazare's arrest, which "showed a lack of sagacity and sobriety" (*Times of India*, August 17, 2011).

101. Table A3.2: Del-46, Del-49, Del-36b, Del-14. See also *Times of India,* August 5–6, 2011.

102. *Times of India,* August 6, 2011.

103. Nearly two years later, Rahul Gandhi would once again undermine Prime Minister Singh by opposing a government-drafted ordinance on providing convicted legislators with a limited period to participate in legislative procedures, but without voting rights, while they went through the appeals process. Singh, who was away in New York at this time, not for the first time considered resigning from office as government fault lines continued to open (Ahluwalia, *Backstage,* 340–43).

104. Rahul Gandhi, "Speaking on Lokpal in Parliament," Indian National Congress, August 26, 2011, https://bit.ly/39jbJEZ (accessed November 1, 2020).

105. A recent finding in the civil wars literature is that ideological challengers from the same family tree are particularly threatening to one's group cohesion. Though distinct contexts, this finding is instructive in helping us think about how ideological coherence or consolidation can be threatened in dynastic political contexts (Mohammed Hafez, "Fratricidal Rebels: Ideological Extremity and Warring Factionalism in Civil Wars," *Terrorism and Political Violence* 32, no. 3 [2017]: 604–29).

106. Table A3.2: Del-26.

107. Table A3.2: Del-35.

108. Ibid.

109. Table A3.2: Del-10b, Del-19. A full bill did not pass, as some members of the government, coalition partners such as the DMK, and several regional parties who had supported the UPA as non-coalition partners (such as the BJD, BSP, and AIADMK) stood against the inclusion of the full lower bureaucracy and the mandating of Lokayuktas, which, these parties argued, would undermine state autonomy.

110. Table A3.2: Del-36b; Del-14. Due to opposition from both inside and outside the government to a full vote on the bill, this "Sense of the House" resolution was an in-principle agreement with respect to the three issues discussed here, and was forwarded to the Standing Committee in lieu of seeking a firm commitment from parliament.

111. Misra, *Revisiting Regional Growth Dynamics in India in the Post Economic Reforms Period.*

112. Table A3.2: Del-33, Del-34. Key state-level elections that could impact coalition numbers at the center were four months away.

113. Table A3.2: Del-14, Del-36b, Del-75, Del-12.

114. *Times of India,* December 14, 2011.

115. Ibid., December 28, 2011.
116. Ibid., December 11, 2011.
117. Ibid., December 12, 2011.
118. The Congress would win a majority of the Manipur seats in March 2012.
119. Table A3.3: 2015-fgACTV, 2015-fgPRIJ. In March 2012, Congress also lost a key state election in UP, which weakened the coalition's sense of self, and the party began to lose its grip on another crucial state, Andhra Pradesh, due to the separation movement around the new state of Telangana and the rise of and opposition to Telangana from Y. S. Jaganmohan Reddy, whose father had been a key Congress ally until his sudden death in 2009 at the start of UPA-2.
120. *Times of India*, March 26, 2012.
121. Ibid., May 30–31, June 1, 2012; Table A3.2: Del-1.
122. *Times of India*, June 1, 2012.
123. Table A3.2: Del-75, Del-26, Del-34, Del-10b; Table A3.3: 2015-fgBURC.
124. In July, the Prime Minister's Economic Advisory Council (PMEAC), among others, conceded that business sentiment and investor outlook had been negatively impacted during the IAC agitation. The PMEAC's *Economic Outlook 2011/12* stated: "The spate of corruption-related controversies that has emerged over the past one year has consumed energies of government and has led to an unintended slowing down of initiatives to restore investment and economic confidence" (Economic Advisory Council to the Prime Minister, *Economic Outlook 2011/12* [New Delhi: Government of India, July 2011], https://bit.ly/2Ydu2Vr [accessed January 17, 2020]).
125. Table A3.2: Del-8b.
126. Table A3.2: Del-5.
127. Table A3.2: Del-29.
128. Table A3.2: Del-28. Pranab Mukherjee's addition of the retroactive tax to the budget was a contentious issue for the prime minister, and contributed to the "general negative mood" in the nation (*Times of India*, June 28, 2012). Global conditions did not help the situation, as the European recession swelled. Over the next few months, returning Finance Minister P. Chidambaram, Planning Commission chief Montek Singh Ahluwalia, PMEAC chief C. Rangarajan, and newly appointed Chief Economic Advisor to the Ministry of Finance Raghuram Rajan became more active in shaping the economy's revival. These figures backed the prime minister's proposal for an increase in the price of diesel and cooking gas, as well as the proposal to ease FDI rules regarding civil aviation and retail among other areas to manage the credibility crisis.
129. Table A3.2: Del-33.
130. Table A3.2: Del-11.

131. Ibid.
132. Table A3.2: Del-35. In his 1991 budget speech where he announced the liberalization reforms to the Indian parliament (and the world), Singh's support for business and market opening were both important ingredients of state policy. The state was an active protagonist, beyond its role in managing the liberalization of licensing and trade opening. Singh's parliament speech is instructive:

    > Farmers will be compensated for the proposed increase in the price of fertilisers through suitable increases in procurement prices.... We would continue to ensure that 50% of the plan resources are invested in the agricultural and rural sector. The provision for the continuing schemes for assistance to small and marginal farmers for dug wells and shallow tube wells would be doubled.... New schemes are being drawn up to popularise small tractors and matching implements, drip and sprinkler irrigation in areas where water is scarce, and quality seeds in low yield areas. (Manmohan Singh, Minister of Finance, "Speech on Budget, 1991–92," July 24, 1991, https://bit.ly/33Mdynw, p. 10 [accessed October 1, 2020])

133. Table A3.2: Del-34.
134. Table A3.2: Del-12.
135. Table A3.2: Del-33, Del-10b. The NAC, meanwhile, was adamant that the Lokayukta be a key part of the Lokpal bill, a position in contrast to coalition allies.
136. Table A3.2: Del-8b.
137. Table A3.2: Del-26.
138. Table A3.2: Del-8.
139. Table A3.2: Del-19.
140. Table A3.2: Del-34.
141. Table A3.2: Del-10b, Del-12.
142. Congress general secretary Digvijaya Singh, for example, consistently called for Rahul Gandhi to hold a more active role in the party (*Times of India*, July 16, 2012). During this time, Gandhi joined the government's Core Committee, a closed group of select ministers and senior officials that discussed pressing policy matters (Table A3.2: Del-26, Del-34). In contrast to Rahul Gandhi's early promotion as prime ministerial candidate for the Congress in 2014, Narendra Modi, who would sweep that general election, was only revealed as the BJP's candidate in September 2013.
143. Table A3.2: Del-15.
144. In one of my interviews with the late Naresh Chandra, former Cabinet Secretary during the 1991 liberalization reforms (discussed at length in the next chapter) and former Indian Ambassador to the US, Chandra recounted a

story of a private meeting he arranged between former US Secretary of State Henry Kissinger and Rahul Gandhi on the sidelines of an evening reception. Kissinger, Chandra thought, would be able to size up the political guile and potential of Gandhi having dealt with some of South Asia's strongest modern-day leaders. After a thirty-minute discussion, Kissinger found Chandra and simply said about Gandhi: "He doesn't have it."

145. Table A3.2: Del-29.
146. Table A3.2: Del-19.
147. Table A3.2: Del-34, Del-33, Del-35, Del-54, Del-14.
148. *Times of India*, August 15, 2012.
149. Table A3.2: Del-34, Del-33, Del-35.
150. Table A3.2: Del-1, Del-2. Activists also targeted Sonia Gandhi's son-in-law, businessman Robert Vadra, regarding his allegedly corrupt dealings with commercial real estate developer DLF. Reportedly, concessions were made by the Congress government through land acquisition in Haryana to the real estate developer, and which echoed the Sanjay Gandhi Maruti deal facilitated by Haryana chief minister Bansi Lal (see Chapter 3).
151. *Times of India*, July 31, August 27, 2012. Fifteen policemen and six protestors were injured; 974 people were detained, and all were released by the evening (ibid., August 27, 2012).
152. Table A3.2: Del-26; Table A3.3: 2015-fg-BURC, 2015fgPRIJ; *Times of India*, July 30, 2012.
153. *Times of India*, August 14, 2012; relatedly, see also ibid., August 3, 2012.
154. Ibid., August 4, 2012.
155. Ibid., August 13, 2012.
156. Ibid., July 29, 2012.
157. Table A3.2: Del-7, Del-31, Del-3. The Lokpal and Lokayukta bills that were made law in 2013 eventually incorporated the IAC's chief concern—that the prime minister fall under the jurisdiction of the ombudsman. Unlike the unbound version of the Jan Lokpal, however, the inclusion of the prime minister in the government bill came with important caveats: exception on matters pertaining to international relations, external and internal security threats, public order, and atomic energy and space. This version of the bill was shaped by the NAC.

6

United Progressive Alliance
Technocrats and Transformations

I do not minimize the difficulties that lie ahead on the long and arduous journey on which we have embarked. But as Victor Hugo once said, "No power on earth can stop an idea whose time has come." I suggest to this august House that the emergence of India as a major economic power in the world happens to be one such idea. Let the whole world hear it loud and clear. India is now wide awake....

—Manmohan Singh, Budget speech, 1991

With industrialization and economic growth people had often forgotten old reverences. Men honored only money now. The great investment in development over three or four decades had led to this: To "corruption," to the "criminalization of polities." In seeking to rise, India had undone itself.

—V. S. Naipaul, 1990

Social and Economic Development

The ideational lenses through which UPA decision-makers viewed the IAC illustrate a cognitive divergence among market liberal economic reformers, the rights-based social reformers, and Congress Party secular nationalists. On one end of the scale, some state elites felt sympathy for the aims of the IAC, specifically its public action and reformist perspectives; on the other end, some elites who held secular nationalist perspectives were more hostile toward the IAC, viewing the movement as mobilized by right-wing groups and opposition parties. Yet others who held a market liberal perspective wanted as little direct engagement as possible with the movement, as these elites narrated the solution to anti-corruption protests in, and symptomatic of, urgent economic progress and reform. Crucially, these divergent perspectives were rooted in an intellectual lineage exogenous to the IAC crisis. This chapter will consider proxy cases in which UPA decision-makers' ideas drive political behavior in line with the aforementioned narratives, especially in the face of material pressures, and will consider the mechanism of checks and balances that emerged from the heterogeneity of these ideas interacting with the polycentric policymaking environment within the UPA government to shape response to the IAC.

Decision-makers in the UPA government held various perceptions of the IAC. There existed specific ideational clusters among those decision-makers in authoritative positions of power who composed UPA institutions and committees between 2004 and 2014. These diverse cognitive frames are closely linked to the professional and educational backgrounds of elite government leaders.[1] Once in government, the bearers of these divergent ideas entered informal and formal networks of decision-making that reinforced specific constellations of ideas that served to intellectually underpin governmental institutions. Elites with diverse and divergent ideas provided a system of checks and balances in policy debates and government output throughout the UPA.

Three dominant perspectives permeated elite decision-making in the UPA (for shorthand): market liberal, social reformist, and secular nationalist. These distinct cognitive frameworks provided the lenses through which elites assessed the IAC movement. Market liberals could be found primarily in the cabinet, the PMO, and the Planning Commission; social reformists, meanwhile, dominated the de facto parallel cabinet or NAC, but found sympathizers in the cabinet, as well as in the Congress Party; and secular nationalists were often Congress Party politicians, some of whom served in the cabinet, but most of whom served in the Lower and Upper Houses of parliament.[2] Decision-makers allied with these perspectives were prevalent among the advisory and parliamentary committees that shaped executive action toward the IAC and indeed policy design throughout the UPA. As such, the state experienced a Polanyian double transformation in which decision-makers favored markets and managed political and social consequences by developing a welfare state concurrently during the government's tenure.

In sum, government institutions advocated diverse strategic approaches to the IAC, making an arbitrary response less likely than in the case of Indira Gandhi and the JPM, and the constraints posed by these divergent perspectives produced a system of ideological checks and balances throughout the UPA government that made negotiated concessions with the IAC the most likely outcome.

Diverse Decision-Makers and Perspectives

Three dominant perspectives emerged among government elites in the UPA: (*a*) The *market liberal* perspective, which was espoused primarily by those technocrats and senior bureaucrats who pursued limited engagement with the IAC and believed that the movement sought to discredit the government by conflating economic growth mechanisms with corruption. (*b*) The *social reformist* perspective, which was espoused primarily by those technocrats and activists in government who viewed the IAC in sympathetic terms and who sought full engagement with the movement acting, in their view, against widespread corruption that stemmed from the distorted mechanisms of economic liberalization. (*c*) The *secular nationalist* perspective, which was espoused primarily by Congress Party politicians who hostilely viewed the IAC in association with the main opposition party, the BJP, and the religious nationalist RSS.

The Secular Nationalist Perspective

The secular nationalists in the UPA government were mainly Congress Party politicians who spent their careers as elected or nominated MPs.[3] Various generations of politicians served in the UPA coalition at this time, and while many of these politicians belonged to the Congress Party, others did not. These secular nationalists viewed the IAC as a movement brought about by political and social forces from the Hindu nationalist right, namely the RSS and the BJP.[4] The BJP had been the Congress's chief political opponent at the center for two decades, and went on to defeat the incumbent UPA coalition in a landslide victory in the 2014 elections. To Congress politicians, the rise, appeal, symbolism, and focus of the IAC suggested that the movement was an extension of the BJP and RSS, and thus aimed to topple the government. Consequently, these decision-makers viewed the movement antagonistically, and sought no, or even forceful, engagement with the movement.

As one parliamentarian in the Lok Sabha who represented a party in coalition with the Congress at the center noted to me, "There is no question about the fact that they [the IAC] were an extension of the BJP. Their [BJP] hands were all over the movement."[5] A Congress minister in the Rajya Sabha who advised party president Sonia Gandhi at the time of the IAC argued that although corruption scams increased, "more importantly perhaps, the BJP was definitely propping up the IAC leadership. I knew this for a fact from my sources close to the movement."[6] A Congress Party spokesperson further elaborated this point, underscoring the hostility between Congress politicians and the purported RSS–BJP support for the IAC. In years past, he argued, the fight against corruption was a nonpartisan issue, "but then it got captured by the RSS and took on this strong anti-Congress tone." This spokesperson noted that some party members "saw the RSS influence, but also saw the fact that corruption was a serious issue, and we needed to communicate it to the public while there was no backlash. *Others just saw the RSS influence and couldn't look beyond it.*"[7] For one cabinet minister, the rise, strength, and endurance of the IAC clearly signaled that the movement was backed by the BJP, who used the streets to undermine parliamentary politics:

> The problem of protests and opposition on the streets is systemic. What I mean is impatience about being in opposition. *The BJP doesn't want to be in opposition no matter what. So, unless you go to the street, there is no opposition. And that's what they took advantage of with the IAC.* It is actually remarkable how much impact they were able to have.[8]

Thus, in the view of this cabinet minister, to understand the function of the IAC, one must first understand that the movement's leadership was "political from the start." He continued:

> The guys at the top of the IAC were very sharp; they were careerists. There is a distinct difference between social service and social activism. The IAC types are the latter; they are activists, they are lobbyists. They don't run schools; they are people who tell you how schools should be run. *So they have a strong political agenda.*[9]

Because the IAC was widely perceived as an extension of the RSS–BJP nexus, many politicians harbored the view that the Congress leadership could easily manage the movement through aggressive communication campaigns to undercut the opposition. They argued that the UPA leadership, chiefly the prime minister, should have communicated more vociferously to citizens that the slew of scams emerging from the government would be handled case-by-case, and that, more gravely, it was important to shut down the RSS–BJP hold over the anti-government narrative.[10] As one senior Congress minister in the Rajya Sabha who worked closely with both Singh and Sonia Gandhi noted, poor government communication regarding the political nature of the IAC allowed the RSS–BJP to greatly heighten anti-government fervor. The prime minister, he argued, had an "excellent mind" and was a "clean" rather than a corrupt man, but was "an atrocious communicator" who failed to communicate with the public, which heightened the influence of activist groups.[11] A Congress politician in the Lok Sabha who conducted back-channel discussions with the IAC likewise noted: "A technocrat [prime minister] doesn't understand the norms of the people. *The prime minister never understood what was happening outside. So the BJP stepped in.*"[12]

A senior spokesman for the Congress Party commented that, in his view, in part due to the critical role of the RSS in organizing the IAC, the anti-corruption movement had set its eyes firmly on entering government after agitating in the streets and thereby undermining Indian democracy. This, he argued, made it all the more likely that the BJP had backed the IAC to discredit the UPA:

> These people [the IAC] just wanted to gain access to power; they wouldn't be caught dead in a slum or with poor people. *They wanted to disrupt the system and shake up the institutional framework.* But they wanted to do it from the outside; not sacrifice and actually enter politics. The BJP gave them the support they needed for this. What angers me most is that our party's communication on this was terrible!"[13]

This perspective was prominent at the time of the movement, as UPA politicians consistently warned that the IAC ultimately sought political office and to supersede democratic institutions. AICC spokesperson Abhishek Singhvi, for example, commented at the height of the IAC demonstrations in June 2011: "It is most unfortunate that this common crusade against corruption is allowed to be remote-controlled or hijacked by vested political interests."[14] Later, at the June CWC meeting that year, Congress leaders dismissed the IAC as a front for the RSS–BJP, and vowed not to bow before the movement.[15] Home Minister P. Chidambaram furthered this promise when Baba Ramdev joined the anti-corruption demonstrations: "This is not an agitation by a yoga teacher or yoga guru, this is a political agitation which is fully backed by the RSS and its front organizations.... We will allow peaceful protests, but we will not allow anything that will trigger a [communal] conflagration."[16]

Baba Ramdev's role in the IAC, and the suppressive government response to his demonstrations, underscores the influence of the secular nationalist perspective and its strategy to combat the anti-corruption movement. Yoga guru Baba Ramdev, who increasingly mobilized for the IAC, took up the issue of "black money" hidden by corrupt officials in foreign banks.[17] Following the "presumptive loss" logic of the CAG, Ramdev argued that if this "black money" were returned to India from Europe, the economic outlook of the country and the prosperity of the Indian people would improve dramatically. Ramdev's first demonstration ended abruptly when he and his supporters were beaten and chased from Delhi in the night by police.[18] In the days that followed, leaders of the opposition and BJP senior politicians Sushma Swaraj and Arun Jaitley demonstrated in solidarity with the saffron-clad Ramdev at Rajghat in Delhi.[19] Jaitley, who had been an active protestor against Indira Gandhi, even likened Ramdev to JP. Ramdev continued to demonstrate, both alone and with the IAC, and often invited high-ranking BJP leaders and their allies to join him, including Nitin Gadkari and Sharad Yadav.

By the end of 2012, Ramdev's mantra had transformed from removing corruption to removing Congress: *Congress hatao, desh bachao* (remove Congress, save the country). On one occasion, joined by BJP politician Ram Jethmalani on stage, Ramdev took his message further: "We have decided not to vote for Congress. You have to tell people that it is Congress which has pushed you to poverty and is responsible for the price rise. Next time in the elections, we should ensure that not a single Congress leader gets elected to Parliament."[20] The overt associations between Ramdev and the BJP caused some UPA decision-makers to associate the IAC wave with the religious nationalist right. A senior cabinet minister who served as chief negotiator with the IAC at the appointment of the prime minister in 2011 echoed this perspective:

> This IAC was purely populist. They weren't interested in corruption and governance and the common man, as they claimed. They simply said, "whoever does anything wrong, we will put them in jail." That was their version of a Lokpal. It's populist. *And so you can see the elements of RSS fascism to it.*[21]

In sum, many UPA decision-makers, chiefly the secular nationalists of the Congress Party, believed that the religious nationalists of the RSS and BJP supported and mobilized the IAC. These dueling nationalisms led party politicians in the government to view the IAC in hostile terms, which caused

MPs and the cabinet to advocate against engagement with, and even to promote suppression of, the IAC movement.

The Social Reformist Perspective

The social reformist faction of the UPA government was composed principally of technocrats and activists who entered the government as part of the de facto parallel cabinet, the NAC, that Congress Party president Sonia Gandhi formed in 2004. Decision-making elites with reformist perspectives viewed the IAC as a movement that exposed grand corruption that had not been sufficiently resolved by multiple governments. This corruption, they believed, was linked to the mechanisms of liberalization that had concretized the political–business alliance that fueled corruption and that undermined state mechanisms for social service delivery and accountability. Among those with a reformist perspective were activists in the NAC, who came to prominence as anti-corruption campaigners in the rights-based reform movements of the late 1990s and early 2000s. Their entry into government fundamentally changed the vocabulary in which citizens made claims on public institutions and services. This civic action led the state to grow newly open to litigation, and these elites were therefore highly sympathetic toward the IAC.

To the social reformist perspective, the widespread corruption of the UPA was integral to the nature of the growth process pursued by that government.[22] These decision-makers considered the IAC movement to be a direct demonstration against the non-inclusive growth strategy pursued by market liberal technocrats in the UPA government, who proactively provided benefits to large businesses to generate growth. Reformist decision-makers considered this approach to sideline effective redistribution and deepen inequality. As one reformist NAC member claimed, the market liberal growth strategy could not be considered blind "crony capitalism" as such, but the strategy diverted investment in infrastructure development and social service delivery schemes whose inadequacy led people to rise against government corruption:

> *The government had an explicit strategy to make land and other resources available to large capitalists for cheap.* They reasoned that if we [the government] provide big businesses with large capital then they would help bring down prices for energy, telecommunications, and other inputs. And in some cases prices did come down. *But none of these big business houses is going to spend on infrastructure*

on their own, or through the infrastructure fund. They expect the public sector to do all that and only then will they [businesses] spend. *Neither side followed through.* What's the result? Clogged ports, terrible transport infrastructure, inadequate power supply, etc.—all this affects the ease of doing business for the common man. *What did people think? The government is only set up for the big guy and fails to deliver.* Of course they [the IAC] are going to protest.[23]

A senior minister extended this rationale, arguing that the liberalization reforms pursued by market liberals had resulted in inadequate redistribution that created social and economic inequalities, and citizens attributed these inequalities to a corrupt and unaccountable system of governance. "Ultimately," he conceded, "there was a contradiction in what was being tried during liberalization. We let the private sector take control of a variety of state functions that were inefficient, and the contracts were skewed to favor the private sector." During his time in office, he states, he inquired about the terms of agreements for public–private partnerships (PPPs) and "no one knew." He quickly realized that *"if private sector partners do something wrong they won't get caught; and if they get caught they won't get punished.* In this way PPPs are very good for immediate corruption; you make quick money off of a deal. And lots of it."[24]

Decision-makers held sympathy for the IAC not only because it fought corruption, but also because the collective action it provoked pressured the government to institute anti-corruption reform measures. Social reformists fully backed the IAC's momentum and its call for a Lokpal bill.[25] Despite differences among the NAC and IAC regarding the scope of the Lokpal, the former strongly believed that the IAC fought against India's paramount political problem—large-scale corruption—and that the IAC's approach of supra-level activism was a critical driver of social and economic development. These elites firmly believed that the fight against corruption would be strengthened by bottom-up public action that would hold public institutions accountable. Corruption, in their view, was the result of the government's approach to economic and social governance, which privileged crony business elites. In this way, they believed, public action could reduce social inequalities by empowering the state to combat corruption.[26]

Consequently, the NAC and IAC enjoyed a cooperative relationship. For example, the NAC-led Working Group on Transparency, Accountability, and Governance consulted with IAC activists during the early months of the IAC agitation in 2011. This led to the establishment of a subcommittee on the Lokpal bill. Although these consultations eventually collapsed due to the cabinet's intransigence regarding the content of the bill, members of the NAC continued to implicitly support the IAC movement, and vice versa. In a letter to Prime Minister Manmohan Singh on April 6, 2011, Anna Hazare stated: "The NAC sub-committee has discussed Jan Lokpal Bill. But what does that actually mean? *Will the government accept the recommendations of NAC sub-committee? So far, UPA II has shown complete contempt for even the most innocuous issues raised by NAC [sic].*"[27] On another occasion, when the government accused the leader of the IAC of bribery, members of the NAC and other civic activists made a public statement that claimed: "We stand with them [the IAC] in their battle for cleaner and more accountable governance and for the strengthening of democratic institutions. *We will oppose all efforts that seek to sideline the central issue of establishing strong and effective mechanisms to tackle endemic corruption in the country.*"[28] Moreover, when Anna Hazare was branded as "corrupt" by some UPA legislators and was arrested for allegedly violating prohibitory orders, some NAC decision-makers came out strongly against the government and protested with the IAC against Hazare's detention. After all, some of these reformists were activists by profession, and did not consider themselves bound by their ties to the UPA government. Sometimes, one senior member of the NAC noted, he and his colleagues "held a meeting on a policy issue with Mrs. [Sonia] Gandhi and other people from government, and we had protested the day before saying this government was a sham. And she [Sonia Gandhi] never said anything to us."[29]

Social reformist elites took a very different approach than their market liberal colleagues to the reformist mechanisms that had exposed several of the central government corruption scandals in the UPA and that fueled the IAC—namely the CAG reports. Some members of the NAC enjoyed a cooperative relationship with the CAG Vinod Rai, whose reports, which detailed a "presumptive loss" to the exchequer resulting from favors that the government allegedly provided to large businesses, caught the media and citizens' attention in the lead-up to the IAC movement to fuel the corrupt state narrative. As one member of the NAC who explicitly advised the CAG during this time stated:

> When the scams started hitting, they [the PMO and cabinet] lost their way.
> I think the CAG himself was very active, and was a lot like [T. N.] Seshan
> [former chief of the Election Commission widely credited for clamping down

on election fraud and violence in the 1990s]. *Vinod Rai completely transformed the CAG. And he had an advisory group, I was a member, and we gave him ideas on what was going on in government and what to do.* This notion of presumptive loss, that he came up with on coal and 2G, really caught the imagination of the people. *It was really very clever and exposed wrongful policies.*[30]

This admission by a leading member of the NAC is quite striking, especially when one considers the effect that these reports had on the IAC and on many others in the government, chiefly those market liberal elites who felt that the presumptive loss logic of the CAG was misleading.

Overall, the view of social reformist decision-makers that public office was abused by ministers to enrich themselves and to cede state functions to the private sector is precisely the logic that underscored the CAG reports that crystallized the corrupt state narrative and struck fury among citizens. This framework formed the ideational foundation of the NAC and other decision-makers in the UPA who sought to fully negotiate with the IAC movement.

The Market Liberal Perspective

Market liberals in the UPA government became crucial decision-makers during the 1991 balance-of-payments crisis. During this crisis, the technocrats who would later hold authoritative positions in the UPA, including the prime minister, finance minister, deputy head of the Planning Commission, and leaders of the Reserve Bank of India (RBI), played key roles in the lobbying, design, and implementation of liberalization reforms. Although all decision-makers who held a market liberal perspective accepted that the IAC had directed the public's attention to the important issue of corruption, these elites believed that the IAC sought to discredit the government by conflating economic growth mechanisms with corruption.[31] This is evident, in part, in the market liberals' attribution of the foundational logic of the anti-corruption movement to the CAG reports.

Between August 2010 and March 2012, the office of the CAG released reports that underscored the "presumptive loss" to the exchequer that had resulted from alleged favors provided by the UPA government to large corporate houses for contracts pertaining to the 2G telecommunications spectrum and extractive industries such as coal. Market liberal elites believed that, although some ministers in the UPA had pocketed illicit funds from the allocation process, the CAG's logic, which was fully adopted by the IAC, was flawed in its understanding of the government's push for economic growth in a politically intransigent parliament. These elites noted also that those who had allegedly profited from the favors were subsequently sidelined by the government and in some cases arrested. One senior official who was also a close advisor to the prime minister and who headed a core institution under the UPA argued that, while the IAC movement raised the vital issue of corruption, the leaders of the movement "*were feeding off the CAG reports*, which had over-extended their ambit and did not understand why we followed the processes that we did." There were, he concedes, "ministers from the coalition parties that skimmed and the authorities rightly looked at this. *But this presumptive loss logic was bogus.*"[32] Certain state institutions, as discussed in Chapter 2, have historically and spatially developed more autonomy in India, and the CAG is no different. Some decision-makers who held a market liberal perspective claimed that the anti-corruption movement actively manipulated the CAG reports by failing to entertain the possibility that the economic growth strategy pursued by the government was warped by an intransigent political environment in which a more transparent system of contract procurement had been tabled but held up in parliament by the opposition party. One senior cabinet member recounted to me:

> We always started [in 2004 when the UPA came to power] from the belief that competitive bidding was the best process to auction contracts, but it was so difficult to put this through parliament and get the states on board. Meanwhile, people were saying, "The economy has to grow at 9 percent!" And so for that you need coal, you need power, and 2G was part of those inputs. In fact, because there were problems in the TRAI [Telecom Regulatory Authority of India], they themselves said that as far as 2G is concerned we cannot go the competitive bidding route because this would mean too high a price being paid, and that processes of big enrollment of Indian consumers would not run smoothly. But they said maybe with 3G there could be competitive bidding. The irony was that we had been trying to get competitive bidding through parliament for some time [*sic*].[33]

He continued:

> I spoke in parliament on 2G and coal, but to no avail. We said again, "'Let's move toward competitive bidding," but there was opposition from the state governments which produce coal, many of them are BJP-led, so we could

not get this thing moved successfully through the political process of the standing committees. It took us three to four years. By 2012, we were able to put forward the law that made competitive bidding a possible route. But by then the entire government was painted with these scams. *It was not just face saving. It was the only way we wanted to get legislation approved by Parliament.* BJP blocked us at every path in states where they had a majority. Their [the IAC's] feeling was that we had purposefully kept these things [procurement of government contracts] in the dark and taken money and pocketed it all to the detriment of the common man. *No one understood that it took time for us to get competitive bidding legislation through, while we had to keep the country moving forward through [economic] growth. So my own feeling was that the movement manipulated these CAG reports. I had no reason to believe that anything good was a real motivation behind these reports and their [the IAC's] uproar.*[34]

A senior member of the PMO corroborated this perspective, and argued that the IAC movement conflated the allocation process and corruption to discredit the government:

> *All these so-called scams; these losses, notional losses, putative losses—they have no connection to reality or the complexity of government decision-making.* I mean government is not a company that sits there and maximizes profit. *It sits there and ensures sectors grow, for example in telecom, and that prices stay low. This is not corruption. That's what we did.* Look at subsequent low prices in the telecoms sector and the way the sector has boomed. *He [the head of the CAG] grabbed a narrative without understanding the economic logic and the movement ran with it.* They wanted to discredit the entire government without understanding how the economy works.[35]

A senior cabinet minister likewise complained that the CAG reports were a "personal attack," accusing the CAG of "handing over the reports to the media to create a frenzy. *The movement's purpose was not corruption, but to discredit us, and I believe they succeeded.*"[36] Indeed, many market liberal state elites believed that the IAC used the CAG reports to actively manipulate the narrative of the economic growth strategy that the UPA had pursued to blanket the entire government as corrupt. For these decision-makers, the notion of "presumptive" losses made little economic sense, as prices for telecommunications, coal, and other inputs had been artificially lowered for citizens due to the allocation processes that followed. The IAC, however, considered any concessions to a select few businesses as naked crony capitalism and the chief cause of rampant government corruption.[37] This divergence in perspective led to increasing antagonism between market liberal decision-makers and the IAC. As one senior advisor in the PMO who attended early meetings between the prime minister and the IAC argued, the movement "was essentially CAG reports spilling into street politics," which incited "rallies against what they [the public] saw as crony capitalism. The PM wanted to accommodate [them] but he wasn't prepared to sit and negotiate a parliamentary matter [Lokpal bill] with a group of activists who wanted to handicap our progress."[38] Market liberals during this time strongly rejected the IAC's conflation of economic liberalization and corruption. For example, in a speech at the Indian Institute of Management (IIM) in Kolkata on August 22, 2011, Prime Minister Manmohan Singh argued:

> There are some who argue that corruption is the consequence of economic liberalization and reforms. This is of course completely mistaken. *Many of the areas, which have actually seen systemic reforms, have also seen the disappearance of corruption. Industrial licensing, import licensing and rationing of foreign exchange are good examples.* These areas were earlier associated with widespread corruption. The abolition of licensing has eliminated corruption in these areas.[39]

Prime Minister Singh's defense here is instructive. In fact, three days after his speech in Kolkata, during an address on the IAC movement in a parliamentary debate on August 25, 2011, the prime minister asserted that the liberalization process had no direct link to corruption. "Corruption sources," he argued, "are numerous," but the *"liberalisation that we brought about has ended that part of this corruption story."*[40] In this speech, Singh referenced the technical interventions that facilitated the liberalization reforms—such as leaner regulation, increasing competition, and taxation, among others—as mechanisms that have thwarted corruption in India.[41] Some market liberal elites even explicitly tied government corruption to the pre-liberalization era, when an activist ideology permeated the government and the state invasively intervened in the daily lives of citizens:

> *Some of these guys [in the IAC] prefer the pre-1991 days, when there was absolutely no transparency in bureaucratic decisions.* When no questions were asked. *The*

1991 reforms cleansed the system and helped bring corruption down. That's not to say one should ignore corruption today. *But the system should be allowed to correct itself.* For the movement to go out and call everything we did a scam, without understanding why and to what effect, is absurd. *All they ended up doing was creating an atmosphere of suspicion and fear that stifled the bureaucracy.* This probably harmed the country more, yet they couldn't have cared less about this aspect.[42]

By the end of the IAC agitation, as market liberals attempted to revive the economy to combat the conditions that had, in their view, precipitated the IAC movement, the prime minister argued that the anti-corruption demonstrations had created a "mindless atmosphere of negativity and pessimism" that could "do us [India] no good."[43]

Market liberal decision-makers believed that the impetus of anti-corruption collective action lay in deteriorating economic conditions that manifested most prominently in the nation's rising inflation. The precarious fiscal environment nodded at the movement's argument that the government had chosen to line its own pockets rather than ensure political transparency and improve the welfare of its citizens, as the nature of the corruption scandals suggested that rampant discretionary powers were enjoyed by the political class.[44] Although this claim made little economic sense to market liberal decision-makers, it certainly allowed the IAC to capture the support (and imagination) of the nation. The growing appeal of the IAC led to further limiting engagement with the movement by market liberal elites, as they increasingly focused their energy on reviving the economy. Market liberals hoped that a revived economy would placate the urban, middle-class citizens who supported the movement. A senior technocrat who rose to prominence during the liberalization reforms and who is often viewed as the chief driver of India's liberal-capitalist policies over the past two decades reflected: "The problem in the end was inflation. It is the chief economic indicator that rules people's minds in India. There was an impression that inflation goes up because of the rapacious *baniya* [merchants] looting the public."[45] A senior advisor in the PMO corroborated this view, asserting that the IAC "developed mass support because the economy slowed down." The world economy, he noted, "was shutting down, and after experiencing 7–8 percent growth in India for a decade, 4–5 percent just didn't work for people. So the people took to the streets" (see Table 6.1).[46]

Table 6.1 Growth Rate of India's GDP at Constant Prices, 1980–2011

Years	GDP (%)	Per Capita GDP (%)
1980/81–1990/91	5.2	3.0
1990/91–2000/01	5.9	4.0
2000/01–2010/11	7.6	6.0

Source: Government of India, *Economic Survey 2011–12* (New Delhi: Ministry of Finance, 2012).

It is noteworthy that market liberal elites believed that internal government wrangling led to the mismanagement of the economy, which further fueled the IAC movement. The Indian economy experienced rapid growth between 2003 and 2004, and between 2005 and 2008 India was ranked among the fastest-growing economies in the world, providing the government an exponential increase in revenue. In addition, the nation's total tax revenue had increased by 31 percent per year since 2003, so that by 2009 the government budget was four times larger than that of 2003.[47] Thanks to this financial windfall, the UPA was able to unveil the largest-ever post-independence expansion of government expenditure to address social welfare.[48] However, this momentum was interrupted by the global financial crisis of 2008, after which, despite an uptick of economic growth in 2010 (10.3 percent), at the height of the IAC from 2011 to 2012, GDP growth fell to 6.6 percent and then 4.7 percent, respectively.[49] The simultaneous exposure of large-scale corruption scandals and plummeting economic growth heightened fears that India's growth trajectory fell hand-in-glove with crony capitalism. Market liberal elites wanted to push forward mechanisms and reforms to kick-start economic growth, and believed that decision-makers in the NAC and Congress Party hampered these efforts.[50] A cabinet minister who held two consequential portfolios during the UPA's rule highlighted one particular case to me:

> We got overwhelmed by the backlash of wrong fiscal policies. We allowed the fiscal deficit to go bust, and started enormous borrowing. A fiscal deficit that had been brought down to 2.5 percent of GDP by us had been allowed to go up to 5.7 percent by others. I had another portfolio at the time and was asked to return [to the Finance Ministry] in order to manage this out-of-control economy. I said to the PM on my return, "How did you let this happen? You know how this [economy] works better than others." He nodded. *Fact is he couldn't overrule Pranab Mukherjee [the incumbent finance minister]*

who was much senior to him in the party and close to Mrs. Gandhi. And what happened with this kind of indecision? Indiscriminate borrowing following a monetary stimulus. The fiscal deficit crossed limits, inflation crossed limits, oil prices had gone up, and the rupee depreciated. *When people are hurting in their stomach, anything goes. So the fact that the movement erupted like that is not surprising.*[51]

The fiscal deficit and inflation rate spiraled out of control during UPA-2. The fiscal deficit, which had been on a correction path until 2007–08, rose to 6 percent in 2008–09, and then to 6.4 percent in 2009–10. This rise was due in part to a stimulus package implemented in 2008–09, in the aftermath of the global financial crisis, which offered tax cuts, invested widely in infrastructure, and increased expenditure on government consumption to support aggregate demand.[52] According to the aforementioned cabinet official, this spending should have been more tightly controlled by reigning in populist welfare schemes.[53] However, by the emergence of the IAC in 2011, inflation had spiked, and market liberal elites had no choice but to engage the IAC to a certain degree, as the movement had come to represent the nation's discontent with the government's poor economic management. As another senior cabinet minister reflected to me that he "worried a great deal" about this backlash against the government's economic management, but that "there was nothing we could do. *In the end, inflation became an issue for the movement's followers that we were not able to handle effectively.*"[54] Overall, market liberal elites assessed the IAC as a movement that sought to discredit the UPA by conflating the mechanisms through which economic growth was pursued with corruption. This narrative suggested that the movement played a proximate role in the public's growing suspicion of the government's liberalization reforms. An unstable macroeconomic environment, which market liberals believed to be the result of government mismanagement of fiscal policy, exacerbated these conditions. Although market liberal decision-makers conceded that corruption was endemic to India and presented a major challenge to the government, they did not agree with the IAC stance that this corruption was intimately linked to processes of economic growth. Thus, market liberal decision-makers were unsympathetic to the movement, and sought limited engagement with the IAC. Instead, they proposed to design for and focus on mechanisms to improve the economic conditions that they believed to be at the root of the collective action.

Exogeneity

Understanding the three dominant perspectives among decision-making elites helps us to understand why divergent government strategies were advanced during the IAC agitation. The juxtaposition of these divergent ideas, alongside the structural dynamics discussed in Chapter 5, created a system of ideational checks and balances that regulated government behavior. To illustrate the weight of decision-makers' ideas in government within this system of checks and balances, it is crucial to note that these ideas have a source exogenous to the case of the IAC. The ideas held by UPA decision-makers were both external and antecedent to their engagement with the IAC. Without tracing these ideas, we can straightforwardly view the decision-makers' accounts in these chapters as retroactively (and conveniently) blame-shifting for government failures. Exogeneity is illustrated by the entry of proponents of new ideological frameworks to the Indian government, such as the market liberal technocrats who came into government mainly in the 1980s and 1990s, and the reformist technocrats and activists who entered government in the early 2000s. Together, they contributed to the Lakatosian evolution of the Congress Party's ideas, whose "hard core" of secular nationalism—discussed at length in Chapters 3 and 4—remained intact.[55]

Market Liberal Idea Carriers

The 1991 Financial Crisis and Economic Liberalization

The 1991 balance-of-payments crisis provided an entry point for market liberal idea carriers to enter positions of government decision-making power. By Indian standards, the crisis substantially revised the relationship between the state and the market, especially regarding socioeconomic development.[56] Market liberal elites sought to reduce the ambition of the state, which they believed to be riddled with corruption and inefficiency, by re-embedding large areas of social and economic life into new, limited regulatory institutions that functioned in tandem with the private sector.[57] Overall, the aim of these decision-makers was *first* to increase economic growth through export promotion and a more permissible regulatory architecture among other measures, which would *then* permit the reduction of social issues such as wage inequality and government corruption. These actors would later hold such positions as prime minister, finance minister, deputy head of Planning Commission, and home minister, among other cabinet and PMO positions that held primary decision-making power in India during the UPA government (2004–14).

Pre-liberalization India was wracked with state corruption driven by government quotas, licenses, and permits, which led the country's political economy to be widely referenced as the "license–permit–quota raj."[58] This corruption meant that the state sector was enormously powerful, and that citizens were at the mercy of bureaucrats and government officials who used everyday state practices, from routine forms to the supply of telephone lines, to perpetuate corruption.[59] The narrative of the corrupt state, which gathered pace under Indira Gandhi's tenure, especially during the Emergency, bolstered the market liberal critique of the distortions created by external protection and domestic licensing. At the dialectic level, ideas supporting economic liberalization had emerged in the upper echelons of the Indian government since the mid-1970s, notably during the Janata Party government (1977–80), as well as globally among thinkers and economists across development circles.[60] However, the economic ideas that drove such capitalist reforms did not take firm hold until the Indian economy faced the 1991 balance-of-payments crisis.[61] This crisis, in the words of the prime minister's special advisor on the economy, was a "necessary shock that allowed us to bring in the correct changes. There were no socialist answers to what we needed to do."[62]

Narasimha Rao was sworn in as prime minister of India on June 20, 1991, during the national balance-of-payments crisis. Two days later, Rao informed Manmohan Singh that he would be finance minister, and would lead the monumental changes to the architecture of India's political economy. Although Prime Minister Rao provided political capital to these reforms, without which the Congress's minority government would not have been able to respond sufficiently to the crisis it faced, the vision and content of the reforms can be squarely situated in the network of disparate technocrats and politicians whose liberal-capitalist economic ideas came to the fore as the financial crisis burst open negotiation possibilities with a historically uncompromising executive branch. Chief among these technocrats was the future prime minister of the UPA government, Manmohan Singh.[63] As a long-time colleague of Singh recounted to me:

> If any other person would have been finance minister, I don't know what he would have tried. *But given it was Dr. Singh, who had just come back from the South Commission [where he was Secretary General], his instincts were to open up the economy.* I think the solution offered by him and his advisors was the best

one. *Some of us were instinctively in favor, but that was a handful of people.* He had some advisors that disagreed with his ideas, but they left shortly thereafter. In fact, his chief economic advisor at the time, who disagreed with the content of the reforms, left.[64]

The influence and professional networks of such international institutions as the South Commission extends also to the Bretton Woods twins, the IMF and the World Bank, as well as to international graduate programs where market liberal ideas swelled at this time.[65] As Secretary General of the South Commission prior to his call from Rao, Singh interacted closely with IMF managing director Michel Camdessus and with World Bank officials.[66] Also elevated to cabinet meetings and steering committees were bureaucrats who had drafted white papers between 1985 and 1991 on possible pathways to liberalization, including S. Venkataraman (doctorate from Carnegie Mellon), A. N. Verma, Gopi Arora, Jairam Ramesh, Raja Chelliah, and the Rhodes Scholar Montek Singh Ahluwalia, who spent several years among Washington economists while working with the World Bank. In the 1970s, the World Bank emerged as one of the most intellectually vibrant institutions for research in economic development, especially among young economists from emerging markets.[67] In addition, pro-liberalization economists such as Arvind Virmani (doctorate from Harvard), Rakesh Mohan (doctorate from Princeton), C. Rangarajan, Jagdish Bhagwati (doctorate from MIT), and Ashok Desai joined the team as advisors, as did several elected officials, namely P. Chidambaram, a lawyer and Harvard Business School graduate who was known for his no-nonsense approach to the bureaucracy, and who would spearhead the opening of India's trade policies.[68] Beyond their professional exposure, many of these policymakers were educated internationally at the graduate level.[69]

The intellectual lineage of Manmohan Singh's ideas is worth considering in depth here to provide a fuller understanding of the market liberal approach to diagnosing the IAC crisis. From his time as an undergraduate at the University of Cambridge to his doctoral work at the University of Oxford, Manmohan Singh became skeptical and then critical of India's prevailing *dirigiste* political economy.[70] At Oxford, Singh was supervised by I. M. D Little, whose landmark book *Critique of Welfare Economics* employed logical positivism to counter the claim that welfare economics could provide an objective criteria of justice.[71] Singh studied at Nuffield College, which Little had transformed into a distinguished center of development economics. The pro-trade, anti-*dirigiste* scholar Jagdish Bhagwati, a fellow economist whom Singh knew well from his time as an undergraduate at St. Johns College, Cambridge, also taught at Nuffield at this time.[72] Bhagwati and Singh would find this academic atmosphere the ideal space for intellectual exchange, and Bhagwati would significantly influence Singh's dissertation.[73] The pair remained close for many years, and Bhagwati would be appointed as a member of special steering committees and advisory groups formed by Singh during his time as finance minister and as prime minister in the UPA.[74]

Manmohan Singh's well-reviewed book *India's Export Trends and the Prospects for Self-Sustained Growth* built its argument from the fresh work of Ragnar Nurkse and other classical development economists, and examined the role of foreign trade in India's quest for self-reliance.[75] Singh's study was the first scholarly work to hypothesize that India's poor export record was due to indigenous factors rather than a lack of world demand. He wrote this monograph at a time of salient export pessimism (and at the height of import substitution) among the technocracy of Indian policymaking.[76] Singh's work proposed the potential benefits of export orientation for the Indian economy.[77] In line with Nurkse's thinking, Singh hypothesized several important factors among industrialized countries that prevent the rapid growth of exports in developing economies. In these cases, international trade was no longer an effective engine of economic growth and, Singh argued, that developing nations should instead focus on balanced growth. This meant the significant expansion of several sectors such that one industry might serve as the domestic market for another. In the long run, Singh concluded, the country would have no choice but to finance many of its imports with a strong export drive. Import substitution, although viable in the very short-term, would be quickly exhausted. During his early years in government service, Singh and others found that those who spoke against the existing *dirigiste* framework of political economy were sidelined, and so the conclusions in his book can be read as far starker.[78] Singh's tenure as finance minister and prime minister allowed him to implement the market mechanisms in which he deeply believed.

In sum, internationally influenced and trained leaders entered government during the liberalization process who would take up authoritative positions of policymaking power in the UPA. The introduction of these elites to the Indian government was the result of the accumulation of anomalies in India's planned economy that led to the crisis of 1991. The shifts in India's political economy architecture would cement the place of market liberal decision-makers in future Indian governments, most notably the UPA. However, it is important to note that these actors lay waiting in the periphery of the state apparatus for some time before they rose to power in 1991. This is important to emphasize, as is the power of their ideological framework years later during the UPA, because it highlights that they did not conveniently adopt market liberal ideas, but held these beliefs independently.

The Stability of Market Liberal Ideas

Market liberal technocrats had long circled the periphery of the Indian government as academics, experts, bankers, and other professionals, quietly influencing as many political elites as possible to recognize the expediencies of the liberal-capitalist reforms that they believed India required.[79] They had held these perspectives long before their ascent to power, and their influence gathered pace in part because the corrupt state narrative, in the aftermath of the Emergency, had bolstered the liberal-market critique of the distortions created by external protection and domestic licensing.

Serious consultations regarding a reified liberalization reform package began in earnest five to ten years before the 1991 crisis during the Rajiv Gandhi administration (1984–89). The prime minister spoke with finance heavyweight S. Venkitaramanan and Berkeley economist Vijay Kelkar, who would later advise a series of finance ministers in the UPA government, about mechanisms to remove the license regime that slowed Indian growth.[80] Simultaneously, Gandhi turned to younger bureaucrats such as Jairam Ramesh, who would later become Minister of Environment and hold other senior posts in the UPA, and Montek Singh Ahluwalia, an economist who would later become the deputy chairman and de facto head of the Planning Commission under the UPA government. By the time V. P. Singh replaced Rajiv Gandhi, Ahluwalia and other economists such as Rakesh Mohan, who would hold senior positions such as the Chief Economic Adviser to the Finance Minister in the UPA, began to formulate the broad framework of a possible reform program.[81] They were later joined by C. Rangarajan, who would become chairman of Prime Minister Singh's Economic Council. These papers, as well as the final policies therein, touched upon five key areas of reform.[82] The proposed framework encouraged a move from public investment to growth driven by the private sector, and from industry and agriculture to services and technology. The emphasis thus shifted from *purely* state-led distributive justice to the state acting as a protagonist in private initiatives to accelerate high growth—support for market opening was a vital ingredient of state policy.[83] This shift was intended to encourage a distribution of income that favored the middle classes, and would successfully do so in the years to come.[84] In this way, technocrats who would take up influential posts in the UPA government carried forward a clear blueprint for India's turn toward market interventions for social and economic development during and after their time in office.

Moreover, these policymakers' ideas did not waver even under pressure from external material interests. When the Rao administration took power in May 1991, Congress held only a precarious minority government that came to power after some of the shortest-lived coalition governments in India's history to date. Furthermore, Rao had been selected as prime minister after Rajiv Gandhi's sudden demise when his widow, Sonia Gandhi, refused to take the mantle. That the very pro-liberalization ideas that were anathema to the political class gathered steam and became a reality during this period indicates that some government decision-making was not based on external material interests. For example, the decision by Finance Minister Manmohan Singh to devalue the currency by a cumulative depreciation of about 19 percent disturbed Prime Minister Rao (at first), his cabinet, his allies, and some of the business community. Many still had unfavorable memories of the 1966 devaluation experience. Although markets reacted positively to the devaluation, the parliament, and even members of the Congress Party, were furious.[85] In addition, the IMF-driven transfer of gold to the British government the following day agitated the parliament even further, illustrating the perilous political environment under which ideas edged material factors from decision-making processes during the crisis. As a key decision-maker in the liberalization process recounted:

> *Since we [decision-makers who advanced market liberal policies] came into government, opposition to anything we have tried to do has been ideological.* Take, for instance, the 1991 reforms. Within the party, there were these old retainers from Indira Gandhi's time, they were in the cabinet of Mr. Rao and they opposed it. And outside the party the communists were there in significant numbers, and the regional parties had been weaned on a diet of socialism—but they didn't have an ideology. *There was opposition, from within the party and outside.* Remember, we had a weak coalition. But no one had an alternative answer. No one had an answer to what we were doing. The opposition was— "reforms will negatively impact the poor; and that we were departing from the path laid down by Nehru and Mrs. Gandhi." We just went ahead and said:

"This is the way the world is moving, this is the way smaller countries like India, poor countries like us—Korea, Malaysia—that were actually poorer than us are making themselves richer." The record was clear—only open economies flourished, not closed economies. *And so we pushed ahead.*[86]

Prime Minister Rao's Cabinet Secretary at this time, Naresh Chandra, confirmed this perspective to me, noting that while electoral and material pressures were stiff, those supporting market liberals felt the need to advocate their approach to the crisis:

When Rao came to power in 1991, Congress did not have a full majority in the Lower House, and yet during that period, we implemented more reforms than any other administration. My job, as his Secretary, was to work with all our partners. *But we had to push through cabinet level orders and through back-channel meetings. We had no choice but to do it by stealth.* We put out more orders to ensure that while we were fixing the economy in 1991 no Minister acted without any approval from the cabinet. These Ministers used to make money by giving a petrol pump permit or a phone line or allotment for railways, and we put a stop to that by centralizing the ability to get permission to the cabinet. Outside, the opposition and others were creating a fuss about the inflation rate and then the Air India staff leaked the story of the gold transfer to the UK. *Then people like myself supported Montek and others [with market liberal perspectives] and held continuous meetings with the media to say: "Look, we are in peril, and we have to go for structural reforms and follow what the IMF has advised us and get some proper fiscal management going in the country." It was off the record and they played ball. This is what we had to do to fight against the outside pressures. We did it [liberalization] in the night so that politicians didn't derail us.*[87]

Finally, the landmark budget was announced on July 24, 1991, and Manmohan Singh called India's path to liberalization, borrowing from Victor Hugo, "an idea whose time has come."

In sum, the ideological framework through which market liberal decision-makers assessed the IAC had been long held by these elites. This framework was shared through policy networks or processes of political socialization, and carried into specific state institutions during the 1991 liberalization reforms and beyond, which elevated market mechanisms for economic and social development. Market liberal elites maintained positions of authority in the UPA government through institutions such as the PMO, the Planning Commission, and the cabinet. There is clear intellectual coherence between market liberal perspectives and their idea carriers' diagnosis of the IAC. However, the post-1991 retrenchment of the state would create a vacuum in which civic action would swell, and rights-based activists would also rise to government office, most notably with the NAC, and flourish. These elites who held a reformist perspective counterbalanced the market liberals in the UPA government, especially when faced with anti-corruption collective action.

Social Reformist Idea Carriers

2004 "India Shining" and Rights-Based Movements

The BJP-led National Democratic Alliance's (NDA) "India Shining" campaign in the lead-up to the 2004 elections illustrated the political context in which social reformist idea carriers came into positions of authority in the UPA.[88] On August 9, 1997, as Sonia Gandhi sought to redeem her family's dynasty as leader of the Congress Party, she spoke to party members for the first time with ballast:

> What has become of our great organization? Instead of a party that fired the imagination of the masses throughout the length and breadth of India, we have shrunk, losing touch with the toiling millions. It is not a question of victories and defeats in elections. For a democratic party, victories and defeats are part of its continuing political existence. *But what does matter is whether or not we work among the masses, whether or not we are in tune with their struggles, their hopes and their aspirations.*[89]

In the general election of 2004, Sonia Gandhi's Congress stitched together a left-of-center coalition government that appealed to the common man (*aam aadmi*) to defeat the rightist NDA government whose policy performance was deemed to be out of step with the BJP's claims of an India "shining" economically and geopolitically.[90] In attempting to bring down this empty edifice, the Congress put together a coalition that would not only need the support of leftist parties to remain in power, which would give Gandhi's administration a distinct ideological dimension, but would also formalize the government role of social reformist technocrats, senior bureaucrats, and activists through the establishment of the NAC on June 4, 2004.[91]

The NAC was a high-profile advisory body of social reformist elites that was formed and chaired by Congress president Sonia Gandhi. Gandhi's creation of this board directly pitted the PMO and the cabinet against a new institution, a de facto parallel cabinet, in policymaking power.[92] The NAC would actualize social reformist ideas in UPA policy, thereby counterbalancing the prescriptions of market liberal decision-makers. The NAC sought to enforce the coalition's Common Minimum Program (CMP), which explicitly supported an activist state that would bring about social and economic equity through redistribution.[93] Specifically, the CMP urged the provision of immediate economic relief to citizens and rejected the BJP-led NDA's reliance on pseudo trickle-down effects, or promise, of higher growth. Under Gandhi's leadership, the state was considered responsible for providing this economic relief.

Many NAC members rose to positions of authority in the UPA government through their role in the rights-based movements of the 1990s and early 2000s. Such members included Aruna Roy, Nikhil Dey, Harsh Mander, A. K. Shiva Kumar, N.C. Saxena, and Jean Drèze, among others. The most prominent rights-based movement of this era was the National Campaign for People's Right to Information (NCPRI), which spread anti-corruption advocacy efforts that aimed to create greater transparency at the lower levels of bureaucracy. This movement led to the establishment of the Right to Information (RTI) bill as part of the Congress's 2004 campaign pledge, which became law in 2005.[94] Once they became members of the NAC, these activists and technocrats helped design and advocated for the UPA government's state-led and rights-based social security schemes, and acted as the administration's effective liaison with civil society.[95]

The intellectual lineage of the administration's focus on these political mechanisms is illustrated in part by the ideas of Amartya Sen and Jean Drèze, who deeply influenced members of the NAC regarding the primacy of the state, and the ability of public action through social movements to bring about participatory growth and social development. These thinkers argued that liberalization had been severely impaired by India's "backwardness" in basic education, elementary healthcare, gender inequality, and limitations on land reforms.[96] This "backwardness" meant that the expansion of social opportunities through the development of human capital necessarily preceded economic growth. Only the development of human capacities through the supply of basic services that had been impeded by corruption and crony capitalism could create participatory growth.[97] The rapid expansion of human capabilities, they argued, could be encouraged by state intervention and public action.

Drèze and Sen argued that, since the 1991 economic reforms, the constructive role of the state in economic development had not been appropriately harnessed. In their book *An Uncertain Glory: India and Its Contradictions*, which they wrote during the IAC movement, Drèze and Sen argued that public discontent against corruption did not stem from slowed growth, as some government officials argued, but from bias in the growth process, which "made the country look like islands of California in a sea of sub-Saharan Africa."[98] The heightened inequality and corporate state capture that led to the anti-corruption agitation were hand-in-glove for these thinkers.[99] Drèze and Sen acknowledge that, prior to economic reforms, the role of the state was certainly negative in its restrictions on trade and general citizen exchange, but the pair also argue that this role has been left unimagined post-1991 due to apathy toward the public sector among market liberals.[100] For Drèze and Sen, the social incentives to which citizens and politicians alike are beholden "can hardly be reduced to the narrow—though often important—role of markets and profits" prioritized by the private sector. This focus on markets and profits, they argue, has weakened the state's capacity to enhance social development. They view social movements as a positive force for economic and social development by pressuring the government to act.[101] The outcome of social movements, especially anti-corruption collective action, holds crucial bearing on the prospect of a constructive influence of the state on the lives of citizens.[102] The influence of the state should include the provision of basic social security, protections, building infrastructure, and bulwarks against corruption. The vigilance and involvement of the public through collective action can be consequential not only to ensure an adequate expansion of essential welfare services, but also to monitor their functioning. Collective action takes two forms: *collaborative* action, such as public health campaigns, literacy drives, land reforms, and other endeavors; and *adversarial* action that goads the government to respond appropriately to pressure from public demands, such as battling corruption.[103] The roots of the NAC, as well as its sympathy for the IAC, stemmed from this push for civil society to shape and enhance the state.

Though one risks oversimplifying the intellectual lineage (the tussle between market-based capitalism and social provisioning reform has a long history in India and many developing countries) through recourse to the works of Sen and Drèze, the aforementioned ideas were clearly transmitted to NAC members through idea carriers—particularly the two most influential economists in the institution, A. K. Shiva Kumar (whose doctoral supervisor at Harvard was

Sen) and Jean Drèze himself.[104] Congress Party president Sonia Gandhi had a close relationship with many of these figures, particularly NCPRI activists Aruna Roy, Nikhil Dey, and Harsh Mander, who influenced the Congress manifesto in the lead-up to the 2004 elections.[105] Together with academics such as Drèze and Shiva Kumar, and with technocrats such as N. C. Saxsena, M. S. Swaminathan, and Jayaprakash Narayan (no relation to JP), among others, the ideas of these thinkers supported the intellectual and ideological justifications for the NAC.

The Stability of Social Reformist Ideas

The NCPRI precipitated the formation and spread of right-to-information movements across Indian states in the 1990s, and became the model of national anti-corruption reform organizations that would later heavily influence and cultivate the leaders of the NAC and the IAC.[106] Right-to-information activism focused on the highly centralized system of public documents and the asymmetry of power that left citizens uninformed about important government matters from social quotas to wheat yield percentages in their state. This constituted a systemic problem within the government bureaucracy that activists argued allowed widespread corruption. The chief impetus of this deep-seated corruption, activists reasoned, was the degradation of the Indian state. Many movement leaders had observed this first-hand as members of the Indian bureaucracy.

The quality of India's public-sector institutions, chiefly its administrative services, struggled to keep pace with the nation's considerable economic progress post-1991. For most of India's post-independence history, the country's bureaucracy, which India inherited from a colonial framework, was revered as the nation's most efficient and disciplined institution, and was considered both devoted and adequate to secure India's future development. The top echelon of this bureaucracy included India's famed Indian Civil Service, later named the Indian Administrative Service (IAS). Yet over the past three decades, there has emerged the increasingly prevalent view that the corruption and politicization of the administrative bureaucracy have only become deeper entrenched.[107] This is the consequence, scholars argue, of a confluence of factors. Government service is no longer among the most prestigious and lucrative jobs in the country; political leaders enact increasingly arbitrary management of bureaucrats, including ad hoc transfers between posts and even unjustified removal of office by chief ministers; state functions are increasingly outsourced to the private sector; and government service offers a low investment in its human capital.[108] Over time, the decline in government trust and general disinvestment in the bureaucracy by the political center provided the backdrop against which many civil servants moved toward civic activism in the 1990s.

In 1987, bureaucrat-turned-activist Aruna Roy, who would become a key advisor to Sonia Gandhi in the NAC, brought together a team of activists and former bureaucrats to form the Mazdoor Kisan Shakti Sangathan (MKSS).[109] The group began with the modest aim to better understand the issues that led to the denial of state benefits to the poor. The activists proposed an informal information system such that nothing could happen in the district without the knowledge of its citizens. They proposed that a public information exchange be organized in the center of the village square to enable the government bureaucracy to share information and to allow public auditing of official claims. Thus was born the *jansunwaai* (social audit) and the public demonstrations that would form under the NCPRI banner. [110] Many of the elite activists who campaigned for the RTI Act—and later similar Acts for the right to work (NREGA), food (PDS), education (RTE), and others—had careers in the Indian bureaucracy, and knew that many bureaucrats benefitted from the prevailing system, either through rents or the power to maneuver the policies of their political bosses to gain political capital.[111] Nevertheless, while the government and many state agencies resisted the NCPRI movement, other former bureaucrats, intellectuals, journalists, and members of the business community supported the movement.[112]

The logic of this rights-based movement was driven by activists' aim to strengthen the state through civic activism.[113] As one leader of the NCPRI noted to me: "We essentially have a systemic problem of corruption which needed us to empower people before we could create change in government practices. This is why ours was a citizen empowerment movement."[114] Former bureaucrat Arvind Kejriwal, who would become a leader in the IAC movement, became acutely interested in the RTI's potential to expose corruption in Delhi with his own NGO, Parivartan (Change), in the early 2000s.[115] There was, however, a crucial analytical divergence between the approach to anti-corruption reform taken by Kejriwal and the IAC and that taken by NCPRI activists. The latter understood political corruption to originate in complex organizational structures that needed to be targeted and reformed piecemeal, while the IAC focused on the moral degradation of politicians and the failing credibility of government officials. In this sense, it sought to expose, or undermine, mechanisms of procedural democratic governance.[116] However, the two movements certainly shared a common genealogy. One technocrat who was a core member of the NCPRI and held a senior bureaucratic position in the UPA government stated that he "admired" the IAC, as they successfully "created an aura of not tolerating corruption—they really stood up to the government, just like we [the NCPRI] had before them. They convinced everyone that their movement would remove corruption." Observing the evolution of the IAC movement, he praised, "was like observing the pumpkin turn into a chariot. They brought the government face-to-face with corruption and the sentiment of the people. This is how anti-corruption efforts must work."[117] There is clear intellectual symbiosis here with the work of Sen and Drèze as well as with the activist ideology of the rights-based movements that led to the formation of the NAC in the UPA government.

In the view of many activists involved in these rights-based movements, although the Congress Party government had long been associated with grand corruption, the issue became entrenched with putative crony capitalism in the UPA government.[118] One academic who supported and then joined these movements in the early 2000s noted:

> First it was Congress, the mother of corruption, and people thought there is a DNA problem with Congress. They cannot be cured. Then the left witnessed corruption in Bengal. They all became millionaires. In Kerala, also the same. So, regional parties started becoming embroiled too: Jayalalithaa in Tamil Nadu, Lalu Yadav with the Fodder Scam, Mulayam Singh with disproportional assets, so gradually the entire political class became corrupt. It was no longer the Congress. *Over the last seven to eight years, everything has had a price.* The politicians created an illusion of equality. Mandal [Commission] created a safety wall, and led to the emergence of the lower middle class. But by the end of the BJP [2004] the charm of liberalization had begun to fade. *And what we see today is disenchantment with liberalization—it has caused the rich to get richer and the political class to fill their pockets. Liberalization doesn't talk the language of development; it talks only about growth.*[119]

According to these activists, the non-inclusive liberalization pursued by Indian governments since 1991 brought larger opportunities for kickbacks, which become more extractive in an increasingly globalized political economy.

The reformist cited here asserted that, after several years of "enchantment with liberalization and globalization," the public began to recognize the "crony capitalism" and "global levels of corruption" at its core. Liberalization, he argued, "gave an open field for grazing and looting, and the top was indifferent. It became a virus across all parties, and popular concern went out."[120]

Throughout their time in the UPA, NAC members and their allies, such as leftist parties, explicitly argued that existing liberalization reforms were not inclusive, and had entrenched a political–business nexus that not only prevented effective state-led redistribution, but also perpetuated government corruption.[121] The chief concern of these social reformists was the dilution of public sector power, especially in the area of service delivery, and the creation of transparency and accountability to combat government corruption. As economic conditions worsened leading up to the IAC, and the corrupt aspects of the business–state nexus became more salient (and publicly exposed) to these elites, the more the quality of public services failed to improve. One advisor to the NAC noted that the "roll back" of effective state mechanisms, which the government should have primed, were sidelined to promote private mechanisms in developmental activities through PPPs, which promoted inefficiencies rooted in corruption.[122] A senior social reformist who attended NAC meetings furthered this claim, noting the market liberal push for PPPs and the tempering of public sector functions on one hand, and the resultant corruption scams throughout the UPA administration on the other:

> *PPPs created avenues for corruption, not efficiency.* Businesses that were selected as partners created both a certain degree of uncertainty accompanied by a certain fight for turf. The uncertainty was in the ownership. It wasn't as clear-cut as the government saying, "You [private contractor] build the road, you maintain it for 10 years, and you take tolls. And we just own it and it comes back to us after a certain period of time." No, this is not how it was. What happened is that PPPs allowed for different ministries to extract rents as they did in the past. That is, ministers saw something up for grabs. Why not take the booty? Because in the previous system, booty had been collected. Contractor would give the minister a payoff. So with PPPs corruption became explicit, and the amounts went up. And another thing happened. When the private contractors realized they couldn't build infrastructure on the low amounts they promised government, especially after the downturn [during the 2008 financial crisis], they did what they do best, which is go up to the government and say, "We can't possibly build this the way we said we would, so change the contract.

Give us a higher amount to finance this. Or allow us to increase the tolls." *Sometimes there were extra funds, more often there were not. So to make matters worse, the infrastructure remains half-built! And this is where the corruption scams came along: Coal, 2G, and others, all of them were related to this story, though with different successes. Spending of government went up and, ironically, leakages not in service delivery, as they [market liberal elites] argued, but in PPPs go up!* So citizens demonstrating [with the IAC] rightly think they are not getting what they were promised while everyone appears to be lining their pockets.[123]

Supporting these assertions, one cabinet minister speculated that "the PM thought that 'if I take money away from corrupt bureaucracies through PPPs, ultimately then there will be less corruption'."

It is noteworthy to compare the above-mentioned perspective that PPPs perpetuate corruption with that of the market liberal perspective, which viewed the policy tool as a panacea for combating corruption. Social provisioning, for market liberal elites, should be provided by the state as soon as it can be afforded—for Singh and others, this would emerge from effectively managing the consumption–investment balance, or what has popularly been referred to as "liberalization with a human face." As discussed earlier, the 1991 architects and their successors are rather removed from a belief in fully self-regulating markets for all. However, the failure to build effective capitalist institutions, together with a distrust of the bureaucratic architecture, made this approach more conjectural than impactful, especially during the IAC crisis. As one senior cabinet minister argued, "corruption takes place because of poor public administration in India," and that this formed the "major motivation for why we pushed the PPPs. The public sector doesn't have the management skills." The public sector, he reasoned, "needs management skills, and private sector needs resources to get the job done. But it proved far more complicated and has been a mixed experience."[124] Another market liberal elite who led an apex economic and social policy institution in the UPA noted:

Our overall aim was to make the state more productive, for which investment in the public sector simply wouldn't cut it, and so we turned to the private entities. For example, with the NREGA program we were able in the Planning Commission to insist on guidelines that gave both the states more flexibility and direct resources for productive use—namely water, which is the key resource constraint. *Huge resistance! People like Jean Drèze [member of the NAC] and his ilk would say we are trying to hijack what is meant to be an employment guarantee program into a productivity enhancement program.* Their view was, "You want to do productivity enhancement, do it, we are not against it, but don't do it with NREGA." The problem with these guys [social reformist elites] is that they don't think about budget constraints. So if someone comes and asks for a day's work, he should get it—never mind that there is no project worked out (and that there is a project 8 kilometers away that actually needs him!). No, he should be given the job there by us [the government]. *None of these people [in the NAC] had been given a reorientation that the economy had changed.*[125]

One Congress politician, noting the effect of ideological division on the rise of the IAC, claimed that many of his generation had grown accustomed to an "ever-present government" in which "development and growth were not everything." After the liberalization reforms of 1991, he argued, "cities were no longer recognizable," and the "India Shining" campaign left few examples of successful development schema. "We lost the people to these movements [such as the IAC]," he argued, "because we didn't sufficiently continue these things. The technocrats like the Prime Minister just didn't get this."[126] Although PPPs started off well (2008–12), in the second UPA administration, beginning with the roads sector, problems began to emerge from delays in getting environment and forest clearances to demand plummeting and investors struggling to raise finance after the 2008 crisis. Consequently, private licensees sought modifications to agreements and contracts, while those that were able to turn to and secure large loans from public sector banks "raised suspicion that unscrupulous investors may be siphoning off the surplus from the project and then recycling them back to their own equity contribution."[127]

***

The debate surrounding PPPs represents a proxy issue that illustrates the ideological divisions in the government during the UPA's tenure in which decision-makers favored markets and managed political and social consequences by developing a welfare state concurrently. It is an example of the lack of state exit in key areas of the economy that then protects poorly performing capital interests as well as obdurate unions. As such, India under the UPA experienced a simultaneous Polanyian double transformation. Indeed, dissonant ideas can be held over the same domain, at the same time, with observable implications on policy. Another pertinent example being NREGA, viewed on the one hand as the hallmark of a modern welfare state, while on the other as the democratization of collusive corruption through the creation of new rent networks, or as vacuous populism—or all three. In the same vein, this divergence was in full swing during the IAC movement. As one NAC member who worked closely with both Manmohan Singh and Sonia Gandhi reflected: "There was always a debate between pro-growth and pro-redistribution. The PM and FM were not in favor of prioritizing the welfare state but the NAC and Mrs. [Sonia] Gandhi certainly were."[128]

Social reformists argued that the UPA should have further strengthened state mechanisms of social service delivery and public welfare. That the government did not—or had to be strongly pushed to do so—is directly linked, according to this narrative, to the economic liberalization pursued by market liberals in positions of government authority. One social reformist in the UPA argued that the government did not sufficiently support social welfare policies, and noted that "corruption doesn't become an issue for people in India so long as governments are delivering and own their delivery systems." Had Manmohan Singh "understood what we were trying to do from the start," he argued, "corruption would not have troubled the Indian citizen in the way it did."[129] Together, the force of their ideas and their political elevation by Sonia Gandhi meant that decision-makers in the NAC could not be disregarded or overlooked by the cabinet and the PMO.[130] The NAC persisted throughout the tenure of the UPA government (2004–14), even when the support of leftist parties, for whom the CMP was established, was no longer needed in UPA-2. These decision-makers became increasingly agitated by rising inequality and by slowed state intervention in social and economic policy issues such as corruption.

Ideational Checks and Balances

The mechanism of an ideational checks and balances in the UPA government emerged from the heterogeneity of decision-makers' ideas interacting with the polycentric policymaking environment within the UPA government to shape response to the IAC. In the UPA coalition, policymaking was bifurcated among elites associated with two centers of power: Congress Party president Sonia Gandhi and Prime Minister Manmohan Singh. These two policymaking loci had an institutional basis that allowed the establishment of the NAC under the chairpersonship of coalition leader Gandhi alongside the traditional cabinet and executive offices of Prime Minister Singh. The separation of powers among diverse parties and institutions across and within the UPA government created institutional constraints that made an arbitrary government response to the IAC unlikely. This polyvocality manifested at both the dialectic and institutional levels in public statements, actions, and protests as well as in negotiating committees and subcommittees that involved decision-makers in the NAC, PMO, cabinet, parliament, Planning Commission, and the Congress Party.

Despite its knowledge of several corruption scandals, the sheer magnitude of the IAC movement and the credibility crisis it generated caught the UPA by surprise. In this environment of uncertainty, the crisis had to be diagnosed before it could be resolved. The government mobilized diverse strategies that included limited engagement with the movement, full negotiation with the movement, and a few short-lived cases of clampdown on protestors. The coalition era in India, specifically, has opened opportunity structures allowing divergent idea carriers to enter government and to hold authoritative positions of power, and these decision-making elites entered formal and informal networks within, and sometimes across, institutions. These elites often weaponize their ideology to delegitimize alternative ideologies, and this ideational power struggle over credible visions necessarily shapes institutional contestation.

Diverse decision-making elites accepted, appropriated, deployed, and contested various combinations of ideas regarding social and economic development (market liberal/social reformist) and concepts of the nation (secular nationalist)—both to explain and to resolve the crisis of the nationwide IAC movement. Technocrats, bureaucrats, and activists brought into the NAC by Sonia Gandhi immediately after the left-of-center coalition was struck by the Congress in 2004 held social reformist ideas. Other technocrats, bureaucrats, and officials led by Prime Minister Manmohan Singh, who came to prominence in government during the 1991 dismantling of India's *dirigiste* political economy, held market liberal ideas. Party politicians in the Congress mostly held secular nationalist frameworks that were consistent with the party's historical discourse (and ideological "hard core") against religious nationalists as seen in Chapters 3 and 4. Each set of decision-making elites were empowered to prevent actions by other elites throughout policy design and implementation during the UPA. In this way, the state experienced a Polanyian double transformation in which decision-makers favored markets and managed political and social consequences by developing a welfare state concurrently. These decision-making elites approached the roots and rise of the IAC from diverse frameworks, and therefore proposed contrasting strategies to respond to the movement.

Thus, the fragmented, segmented, and stratified structure of the UPA coalition government prevented arbitrary action against the IAC, and instead pushed dialogue and negotiation with the movement. The polycentric structural environment interacting with elites' divergent ideological frameworks produced a system of ideational checks and balances on government behavior in the face of anti-corruption collective action.

Notes

1. See Tables A4.2 and A4.3 in Appendices.
2. These classifications of narratives should not imply that no politicians held market liberal or reformist views, or were sympathetic to such views. I use this illustration to convey the dominant associations of those who were primary idea carriers, and to note their institutional affiliation.
3. As mentioned in Chapter 3, one of the two major "master narratives" of Indian nationalism since the turn of the twentieth century has been *secular nationalism*. Indian secularism, which denotes religious equidistance rather than non-involvement by the state, was principally represented by the Congress Party during and after the independence movement. The second "master narrative" is *religious nationalism*. This narrative views Hinduism not only as India's majority community, but also as the "hard core" (my formulation of ideas in Lakatosian terms) of India's distinctive national identity. The aim of Hindu nationalists is to build Hindu unity. This nationalism is often called "Hindutva" (Varshney, *Ethnic Conflict and Civic Life*, 56–57).
4. The BJP is heir to the Jana Sangh party discussed in Chapters 3 and 4.
5. See Table A3.2 in Appendices for interviews with elite respondents: Del-5.
6. Table A3.2: Del-8.
7. Table A3.2: Del-3.
8. Table A3.2: Del-26.
9. Ibid.
10. Table A3.2: Del-11, Del-84; see Table A3.3 in Appendices for focus groups: 2015-fgPRIJ.
11. Table A3.2: Del-8.
12. Table A3.2: Del-7.
13. Table A3.2: Del-3.

14. *Times of India*, June 5, 2011; he repeated this statement later, as well (ibid., December 12, 2011).
15. Table A3.2: Del-10b, Del-15, Del-79c.
16. *Times of India*, June 9, 2011.
17. Naqvi, *Capital Conquest*, 13. The accusation that politicians and other elites embezzled public funds and stashed them away in secure banks abroad to the detriment of the common man is a particularly salient charge, which, whether economically borne out or not, has consistently captured the imagination of citizens across South Asia. The recently released "Panama Papers" added more fuel to this fire, and certainly incumbent Prime Minister Narendra Modi's 2016 demonetization policy captivated (and capitalized upon) this imagination.
18 It is important to note that, as Indian historian Ramachandra Guha observed, the "threat to India from Hindutva [Hindu nationalist] bigotry was at its most intense from about 1989 to about 2004," in which the nation saw large-scale riots and killings. The specter of the Hindutva RSS backing—or, even worse, birthing—the IAC was perhaps even greater in the mind of some secular nationalists in the UPA than it was to Indira Gandhi and her Congress government in the early 1970s (Ramachandra Guha, *Patriots and Partisans* [New Delhi: Penguin Books, 2013], 7–8).
19. Table A3.2: Del-16; *Times of India*, June 6, 2011.
20. *Times of India*, August 15, 2012. He had also made a similar statement earlier in his career (ibid., August 13, 2012).
21. Table A3.2: Del-26.
22. Table A3.2: Del-11, Del-36b, Del-57, Del-62.
23. Table A3.2: Del-36b.
24. Table A3.2: Del-12. This will be considered in greater depth later in this chapter.
25. Table A3.2: Del-14, Del-36b, Del-31. Indeed, it is important to point out that there were substantive differences between some NAC members, particularly Aruna Roy, and leaders of the IAC regarding the content and scope of the Lokpal bill.
26. Table A3.2: Del-75, Del-32.
27. Anna Hazare, "Anna Hazare's 5-Point Letter to PM," NDTV, April 6, 2011, http://bit.ly/2oDb23s (accessed October 1, 2020).
28. *Times of India*, April 20, 2011.
29. Table A3.2: Del-14.
30. Ibid.
31. Table A3.2: Del-33, Del-34, Del-35; Table A3.3: 2015-fgINTL. Prime Minister Manmohan Singh's letter to Hazare during his August 2011 fast

makes explicit recourse to the "scourge of corruption" that needed to be eradicated from everyday Indian civic life (*Times of India*, August 23, 2011).

32. Table A3.2: Del-35.
33. Table A3.2: Del-34.
34. Ibid.
35. Table A3.2: Del-21.
36. Table A3.2: Del-33.
37. Table A3.2: Del-1, Del-30; Table A3.3: 2015-fgACTV, 2015-fgNGOW.
38. Table A3.2: Del-19.
39. NDTV, "Full Text: Prime Minister's Speech at IIM Calcutta," August 22, 2011, http://bit.ly/2qdFUay (accessed October 1, 2020).
40. NDTV, "PM's Entire Speech on Anna, Corruption," August 26, 2011, http://bit.ly/2ps9zfq (accessed October 1, 2020).
41. Manmohan Singh was not a purist, classical liberal, as he emphasized his strong commitment to the goal of alleviating poverty. However, for Singh, economic growth was an indisputable necessary condition to address inequality and to enhance social development. Indeed, and as we will see later in the chapter, in the very articulation of the liberalization reforms Singh seeks to *build* on the Nehruvian dirigiste past.
42. Table A3.2: Del-35.
43. Malavika Vyawahare, "From India Shining to India Whining?" *New York Times: India Ink*, October 10, 2012, http://nyti.ms/2oYmzdX (accessed October 1, 2020).
44. These powers were widely noted by the CAG to have been used to extract and favor large private players in procurement contracts, from mining rights to the telecom spectrum. This much was assumed by market liberals such as the prime minister, who felt that he needed to ensure that pathways to corruption, although undesirable, did not impede economic growth or broader social and economic welfare (Table A3.2: Del-34). Beyond the CAG reports, the government gave incentives to the corporate sector through tax concessions and a significant reduction in the corporate income tax rate, which was in line with its economic growth push.
45. Table A3.2: Del-35.
46. Table A3.2: Del-21.
47. Manor, "The Congress Party and the Great Transformation."
48. Centre for Budget and Governance Accountability (CBGA), "How Did the UPA Spend Our Money? An Assessment of Expenditure Priorities of Resource Mobilisation Efforts of the UPA Government" (New Delhi: CBGA, 2009).
49. Internationally, leading investors became increasingly fearful that India, along with other emerging markets (namely Turkey, Brazil, South Africa,

and Indonesia), were too dependent on volatile foreign investments to finance their growth ambitions. This trend eventually led to the designation of these countries as the "Fragile Five" in a 2013 Morgan Stanley report, which became another tipping point for macroeconomic insecurity in India (*Morgan Stanley Research*, "Global EM Investor: The Fragile Five," August 5, 2013, http://nyti.ms/2qdW0kK [accessed October 1, 2020]).

50. For example, the prime minister planned to install market liberal technocrat Montek Singh Ahluwalia as finance minister during the crisis, but was overruled by Sonia Gandhi (Table A3.2: Del-34, Del-54).

51. Table A3.2: Del-33.

52. Misra, *Revisiting Regional Growth Dynamics in India in the Post Economic Reforms Period*, 8.

53. Table A3.2: Del-33.

54. Table A3.2: Del-34.

55. See Chapter 2 sub-section "Change and Continuity."

56. James Manor, "Did the Central Government's Poverty Initiatives Help to Re-Elect It?" in *New Dimensions of Politics in India: The United Progressive Alliance in Power*, ed. Lawrence Saez and Gurharpal Singh, 13–25 (London: Routledge Press, 2011); Isher Judge Ahluwalia and I. M. D. Little, *India's Economic Reforms and Development: Essays for Manmohan Singh* (New Delhi: Oxford University Press, 2012), 5. The Soviet Union and East European socialist regimes had collapsed, and global entities poured scorn on the feasibility of socialist models. China, meanwhile, was well on its way to opening up the economy.

57. The *Times of India* noted: "A change of considerable significance is taking place in India … the emphasis has shifted from distributive justice to growth" (*Times of India,* Editorial, February 22, 1991).

58. Jagdish Bhagwati and Arvind Panagariya, *Why Growth Matters: How Economic Growth in India Reduced Poverty and the Lessons for Other Developing Countries* (New York: Public Affairs, 2013).

59. Akhil Gupta, *Red Tape: Bureaucracy, Structural Violence, and Poverty in India* (New Delhi: Orient Blackswan, 2012). Though this dichotomy (between pre- and post-liberalization) is rather simplistic when one looks at the longer arc of reforms, the 1991 program does reflect the point of shift in India's political economy from "a reluctant pro-capitalist state with a socialist ideology to an enthusiastic pro-capitalist state with a market liberal ideology" (Kohli, *Democracy and Development in India*, 195; Mihir Sharma, *Restart: The Last Chance for the Indian Economy* [New Delhi: Random House India, 2015]).

60. Frankel, *India's Political Economy*; Barbara Harris-White and Anushree Sinha, eds., *Trade Liberalization and India's Informal Economy* (New Delhi: Oxford

University Press, 2007); Kunal Sen, "Why Did the Elephant Start to Trot? India's Growth Acceleration Re-Examined," *Economic and Political Weekly* 42, no. 43 (2007): 37–47; Mukherji, *Globalization and Deregulation*.

61. In the spring of 1991, the RBI, with the country holding only enough reserves of foreign exchange to pay for two weeks of imports, secretly pledged 47 tons of gold to the Bank of England to borrow USD 400 million to pay its creditors (for a compelling retelling of this episode, see Shankkar Aiyar, *Accidental India: A History of the Nation's Passage Through Crisis and Change* [New Delhi: Aleph Books, 2012]).

62. Table A3.2: Del-27.

63. P. C. Alexander, *Through the Corridors of Power: An Insider's Story* (New Delhi: Harper Collins India, 2004); Ramaswamy Venkataraman, *My Presidential Years* (New Delhi: South Asia Books, 1994); Table A3.2: Del-35, Del-54, Del-82.

64. Table A3.2: Del-33.

65. As Eleni Tsingou notes, the rising dominance of market-friendly ideas was in part due to them being hatched inside transnational networks of experts held together by elite peer recognition and an ambition to provide global public goods in line with the values its members considered honorable (Eleni Tsingou, "Power Elites and Club-Model Governance in Global Finance," *International Political Sociology* 8, no. 3 [September 2014]: 340–42).

66. Table A3.2: Del-33, Del-24b, Del-27. As one scholar has posited, internationally trained state elites mentioned here lacked "insularity in their thinking [which] enabled them to see India's problems in a broader perspective ... and counter some of the ingrained habits of many Indian economists, in academia and in government" (Deena Khatkhate, "Looking Back in Anger," *Economic and Political Weekly* 38, nos. 51–52 [December 27, 2003]: 5350–53, quoted in Kapur, *Diaspora, Development, and Democracy*, 151). Of course, it is important to note that there is no isomorphic mapping between the international institutions mentioned here and support for liberalization—several state elites also linked to these same institutions held divergent views (as noted in this chapter and elsewhere).

67. Kapur, *Diaspora, Development, and Democracy*, 23. One of the most fascinating distinct tones of recognizing political constraints while pushing through ideas on opening and liberalization.

68. In a PBS interview in 2002, Chidambaram had the following to say about his time at Harvard:

> Let me tell you very frankly, when I went to the Harvard Business School I was more or less a committed socialist. Even in the Harvard Business School I don't believe I quite gave up my admiration for socialism, *although remaining in the U.S. for two years exposed me to another model, which appeared*

to be more successful, which appeared to have brought jobs and incomes and prosperity to a much larger proportion of people. But I must confess that I still remained quite pink when I was there. (Emphasis added; Palaniappan Chidambaram, Interview, *Commanding Heights: The Battle for the World Economy,* PBS, 2002, https://to.pbs.org/2R0porA [quoted in Kapur, *Diaspora, Development, and Democracy,* 22])

69. This is a salient factor when comparing the backgrounds of elites in positions of authority in the Congress (1971–75) and UPA (2004–14) governments at the time of the anti-corruption movements (Tables A4.1–A4.3 in Appendices). In the UPA government, 14 percent of elites in the cabinet, including the prime minister and ministers of finance, home, law, and justice, among others, studied internationally (not including those officials with similar backgrounds in the RBI and the Planning Commission). Furthermore, 50 percent of the NAC were educated abroad. In total, 25 percent of decision-makers came from technocrat, bureaucrat, or activist backgrounds. In contrast, in the far smaller cabinet in the Congress government under Indira Gandhi, 8 percent of elites in positions of authority had been educated internationally, namely the prime minister, steel minister Mohan Kumaramangalam, West Bengal chief minister S. S. Ray, and, of course, P. N. Haksar. In that administration, 6 percent of decision-makers came from technocratic backgrounds, the most prominent being secretariat head P. N. Dhar. Overall, it is important not to make a qualitative assertion about the nature of studies in India and abroad, but to note that those who studied abroad held different and distinct training methods and ideational networks that plausibly influenced their worldviews.

70. At Cambridge, Singh deeply admired the monetarist Dennis Robertson (Daman Singh, *Strictly Personal: Manmohan and Gursharan* [New Delhi: Harper Collins India, 2014], 116–17). Singh graduated with the prestigious Adam Smith prize for the best tripos result related to his essay on international investment and development, in which he argued that developing nations such as India had to build a domestic market and therefore generate capital at home in order to grow (ibid., 122, 146). In his own words, he gained "a better idea of how the economy works, and what can be done to kick-start an economy" (quoted in ibid., 141).

71. I. M. D Little, *A Critique of Welfare Economics* (Oxford: Oxford University Press, 2003 [1950]).

72. Incidentally, Little's successor at Nuffield College was Amartya Sen, who we will see later represents the opposing intellectual view of India's political economy of development to Jagdish Bhagwati.

73. D. Singh, *Strictly Personal,* 158, 167. Economists such as T. N. Srinivasan and Jagdish Bhagwati were among the earliest to link the policy of state control

to low growth. Indeed, the first intellectual treatment of India's economic policies was written by Jagdish Bhagwati and Padma Desai. Manmohan Singh reviewed this book in 1972 in *The Indian Economic and Social History Review* when he was Chief Economic Advisor in the Ministry of Finance. It is interesting to note his concluding remarks: "It would be tragic if we were to become prisoners of instruments which, howsoever suitable at one stage of development, turn out later to be fretters on further development." He further stated that he did not believe that "more controls are better than less controls" (Manmohan Singh, "Book Review: Jagdish Bhagwati and Padma Desai, India: Planning for Industrialization; Industrialization and Trade Policies since 1951 (Oxford University Press, 1970)," *The Indian Economic and Social History Review* 9, no. 4 [December 1972]: 413–17, 417).

74. Del-34.

75. Manmohan Singh, *India's Export Trends and the Prospects for Self-Sustained Growth* [Oxford: Clarendon Press, 1964]. Singh wanted to write a dissertation that challenged the dominant hypothesis at the time, which suggested that India should continue with an anti-trade, autarkic policy (D. Singh, *Strictly Personal*, 163). His project developed as he became heavily influenced by the work of Ragnar Nurkse and other classical development economists who argued, contrary to established trends, that financing for development should come to a large extent from the developing country itself ("capital is made at home"), and that key areas to be financed needed to exhibit increasing returns in order to trigger the dynamics of development or virtuous circles of growth. In short, for a poor country, as India was then, to be sustainable in the long term, it needed to formulate a balanced method to finance its development (Ragnar Nurkse, *Equilibrium and Growth in the World Economy: Essays by Ragnar Nurske*, ed. Gottfried Haberler and Robert M. Stern [Cambridge, MA: Harvard University Press, 1961], 141).

76. The policy of import substitution was especially emboldened since the Indira Gandhi years, and was a corollary to state-driven intervention in economic and social life. India's massive import bills would lead to foreign exchange or deficit crises in 1956, 1966, and beyond, most notably in 1991. Exports simply did not feature in the matrix of India's political economy. Proponents of export "pessimism" believed that the world would not offer a growing market to products from developing nations. Manmohan Singh sought to challenge this fundamental assumption. See also Mukherji, *Globalization and Deregulation*.

77. That is, the solution to India's precarious financial architecture did not lay in multiple IMF loans or domestic borrowing, which would fail to address the fundamental issues at hand and heighten the fiscal deficit, but in India opening and stepping up its exports (Table A3.2: Del-34, Del-82b).

78. D. Singh, *Strictly Personal*, 173. After defending his dissertation, Singh joined the Ministry of Foreign Trade in Indira Gandhi's newly installed government in 1971. After serving as governor of the RBI from 1982 to 1985 and as deputy chairman of the Planning Commission from 1985 to 1987, Singh joined the UN-backed South Commission as Secretary General in Geneva. In 1991, when crisis called, he would return to India to take up the post of finance minister.

79. Serious debates emerged at least as far back as the Janata government (1977–80) and in the public domain among economists such as Jagdish Bhagwati and T. N. Srinivasan into the 1980s as well as at this time at think-tanks such as the Delhi-based Indian Council for Research on International Economic Relations (ICRIER). The difficulties with the existing strategy had received more detailed empirical support from analysis of the problems of low productivity, and low productivity growth within Indian industry.

80. Table A3.2: Del-80b, Del-35, Del-27.

81. Table A3.2: Del-28, Del-62, Del-35. Ahluwalia, we now know, was the author of the famous "M Document" written in 1990 that "presented an integrated strategy for reform—of fiscal policy, industrial policy, trade policy, and exchange rate policy." This document was leaked in the *Indian Express* on July 11, 1990, and started a broader public discussion among economists. Many of its ideas would be implemented in the subsequent reforms. For a fascinating account of the "M Document" and internal government debates, see Montek Singh Ahluwalia, *Backstage: The Story behind India's High Growth Years* (New Delhi: Rupa, 2020).

82. The causal weight of ideas here is highlighted by the market liberal elites' elaborate package of economic restructuring, which reached beyond the crisis of liquidity they faced (Arjun Sengupta, "Financial Sector and Economic Reforms in India," *Economic and Political Weekly* 30, no. 1 [January 1995]: 39–44). The crisis posed the opportunity for these actors to diminish state intervention in the lives of citizens. Indeed, Manmohan Singh called for "bold measures" to "convert the crisis into an opportunity to build a new India, to do things which many people before us have thought and said should be done, but somehow were never done [*sic*]" (Manmohan Singh interview with Zoya Hasan, quoted in Hasan, *Congress after Indira*, 54).

83. This can be seen in three main ways, that are largely intact to the present day: (*a*) The state continues to control a significant part of the corporate sector through ownership. (*b*) The state plays the role of a handmaiden of the institutionalization of capitalism. (*c*) The state has played a major role in industrial strategy, both historically and since 1991.

84. Ibid., 124.

85. Kohli, *Democracy and Development in India*, 140–64.
86. Table A3.2: Del-33.
87. Table A3.2: Del-27.
88. "India Shining" was the slogan of the incumbent BJP-led NDA alliance during the 2004 general election campaign that sought to build a narrative of economic and social optimism and globalization in India.
89. Sonia Gandhi, "Meeting of All India Congress Committee (AICC); Opening Remarks by the Congress President," New Delhi, April 6, 1998, http://bit.ly/2qeb8Pb (accessed October 1, 2020).
90. It is worth noting the irony that an explicitly *aam aadmi* (common man) movement against corruption, the IAC, would be the UPA government's undoing, which rose to power on a campaign of *Congress ka haath aam aadmi ke saath* (Congress's hand is with the common man).
91. Despite that her party and its key decision-makers, including her chosen prime minister, were the chief architects of the liberalization reforms of the early 1990s, Sonia Gandhi saw her party and coalition's fundamental mandate as a bulwark against the BJP's "India Shining" campaign and its focus on further liberalization.
92. Table A3.2: Del-26, Del-8b, Del-14. After the syndicate of the 1960s, this was the first time that power in a Congress government had been vested in a group outside the office of the prime minister. As detailed in Chapter 5, the establishment of the NAC created a secondary center of power and influence in government that resulted in a coalition between followers and supporters of Sonia Gandhi's center of power under the NAC on one hand and the coalition of Prime Minister Manmohan Singh under the PMO and the cabinet on the other.
93. The CMP committed itself to furthering the "welfare of farmers, agricultural labor ... and the weaker sections of society [and] to the well-being of the common man across the country" (quoted in Hasan, *Congress after Indira*, 87). Although the CMP became obsolete after UPA-1, the NAC continued to press its reformism on central policymaking.
94. The RTI bill first found its way to the floor of parliament in 2002. The then-ruling BJP-led coalition government passed the bill in January 2003, but the bill was deemed by NAC elites as a diluted draft, especially considering the series of corruption scams and the pogrom of Muslims during ethnic riots in Gujarat in 2002. Politicians of all stripes, and in both houses, feared that the law, in its original form, would offer retrospective review, and could be used to blackmail state officials, thus stifling the everyday workings of the bureaucracy (Table A3.2: Del-25, Del-25b, Del-33). However, activists refused to back down, and continued to lobby the government to overturn what they

considered a weak bill and to promote the stronger RTI Act in its original form.

95. Including Bharat Nirman (a cluster of six infrastructure programs), Sarva Shiksha Abhiyan, Mid-Day Meals Scheme, NREGA, Total Sanitation Campaign, National Rural Health Mission (NRHM), Integrated Child Development Services, Jawaharlal Nehru National Urban Renewal Mission (JNNURM), and polio eradication, among others.

96. Amartya Sen and Jean Drèze, *India Economic Development and Social Opportunity* (Oxford: Oxford University Press, 1995), 180.

97. Jean Drèze and Amartya Sen, *India: Development and Participation* (New Delhi: Oxford University Press, 2002), 322–23. From the 1980s and early 1990s, in particular, see also Jean Drèze and Amartya Sen, *Hunger and Public Action* (Oxford: Oxford University Press, 1989); Sen and Drèze, *India Economic Development and Social Opportunity*; Amartya Sen, *Poverty and Famines: An Essay on Entitlement and Deprivation* (Oxford: Clarendon Press, 1981); Amartya Sen, *Choice, Welfare, and Measurement* (Oxford: Basil Blackwell, 1982); Amartya Sen, *Resources, Values, and Development* (Oxford: Basil Blackwell, 1984); Amartya Sen, "Public Action for Social Security," in *Social Security in Developing Countries*, ed. E. Ahmad, 3–32 (Oxford: Clarendon Press, 1990); Jean Drèze, "Economic Development, Public Action, and Social Progress," *Canadian Journal of Development Studies* 15, no. 3 (December 1994); and Jean Drèze, "Distribution Matters in Cost–Benefit Analysis," *Journal of Public Economics* 70, no. 3 (1998): 485–88.

98. Jean Drèze and Amartya Sen, *An Uncertain Glory: India and Its Contradictions* (Princeton: Princeton University Press, 2013), ix.

99. Ibid.

100. Sen and Drèze, *India Economic Development and Social Opportunity*, 19–22, 184–90.

101. In 2013, the duel between market liberal and reformist ideas came to general public attention with the writings of Drèze and Sen on one hand and Bhagwati and Panagariya on the other. See Gardiner Harris, "Rival Economists in Public Battle over Cure for India's Poverty," *New York Times*, August 21, 2013, http://nyti.ms/2qdPXcO; Pankaj Mishra, "Which India Matters?" *New York Review of Books*, November 21, 2013, http://bit.ly/2pt7dwQ; David Rieff, "A Battle for the Soul of India," *National Interest*, September 4, 2013, http://bit.ly/2qmbrUq (all accessed October 1, 2020).

102. Drèze and Sen, *An Uncertain Glory*, 103.

103. Drèze and Sen, *Hunger and Public Action*.

104. As one of his colleagues in the NAC told me, Jean Drèze "led many of our meetings. The food security bill, for example, was presented to us all by Jean

[Drèze] and Harsh Mander, who put in a lot of time and effort into the bill and many of our discussions in shaping the large UPA schemes" (Table A3.2: Del-14).

105. Table A3.2: Del-36b, Del-75, Del-12.

106. The anti-corruption fervor of this period was emboldened by several non-governmental organizations (NGOs). Chief among these were the Association for Democratic Reforms (ADR), which sought to bring transparency to party politics, focusing particularly on bringing political parties under the RTI Act and reforming campaign funding, and Janaagraha (or "force of the people"), which aimed to strengthen democracy in India by working toward citizen participation in urban local government (Table A3.3: 2015-fgNGOW).

107. Anirudh Krishna, "Continuity and Change: The Indian Administrative Service 30 Years Ago and Today," *Commonwealth and Comparative Politics* 48, no. 4 (2010): 433–44; Gupta, *Red Tape*. Data from a 2006 World Bank study of India's administrative services shows a steady decline over time in the bureaucracy's effectiveness in policy formulation and implementation (World Bank, "Reforming Public Services in India: Drawing Lessons From Success," Washington, D.C., 2006).

108. Bussell, *Corruption and Reform in India*; Lakshmi Iyer and Anand Mani, "Traveling Agents: Political Change and Bureaucratic Turnover in India," *Review of Economics and Statistics* 94, no. 3 (2012): 723–39. For a thorough review of these factors, see Milan Vaishnav and Saksham Khosla, "The Indian Administrative Service Meets Big Data," Carnegie Endowment for International Peace, September 1, 2016.

109. Beginning in the mid-1990s, an entire generation of technocrats- and bureaucrats-turned-activists rallied against corruption at all levels, and in all forms, through NGOs and other grassroots organizations and rights-based movements (Table A3.3: 2015-fgNGOW, 2015-fgBURC). This is substantiated by the many primary accounts by former-bureaucrats-turned-activists regarding government corruption at the center. These works include Promila Shankar, *Gods of Corruption* (New Delhi: Manas Publications, 2015); P. C. Parakh, *Crusader or Conspirator: Coalgate and Other Truths* (New Delhi: Manas Publications, 2014); Sahai, *Lokpal Bill*; Kejriwal, *Swaraj*; C. P. Srivastava, *Corruption: India's Enemy Within* (New Delhi: Macmillan Press, 2001). Among these reformists, corruption is considered the single biggest impediment to the development of India (Table A3.3: 2015-fgBURC).

110. At the center, existing Indian legislation regarding government records and information was a direct vestige of the colonial era. Consider, for example, the Official Secrets Act of 1923, which was enacted to prevent spying and to

punish anyone who disclosed government information, and which was designed to enable imperial masters to deny power to Indian natives. This Act created informational asymmetries that kept citizen complaints to a minimum, and thus widened the potential for the abuse of public office for private gain.

111. Table A3.2: Del-13, Del-72b; Table A3.3: 2015-fgBURC.

112. Table A3.2: Del-44, Del-74, Del-55; Table A3.3: 2015-fgBUSN.

113. Table A3.2: Del-14, Del-53, Del-1; Table A3.3: 2015-fgACTV.

114. Table A3.2: Del-32.

115. Rashmi Bansal, *I Have a Dream: The Inspiring Stories of 20 Social Entrepreneurs Who Found New Ways to Solve Old Problems* (New Delhi: Westland Ltd., 2011), 269.

116. Table A3.2: Del-14, Del-36b. This also allows us to assess how the IAC rose synonymously with a larger schism that had long been widening between the bureaucracy, from which many anti-corruption activists emerged, and the political establishment, beginning in the early 1990s. The IAC's Jan Lokpal was a far more stringent bill that dictated that the ombudsman have full jurisdiction over the prime minister, without concessions, and which proposed to exclude NGOs from any punishment.

117. Table A3.2: Del-32.

118. In an innovative piece, Aditi Gandhi and Michael Walton argue that 43 percent of the total number of billionaires, who account for 60 percent of billionaire wealth in India, located their primary sources of wealth in rent-thick sectors such as real estate, construction, infrastructure, ports, media, cement, and mining—in other words, the areas in which government has discretion (Aditi Gandhi and Michael Walton, "Where Do India's Billionaires Get Their Wealth?" *Economic and Political Weekly* 47, no. 40 [October 6, 2012]: 10–14; see also James Crabtree, *Billionaire Raj: A Journey through India's New Gilded Age* [New York: Penguin Random House, 2018]).

119. Table A3.2: Del-1.

120. Ibid.

121. As one member of the NAC outlined:

The entire thinking on social policy during UPA was outsourced to the NAC. And it was a brilliant move by Mrs. [Sonia] Gandhi. The other side [cabinet and Planning Commission] had no appetite, no interest, and no understanding for what we were working on. *Without us you would have had a runaway [market] liberal government, and Mrs. Gandhi knows the political fallout of that.* (Table A3.2: Del-14)

122. Table A3.2: Del-54.

123. Table A3.2: Del-10.

124. Table A3.2: Del-34.
125. Table A3.2: Del-35.
126. Table A3.2: Del-7.
127. Ahluwalia, *Backstage*, 316–18.
128. Table A3.2: Del-12.
129. Table A3.2: Del-53.
130. Duncan Green, *From Poverty to Power: How Active Citizens and Effective States Can Change the World* (Oxford: Oxfam International, 2008).

7

The Politics of Ideas in India and Developing Democracies

Every man, wherever he goes, is encompassed by a cloud of comforting convictions, which move with him like flies on a summer day.

—Bertrand Russell, 1928

The Politics of Ideas in India: Past and Present

One of the main goals of my project has been to show that elite ideas need to be taken seriously. This much may seem obvious when we discuss and write about government behavior in the developed world, but once we interrogate the leading monographs and theories on government decision-making in India and other developing contexts, ideas are given little to no sway. I have also sought to go deeper, by exploring where ideas come from, how they might be chosen, and when they are the most salient for explaining political behavior. This book therefore provides a useful balance to the current comparative work on Indian politics and political economy. To illustrate, I have argued that government response to a credibility crisis, as evidenced by decision-makers' treatment of a nationwide anti-corruption movement, is conditioned by the interaction between the ideas of state elites and political and state structures. Ultimately, we observe ideas play out in two ways in the empirical analysis. The first is through activating populism and the second is through an ideational checks and balances mechanism.

The number of populists in power have increased fivefold since 1990, with a firm anchoring in distinct concepts of the nation.[1] Whereas populism was once found primarily in developing democracies, populists, and their visions of the nation, are increasingly gaining power in systemically developed institutional contexts too.[2] Consider the words of US Attorney General William P. Barr during a closed-door speech at the University of Notre Dame on October 11, 2019: "Secularists, and their allies among the 'progressives,' have marshalled all the force of mass communications, popular culture, the entertainment industry, and academia in an unremitting assault on religion and traditional values."[3] On the same day, around 450 miles south in Nashville, Tennessee, Secretary of State Mike Pompeo gave a speech on "Being a Christian Leader" at the American Association of Christian Counselors. The event was showcased on the State Department's homepage all week.[4] Beyond its bluster, populism is a "thin-centered" ideology "that considers society to be ultimately separated into two homogenous and antagonistic groups, 'the pure people' versus 'the corrupt elite,' and which argues that politics should be an expression of the *volonté générale* [general will] of the people."[5] Such a treatment of populism has echoes of George Orwell's measure of contemporary nationalism in a 1945 essay as "the habit of assuming that human beings can be classified like insects."[6] The secular–religious nationalism pivot, which fervently plays a constitutive role in political realignments in many distinct countries, foregrounds how moral boundaries between groups are redrawn confrontationally in politics and how categories of "us" and "them" emerge. This was not only the case in India nearly half a century ago in the lead-up to the Emergency, but reverberations are also witnessed across the country today. Though at the time of writing the BJP government led by Prime Minister Modi has not yet faced the type of credibility crisis outlined in this book, what predictions or instruction might my analysis imply of the likely outcomes for the current set of state elites in India?

Since its rise to power in 2014, concepts of the Indian nation have been a hallmark of Prime Minister Narendra Modi's BJP government and its populist politics.[7] They revolve around religious, specifically Hindu, nationalism. Despite the promise, and often inconsistent delivery on campaign promises, of a less corrupt and more accountable and productive state administration, it is Modi's populism that has roared with full force. On the day of the 2019 election success, the secular–religious nationalist divergence was weaponized and laced the prime minister's victory speech at the BJP headquarters: "Secularism was a tax that used to be paid till today. Fake secularism and its leaders [that is, Congress Party] who were calling for the secular forces to unite have been exposed and have fallen silent over the past five years."[8] The 2019 general election brought consolidation of political power under Modi, and firmly established the BJP as the new dominant force in Indian politics.[9] The victory marks the first time since Indira Gandhi's electoral sweep in 1971 that a sitting prime minister returned to power winning an outright majority in two consecutive elections. Just as it was the case nearly five decades ago with the Congress Party and Gandhi, the BJP's victory is in significant part a mandate on Narendra Modi and his worldview, which has thrived in step with the type of centralization of state power laid out in Chapter 3.[10] Though we should be careful not to overextend historical parallels, populism is at the heart of both leaders' governance style and tactics.

In a recent essay, political scientist Ashutosh Varshney outlined two variants of populist politics that resonate in India—left-wing populism and right-wing populism. What they share is the type of undercutting of independent state institutions and primacy placed on the elected realm that we saw evidenced in Chapters 3 and 4.[11] Where they differ, Varshney argues, is in their definition of "the people"—for left-wing populists such as Indira Gandhi, "the people" are the poor, while for right-wing populists "the people" are the ethnic, racial, or religious majority.[12] In other words, each populism views "the nation" divergently.

As argued in this book, the concepts of the nation under the Congress Party government led by Indira Gandhi were anchored in secularism with a preference for a socialist economy and focus on minority rights. The concepts of the nation under Narendra Modi's BJP government are anchored in Hindutva with a sidelining of minority rights.[13] In terms of its economic outlook, the story is somewhat mixed. As well as popular policy schemes, Modi's record does not depart from practices in multiple administrations since liberalization in slowly allowing private actors to operate in newer sectors and services (telecoms, healthcare, IT) while keeping control of the industrial backbone (power, oil, heavy industry, utilities, mining). And while there is a clear nativist hue in the economic order under Modi and the BJP, it is not as overtly as anti-elite.[14] Ultimately, for the present analysis, the "hard core" of this populism remains anchored in religious nationalism. This ideology interacts with an executive which, similar to that under Indira Gandhi, harnesses state power to reshape society; a process that begins by centralizing executive power to monopolize decision-making.

Consider, for example, the perspectives of those technocrats who have served within the Modi administration and who view the twin pillars of populism and centralization as undercutting India's economic performance. While delivering the OP Jindal Lecture on the Indian economy at the Watson Institute of International and Public Affairs at Brown University on October 9, 2019, former governor of the RBI under the Modi government, Raghuram Rajan, affirmed:

India has become too big an economy to be run from the top. Unfortunately, the experience so far is that it simply doesn't work. *This government is extremely centralized which puts a lot of pressure on the leadership. The leadership doesn't have a consistent and articulated vision on how to achieve economic growth.* Today what we have is a PMO which essentially works through the bureaucracy. The ministerial level is often bypassed [and] disempowered for the most part.[15]

Rajan's comments come against the backdrop of a slowdown in economic growth to a six-year low of 5 percent and with populist measures, according Rajan, signaling "a dark and uncertain path" ahead for the Indian economy.[16] This analysis closely matches those of other technocrats who have served the Modi government, notably Arvind Subramanian, Chief Economic Advisor to the Prime Minister from 2014–18, who remarked in 2017 that centralization as well as "nativist" impulses in the BJP government will hold back economic and developmental progress.[17] These comments together with the process and performance of policy design in the Modi administration give a nod to the impression that ideational checks and balances, as studied and revealed in Chapter 6, are conspicuous by their absence in the BJP government. [18]

We know from a range of long-standing academic scholarship and thinking that a separation of powers reduces arbitrary behavior among government officials.[19] But which mechanism does the counterbalancing needs explication, case by case. In existing explanations on India, there are two main ways checks and balances affect arbitrary government behavior. The first is institutional, in the spirit of *The Federalist Papers*; for example where the Supreme Court, the Election Commission, and the presidency, among others, act as "referee" institutions to keep arbitrary government behavior in check.[20] Populists such as Gandhi and Modi have actively superseded non-elected public institutions and, in both cases, their governments have weakened accountability.[21] The second is political interests, where coalition or minority government survival is conditional on the goodwill and support of smaller party partners typically at the state level and sometimes even the opposition, and therefore politicians accountable to different constituencies check one another's authority in government.[22] As development expert at the Centre for Policy Research Yamini Aiyar points out in a recent essay, the natural victim of the centralization and ideological homogenization taking shape under Modi and the BJP has been the checks and balances incubated within Indian federalism, which had thrived in the years since the breakdown of the Congress's dominance.[23] The third mechanism, as introduced in Chapter 6 and this book, is an ideational checks and balances, the absence of which has led the Modi-led BJP government to signal that it is likely to behave more like the Indira Gandhi government did if it were to face a credibility crisis—by activating populist steps given content and shape by its dominant, religious, nationalism.

On August 5, 2019, thousands of Indian state troops shifted tactically in Jammu and Kashmir (J&K) to enforce that state's new Reorganization Act. A major Hindu pilgrimage was cancelled, schools and colleges were shut, tourists were ordered to leave, telephone and internet services were suspended, and democratically elected regional party leaders were placed under house arrest. In his annual Independence Day address ten days later, Prime Minister Narendra Modi declared that he was proud that the revocation of Article 370 in Kashmir, which had granted the state semi-autonomous status, had made "one nation, one constitution" a reality.[24]

In the immediate aftermath of the overturning of Article 370 in the contentious Muslim-majority state of J&K, state authorities detained some 2,000 citizens—including politicians, businessmen, activists, and journalists—to prevent them from protesting.[25] In a vivid, though inverse, reminder of the language used by Indira Gandhi during the Emergency, Prime Minister Modi and the ruling BJP asserted that their government is integrating Kashmir into the Indian nation. Yet in practice, at the time of writing, detentions have continued (and increased) while there is limited movement and media reportage.[26] And despite losses to the state's exchequer of a reported USD 5.4 billion against the backdrop of a national economic slowdown and the coronavirus pandemic, the clampdown continues.[27] A sincere reading of the BJP's election manifesto and a longitudinal study of the party and Narendra Modi's ideological roots would have largely presaged the Kashmir decision as well as the strategy pursued by the government's decision-makers in the face of dissent overall. Over the past six years under Narendra Modi's tenure, the government has superseded public institutions, undercut courts, introduced unilateral populist measures to alter sections of the economy, and adversely targeted communities that are considered oppositional to the ideology of Hindutva, mainly Muslims.[28]

In another case a few months later, on December 11, 2019, the BJP government passed the Citizenship Amendment Act (CAA), which gave immigrants from neighboring countries a pathway to Indian citizenship so long as they belonged to a select group of religions—excluding Islam.[29] The Act ushers religion as an official principle for citizenship for the first time and passed on the heels of the government's push for related nationwide citizenship verification processes, through a National Population Register (NPR) and one of its core campaign promises, a National Register of Citizens (NRC), together fueling a narrative of state-sanctioned assault against India's Muslims.[30] Despite the prime minister's claims that the CAA sought only to provide "citizenship to those facing discrimination," the new law incited widespread criticism domestically, among international allies and multilateral organizations, and set off a series of protests across the country with peak crowds reaching as many as 100,000 in the city of Hyderabad.[31] What followed was a brutal crackdown in the nation's capital, Delhi, resulting in communal clashes and a pogrom by state-controlled security forces there using tear gas, batons, and assault rifles—instances of which were caught on video.[32] Counter-protests led by BJP politicians incited further suppression.[33] The coronavirus pandemic forced protests to end on March 22, 2020, as a nationwide lockdown was enforced, by which time at least 30 people had died during the anti-CAA protests in BJP-governed states and 50 during the communal violence stemming from it. More than 800 people had been arrested mainly under the Unlawful Activities Prevention Act (UAPA), which is generally used for terrorists.[34]

Though the above sketches from present-day India are not a case of a government facing a credibility crisis in the manner explored in this book, specifically the absence of an anti-corruption movement and that government leadership—chiefly Prime Minister Modi—remains popular, the central mechanisms that inhere in my argument reverberate in the current BJP government's response to collective action on the streets.

Cross-National Perspectives: Developing Democracies

While this book has been a comparative study of two governments in one country, its central argument resonates with accounts of political behavior during credibility crises broadly, and government response to anti-corruption movements specifically, in other parts of the world—albeit imperfectly.[35] Here, I specifically examine contexts like India, namely stable, multi-party, developing democracies that have faced nationwide anti-corruption movements. Importantly, these cases are from low- and middle-income countries where rent-seeking and other material external pressures would be considered tougher constraints on government behavior over and above ideology.

Indeed, the post-2008-financial-crisis global economy remains deeply in flux, and academics and policymakers around the world continue to debate how states and markets interact to produce optimal growth. Equally as volatile have been the political and sociological phenomena driving and emerging from this crisis milieu. Chief among them, citizens' collective action the world over against elite decision-makers who have been exposed or accused of corruption, economic mismanagement, and poor governance more broadly. In such cases, government reputations have plummeted, and uncertainty has overwhelmed the political arena.

Brazil

Dilma Rousseff was elected as the first female president of the country in 2011, and won reelection in 2014. Rousseff's involvement in politics began at a young age, when she became involved with the left-wing militant group National Liberation Command (Comando de Libertação Nacional).[36] Although Rousseff was arrested in 1970, her release three years later failed to wane her interest in politics, and, in 1986, she was appointed to public office for the first time. Over the next fifteen years, Rousseff alternated between the public and private sectors, as well as continuing to pursue advanced degrees in economics. Rousseff maintained her left-wing political alignment during this time, supporting the Workers' Party coalition (Partido dos Trabalhadores, or PT) from 1999 on, under the leadership of Luiz Inácio Lula da Silva (or Lula). When Lula was elected president in 2002, Rousseff accompanied him on his rise to power, and was appointed the chair of Petrobras, the country's state-controlled oil company. In 2005, Lula named Rousseff his Chief of Staff, and, six years later, Rousseff herself was elected president, running on a PT ticket. Her platform was in line with the party's leftist ideology. Rousseff's domestic agenda focused on social welfare issues, such as job creation for all, steep poverty eradication, and economic stability, while her foreign policy agenda emphasized the protection of human rights. Despite Rousseff's successful rise to power, her administration faced opposition and accusations of corruption from the beginning.[37] In fact, many of the accusations had begun under Lula's presidency, before Rousseff had been elected to high office. However, the accusations of corruption did not escalate into street protests until 2013 and went on in subsequent waves until 2015. The anti-corruption demonstrations began innocuously against an increase in transportation costs, but quickly transformed into a full-scale investigation of PT members within the federal government.[38] The government provided concessions to the anti-corruption movement while key decision-makers from the government, including Rousseff, were eventually investigated and removed from office.

A hybrid of consensual and majoritarian rule has come to signify governance at the center in Brazil, where coalitions have become dominant and larger since Fernando Henrique Cardoso's term in the late 1990s.[39] Since the PT's rise to power, ideological balancing within the government has been a critical factor in policymaking and governance.[40] Over time, this has meant that cabinets have become more ideologically diverse, larger, and often conflictual. This was evident in the Dilma Rousseff government that faced the 2013–15 anti-corruption wave.[41] President Rousseff built a heterogeneous, oversized, and over-concentrated governing coalition, denoting internal factions within the PT government.[42] The ideological spectrum of this government stretched from left- to right-wing parties, including a variety of technocrats such as Rousseff.[43] After meeting with leaders of states as well as representatives of the anti-corruption agitation at the end of June 2013, President Rousseff announced a "national pact" of reforms pertaining to, among other things, social services reforms and anti-corruption measures.[44]

A few factors may help explain Rousseff and her government's actions during this time. It is plausible to assert that the tolerant and quick turnaround in government response (within a month of the demonstrations starting) was in part born out of an ideologically plural cabinet environment that placed a check and balance on arbitrary executive action in response to the anti-corruption movement.[45] It is also possible that the quick turnaround in government response was due to increasing international pressure regarding Petrobras, which was involved in corruption at the highest levels of government. Although the corruption scandal did not fully surface until 2014, accusations had begun six years prior, deeply implicating Rousseff, many high-level Brazilian politicians, as well as the Brazilian construction giant Odebrecht.[46] As Rousseff's popularity took a deadly hit with the reveal of her involvement in the Odebrecht scandal, it is quite possible that Rousseff was trying to mitigate any potential loss of support and create the image of a stronger stance on corruption, should allegations of misconduct or corruption surface in her future.

Finally, a cooperative response to accusations of corruption is in line with Rousseff's decision-making style. As a member of the PT, Rousseff was a professed democratic socialist, appealing to workers and opposing oppressive governments like the one that had preceded the PT-dominated era. Having been imprisoned by the government when she was part of a guerilla movement in her early political years, Rousseff likely had personal reasons for not wanting to be associated with a suppressive regime.

Turkey

The Justice and Development Party (Adalet ve Kalkinma Partisi, or AKP) government's intolerant response under Prime Minister Recep Tayyip Erdogan toward two anti-corruption movements in 2013 also echoes this book's core arguments. The AKP came to power in 2002 and increased its vote share in every subsequent election until 2011. Turkey's relatively high electoral threshold of 10 percent intensified the effects of this increasing vote share by conferring AKP-majority governments with an outsized allocation of seats that shielded the party from the need to form coalitions. Simultaneously, during this time, the AKP undercut traditional poles of power, namely the "Kemalist" institutions that historically enforced the secular, Western-oriented ideology inspired by Mustafa Kemal Ataturk.[47] This ideological undercutting took shape in institutions such as the judiciary, parliament, and military, through constitutional amendments and other means to weaken challenges to the government that threatened its core ideology.[48] If Indira Gandhi came to power on a populist platform rooted in concepts of secularism, socialism, and minority rights, then Erdogan and the AKP government's populism can be understood in terms of Islamic ethics, economic liberalism, and a focus on the Sunni Anatolian heartland.[49] Similar to the Gandhi case, the will of the nation was to be expressed through the personality of Recep Tayyip Erdogan via a powerful, centralized state.

However, after 2012, Erdogan's populist star began to fall as the economy ebbed and his government faced a series of political and corruption crises. Inter-elite competition over ideology and power, which has been the hallmark of Turkish politics throughout the rise of the AKP—between Islamists, Gulenists (Hizmet), Kemalists, and others—ruptured and came to a crescendo in the lead-up to, and during, the 2013 anti-corruption demonstrations in Gezi Park. In the investigations that initiated the crisis, prominent government officials and ministers were implicated in widespread allegations of corruption in public tenders, smuggling, and sanctions evasion. These allegations came to a climax with the release of alleged recordings of Prime Minister Erdogan himself ordering his family to hide dubiously obtained cash. These allegations clashed with the AKP's platform of transparency and proposals for anti-corruption legislation. Like Indira Gandhi in 1975, Erdogan believes himself to be the custodian of the national interest, specifically the conceptualized nation epitomized by pious Anatolians.[50] Thus, the AKP majority government viewed the function of the anti-corruption movements, mobilizing several disparate social and political groups, in hostile terms, by focusing on secular-national Kemalists and erstwhile allies, the Gulenists, who, in the eyes of the AKP, attempted to defile and discredit the government.

The changing nature and ideological position of the Turkish presidency added to the process of ideological homogenization and the removal of rival ideological and power bases within the AKP government. Prior to the rise of the AKP, the Turkish presidency was designed as a typical apolitical, secular office within a European-style split executive system where the president served as the head of state. Abdullah Gul's nomination to the Turkish presidency and the subsequent referendum on constitutional changes to the presidency began a new era of centralizing state power under the AKP.[51] Abdullah Gul, a former staunch Islamist and co-founder of the AKP, was sworn in as president, which meant that both elements of the split executive were now controlled by AKP founders and ideologically uniform—reducing the incentive for conciliation with the movement and increasing the incentive for internal cohesion during the above-sketched crisis.[52] Given the AKP majority, control over both levels of the split-executive, and increasingly homogenous ideological orientation, suppression of the anti-corruption protests became a likely course of action.

As well as using state security forces to suppress protestors, the AKP's response included targeting police and judiciary officials for dismissal while simultaneously accepting the resignation of a number of ministers. This part of the government's response is also in line with the predictions of this book's core argument. Erdogan's rhetoric regarding the corruption investigations framed the crisis as a shady plot orchestrated by "dark circles" and "criminal gangs" and initiated by "organizations acting under the guise of religion but being used as the tools of certain countries."[53] This was an allusion to the Gulen movement and its founder, Fethullah Gulen, who resides in the US outside Saylorsburg, Pennsylvania, and whose students made up many parts of the Turkish bureaucracy, including in the police and courts, at that time. In reaffirming the AKP's concretizing view, Erdogan claimed in typical populist fashion that "neither the nation nor we will give permission to those who seek to settle their scores outside the ballot box." The AKP's centralized power under Erdogan and relatively (and at that time increasingly) uniform ideology incentivized Prime Minister Erdogan to concentrate on intra-AKP unity, and purge investigators and challengers as nefarious plotters.

The Turkish case presents an interesting divergence from the Indian case as well as others mentioned here, in that the anti-corruption challenge did not come from a largely apolitical prosecution force or from a bottom-up popular movement. As noted above, core elements of the Turkish state such as the judiciary had been controlled by the Kemalist elite but, following AKP actions to target Kemalist influence, some institutions fell under the influence of the Gulenist movement. Gulenists were widely seen to be behind the corruption cases as the two erstwhile allies, Erdogan and Fetullah Gulen, engaged in a power struggle through various spheres of control within the Turkish state. This power struggle itself was partly the result of ideological disagreements. The Gulenist faction desired a greater focus on liberalism, less hostility toward Israel, and a foreign policy reorientation toward western Europe and away from the Middle East. The contest was primarily, however, a struggle over power and control over the direction of the conservative Islamist movement and their shared electorate. Therefore, the AKP response to the crisis was perhaps harsher than other cases we have seen here, as the challenge was "internal" insofar as the Gulenists comprised large factions of the AKP government and base.

Indonesia

Similar to the Brazil case, the Indonesian political structure encourages a strong presidency together with a fragmented multi-party parliament. Against the exposure of corruption scandals, chiefly the Century Bank outrage that implicated senior officials in government, anti-corruption demonstrations spread across Indonesia from November 2009 onward. Chief financial officials were accused of improperly bailing out Century Bank as the bank was reportedly not facing a solvency crisis, nor needed the excess liquidity provided by the government. The crisis ensnared key ministers such as the minister of finance and the vice president. The President Susilo Bambang Yudhoyono (SBY)–led coalition government responded largely tolerantly by engaging in parliamentary investigations and hearings.

The Indonesian parliament, the People's Representative Council (DPR), has in recent years become a hallmark for coalitions from across an ideological spectrum within the country's sixteen political parties, ranging from rising conservative Islamic to secular parties, among others.[54] Cabinet positions during this time were spread equally between technocrats, including economist Boediono as vice president, and party politicians.[55] Hence SBY termed the thirty-four-member cabinet Kabinet Indonesia Bersatu (the United Indonesia Cabinet). These cabinet members hailed from parties across the ideological spectrum such as those committed to *pancasila* (five principles), the founding ideology of the Indonesian state that emphasizes pluralism, and those committed to a more assertive role for Islam in the government. Thus, the cabinet itself contained some of the ideological fault lines within Indonesian politics.[56] Meanwhile, the party under SBY's leadership, the Democratic Party, had only secured barely north of 20 percent share of the electorate.

This "United" cabinet did not ensure harmony within the government, as expected by the president, and parties within the same coalition often disagreed and even vociferously criticized the policy initiatives, thus underscoring their divergent ideological anchoring.[57] It was coalition partner parties Golkar and Prosperous Justice Party (PKS) who began a parliamentary investigation into the alleged irregularities in the bailout fund for Century Bank led by Boediono and Finance Minister Sri Mulyani.[58] This internal ideological and political power balancing within the government most plausibly played an important role in the absence of arbitrary, intolerant action against the anti-corruption demonstrations. The Democratic Party's centrist ideological roots likely played a role as well. The SBY-led Democratic Party marketed itself as centrist, reformist, and rooted in the more liberal and pluralistic ideological leanings of *pancasila*.[59] This likely encouraged a tolerant approach by avoiding framing the challenge as arising from oppositional "others." Golkar, the main coalition partner, also evolved into a more democratic party that maintains ideological diversity through a trend of factionalization.[60]

Demonstrators' criticism against the government mostly focused on the technocratic officials involved with the bailout decision, namely Finance Minister Sri Mulyani Indrawati and Vice President Boediono, rather than directly implicating President SBY in corruption.[61] This targeting of specific ministers, both of whom were technocrats, reduced the exposure of the political leadership in graft allegations, contributing to the incentive to respond tolerantly. Had the investigations directly implicated SBY and Democratic

Party officials, there perhaps would have been an incentive to respond at least partly intolerantly. Thus, a credibility crisis may encourage entrenched political players to employ junior, especially technocratic, officials as "scapegoats" to preserve the party's reputation and pacify some opposition while appearing to respond tolerantly.

Malaysia

In contrast to the Indonesian case, another study from Southeast Asia, namely Malaysia, shows an intolerant government response to the anti-corruption Bersih (clean) movement. Bersih's demonstrations began after the controversial 2008 election and against the backdrop of deteriorating economic conditions. Bersih evolved from a movement of opposition parties into a widespread, diverse effort comprised of dozens of major NGOs and political parties. The demonstrations were primarily channeling anger over government corruption, chiefly targeting the alleged embezzlement of hundreds of millions of US dollars by Prime Minister Najib Razak from the suffering 1 Malaysia Development Berhad (1MDB). This has since been deemed one of the largest corruption scandals in history. Populist Razak was the leader of the Barisan Nasional (BN) government, a conservative coalition run by the United Malays National Organization (UMNO). It is a coalition in name only (registered as a single party) with the UMNO the historically dominant player and particularly powerful since 2013.[62] The UMNO's right-wing, ultra-Malay nationalism concretized during the Razak administration, witnessing the government become a fiercer vehicle for majoritarian, or *bumiputra* (indigenous Malay), interests.[63] The party's ideological emphasis on "indigenous" ethnic Malay interests, rather than appealing to a diverse constituency, also created an incentive for intolerant response to demonstrations since an ethnic-based nationalism is fertile for the politics of division and alienation of out-groups.

The UMNO viewed the system of ethnic preferences as critical to maintaining electoral and government control.[64] Crucially, prior to the rise of anti-corruption demonstrations, the UMNO had cemented control through decades in power since Malaysia's independence, which also allowed UMNO supporters to take control over major sectors of the economy through patronage extended through privatization schemes.[65] This is reflected not only in the roster of government ministers and decision-makers but also in the co-optation of the judiciary.[66] As the traditionally ethno-nationalist cleavages have hardened since the emergence of a two-party bloc in 2008, the BN government, averring its rising nationalist suspicions, became more suppressive against the Bersih.[67] Throughout the movement's demonstrations, the government intensified its crackdown, detaining movement leaders and sympathizers under draconian anti-terrorism and anti-sedition legislation as well as shutting down websites.[68] These efforts were insufficient to quash Bersih's momentum, however, which eventually was able to end the BN/UMNO government for the first time since Malaysian independence.

Critical to bringing down the Razak government was the role of former Malaysian prime minister Mahathir Mohammed, who previously led the UMNO government. Mahathir, in a remarkable evolution, founded a new opposition party, the Malaysian United Indigenous Party (Bersatu), and allied himself with an opposition he himself had targeted while premier. Similar to the power struggle which erupted within the AKP in Turkey between rival factions, Mahathir's defection from his party represented a power struggle between two prominent UMNO figures rather than a pure fracturing along ideological lines as seen in coalition or more fissured government responses to protest movements. This new opposition alliance ended nearly six decades of UMNO rule by capitalizing on shifting power balances. Had Mahathir maintained his old party line and kept with party ranks, the Razak government could have had greater leverage through internal cohesion and sought to maintain power even in the face of electoral defeat. As an extension of the argument presented in this book, the personalization of party factionalization can facilitate internal power struggles that may manifest if the ruling party's leadership is fractured along rival centers of power and influence. These power contests demonstrate an instance in which governments primed toward intolerant responses may be unable to maintain internal cohesion and can present an opportunity to force conciliatory moves or resignation from a previously obstinate government. Arguably, we saw this type of power dispersal between the Congress Party and executive in the UPA government.

There is yet another instruction that can be extracted from the Malaysia case study which speaks to the India case. The incumbent party's long stint in government and monopolized control over Malaysian politics reduced any incentive for the UMNO government to acquiesce to outside demands. Long-term durations in power often accompany patronage networks as corruption seeps into the broader economy, a phenomenon seen widely in Malaysia (and in India). While considering the role of ideology and the diffusion of power, in future research it is also worth examining the duration and depth of dominant single-party rule, which can be seen to be settling in from the AKP in Turkey, the BJP in India, and the UMNO in Malaysia. Monopolized control and the accompanying patronage networks may act as a double-edged sword in which governments initially engage in corruption as a benefit and means of control, and later become shackled to the same linkages to avoid future punishment. Moreover, political leaders responding intolerantly likely believe the support of their political base is "sticky" since there is financial incentive within the patronage network to remain steadfast in the face of a crisis. Thus, the role of duration and depth of single-party dominance should be an additional factor of analysis when examining the role of ideas and power to make analysis of government incentives more multidimensional.

In the final two cases, from Bulgaria and Romania, we see how ideologically heterogenous elite decision-making can often capitulate to anti-corruption movements, before a checks and balances mechanism can fully produce a negotiated response.

Bulgaria

The argument presented in this book also appears to resonate with developing democracies facing significant external institutional pressures such as Bulgaria, a European Union (EU) member state. Throughout 2013 and 2014, a wave of anti-corruption protests erupted against the government led by Prime Minister Plamen Oresharski. Despite the influence of powerful external institutional actors like the European Union, Bulgaria ranked seventy-seventh in global corruption indexes with noted rampant corruption.[69] Moreover, Bulgarian governments at this time were characterized by instability, epitomized by the Oresharski cabinet being preceded and succeeded by short-lived caretaker governments and facing various large protest movements. The six previous Bulgarian governments had won against incumbents.[70] As for ideological diffusion, Bulgarian political parties represented in recent parliaments include the major center-right and center-left parties, as well as nationalist alliances, pro-Turkish minority parties, and ultra-nationalists. Notably, external actors, such as the EU, have often been ideological tools of advancement for veteran Bulgarian politicians rather than institutional constraints.[71]

The Oresharski government assumed power in May 2013 following nationwide protests over austerity measures and deteriorating economic conditions. Oresharski, a former finance minister and economist, served as the technocratic head of a coalition government that relied on the support of the center-left Bulgarian Socialist Party, the Turkish-minority-focused Movement for Rights and Freedoms, and some ministers within the ultra-nationalist Ataka Party.[72] Thus, the ideological spectrum supporting the government spanned from pro-EU, pro-minority rights stances to ethnic nationalism and Euroskepticism. As an example of the ideological contradictions inherent in this base of support, Ataka opposed the EU's efforts to force the use of the minority Turkish language in public broadcasts while the pro-ethnic Turkish party sought EU support precisely because of their protections for minority language rights.[73] Meanwhile, Oresharski himself was not a member of any political party and was considered a reformist technocrat tasked with revitalizing the Bulgarian economy. Thus, the prime minister did not have an independent political base of support to withstand potential challenges while the parliamentary base of support relied on ministers from opposite ends of the ideological and nationalist spectrum.

The Oresharski government quickly came under significant pressure from massive protests in the capital Sofia following the appointment of Delyan Peevski—a prominent media mogul and symbol for many Bulgarians of an economic elite enriched through cronyism—as the head of the Bulgarian security service.[74] Protests, some exceeding 10,000 in Sofia, continued unabated in light of persistent economic woes and controversial political appointments as Oresharski refused to step down.[75] Outrage soon erupted over the bailout of a Bulgarian bank owned by politically connected elites after a series of bank runs on vulnerable domestic financial institutions.[76] Persistent protests, EU pressure, and opposition from the Bulgarian president eventually forced the resignation of the Oresharski cabinet and forced snap elections.[77] The key moment resulting in the collapse of the government was the withdrawal of support by the Movement for Rights and Freedoms party, which deprived the government of its near-majority.[78] The diffusion of power and the coalition partner's reliance on a base of support rooted firmly in an ethnic minority led to government collapse in the face of mass protests. The government resigned, called for snap elections, and power eventually returned to the center-right coalition that had fallen before Oresharski's term.

Romania

To illustrate another example from Europe, the case of anti-corruption demonstrations in Romania and the divergent nature of the government's response closely aligns with the arguments made in this book. In early 2017, the Romanian government, led by the center-left Social Democratic Party (PSD), unveiled an executive decree to decriminalize public officials' graft offences under USD 47,500. A draft bill, which would free prisoners serving sentences of up to five years for non-violent crimes, including corruption, was also sent to parliament. These decrees and legislative attempts triggered massive anti-corruption demonstrations around Romania, notably in front of government headquarters, in the Piata Victoriei square.[79] Within a few days, the government repealed the decree with no confrontation between the movement and security forces, signaling a tolerant response.

The efforts were largely seen through partisan lenses, as one of the assumed beneficiaries of the new clemency would be PSD leader Liviu Dragnea, who held a firm grip on internal party power, was charged with corruption offenses, and had a personal stake in ensuring the PSD's attempts to decriminalize corruption succeed. The ruling coalition government was comprised of the left-wing PSD and the center-right Liberal-Democrat Alliance (ALDE), with outside support from the minority-oriented Democratic Alliance of Hungarians in Romania (UDMR). Though UDMR pledged to cooperate with the ruling coalition, their behavior suggested otherwise, and they were vocal in their criticism of the amnesty to corrupt officials, while others resigned from government as a stand against the decree.[80] The coalition government's cabinet included twenty-six ministers—the largest in seventeen years—with a mix of center-right and left politicians as well as technocrats, controlling only 53 percent of seats in parliament. Indeed, Romania's recent national politics have been filled with unstable coalitions often with mixed ideological factions along both ethnic nationalism and left–right scales.[81] There have also been semi- and full-technocratic governments during this time.[82] To add to governance instability, the government–president fraught relationship is an idiosyncrasy of the Romanian political system.[83] The Romanian president has tended to side with protestors and condemn efforts to undermine anti-corruption campaigns. These political fissures and ideological conditions prevented a more suppressive and arbitrary response to the movement.

Following subsequent elections that returned the PSD to power, however, the government doubled down on defanging anti-corruption efforts by pressuring the Romanian president to dismiss an anti-corruption investigation leader and reintroducing similar legislation that initially provoked the movement. Likewise, the government has repeatedly deployed riot police that have responded with a level of force deemed excessive by the president. Additionally, the government has pressed on despite threats from EU officials to trigger Article 7, asserting that Romania is in violation of the rule of law through their corruption decriminalization efforts. This would signal an increasingly intolerant response. Further intolerant responses may have reached a ceiling by the aforementioned electoral demands for coalitions and the inclinations of the president to reign in government excesses. Since the inception of the unresolved demonstrations, the president fully supported the anti-corruption movement while calling riot police responses excessive. Similarly, the EU criticized the PSD-led efforts through the Venice Commission's official recommendation that the supposed reforms be withdrawn and recalibrated to fit EU norms and standards.[84]

The uneven allocation of power in this context provides an interesting case study. Internal PSD politics are cemented around long-time political bosses while the PSD regularly comes in as the top vote-getter in parliamentary elections. But institutional power is also diffuse among coalition members, the split executive, and the supranational EU. In both Romania and Bulgaria, there remain continued citizen efforts to protest government corruption with mixed response.[85] Thus, the government likely fell short of current limits without risking new coalition defections and more severe rebukes from the president and the EU.

Elite Decision-Making in India: Rules, Deals, and Ideas

The performance of the Indian state varies greatly—the government successfully manages many large-scale tasks in times of crisis, while performing poorly on seemingly basic ones. The state's dismal performance in a host of basic public services has led one scholar to describe India as a "flailing state."[86] Nevertheless, the state remains central to the interface between decision-makers and civil society, from Nehruvian grand designs and distrust of the bureaucracy to citizen demands to redress corruption. This has made the Indian state, according to Lant Pritchett, Kunal Sen, and Eric Werker, a nexus of both deals (selectively enforced) and rules (impersonally enforced) between political and economic elites.[87] But both deals and rules are the result of a substantive and cognitive coalition between special interest groups, activists, bureaucrats, and politicians, which breeds divergent and dissonant elite perspectives on the state and its capacity for social and economic development—in other words, the realm of ideas. This distinction is not just semantic but has important conceptual implications, chiefly that political action, whether in economic development, as the aforementioned authors discuss, or in the political economy of government decision-making, as this book privileges, is agency centered. Consider, for example, two of the prominently featured leaders in this book, Manmohan Singh and Indira Gandhi, and their worldviews.

Leaders may not be generalizable, but their cognitive frames can be—both spatially and longitudinally. In the case of the former, we see ideas spread from institutions and countries distinct from India through transnational epistemic networks into policy design in Delhi, while in the case of the latter, Indira Gandhi very much took on the ideas of Congress Party founders and leaders into her government. Gandhi was to a large extent a product of her historical and institutional environment—selected by the party organization due to her father's prominence and the perception among party elites of her malleability. But she also ended up transforming the executive branch as well as institutions across the state, from the Supreme Court to the Election Commission, with significant, arguably negative, consequences that echo until this day. Meanwhile, Manmohan Singh, while circumscribed by the constraints of both his party and the patchwork of a coalition system, arguably changed the course of contemporary Indian politics with the 1991 reforms. In both cases, these leaders represented a particular set of ideas that became especially salient at specific critical junctures.

Ideas give leaders and decision-makers guidance on how to make sense of the world and act within it. And a plausible candidate for ideas that resonate across contexts is the concept of the nation and its constituent parts. We have observed this over many decades certainly in postcolonial contexts, with leaders such as Kemal Ataturk, Golda Meir, Gamal Abdel Nasser, and Nelson Mandela, to name but a few distinct, varied, leaders, who all leant on concepts of the nation to govern. Such leadership, and such ideas as I have mapped earlier, are particularly salient during crisis moments—from independence to droughts, regional wars, nationwide protests, economic disruptions, and more.[88] Decision-makers are therefore best seen as the vanguard of a particular set of ideas, before any rationalist rules are designed or deals are struck. After all, from literary canons to great cinema, protagonists are driven by complex emotions. Rational calculation is often found wanting, and is instead replaced by a mosaic of loyalty, lust, envy, and even guilt and conscience. These cannot be simply relegated to fiction as they resonate with us all, transcending space and time. Thus, when it comes to complex human motives, material gain in just one motivation.

I do not completely disagree with the rationalist view. There is enough evidence that for the most part such a calculus of behavior prevails in the world—but not always. My argument is that while most decision-makers often behave in the manner that rational choice models posit, there are conditions when they do not. And while rational choice models ignore the few, I believe that the few, especially those studied here such as Indira Gandhi and Manmohan Singh, have far greater effects on political life than assumed by rational choice models. Decision-makers' ideas matter and can explain both epochal reform events—like the breakup of the Soviet Union—as well as incremental reform, as in the case of liberalization in India: in other words, large effects that can result from a few. A standard riposte is, can we model this? One way would be for us to use a Poisson distribution—which captures rare events, but with large weights attached to the events. Consider, for example, the most common assertion about politicians and bureaucrats in India (and other weakly institutionalized contexts)—that they are corrupt or at least easily corruptible. But for policy to be effectively designed and executed, even a corrupt minister needs an effective bureaucrat, that is, with a clear set of ideas and plans for implementation. As we saw in Chapter 6, an effective minister, such as Narasimha Rao, with an effective set of bureaucrats and technocrats, such as Naresh Chandra and Manmohan Singh respectively, is a rare event—but when it happens one does get reforms and shifts. Uncommon events but with large consequences that are akin to a Poisson distribution.

To reduce politics, solely or even predominantly, to material interest and strategic calculations undermines what it means for a society to be democratic. Individually and collectively, it is in the exchange of ideas that we define who we are and what we hope to become. In democracies, therefore, policymaking power is largely about collective action, which involves coordination efforts and the ability to affect others' preferences to shape specific, and eventually shared, political outcomes. At a time when fake news and disinformation threaten democratic governance around the world, society and scholars need to focus even more on people's worldviews and cognitive filters: how individuals or groups see themselves, who they identify with, and the courses of action considered "legitimate" within recognized norms. Without this, certainly without regard for this process, we dilute and denigrate democracy.

As argued in this book, there are no objective readings of interests—be they votes and rents; deals or rules—without recourse to ideas. Perceptions of the outside world are mediated through ideational processes, which can take different forms. No mechanism for this deliberation took shape in the Congress government under Indira Gandhi leading up to and during the crisis she and her government faced. In fact, Gandhi's power and support in her government were such that she was able to despotically subsume all collective institutions and committees, chiefly her own cabinet, to institute the suppressive Emergency decree. Meanwhile, there was a proliferation of committees and cabinet meetings in the UPA, especially during the crisis from 2011 to 2012, which acted as one of the arenas for where we observed the ideational checks and balances take form.

Cognitive frames, therefore, make it possible for decision-makers to diagnose a crisis by acting as interpretive frameworks that describe the workings of the political, economic, and social world through defining its constitutive elements and providing a general understanding of their proper and improper causal interrelations. Hence, by deploying their ideas, decision-makers reduce courses of government action to re-establish their credibility. This is most notably the case under situations of high uncertainty.

Notes

1. Jordan Kyle and Limor Gultchin, "Populists in Power around the World," Tony Blair Institute for Global Change, November 2018,
2. Jim Mattis, upon resigning as US Secretary of Defense under the Trump administration, wrote:

   We must do everything possible to advance an international order that is most conducive to our security, prosperity and values, and we are strengthened in this effort by the solidarity of our alliances…. Because you [President Trump] have the right to have a Secretary of Defense whose views are better aligned with yours on these and other subjects, I believe it is right for me to step down from my position. (Helene Cooper, "Jim Mattis Defense Secretary, Resigns in Rebuke of Trump's Worldview," *New York Times*, December 20, 2018, https://nyti.ms/2RcR64j [accessed October 1, 2020])

3. Attorney General William P. Barr, "Remarks to the Law School and the de Nicola Center for Ethics and Culture," University of Notre Dame, October 11, 2019, https://bit.ly/2QNVVky (accessed October 1, 2020).

4. Secretary of State Michael R. Pompeo, "Being a Christian Leader," American Association of Christian Counselors, Nashville, Tennessee, October 11, 2019, https://bit.ly/2D8SE7m (accessed October 1, 2020).

5. Mudde, "The Populist Zeitgeist," 543.

6. George Orwell, *Notes on Nationalism* (London: Penguin Classics, 2018 [1945]).

7. Prashant Jha, *How the BJP Wins: Inside India's Greatest Election Machine* (New Delhi: Juggernaut, 2017); Neelanjan Sircar, "The Politics of Vishwas: Political Mobilization in the 2019 National Election," *Contemporary South Asia* 28, no. 2 (May 2020): 178–94.

8. "Lok Sabha Election Results: In Victory Speech, Narendra Modi Likens 2019 Polls to Mahabharata, Says Will Take Rivals Along Too," *News18.com*, May 23, 2019, https://bit.ly/2DcIiTW (accessed October 1, 2020). Noted Indian journalist Mihir Sharma wrote within a few hours of the election result, the "Congress has lost this election not because it failed to strike a few alliances, or because of the personality of Rahul Gandhi, or because it was poorer than the BJP and had fewer levers of influence. It lost because it has lost the ideological argument" (Mihir Sharma, "Don't Blame RG; He Is Not Why Modi Has Crushed Congress," NDTV, May 23, 2019, https://bit.ly/2Y9F79m [accessed October 1, 2020]).

9. For example, of 191 head-to-head contests between the BJP and its main rival, the Congress Party, the BJP won 175. Moreover, the average BJP candidate's winning margin thickened from 16 to 20 percent between the previous election in 2014 and 2019 (for more, see Neelanjan Sircar, "Lok Sabha Results 2019: BJP's Win Margins Rose in 2019," *Hindustan Times*, May 25, 2019, https://bit.ly/2OGRTYu [accessed October 1, 2020]).

10. Pratap Bhanu Mehta, "Staggering Dominance: The Only Authentic Analysis of This Election Is Two Words—Narendra Modi," *Indian Express*, May 24, 2019, https://bit.ly/2XR18K5 (accessed October 1, 2020). The parallels between Gandhi and Modi are striking in terms of style and structure, though not across the board. Specifically, both displayed a disregard for non-elected institutions. The idea of the dutiful and "committed civil servant" came to the fore under Indira Gandhi and that baton has been taken up by Modi, whose loyal cadre of bureaucrats have followed him from his time as chief minister of Gujarat. They both also sought to and succeeded in dominating their party organizations as embodiments of Modi and that machine's value system, and therefore the decision-makers around them are not only loyal but also ideologically aligned (among many pieces on this subject, see Guha, "Indira Gandhi to Modi").

11. Indeed, all populists must have a concrete conception of the nation; but not all nationalists are populists—in part because of the incessant move by populists to undermine and blunt independent state institutions. For example, Hindu nationalist politics at the center from 1998 to 2004, with leaders such as Atal Behari Vajpayee, did not acquire a deeply populist character. Similarly, Jawaharlal Nehru was a staunch nationalist in the Congress tradition (which he helped build) but not a populist statesman.

12. Ashutosh Varshney, "The Emergence of Right-Wing Populism in India," in *Re-Forming India: The Nation Today*, ed. Niraja Gopal Jayal, 327–45 (New Delhi: Penguin Viking, 2019). See also Christophe Jaffrelot and Louise Tillin, "Populism in India," in *The Oxford Handbook of Populism*, ed. Cristóbal Rovira Kaltwasser, Paul Taggart, Paulina Ochoa Espejo, and Pierre Ostiguy, 179–94 (Oxford: Oxford University Press, 2017).

13. As Varshney reflects on Modi's logic, "If India as a nation is collectively 'owned' by its Hindu majority, then Hindu unity has to be viewed as a necessity, conceptually and as a political project" (Varshney, "The Emergence of Right-Wing Populism in India," 337).

14. The two prominent economic policy cases, of demonetization and the goods and services tax (GST), directly hurt small and medium enterprises, traders and shopkeepers rather than the corporate sector. The politics of demonetization in particular are consistent with Modi's populism as sketched here. For more on demonetization, see Jha, *How the BJP Wins*.

15. Raghuram Rajan, "OP Jindal Distinguished Lectures with Raghuram Rajan—India's Economy: How Did We Get Here and What Can Be Done?" Watson Institute of International and Public Affairs, Brown University, October 9, 2019, https://bit.ly/2XIuJVC (accessed October 1, 2020).

16. Perhaps most notably of recent examples, income-support schemes for farmers cover *all* farmers, not just the small and marginal ones at whom it had originally been directed (Yamini Aiyar, "Modi Consolidates Power: Leveraging Welfare Politics," *Journal of Democracy* 30, no 4 [October 2019]: 78–88).

17. "A Quarter Century of India's Transformations," Center for the Advanced Study of India, University of Pennsylvania, October 12, 2017.

18. The BJP government under Modi has developed a reputation as being averse to bringing in internationally trained economists into the policymaking process (Sadanand Dhume, "Gita Gopinath and India's Brain Drain," *Wall Street Journal*, October 4, 2018, https://on.wsj.com/2OEQbXD [accessed October 1, 2020]; M. C. Govardhana Rangan, "Government Invokes Never-Used Powers to Make Urjit Patel Fall in Line," *Economic Times*, October 31, 2018, https://bit.ly/34k8WGs [accessed October 1, 2020]).

19. Alexander Hamilton, John Jay, and James Madison, *The Federalist Papers* (Springville, UT: Sweetwater Press, 2010), No. 51; Torsten Persson,

Gerard Roland, and Guido Tabellini, "Separation of Powers and Political Accountability," *The Quarterly Journal of Economics* 112, no. 4 (1997): 1163–202; Kissinger, *Diplomacy.*

20. Devesh Kapur, "Explaining Democratic Durability and Economic Performance: The Role of India's Institutions," in *Public Institutions in India: Performance and Design*, ed. Devesh Kapur and Pratap Bhanu Mehta, 28–76. (New Delhi: Oxford University Press, 2005).

21. Vaishnav, "India's Elite Institutions Are Facing a Credibility Crisis."

22. Nooruddin, *Coalition Politics.*

23. Yamini Aiyar and Louise Tillin, "'One Nation,' BJP, and the Future of Indian Federalism," *India Review* 19, no. 2 (2020): 117–35.

24. Narendra Modi, "Speech at 73rd Independence Day Celebrations," narendramodi.in, August 15, 2019, https://bit.ly/2XIvEFM (accessed October 1, 2020).

25. Jeffrey Gettleman, Kai Schultz, Sameer Yasir, and Suhasini Raj, "India's Move in Kashmir," *New York Times*, August 23, 2019, https://nyti.ms/34hMIon (accessed October 1, 2020).

26. Meenakshi Ganguly, "Restrictions, Detentions Persist in Kashmir," Human Rights Watch, October 7, 2019, https://bit.ly/2sdph1x; Sobhana K. Nair, "J&K Detentions Made in National Interest: Centre," *The Hindu*, November 20, 2019, https://bit.ly/33b3kwZ (all accessed October 1, 2020).

27. "The Impact of the Lockdowns on Human Rights in Jammu and Kashmir, August 2019–July 2020," The Forum for Human Rights in Jammu and Kashmir (Report Co-Chairs: Justice Madan Lokur and Radha Kumar), https://bit.ly/3nm8dOZ; Tariq Mir, "India Is Using the Pandemic to Intensify Its Crackdown in Kashmir," *Washington Post*, April 30, 2010, https://wapo.st/36AWvdj (all accessed October 1, 2020).

28. Under the Modi-led BJP government, there has been a rise in mob attacks against people accused of eating beef or abusing cows, an animal held sacred to Hindus. Most of those killed have been Muslims. While Modi nominated Yogi Adityanath, a Hindu warrior-priest, as chief minister of Uttar Pradesh, India's most populous state, and a springboard to national leadership. Adityanath has called India's Muslims "a crop of two-legged animals that has to be stopped" and cried at one rally, "We are all preparing for religious war!" (*New York Times*, "India's Turn toward Intolerance," July 17, 2017, https://nyti.ms/33fWENO [accessed October 1, 2020]). This treatment of Islam in the modern Hindu nationalist tradition can be traced to two classic texts: V. D. Savarkar, *Hindutva* (New Delhi: V. S. Prakashan, 1989 [1923]); M. S. Golwalkar, *We or Our Nationhood Defined* (New Delhi: K. Prakshan, 1947 [1939]). For a recent, scholarly treatment of the "ghettoization" of Muslim

voters in India, see Adnan Farooqui, "Political Representation of a Minority: Muslim Representation in Contemporary India," *India Review* 19, no. 2 (2020): 153–75.

29. The CAA bill was introduced by the BJP in 2016. It has been described as demanding

> the assimilation of India's non-Hindu minorities and has already been used by the RSS and its affiliates to justify forcing Muslims to convert to Hinduism, a process euphemistically termed "ghar wapsi" or "homecoming." It would require the assimilation of many Hindus, too, into whatever interpretation of Hinduism the state espouses. (K. Chandra, "The Triumph of Hindu Majoritarianism")

30. The NRC, most controversially, had already been used (or tested) in the northeastern state of Assam where around 2 million people, a quarter of them Muslim, were left out of the updated register. The issue of immigration in Assam came to a crescendo after 1971, when Bangladesh became an independent country amid the India–Pakistan War of that year. Bengali-speaking migrants—both Muslim and Hindu—began crossing the border into Assam, which has a diverse population comprised of hundreds of indigenous tribes belonging to several religions. The NRC aims to exclude anyone who does not have the official documentation to prove that their ancestors lived in India—a messy process given the widespread illiteracy and poverty in the country that can prove fertile ground for politicization. Amidst the controversy, BJP president and close advisor to Modi, Amit Shah, called these undocumented communities "infiltrators" and "termites" (*The Hindu*, "Infiltrators Are Termites, Will Throw Them Out: Amit Shah," April 11, 2019, https://bit.ly/2OCE4KN [accessed October 1, 2020]).

31. Sriram Lakshman, "CAA, NRC Raised during Congressional Hearing on Global Human Rights," *The Hindu*, January 29, 2020, https://bit.ly/3mAOUQO; "New Citizenship Law in India 'Fundamentally Discriminatory'," UN Human Rights Office, December 13, 2019, https://bit.ly/3kS2SNQ; *Guardian*, "India Citizenship Law: 100,000 Attend Hyderabad Protest," January 4, 2020, https://bit.ly/3egvFJj (all accessed October 1, 2020).

32. An eighty-two-page Human Rights Watch report declared that "the police, however, have been quick to arrest critics of the policy and disperse their peaceful demonstrations, including by using excessive and lethal force." Despite this, in recent months early investigations have dubiously absolved the police or ruling-party politicians from playing any role in the pogrom that took place. Human Rights Watch, "'Shoot the Traitors': Discrimination Against Muslims under India's New Citizenship Policy," HRW Report, April 9, 2020, https://

bit.ly/3mChYHw; Vijayta Lalwani, "In Delhi Riots Chargesheet, One Witness with Three Differing Claims about Kapil Mishra's Supporters," *Scroll.in*, July 26, 2020, https://bit.ly/31Z4iP5; Jeffrey Gettleman, Suhasini Raj and Sameer Yasir, "The Roots of the Delhi Riots: A Fiery Speech and an Ultimatum," *New York Times*, February 26, 2020, https://nyti.ms/2Jn3ugh (all accessed October 1, 2020).

33. *First Post*, "Kapil Mishra Leads Pro-Citizenship Amendment Act Protests in Delhi, Crowd Chants 'Shoot the Traitors'," December 21, 2019, https://bit.ly/3jNJ4tE (accessed October 1, 2020).

34. *Scroll.in*, "'The Police Told Us to Throw Stones': BBC Meets Delhi Residents Who Took Part in Communal Violence," March 4, 2020, https://bit.ly/2HUV1At; Mahender Singh Manral, "NE Delhi Riots: 800 Arrests Made as MHA Intervenes," *Indian Express*, April 13, 2020, https://bit.ly/35Sj7UE; Human Rights Watch, "Shoot the Traitors" (all accessed October 1, 2020).

35. No explanatory account is complete without close attention to local dynamics of meaning making; yet no practice is so unique as to foreclose some degree of generality (Vincent Pouliot, "Practice Tracing," in *Process Tracing: From Metaphor to Analytic Tool*, ed. Andrew Bennett and Jeffrey T. Checkel, 237–59 [New York: Cambridge University Press, 2015], 258). This type of partial generalizability enters the realm of middle-range theory. Middle-range theories deal with delimited aspects of social phenomena. Contemporary scholars have argued that this is the way forward for political science, as it is particularly well suited to building theories based on causal mechanisms through process-tracing—such as this book's research (Peter Katzenstein and Rudra Sil, *Beyond Paradigms: Analytic Eclecticism in World Politics* [New York: Palgrave Macmillan, 2010]; David Lake, "Why 'Isms' Are Evil: Theory, Epistemology, and Academics Sects as Impediments for the Iraq War," *International Studies Quarterly* 55, no. 2 [2011]: 7–52).

36. Jeff Wallenfeldt and Michael Ray, "Dilma Rousseff," *Encyclopedia Britannica*, https://bit.ly/2OCXEGJ (accessed October 1, 2020).

37. Ibid.

38. Riordan Roett, *Brazil: What Everyone Needs to Know* (Oxford: Oxford University Press, 2016), 127; M. Melo and C. Pereira, *Making Brazil Work: Checking the President in a Multiparty System* (London: Palgrave Macmillan, 2013), 167.

39. Timothy Power and Matthew Taylor, eds., *Corruption and Democracy in Brazil: The Struggle for Accountability* (Notre Dame: University of Notre Dame Press, 2011), 51.

40. Ibid.; Melo and Pereira, *Making Brazil Work*, 55.

41. Tom Lansford, ed., *Political Handbook of the World 2014* (Thousand Oaks: CQ Press, 2014), 179.

42. Timothy Power, "Continuity in a Changing Brazil: The Transition from Lula to Dilma," in *Brazil under the Workers' Party: Continuity and Change from Lula to Dilma*, ed. Fabio de Castro, Kees Koonings, and Marianne Wiesebron, 10–35 (London: Palgrave, 2014), 10.

43. Power and Taylor, *Corruption and Democracy in Brazil*, 46.

44. *The Economist*, "The Cries Are Answered," June 13, 2013, http://econ.st/2qnzDFS (accessed October 1, 2020).

45. Another illustration of the ideational heterogeneity of the coalition is found in the politics surrounding Dilma Rousseff's impeachment amidst corruption and economic scandals in 2016. Among other factors, the Brazilian Democratic Movement (PMDB) party—which anchored the governing coalition—broke from the PT and, after taking over office on an interim basis until the end of 2018, shifted the government to the ideological right. For more, see Simon Romero, "Dilma Rousseff Is Ousted as Brazil's President in Impeachment Vote," *New York Times*, August 31, 2016, http://nyti.ms/2qnzYbC (accessed October 1, 2020).

46. Daniel Gallas, "Brazil's Odebrecht Corruption Scandal," BBC News, April 17, 2019, https://bbc.in/3jgxYid (accessed October 1, 2020).

47. Ergun Ozbudun, "AKP at the Crossroads: Erdogan's Majoritarian Drift," *South European Society and Politics* 19, no. 2 (2014): pp. 155–67, 138. Indeed, the Turkish political system has become two-dimensional in recent years, encompassed by a left (secularist)–right (pro-Islamist) cleavage (Ali Carkoglu and Melvin Hinich, "A Spatial Analysis of Turkish Party Preferences," *Electoral Studies* 25, no. 2 [2006]: 369–92).

48. Menderes Cinar, "Turkey's Transformation under the AKP Rule," *The Muslim World* 96, no. 3 (2006): 469–86.

49. Tereza Capelos and Stavroula Chrona, "Islamist and Nationalistic Attachments as Determinants of Political Preferences in Turkey," *Perceptions* 17, no. 3 (Autumn, 2012): 51–80. The authors note that the AKP has not pursued overt Islamist policies, but rather has promoted a social and national vision resting on positive attachments to religion and the promotion of Islamic ethics. Indeed, leaders can often have seemingly contrasting tendencies that come together to produce populist platforms. Erdogan has mixed in neoliberalism with Islamism and elsewhere Russia's Vladimir Putin mixes Orthodox Christianity with Russian Eurasianism.

50. The AKP ideology, which had initially appealed to groups as disparate as urban liberals and some left-leaning Kurds, had reoriented further towards its Sunni

Anatolian core following crises such as the Syrian Civil War and Gezi Park protests. This reorientation reduced the influence of rival ideological wings in favor of a more ideologically homogeneous party and government.

51. Toprak Metin and Nasuh Uslu, "The Headscarf Controversy in Turkey," *Journal of Economic and Social Research* 11, no. 1 (2009): 43–67 (accessed October 1, 2020). Abdullah Gul, whose wife wears a headscarf, faced opposition from "Kemalist" institutions in the courts and military. The AKP's overt and over time rising opposition among the traditional bastions of secularism illustrate increasing ideological homogeneity within the Turkish executive.

52. Engin Sahin, "From the Declaration of the Republic to Present Presidential Election Methods in Turkey," *Turkish Journal of Politics* 4, no. 2 (Winter, 2013): pp. 87–105. Abdullah Gul was elected president by the legislature following snap elections in which the AKP increased their vote share to nearly 50 percent.

53. Orhan Coskun and Ece Toksabay, "Hit by Scandal and Resignations, Turkish PM Names New Ministers," Reuters, December 25, 2013, https://reut.rs/35oKXGa (accessed October 1, 2020).

54. Pelin A. Musil, "Emergence of a Dominant Party System after Multipartyism: Theoretical Implications from the Case of the AKP in Turkey," *South European Society and Politics* 20, no. 1 (2015): 71–92; Rodd McGibbon, "Indonesian Politics in 2006: Stability, Compromise, and Shifting Contests Over Ideology," *Bulletin of Indonesian Economic Studies* 42, no. 3 (2006): 321–40; Anies Baswedan, "Indonesian Politics in 2007: The Presidency, Local Elections, and the Future of Democracy," *Bulletin of Indonesian Economic Studies* 43, no. 3 (2007): 323–40; Rizal Sukma, "Indonesian Politics in 2009: Defective Elections, Resilient Democracy," *Bulletin of Indonesian Economic Studies* 45, no. 3 (2009): 317–36.

55. Baswedan, "Indonesian Politics in 2007," 32; Hanta Yuda, "Portrait of the Institutionalization of the Presidential System," *Indonesia 2006* (Jakarta: Indonesian Institute, 2007).

56. Leo Suryadinata, "Pancasila and the Challenge of Political Islam: Past and Present," *Trends in Southeast Asia* 14 (2018): 1–20, 7.

57. Stephen Sherlock, "The Parliament in Indonesia's Decade of Democracy: People's Forum or Chamber of Cronies," in *Problems of Democratisation in Indonesia: Elections, Institutions and Society*, ed. E. Aspinall and M. Mietzner, 160–78 (Singapore: Institute of Southeast Asian Studies, 2010), 174; Edward Aspinall, "Indonesia in 2009: Democratic Triumphs and Trials," in *Southeast Asia Affairs*, ed. Daljit Singh, 113–17 (Singapore: Institute of Southeast Asian Studies, 2010), 110.

58. Dirk Tomsa, "A Storm in a Bank Vault," *Inside Indonesia*, May 1, 2010, http://bit.ly/2qnmRr0 (accessed October 1, 2020).

59. J. T. Paige, "Indonesia Seven Years after Soeharto: Party System Institutionalization in a New Democracy," *Contemporary Southeast Asia* 28, no. 1 (2006): 88–114.

60. L. Suryadinata, "The Decline of the Hegemonic Party System in Indonesia: Golkar after the Fall of Soeharto," *Contemporary Southeast Asia* 29, no. 2 (2007): 333–58.

61. *Wall Street Journal*, "The Bailout of the Century," March 11, 2010, https://on.wsj.com/2XILIHA (accessed October 1, 2020).

62. Meredith Weiss, "Malaysia's 13th General Elections: Same Result, Different Outcome," *Asian Survey* 53, no. 6 (2013): 1135–58, 1148; William Case, "Malaysia in 2013: A Benighted Election Day (and Other Events)," *Asian Survey* 54, no. 1 (2014): 56–83, 56. One author goes as far to say that UMNO "owns" Barisan (Ajay Raina, "Why There Are No Partisan Turnovers in Malaysia: A Perspective," *Asian Survey* 56, no. 5 [2016]: 833–58, 849). UMNO performed better than ever, rising by eighty-right seats—just one seat shy of the opposition coalition Pakatan's entire total. The party's hegemony was restored.

63. Weiss, "Malaysia's 13th General Elections," 1139; Case, "Malaysia in 2013," 62; Raina, "Why There Are No Partisan Turnovers in Malaysia," 850; Clive Kessler, "Malaysia's GE13: What Happened, What Now?," *Aliran Monthly* 33, no. 4 (2013): 9–14.

64. James Chin and Joern Dosch, *Malaysia Post-Mahathir: A Decade of Change* (Singapore: Marshall Cavendish International, 2015), 17.

65. Ibid., 7.

66. Weiss, "Malaysia's 13th General Elections," 1156; Poh Ping Lee, "Malaysia in 2015: A Denouement of Sorts for the Prime Minister," *Asian Survey* 56, no. 1 (2016): 101–07, 105.

67. Case, "Malaysia in 2013," 57; Bridget Welsh, "Malaysia's Elections: A Step Backward," *Journal of Democracy* 24, no. 4 (October 2013): 136–50, 138, 144; *Financial Times*, "Malaysia Intensifies Crackdown on Anti-Corruption Protesters," November 19, 2016, http://on.ft.com/2fe8cvt (accessed October 1, 2020).

68. Human Rights Watch, "Creating a Culture of Fear: The Criminalization of Peaceful Expression in Malaysia," October 26, 2015, http://bit.ly/2oFEqG4 (accessed October 1, 2020).

69. Transparency International, "Corruption Perceptions Index 2013," 2013, https://bit.ly/2pPOka8 (accessed October 1, 2020).

70. Simeon Mitropolitski, "Balkan Politicians, Mostly Immune to the Influence of EU Integration," *Romanian Political Science Review* 14, no. 4 (2014): 367–84.

71. Ibid.

72. *The Economist*, "A New Government at Last," May 30, 2013, https://econ. st/2OgNfBw (accessed October 1, 2020).

73. Natasza Styczynska, "Non-existence of Bulgarian Party-Based Euroscepticism: Why Should We Care?" *Politeja* 33 (2015): 201–14.

74. Tsvetekia Tsolova, "Bulgarians Protests over Media Magnate as Security Chief," Reuters, June 14, 2013, https://reut.rs/2XLOonY (accessed October 1, 2020).

75. BBC News, "Peevski Protests Force Bulgaria PM Oresharski's U-turn," June 19, 2013, https://bbc.in/33bceKF (accessed October 1, 2020).

76. Jack Ewing and Georgi Kantchev, "Feud between Oligarchs Seen as Cause of Bank Run in Bulgaria," *New York Times*, June 30, 2014, https://nyti. ms/2Oe3AXM (accessed October 1, 2020).

77. Tsvetelia Tsolova and Angel Krasimirov, "Bulgaria's Prime Minister Resigns with Bank Crisis Unresolved," Reuters, July 23, 2014, https://reut.rs/2XLQIeG (accessed October 1, 2020).

78. *Deutsche Welle*, "Socialist-Backed Oresharski Cabinet Resigns in Bulgaria," July 23, 2014, https://bit.ly/2OflkSn (accessed October 1, 2020).

79. *New York Times*, "Protests Rock Romania after Government Weakens Corruption Law," February 2, 2017, http://nyti.ms/2l2DDZL (accessed October 1, 2020).

80. Radu-Sorin Marinas, "Romanian Justice Minister Quits after Graft Decree Debacle," Reuters, February 9, 2017, http://reut.rs/2qnf8cj (accessed October 1, 2020).

81. Victoria Stoiciu, "Austerity and Structural Reforms in Romania: Severe Measures, Questionable Economic Results, and Negative Social Consequences," *International Policy Analysis*, Friedrich Ebert Stiftung, August 2012; Toma Burean and Raluca Popp, "The Ideological Mapping of Political Parties in Romania," *Romanian Journal of Society and Politics* 10, no. 1 (2015): 118–36; C. Marian and R. F. King, "Perceiving the Line: The Relevance of the Left-Right Ideological Dimension for Voter Preferences in Romania," *Expert Electoral* 2 (2014): 3–18.

82. McDonnell and Valbruzzi, "Defining and Classifying Technocrat-Led and Technocrat Governments"; Stoiciu, "Austerity and Structural Reforms in Romania." The consideration and subsequent implementation of austerity measures in the last few years have brought in a more conservative quorum of public intellectuals into the government besides the more traditional socialist technocrats.

83. C. Marian and R. F. King, "A War of Two Palaces: Semi-Presidential Government and Strategic Conflict," in *Romania under Basescu: Aspirations,*

Achievements, and Frustrations during His First Presidential Term, ed. R. F. King and Paul Sum, ch. 6 (Lanham: Lexington Books, 2011).

84. European Commission for Democracy through Law, "On Amendments to the Criminal Code and the Criminal Procedure Code," Council of Europe, Opinion No. 930/2018.

85. Vladimir Mitev, "Bulgarian Protests: Battles over Anti-Corruption?" *OpenDemocracy*, July 27, 2020, https://bit.ly/35Sl97e (accessed October 1, 2020).

86. Pritchett, "Is India a Flailing State?"

87. Pritchett, Sen, and Werker, *Deals and Development*.

88. Ann Swidler and Susan Cotts Watkins, "Working Misunderstandings: Donors, Brokers, and Villagers in Africa's AIDS Industry," *Population and Development Review* 38, no. 1 (2013): 197–218.

Appendices

Table A1 Arrests and Affiliations during the Emergency, 1975–77

State/Union Territory	Arrests	MISA Arrests	Opposition Parties Members (% of MISA Arrests)	Banned Organization Members (% of MISA Arrests)	Primary Banned Organization
Andaman & Nicobar Islands	129	41	0	28 (68)	Anand Marg
Andhra Pradesh	1,586	1,135	210 (19)	512 (45)	Communist Party of India (Marxist–Leninist) (CPIML)
Arunachal Pradesh	1	0	0	0	0
Assam	2,921	533	203 (38)	143 (27)	Rashtriya Swayamsevak Sangh (RSS)
Bihar	10,107	2,360	530 (22)	269 (11)	Unknown
Chandigarh	101	27	15 (56)	6 (22)	RSS
Dadra & Nagar Haveli	3	0	0	0	0
Delhi	3,863	1,012	180 (18)	146 (14)	RSS
Goa	113	113	9 (8)	9 (8)	RSS
Gujarat	4,405	1,762	404 (23)	135 (8)	RSS
Haryana	1,279	200	172 (86)	24 (12)	Unknown
Himanchal Pradesh	688	34	17 (50)	8 (24)	RSS
Jammu and Kashmir	777	466	Unknown	Unknown	Unknown
Karnataka	4,502	487	156 (32)	165 (34)	RSS
Kerala	7,924	790	221 (28)	476 (60)	RSS
Lakshadweep	0	0	0	0	0

Contd.

Table A1 *contd.*

State/Union Territory	Arrests	MISA Arrests	Opposition Parties Members (% of MISA Arrests)	Banned Organization Members (% of MISA Arrests)	Primary Banned Organization
Madhya Pradesh	8,141	5,620	1,807 (32)	1,593 (28)	Unknown
Maharashtra	15,272	5,473	780 (14)	1,717 (31)	RSS
Manipur	459	231	14 (6)	2 (1)	RSS
Meghalaya	59	39	2 (5)	14 (36)	RSS
Mizoram	206	70	12 (17)	0	0
Nagaland	99	95	9 (9)	0	0
Orissa	1,170	408	141 (35)	112 (27)	RSS
Pondicherry	117	54	37 (69)	2 (4)	CPIML
Punjab	2,863	440	33 (8)	16 (4)	CPIML
Rajasthan	1,894	542	213 (39)	154 (28)	RSS
Sikkim	4	4	Unknown	Unknown	Unknown
Tamil Nadu	2,671	1,027	570 (56)	139 (14)	RSS
Tripura	176	77	18 (23)	9 (12)	Anand Marg
Uttar Pradesh	31,737	6,956	785 (11)	637 (9)	RSS
West Bengal	7539	4992	41 (1)	6,502 (4)	Anand Marg
TOTAL	110,806	34,988	6,579 (19)	6,356 (18)	

Source: Compiled by author from *Shah Commission Report* (Annexure XIX); and newspaper reportage.

Note: In some cases police officials did not examine group affiliation for arrest (denoted with "Unknown").

Table A2.1 UPA Coalition, Allies, and General Election Performance (Lok Sabha) in 2004 and 2009

Party	Party Type	No. of Seats (2004)	No. of Seats (2009)	Change in Seat Share
United Progressive Alliance (UPA)				
Indian National Congress (INC)	National	145	206	+61
All India Trinamool Congress (TMC)	State	2	19	+17

Contd.

Table A2.1 *contd.*

Party	Party Type	No. of Seats (2004)	No. of Seats (2009)	Change in Seat Share
Dravida Munnetra Kazhagam (DMK)	State	16	18	+2
Nationalist Congress Party (NCP)	National	9	9	-
Rashtriya Janata Dal (RJD)	National	24	4	-20
Jammu and Kashmir National Conference (JKNC)	State	2	3	+1
Janata Dal (Secular) (JD[S])	State	3	3	-
Jharkhand Mukti Morcha (JMM)	State	-	2	+2
Muslim League Kerala State Committee (MUL)	State	1	2	+1
Telangana Rashtra Samithi (TRS)	State	5	n.a.	-5
Independent and other parties (<2 seats)	State	12	12	-
UPA TOTAL		**219**	**278**	**+59**
External Allies				
Samajwadi Party (SP)	State	36	23	-13
Bahujan Samaj Party (BSP)	National	19	21	+2
UPA and ALLIES TOTAL		**274**	**322**	**+48**
Left Parties				
Communist Party of India (Marxist) (CPI[M])	National	43	n.a.	-43
Communist Party of India (CPI)	National	9	n.a.	-9
Revolutionary Socialist Party (RSP)	State	3	n.a.	-3
All India Forward Bloc (FBL)	State	3	n.a.	-3
Other parties (<2 seats)	State	3	n.a.	-3
TOTAL UPA SUPPORT		**335**	**322**	**-13**

Sources: Compiled by author from Election Commission of India website; Lok Sabha website; newspaper reportage.

Notes: Many of the UPA's coalition allies in 2004 were no longer part of the 2009 coalition (denoted with "n.a.").

Table A2.2 Indian National Congress (INC) Party Seats and Vote Percentages in Coalition Era (1989–2009)

Year	2009	2004	1999	1998	1996	1991	1989
Seats	206	145	114	141	140	232	197
Vote Percentage (%)	28.55	26.69	28.3	25.82	29.7	36.5	39.5

Source: Compiled by author from historical reports of the Election Commission of India.

Table A3.1 Exploratory Elite Interviews

Title	Organization	Location	Date
Political Scientist	Jawaharlal Nehru University (JNU)	Delhi	June 3, 2012
Lawyer	Private practice	Delhi	June 4, 2012
IAS officer	Ministry of Commerce and Industry	Delhi	June 5, 2012
Civil society activist	India Against Corruption (IAC)	Delhi	June 6, 2012
Member of Parliament (Rajya Sabha)	Indian National Congress (INC)	Delhi	June 10, 2012
Economist	Indian School of Business (ISB)	Delhi	June 12, 2012
CEO	Major multinational company	Delhi	June 13, 2012
Member of Parliament (Lok Sabha)	INC	Delhi	June 17, 2012
IAS officer	Ministry of Panchayati Raj	Delhi	June 21, 2012
Civil society activist	IAC	Delhi	June 25, 2012
Politician	Bharatiya Janata Party (BJP)	Delhi	3 July 2012
Member	National Advisory Council (NAC)	Delhi	July 10, 2012
Civil society activist	IAC	Delhi	July 13, 2012

Table A3.2 Interviews with Elite Respondents

Code (Del-)	Title	Organization	Location	Date
55	President	PRS Legislative Research (PRS)	Delhi	March 10, 2015
1	Founding member	Aam Aadmi Party (AAP) [India Against Corruption (IAC)]	Delhi	March 11, 2015
56	Vice president	Observer Research Foundation (ORF)	Delhi	March 11, 2015

Contd.

Table A3.2 *contd.*

Code (Del–)	Title	Organization	Location	Date
57	Economist	Jawaharlal Nehru University (JNU)	Delhi	March 12, 2015
72	Co-founder	Association for Democratic Reforms (ADR)	Delhi	March 13, 2015
2	Official	AAP [IAC]	Delhi	March 15, 2015
3	National spokesperson	Indian National Congress (INC)	Delhi	March 16, 2015
37	CEO	Large hedge fund	Delhi	March 17, 2015
58	Chairman	Brookings	Delhi	March 17, 2015
59	Senior consultant	National Institute of Public Finance and Policy (NIPFP)	Delhi	March 17, 2015
4	Senior advisor	United Progressive Alliance (UPA)	Delhi	March 18, 2015
38	Former Secretary General	Federation of Indian Chambers of Commerce and Industry (FICCI)	Delhi	March 18, 2015
78	Deputy Chief of Mission	Embassy of an Indian ally nation	Delhi	March 18, 2015
60	Senior Fellow	NIPFP	Delhi	March 19, 2015
5	Minister of State	UPA	Delhi	March 20, 2015
2b	Official	AAP [IAC]	Delhi	March 20, 2015
15	IAS officer	Ministry of Communications	Delhi	March 22, 2015
6	Advisor to minister	Ministry of Power, Coal, and Renewable Energy	Delhi	March 23, 2015
7	Member of Parliament	INC	Delhi	March 25, 2015
8	Minister of State	INC	Delhi	March 25, 2015
9	Member of Parliament	UPA	Delhi	March 25, 2015
10	Senior official	Planning Commission	Delhi	March 26, 2015
11	Cabinet minister	INC	Delhi	March 28, 2015
79	Journalist	*Times of India*	Delhi	March 30, 2015

Contd.

Table A3.2 *contd.*

Code (Del-)	Title	Organization	Location	Date
80	Journalist	Independent	Delhi	March 31, 2015
39	Senior official	Confederation of Indian Industry (CII)	Delhi	April 1, 2015
40	Senior official	Leading lobbying firm	Delhi	April 1, 2015
79b	Journalist	*Times of India*	Delhi	April 1, 2015
12	Cabinet minister	INC	Delhi	April 5, 2015
41	Senior official	GTI Group	Delhi	April 5, 2015
89	Civil society activist	IAC	Delhi	April 6, 2015
89b	Civil society activist	IAC	Delhi	April 6, 2015
13	Official	UPA	Delhi	April 7, 2015
14	Senior official	National Advisory Council (NAC)	Delhi	April 7, 2015
42	Representative	Intel	Delhi	April 7, 2015
15	Senior advisor	INC	Delhi	April 8, 2015
16	Senior advisor	Bharatiya Janata Party (BJP)	Delhi	April 9, 2015
43	Senior representative	Walmart	Delhi	April 9, 2015
72b	Co-founder	ADR	Delhi	April 10, 2015
89c	Civil society activist	IAC	Delhi	April 11, 2015
44	Senior official	FICCI	Delhi	April 13, 2015
75b	Official	NAC	Delhi	April 13, 2015
39b	Senior official	CII	Delhi	April 14, 2015
81	Senior journalist	*Caravan Magazine*	Delhi	April 14, 2015
61	Director	Centre for the Study of Developing Societies (CSDS)	Delhi	April 15, 2015
82	Journalist	*Indian Express*	Delhi	April 15, 2015
17	Senior advisor	Niti Ayog	Delhi	April 16, 2015
62	Professor	Delhi School of Economics (DSE)	Delhi	April 16, 2015
18	Former Chief Commissioner	Election Commission	Delhi	April 17, 2015

Contd.

Table A3.2 *contd.*

Code (Del–)	Title	Organization	Location	Date
17b	Senior advisor	Niti Ayog	Delhi	April 17, 2015
63	President	Centre for Policy Research (CPR)	Delhi	April 17, 2015
73	Director	Accountability Initiative	Delhi	April 18, 2015
19	Former media advisor	Prime Minister's Office (PMO)	Delhi	April 20, 2015
8b	Minister of State	INC	Delhi	April 21, 2015
74	Senior official	Janaagraha	Delhi	April 21, 2015
64	Former Deputy Governor	Reserve Bank of India (RBI)	Delhi	April 22, 2015
20	Former Governor	RBI	Delhi	April 23, 2015
21	Former National Security Advisor	PMO	Delhi	April 23, 2015
45	Senior official	Reckitt Benckiser	Delhi	April 23, 2015
22	Former Governor	RBI	Delhi	April 24, 2015
23	IAS officer	Ministry of Science and Technology	Delhi	April 24, 2015
46	Former Deputy Secretary General	FICCI	Delhi	April 25, 2015
26	Cabinet minister	INC	Delhi	April 25, 2015
82b	Senior journalist	*Indian Express*	Delhi	April 26, 2015
27	Former Cabinet Secretary	INC	Delhi	April 27, 2015
65	Senior Fellow	CPR	Delhi	April 27, 2015
83	Senior journalist	BBC	Delhi	April 27, 2015
66	Director	NIPFP	Delhi	April 28, 2015
84	Senior journalist	*Hindustan Times*	Delhi	April 28, 2015
75	Official	NAC	Delhi	April 29, 2015
85	Senior journalist	CNN-IBN	Delhi	April 29, 2015
79c	Senior journalist	*Times of India*	Delhi	April 30, 2015
86	Editor	Leading current affairs magazine	Delhi	April 30, 2015

Contd.

Table A3.2 *contd.*

Code (Del-)	Title	Organization	Location	Date
28	Former Chief Economic Advisor	PMO	Delhi	May 1, 2015
29	Member of Parliament	Biju Janata Dal (BJD)	Delhi	May 1, 2015
67	Senior Fellow	Brookings	Delhi	May 1, 2015
80b	Senior journalist	Independent	Delhi	May 2, 2015
24	IAS officer	Ministry of Finance	Delhi	May 2, 2015
30	Official	AAP [IAC]	Delhi	May 2, 2015
31	Senior official	AAP [IAC]	Delhi	May 3, 2015
76	Official	Rajiv Gandhi Mahila Vikas Pariyojana (RGMVP)	Delhi	May 3, 2015
47	Senior official	Aditya Birla Group (ABG)	Mumbai	May 4, 2015
48	Senior official	McCann World Group	Mumbai	May 4, 2015
49	Senior official	Rio Tinto	Mumbai	May 5, 2015
32	Former Information Commissioner	Central Information Commission (CIC)	Mumbai	May 6, 2015
68	CEO	IDFC	Mumbai	May 6, 2015
87	Journalist	*Financial Times*	Mumbai	May 6, 2015
50	Senior official	The Federal Bank Ltd.	Mumbai	May 7, 2015
51	Senior official	Reliance Industries	Mumbai	May 7, 2015
69	Senior Fellow	ORF	Mumbai	May 7, 2015
70	Co-founder	Gateway House	Mumbai	May 8, 2015
52	Senior official	The Chatterjee Group (TCG)	Mumbai	May 8, 2015
53	Official	NAC	Delhi	May 11, 2015
77	Executive Director	Population Foundation	Delhi	May 12, 2015
24b	IAS officer	Ministry of Finance	Delhi	May 13, 2015
88	Editor	Leading national newspaper	Delhi	May 13, 2015
71	Chairman	Centre for Policy Alternatives (CPA)	Delhi	May 14, 2015
25	IAS officer	Ministry of Agriculture	Delhi	May 15, 2015

Contd.

Table A3.2 *contd.*

Code (Del-)	Title	Organization	Location	Date
25b	IAS officer	Ministry of Home Affairs	Delhi	May 16, 2015
33	Cabinet minister	INC	Delhi	May 16, 2015
34	Cabinet minister	INC	Delhi	May 18, 2015
84b	Consultant	UPA	Delhi	May 18, 2015
10b	Cabinet minister	INC	Delhi	May 20, 2015
36	Cabinet minister	INC	Delhi	May 22, 2015
36b	Senior official	NAC	Delhi	May 23, 2015
35	Senior official	Planning Commission	Delhi	May 26, 2015
54	Senior advisor	UPA	Delhi	May 26, 2015

Table A3.3 Focus Groups

Code	Occupation	Participants	Location	Date
2015-fgINTL	Public intellectuals	4	Delhi	April 6, 2015
2015-fgNGOW	NGO workers	5	Delhi	April 10, 2015
2015-fgPRIJ	Print journalists	6	Delhi	April 14, 2015
2015-fgONLJ	Online journalists	5	Delhi	April 22, 2015
2015-fgACTV	Civil society activists	5	Delhi	May 3, 2015
2015-fgBUSN	Small- and medium-sized business owners	5	Delhi	May 20, 2015
2015-fgBURC	Bureaucrats	5	Delhi	May 21, 2015

Table A4.1 Congress Cabinet Ministers and Their Backgrounds, 1971–75

Name	Party Affiliation	Portfolio	Professional Background	Location of Study
		Cabinet Ministers		
Indira Gandhi (Prime Minister)	Congress (R)	Planning; Atomic Energy; Defence; Information and Broadcasting	Party politician	UK
Y. B. Chavan	Congress (R)	External Affairs; Finance	Party politician	India
Uma Shankar Dikshit	Congress (R)	Home Affairs	Party politician	India

Contd.

Table A4.1 *contd.*

Name	Party Affiliation	Portfolio	Professional Background	Location of Study
K. Brahmananda Reddy	Congress (R)	Home Affairs	Party politician	India
H. R. Gokhale	Congress (R)	Law and Justice	Technocrat	India
Swaran Singh	Congress (R)	External Affairs; Defence	Party politician	India
Jagjivan Ram	Congress (R)	Agriculture and Irrigation; Defence	Party politician	India
Bansi Lal	Congress (R)	Defence	Party politician	India
C. Subramaniam	Congress (R)	Finance	Party politician	India
D. P. Dhar	Congress (R)	Planning	Party politician	India
T. A. Pai	Congress (R)	Industries	Technocrat	India
L. N. Mishra	Congress (R)	Railways	Party politician	India
Kamalapati Tripathi	Congress (R)	Railways	Party politician	India
K. Hanumanthaiya	Congress (R)	Railways	Party politician	India
S. S. Ray	Congress (R)	Education and Social Welfare	Party Politician	India
Fakhruddin Ali Ahmed	Congress (R)	Food and Agriculture	Party politician	UK
V. C. Shukla	Congress (R)	Information and Broadcasting	Party politician	India
I. K. Gujral	Congress (R)	Information and Broadcasting	Party politician	India
Mohan Kumaramangalam	Congress (R)	Steel and Heavy Engineering	Party politician	UK
D. P. Chattopadhyaya	Congress (R)	Commerce	Party politician	India
Kotha Raghuramaiah	Congress (R)	Parliamentary Affairs	Party politician	India

Contd.

Table A4.1 *contd.*

Name	Party Affiliation	Portfolio	Professional Background	Location of Study
Moinul Haq Choudhury	Congress (R)	Industrial Development	Party politician	India
Raj Bahadur	Congress (R)	Tourism and Civil Aviation	Party politician	India
Karan Singh	Congress (R)	Health and Family Planning	Party politician	India
K. K. Shah	Congress (R)	Health and Family Planning	Party politician	India

Ministers of State

Name	Party Affiliation	Portfolio	Professional Background	Location of Study
K. L. Rao	Congress (R)	Irrigation and Power	Party politician	UK
L. N. Mishra	Congress (R)	Foreign Trade	Party politician	India
R. K. Khadilkar	Congress (R)	Labour and Rehabilitation	Party politician	India
Sushila Rohatgi	Congress (R)	Finance	Party politician	India
I. K. Gujral	Congress (R)	Works, Housing, and Urban Development	Party politician	India
Sher Singh	Congress (R)	Communications	Party politician	India
K. V. Raghunath Reddy	Congress (R)	Company Law Affairs	Party politician	India
D. R. Chavan	Congress (R)	Petroleum, Chemicals, and Non-ferrous Metals	Party politician	India
Nitiraj Singh	Congress (R)	Petroleum, Chemicals, and Non-ferrous Metals	Party politician	India
Om Mehta	Congress (R)	Home Affairs and Parliamentary Affairs	Party politician	India
R. N. Mirdha	Congress (R)	Home Affairs; Department of Energy	Party politician	India
K. C. Pant	Congress (R)	Home Affairs; Electronics, Atomic Energy and Department of Science	Party politician	India

Contd.

Table A4.1 *contd.*

Name	Party Affiliation	Portfolio	Professional Background	Location of Study
Nandini Satpathy	Congress (R)	Information and Broadcasting	Party politician	India
P. C. Sethi	Congress (R)	Defence Production	Party politician	India
Annasaheb Shinde	Congress (R)	Food and Agriculture	Party politician	India
V. C. Shukla	Congress (R)	Finance	Party politician	India
K. R. Ganesh	Congress (R)	Finance	Party politician	India
A. K. Kisku	Congress (R)	Health	Party politician	India
Sarojini Mahishi	Congress (R)	Tourism and Civil Aviation	Party politician	India
Jagannath Pahadia	Congress (R)	Supplies	Party politician	India
Mohammad Shafi Qureshi	Congress (R)	Steel and Heavy Engineering	Party politician	India
K. S. Ramaswamy	Congress (R)	Home Affairs	Party politician	India
Siddheshwar Prasad	Congress (R)	Education	Technocrat	India
Surendra Pal Singh	Congress (R)	External Affairs	Party politician	India

Source: Compiled by author from newspaper reportage; Foreign and Commonwealth Office (FCO) Records (South Asia), FCO 37, 815, 1971, The National Archives (TNA), Kew, Richmond, UK.

Notes: 1. INC, as it is now, was then the Congress (R) faction (see Chapters 3 and 4 for details); 2. Prime Minister Gandhi did not complete her undergraduate studies at Oxford; 3. During this administration, Indira Gandhi shuffled cabinet portfolios around with a high rate of attrition (often every few months), hence the repetition of departments in the table; 4. Some cabinet ministers would move to different roles during this administration, namely Fakhruddin Ali Ahmed (President of India) and S. S. Ray (Chief Minister of West Bengal); 5. L. N. Mishra died acrimoniously in January 1975 (see Chapter 3 for details).

Table A4.2   UPA Cabinet Ministers and Their Backgrounds, 2009–12

Name	Party Affiliation	Portfolio	Professional Background	Location of Study
		Cabinet Ministers		
Manmohan Singh (Prime Minister)	Indian National Congress (INC)	Atomic Energy; Space; Personnel, Public Grievances, and Pensions; Planning	Technocrat	UK
Sharad Pawar	Nationalist Congress Party (NCP)	Agriculture; Food Processing Industries	Party politician	India
M. K. Alagiri	Dravida Munnetra Kazhagam (DMK)	Chemicals and Fertilisers	Party politician	India
Anand Sharma	INC	Commerce and Industry; Textiles	Party politician	India
Kapil Sibal	INC	Communications and Information Technology; Human Resource Development	Technocrat	US
K. V. Thomas	INC	Consumer Affairs, Food, and Public Distribution; Agriculture	Technocrat	India
Kumari Selja	INC	Culture; Housing and Urban Poverty Alleviation; Social Justice and Empowerment	Party politician	India
A. K. Anthony	INC	Defence	Party politician	India
Paban Singh Ghatowar	INC	Development of Northeastern Region	Party politician	India
S. M. Krishna	INC	External Affairs	Party politician	US
Pranab Mukherjee	INC	Finance	Party politician	India
Ghulam Nabi Azad	INC	Health and Family Welfare	Party politician	India

Contd.

Table A4.2 *contd.*

Name	Party Affiliation	Portfolio	Professional Background	Location of Study
Praful Manohar Patel	NCP	Heavy Industries and Public Enterprises	Party politician	India
P. Chidambaram	INC	Home Affairs; Finance	Technocrat	US
Ambika Soni	INC	Information and Broadcasting	Party politician	India
Mallikarjun Kharge	INC	Labour and Employment	Party politician	India
Salman Khurshid	INC	Law and Justice; External Affairs	Technocrat	UK
Dinsha Patel	INC	Mines	Party politician	India
Farooq Abdullah	Jammu & Kashmir National Conference (JKNC)	New and Renewable Energy	Party politician	India
Mamata Banerjee	Trinamool Congress (TMC)	Railways	Party politician	India
Meira Kumar	INC	Social Justice and Empowerment	Party politician	India
Murli Deora	INC	Petroleum and Natural Gas; Corporate Affairs	Technocrat	India
B. K. Handique	INC	Development of North Eastern Region; Mines	Party politician	India
Dayanidhi Maran	DMK	Textiles	Party politician	India
A. Raja	DMK	Communications and Technology	Party politician	India
Virbhadra Singh	INC	Steel	Party politician	India
M. S. Gill	INC	Youth Affairs and Sport	Party politician	India
Kantilal Bhuria	INC	Tribal Affairs	Party politician	India

Contd.

Table A4.2 *contd.*

Name	Party Affiliation	Portfolio	Professional Background	Location of Study
M. M. Pallam Raju	INC	Human Resource Development; Defence	Party politician	US
Ashwani Kumar	INC	Law and Justice	Technocrat	India
Harish Rawat	INC	Water Resources; Labour and Employment	Party politician	India
Chandresh Kumari Katoch	INC	Culture	Party politician	India
Vayalar Ravi	INC	Overseas Indian Affairs	Party politician	India
V. K. Chandra Deo	INC	Panchayati Raj; Tribal Affairs	Party politician	India
K. Rahman Khan	INC	Minority Affairs	Party politician	India
Pawan Kumar Bansal	INC	Parliamentary Affairs; Water Resources; Railways	Technocrat	India
S. Jaipal Reddy	INC	Petroleum and Natural Gas; Science and Technology and Earth Sciences	Party politician	India
Sushil Kumar Shinde	INC	Power	Party politician	India
Dinesh Trivedi	TMC	Railways	Party politician	US
C. P. Joshi	INC	Road, Transport, and Highways	Technocrat	India
Jairam Ramesh	INC	Rural Development; Environment and Forests	Technocrat	US
G. K. Vasan	INC	Shipping	Party politician	India
M. B. Wasnik	INC	Social Justice and Empowerment	Party politician	India
B. P. Verma	INC	Steel	Party politician	India
Vilasrao Deshmukh	INC	Heavy Industries and Public Enterprises	Party politician	India

Contd.

Table A4.2 *contd.*

Name	Party Affiliation	Portfolio	Professional Background	Location of Study
S. K. Sahay	INC	Tourism	Party politician	India
M. Veerappa Moily	INC	Petroleum and Natural Gas; Law and Justice	Party politician	India
Kamal Nath	INC	Urban Development; Parliamentary Affairs; Road Transport and Highways	Party politician	India
Ajay Maken	INC	Youth Affairs and Sport; Housing and Urban Poverty Alleviation	Party politician	India
Ministers of State				
Vayalar Ravi	INC	Civil Aviation	Party politician	India
Pratik Patil	INC	Coal; Heavy Industries and Public Enterprises	Party politician	India
M. Veerappa Moily	INC	Corporate Affairs	Party politician	India
Vilasrao D. Deshmukh	INC	Earth Sciences; Science and Technology	Party politician	India
Jayanthi Natarajan	INC	Environment and Forests	Party politician	India
Virbhadra Singh	INC	Micro, Small, and Medium Enterprises	Party politician	India
Ajay Maken	INC	Home Affairs	Party politician	India
Manish Tewari	INC	Information and Broadcasting	Party politician	India
Praful Manohar Patel	NCP	Civil Aviation	Party politician	India
Dinsha Patel	INC	Micro, Small, and Medium Enterprises	Party politician	India
Sriprakash Jaiswal	INC	Coal; Statistics and Programme Implementation	Party politician	India

Contd.

Table A4.2 *contd.*

Name	Party Affiliation	Portfolio	Professional Background	Location of Study
K. Chiranjeevi	INC	Tourism	Party politician	India
Jyotiraditya M. Scindia	INC	Power; Commerce and Industry	Party politician	U.S.
K. H. Muniyappa	INC	Micro, Small, and Medium Enterprises; Railways	Party politician	India
Bharatsinh M. Solanki	INC	Drinking Water and Sanitation; Power	Party politician	India
Salman Khurshid	INC	Minority Affairs; Corporate Affairs	Technocrat	UK
V. Narayanaswamy	INC	Planning; Parliamentary Affairs	Party politician	India
S. K. Jena	INC	Statistics and Programme Implementation; Chemicals and Fertilisers	Party politician	India
Sachin Pilot	INC	Corporate Affairs; Communications and Information Technology	Party politician	US
Jitendra Singh	INC	Youth Affairs and Sports	Party politician	India
Krishna Tirath	INC	Women and Child Development	Party politician	India
Shashi Tharoor	INC	Human Resource Development; External Affairs	Technocrat	US
Kodikunnil Suresh	INC	Labour and Employment	Party politician	India
Prithviraj Chavan	INC	Science and Technology; Earth Sciences; Prime Minister's Office; Personnel, Public Grievances and Pensions; Parliamentary Affairs	Technocrat	US
Tariq Anwar	NCP	Agriculture and Food Processing	Party politician	India

Contd.

Table A4.2 *contd.*

Name	Party Affiliation	Portfolio	Professional Background	Location of Study
K. J. Surya Prakash Reddy	INC	Railways	Party politician	India
Ranee Narah	INC	Tribal Affairs	Party politician	India
Adhir Ranjan Chowdhury	INC	Railways	Party politician	India
A. H. Khan Choudhury	INC	Health and Family Welfare	Party politician	Canada
Sarvey Sathyanarayana	INC	Road Transport and Highways	Party politician	India
Ninong Ering	INC	Minority Affairs	Party politician	India
Deepa Dasmunsi	INC	Urban Development	Party politician	India
Porika Balram Naik	INC	Social Justice and Empowerment	Party politician	India
Kruparani Killi	INC	Communications and Information Technology	Party politician	India
Lalchand Kataria	INC	Defense	Party politician	India
E. Ahamed	IUML	External Affairs; Railways	Party politician	India
D. Purandeswari	INC	Commerce and Industry; Human Resource Development	Party politician	India
Jitin Prasada	INC	Defense and Human Resource Development; Petroleum and Natural Gas	Party politician	India
S. Jagathrakshakan	DMK	New and Renewable Energy	Party politician	India
R. P. N. Singh	INC	Home Affairs; Road Transport and Highways	Party politician	India
K. C. Venugopal	INC	Civil Aviation	Party politician	India
Rajeev Shukla	INC	Parliamentary Affairs and Planning	Party politician	India

Contd.

Table A4.2 *contd.*

Name	Party Affiliation	Portfolio	Professional Background	Location of Study
Mahadev Khandela	INC	Road Transport and Highways	Party politician	India
Jitin Prasada	INC	Petroleum and Natural Gas; Road Transport and Highways	Party politician	India
Namo Narain Meena	INC	Finance	Bureaucrat	India
Mullappally Ramachandran	INC	Home Affairs	Party politician	India
Agatha Sangma	NCP	Rural Development	Party politician	UK
Harish Rawat	INC	Parliamentary Affairs	Party politician	India
Pradeep Jain	INC	Rural Development	Party politician	India
Pranabaka Lakshmi	INC	Textiles	Party politician	India
Gurudas Kamat	INC	Communications and Information Technology	Party politician	India
A. Sai Prathap	INC	Steel	Party politician	India
Tushar A. Chaudhary	INC	Tribal Affairs	Party politician	India
Vincent Pala	INC	Water Resources	Party politician	India
Arun Yadav	INC	Youth Affairs and Sports	Party politician	India
Sisir Adhikari	TMC	Rural Development	Party politician	India
Saugata Ray	TMC	Urban Development	Party politician	India
Sultan Ahmed	TMC	Tourism	Party politician	India
Mukul Roy	TMC	Shipping	Party politician	India

Contd.

Table A4.2 *contd.*

Name	Party Affiliation	Portfolio	Professional Background	Location of Study
Mohan Jatua	TMC	Information and Broadcasting	Bureaucrat	India
S. S. Palanimanickam	DMK	Finance	Party politician	India
D. Napoleon	DMK	Social Justice and Empowerment	Party politician	India
S. Gandhiselvan	DMK	Health and Family Welfare	Party politician	India
Preneet Kaur	INC	External Affairs	Party politician	India
Dinesh Trivedi	TMC	Health and Family Welfare	Party politician	US

Sources: Compiled by author from election affidavits posted on myneta.info; profiles on archive.india.gov.in; and newspaper reportage.

Note: Repetition of departments in the table represents portfolios being shifted to (or simultaneously managed by) ministers during the period outlined.

Table A4.3   National Advisory Council (NAC), 2004–14

Name	Professional Background	Location of Study
Sonia Gandhi (Chairperson)	Party politician	Italy
Mihir Shah	Bureaucrat	India
Narendra Jadhav	Technocrat	US
Ashis Mondal	Technocrat	India
Pramod Tandon	Technocrat	India
Deep Joshi	Activist	US
Farah Naqvi	Activist	US
N. C. Saxena	Bureaucrat	India
Anu Agha	Technocrat	India
A. K. Shiva Kumar	Technocrat	US
Mirai Chatterjee	Technocrat	US
Virginius Xaxa	Technocrat	India

Contd.

Table A4.3 *contd.*

Name	Professional Background	Location of Study
Aruna Roy	Activist	India
M. S. Swaminathan	Technocrat	US
Yogendra Yadav	Technocrat	India
Ram Dayal Munda	Technocrat	US
Jean Dreze	Technocrat	UK
Harsh Mander	Activist	India
Madhav Gadgil	Technocrat	US
Jayaprakash Narayan	Bureaucrat	India

Source: Compiled by author from newspaper reports and interview sources.

Notes: 1. Not all members remained in the NAC during its entire tenure; 2. Some departed and returned, while others often remained informal advisors after leaving.

Bibliography

Primary Sources

Archives

Nehru Memorial Museum and Library, New Delhi, India

B. K. Nehru Papers
Henry Austin Papers
Jayaprakash Narayan Papers
P. N. Haksar Papers
Oral History Transcripts: Charan Singh
Oral History Transcripts: I. K. Gujral
Oral History Transcripts: Jayaprakash Narayan
Oral History Transcripts: Madhu Dandavate

National Archives of India, New Delhi, India

All India Radio Records
Ministry of Home Affairs Records
Prime Minister's Secretariat/Office Records

National Archives, Kew, Richmond, UK (Foreign and Commonwealth Office)

Foreign and Commonwealth Office Records (South Asia)
Foreign and Commonwealth Office Records (Information Research)

National Archives, College Park, MD, USA (State Department Records)

General Records of the Department of State (Office of Chief of Protocol)
General Records of the Department of State (Briefing Books)
General Records of the Department of State (Visit Files)
General Records of the Department of State (Central Foreign Policy Files)

University of Chicago, Chicago, US (Center for Research Libraries)

Limaye Papers

Asian and African Studies, British Library, London, UK

Vellore College and Hospital Papers
W. G. Archer and Mildred Archer Papers

Periodicals

Everyman's Weekly (archive available at Memorial Library, University of Wisconsin-
   Madison; R.K. Misra for Lok Niti Parishad).
Times of India (archive available online; Bennett, Coleman & Co. Ltd).

Secondary Sources

Abbott, Kenneth W., and Duncan Snidal. "International 'Standards' and International
   Governance." *Journal of European Public Policy* 8, no. 3 (2001): 345–70.
Acemoglu, D., and J. Robinson. *Why Nations Fail: Power, Prosperity and Poverty*.
   New York: Crown, 2012.
Acemoglu, Daron, and James A. Robinson. *Economic Origins of Dictatorship and
   Democracy*. New York: Cambridge University Press, 2006.
Advani, L. K. *A Prisoner's Scrap-Book*. New Delhi: Prabhat Prakashan, 2016.
Ahluwalia, Isher Judge, and I. M. D. Little. *India's Economic Reforms and Development:
   Essays for Manmohan Singh*. New Delhi: Oxford University Press, 2012.
Ahluwalia, Montek Singh. *Backstage: The Story behind India's High Growth Years*.
   New Delhi: Rupa, 2020
Aidt, T., M. A. Golden, and D. Tiwari. "Incumbents and Criminals in the Indian
   National Legislature." Mimeo, University of California-Los Angeles, 2013.
Aiyar, Shankkar. *Accidental India: A History of the Nation's Passage through Crisis and
   Change*. New Delhi: Aleph Books, 2012.
Aiyar, Yamini. "Modi Consolidates Power: Leveraging Welfare Politics." *Journal of
   Democracy*, 30(4) (October 2019).
Aiyar, Yamini, and Louise Tillin. "'One Nation,' BJP, and the Future of Indian
   Federalism." *India Review* 19, no. 2 (2020): 117–35.
Alexander, P. C. *Through the Corridors of Power: An Insider's Story*. New Delhi:
   Harper Collins India, 2004
Ali, Tariq. *The Nehrus and the Gandhis: An Indian Dynasty*. London: Picador, 1985.

Andeweg, R. B. "Ministers as Double Agents? The Delegation Process between Cabinet and Ministers." *European Journal of Political Research* 3, no. 37 (2000): 377–95.

Andeweg, R. B., and A. Timmermans. "Conflict Management in Coalition Government." In *Cabinets and Coalition Bargaining: The Democratic Life Cycle in Western Europe*, edited by K. Strom, W. C. Muller, and T. Bergman, 269–300. (Oxford: Oxford University Press, 2008.

Appu, P. S. *Land Reforms in India: A Survey of Policy, Legislation, and Implementation*. New Delhi: Vikas Publishing House, 1996.

Arestis, Philip and Malcolm Sawyer. *A Biographical Dictionary of Dissenting Economists*. Cheltenham: Edward Elgar Publications, 2001.

Asch, S. E. "Effects of Group Pressure upon the Modification and Distortion of Judgments." In *Groups, Leadership and Men: Research in Human Relations*, edited by H. Guetzkow, 177–90. Pittsburg: Carnegie Press, 1951.

Aspinall, Edward. "Indonesia in 2009: Democratic Triumphs and Trials." In *Southeast Asia Affairs, 2010*, edited by Daljit Singh, 113–17. Singapore: Institute of Southeast Asian Studies, 2010.

Atran, Scott, and Jeremy Ginges. "Religious and Sacred Imperatives in Human Conflict." *Science* 336, no. 6083 (2012): 855–57.

Austin, Granville. *The Indian Constitution: Cornerstone of a Nation*. New Delhi: Oxford University Press, 1999.

Babb, Sarah L. *Managing Mexico: Economists from Nationalism to Neoliberalism*. Princeton: Princeton University Press, 2001.

Bailey, April H. and Spencer D. Kelly. "Body Posture and Gender Impact Neural Processing of Power-Related Words." *The Journal of Social Psychology* 157, no. 4 (2017): 474–84.

Banerjee, A. V., Donald P. Green, Jeffery McManus, and Rohini Pande. "Are Poor Voters Indifferent to Whether Elected Leaders Are Criminal or Corrupt? A Vignette Experiment in Rural India." *Political Communication* 31, no. 3 (July–September 2014): 391–407.

Banerjee, Abhijit, Rema Hanna, and Sendhil Mullainathan. "Corruption." In *Handbook of Organizational Economics*, edited by Robert Gibbons and John Roberts, 1109–47. Princeton: Princeton University Press, 2013.

Bansal, Rashmi. *I Have a Dream: The Inspiring Stories of 20 Social Entrepreneurs Who Found New Ways to Solve Old Problems*. New Delhi: Westland Ltd., 2011.

Bardhan, Pranab. *The Political Economy of Development in India*. Oxford: Blackwell, 1984.

Baru, Sanjaya. "India and the World: The Economics and Politics of the Manmohan Singh Doctrine in Foreign Policy." ISAS Working Paper No. 53, Institute of South Asian Studies, National University of Singapore, 14 November 2008.

Basweden, Anies. "Indonesian Politics in 2007: The Presidency, Local Elections, and the Future of Democracy." *Bulletin of Indonesian Economic Studies* 43, no. 3 (2007): 323–40.

Bawn, K. "Money and Majorities in the Federal Republic of Germany: Evidence for a Veto Players Model of Government Spending." *American Journal of Political Science* 43, no. 3 (1999): 707–36.

Beckert, Jens. "What Is Sociological about Economic Sociology? Uncertainty and the Embeddedness of Economic Action." *Theory and Society* 25, no. 6 (1996): 803–40.

Beland, Daniel. "The Idea of Power and the Role of Ideas." *Political Studies Review* 8, no. 2 (2010): 145–54.

———. "The Politics of Social Learning: Finance, Institutions, and Pension Reform in the United States and Canada." *An International Journal of Policy, Administration, and Institutions* 19, no. 4 (2006): 559–83.

Beland, Daniel, and Robert Henry Cox, eds. *Ideas and Politics in Social Science Research*. New York: Oxford University Press, 2011.

Bennett, Andrew, and Jeffrey T. Checkel, eds. *Process Tracing: From Metaphor to Analytic Tool*. New York: Cambridge University Press, 2015.

Berman, Sheri. "Ideology, History, and Politics." In *Ideas and Politics in Social Science Research*, edited by Daniel Béland and Robert Henry Cox, 105–26. New York: Oxford University Press, 2010.

———. *The Social Democratic Moment: Ideas and Politics in the Making of Interwar Europe*. Cambridge, MA: Harvard University Press, 1998.

Bermeo, Nancy. "Myths of Moderation: Confrontation and Conflict during Democratic Transitions." *Comparative Politics*, Transitions to Democracy: A Special Issue in Memory of Dankwart A. Rustow, 29, no. 3 (1997): 305–22.

Bevir, Mark. "Governance and Interpretation: What Are the Implications of Postfoundationalism?" *Public Administration* 82, no. 3 (2004): 605–25.

Bhagwati, Jagdish, and Arvind Panagariya. *Why Growth Matters: How Economic Growth in India Reduced Poverty and the Lessons for Other Developing Countries*. New York: Public Affairs, 2013.

Bhargava, Rajeev. "What Is Indian Secularism and What Is It For?" *India Review* 1, no. 1 (January, 2002): 1–32.

Bhattacharjea, Ajit. *Jayaprakash Narayan: A Political Biography*. New Delhi: Vikas Publishing House, 1978.

Birnir, Johanna, and Nil Satana. "Religion and Coalition Politics." *Comparative Political Studies* 46, no. 1 (2013): 3–30.

Blakeslee, David. "Politics and Public Goods in Developing Countries: Evidence from the Assassination of Rajiv Gandhi." *Journal of Public Economics* 163 (July 2018): pp 1–19.

Blyth, Mark. *Austerity: The History of a Dangerous Idea*. New York: Oxford University Press, 2013.

———. *Great Transformations: Economic Ideas and Institutional Change in the Twentieth Century*. New York: Cambridge University Press, 2002.

———. "Powering, Puzzling, or Persuading? The Mechanisms of Building Institutional Orders." *International Studies Quarterly* 51, no. 4 (December 2007): 761–77.

———. "Structures Do Not Come with an Instruction Sheet: Interests, Ideas, and Progress in Political Science." *Perspectives on Politics* 1, no. 4 (December 2003): 695–706.

Boix, Carles. *Democracy and Redistribution*. Cambridge: Cambridge University Press, 2003.

Bolton, G. E., A. Ockenfels, and J. Stauf, "Social Responsibility Promotes Conservative Risk Behavior." *European Economic Review* 74, no. C (2015), 109–27.

Bougheas, S., J. Nieboer, and M. Sefton, "Risk Taking and Information Aggregation in Groups." *Journal of Economic Psychology* 51 (2015) 34–47.

Bourdieu, Pierre. *In Other Words: Essays toward a Reflexive Sociology*. Stanford: Stanford University Press, 1990.

———. *Masculine Domination*. Translated by Richard Nice. Stanford: Stanford University Press, 2002.

———. *Pascalian Meditations*. Translated by Richard Nice. Stanford: Stanford University Press, 2000.

Brady, Henry, and David Collier. *Rethinking Social Inquiry: Diverse Tools, Shared Standards*. 2nd edition. Lanham: Rowman & Littlefield, 2010.

Brass, Paul. *Factional Politics in an Indian State: The Congress Party in Uttar Pradesh*. Berkeley: University of California, 1965.

Brender, Adi, and Allan Drazen. "Political Budget Cycles in New versus Established Democracies." *Journal of Monetary Economics* 52, no. 7 (October 2005): 1271–95.

Brubaker, Rogers. "Why Populism?" *Theory and Society* 46, no 5 (2017): 357–85.

Burean, Toma, and Raluca Popp. "The Ideological Mapping of Political Parties in Romania." *Romanian Journal of Society and Politics* 10, no. 1 (2015): 118–36.

Burgis, Tom. *The Looting Machine: Warlords, Oligarchs, Corporations, Smugglers, and the Theft of Africa's Wealth*. London: Harper Collins, 2015.

Bussell, Jennifer. *Clients and Constituents: Political Responsiveness in Patronage Democracies*. New York: Oxford University Press, 2019.

———. *Corruption and Reform in India: Public Services in the Digital Age*. New York: Cambridge University Press, 2012.

Cammett, Melani. *Compassionate Communalism: Welfare and Sectarianism in Lebanon.* Ithaca: Cornell University Press, 2014.

Campbell, John. "Ideas, Politics, and Public Policy." *Annual Review of Sociology* 28 (2002): 21–38.

Capelos, Tereza and Stavroula Chrona. "Islamist and Nationalistic Attachments as Determinants of Political Preferences in Turkey." *Perceptions* 17, no. 3 (Autumn, 2012): 51–80.

Carkoglu, Ali, and Melvin Hinich. "A Spatial Analysis of Turkish Party Preferences." *Electoral Studies* 25, no. 2 (2006): 369–92.

Carothers, Thomas. "The End of the Transition Paradigm." *Journal of Democracy* 13, no. 1 (January 2002): 5–21.

Carras, Mary. *Indira Gandhi: In the Crucible of Leadership.* Boston: Beacon Press, 1979.

Carroll, Royce, and Gary Cox. "Shadowing Ministers: Monitoring Partners in Coalition Governments." *Comparative Political Studies* 45, no. 2 (2012): 220–36.

Carstensen, Martin, and Vivien Schmidt. "Power Through, Over, and In Ideas: Conceptualizing Ideational Power in Discursive Institutionalism." *Journal of European Public Policy* 23, no. 3 (2016): 318–37.

Case, William. "Malaysia in 2013: A Benighted Election Day (and Other Events)." *Asian Survey* 54, no. 1 (2014): 56–63.

Caselli, F., and W. J. Coleman. "On The Theory of Ethnic Conflict." *Journal of the European Economic Association* 11, no. 1 (2013): 161–92.

Centeno, Miguel Angel. *Democracy without Reason: Technocratic Revolution in Mexico.* University Park: Pennsylvania State University Press, 1994.

Centre for Budget and Governance Accountability. "How Did the UPA Spend Our Money? An Assessment of Expenditure Priorities of Resource Mobilisation Efforts of the UPA Government." CBGA, New Delhi, www.cbgaindia.org, 2009.

Chandra, Bipan. *In the Name of Democracy: JP Movement and the Emergency.* New Delhi: Penguin Books, 2003.

Chandra, Kanchan. "Counting Heads: A Theory of Voter and Elite Behavior in Patronage-Democracies." In *Patrons, Clients and Policies*, edited by Herbert Kitschelt and Steven Wilkinson, 84–109. Cambridge: Cambridge University Press, 2007.

———, ed. *Democratic Dynasties: State, Party, and Family in Contemporary Indian Politics.* New Delhi: Cambridge University Press, 2016.

———. "The New Indian State: The Relocation of Patronage in the Post-Liberalisation Economy." *Economic and Political Weekly* 1, no. 41 (October 10, 2015): 46–58.

———. *Why Ethnic Parties Succeed: Patronage and Ethnic Head Counts in India.* New York: Cambridge University Press, 2004.

Chatterjee, Partha. *The Politics of the Governed: Reflections on Popular Politics in Most of the World.* New York: Columbia University Press, 2004.

Chatterji, Bhola. *Conflict in JP's Politics.* New Delhi: Ankur Publishing House, 1984.

Chaudhri, Kaushik, and Sugato Dasgupta. "The Political Determinants of Central Governments' Economic Policies in India: An Empirical Investigation." *Journal of International Development* 17, no. 7 (2005): 957–78.

Chaudhuri, Rudra. "Re-reading the Indian Emergency: Britain, the United States and India's Constitutional Autocracy, 1975–1977." *Diplomacy and Statecraft* 29, no. 3 (2018): 477–98.

Chayes, Sarah. *Thieves of State: Why Corruption Threatens Global Security.* New York: W. W. Norton & Co., 2015.

Chhibber, Pradeep, and Ken Kollman. *The Formation of National Party Systems: Federalism and Party Competition in Canada, Great Britain, India, and the United States.* Princeton: Princeton University Press, 2004.

Chhibber, Pradeep, and Rahul Verma. *Ideology and Identity: The Changing Party Systems of India.* New York: Oxford University Press, 2018.

Chhibber, Pradeep, Sandeep Shastri, and Richard Sisson. "Federal Arrangements and the Provision of Public Goods in India." *Asian Survey* 44 (June 2004): 339–52.

Chin, James and Joern Dosch. *Malaysia Post-Mahathir: A Decade of Change.* Singapore: Marshall Cavendish International, 2015.

Cinar, Menderes. "Turkey's Transformation under the AKP Rule." *The Muslim World* 96, no. 3 (2006): 469–86.

Clithero, J. A. and A. Rangel. "Informatic Parcellation of the Network Involved in the Computation of Subjective Value." *Social Cognitive and Affective Neuroscience* 9, no. 9 (2014): 1289–302.

Cole, Shawn A. "Fixing Market Failures or Fixing Elections? Elections, Banks, and Agricultural Lending in India." *American Economic Journal: Applied Economics* 1, no. 1 (2009): 219–50.

Collingwood, R. G. *My Autobiography.* Oxford: Oxford University Press, 1939.

Cornell, Svante E., and M. K. Kaya. "The Naqshbandi-Khalidi Order and Political Islam in Turkey." Current Trends in Islamist Ideology, Hudson Institute, September 3, 2015. https://bit.ly/39hU2oW (accessed 1 October 2020).

Cowley, Philip. *Revolts and Rebellions: Parliamentary Voting under Blair.* London: Politico, 2002.

Cox, Robert Henry. "The Social Construction of an Imperative: Why Welfare Reform Happened in Denmark and the Netherlands but Not in Germany." *World Politics* 53, no. 3 (2001): 463–98.

Crabtree, James. *Billionaire Raj: A Journey through India's New Gilded Age.* New York: Penguin Random House, 2018.

Dahl, Robert. *Democracy and Its Critics*. New Haven and London: Yale University Press, 1989.

———. *Polyarchy: Participation and Opposition*. New Haven: Yale University Press, 1971.

Davies, P. H. J. "Spies as Informants: Triangulation and Interpretation of Elite Interview Data in the Study of Intelligence and Security Services." *Politics* 21, no. 1 (2001): 73–80.

De Cleen, Benjamin. "Populism and Nationalism." In *The Oxford Handbook of Populism*, edited by C. R. Kaltwasser, Paul Taggart, Cristóbal Rovira Kaltwasser, Paul Taggart, Paulina Ochoa Espejo, and Pierre Ostiguy, 341–62. Oxford: Oxford University Press, 2017.

De Winter, L., A. Timmermans, and P. Dumont. "Belgium: On Government Agreements, Evangelists, Followers and Heretics." In *Coalition Governments in Western Europe*, edited by W.C. Muller and K. Strom, 300–55. Oxford: Oxford University Press, 2000.

Dencik, Lina, and Oliver Leistert, eds. *Critical Perspectives on Social Media and Protest: Between Control and Emancipation*. London: Rowman & Littlefield, 2015.

Dhar, P. N. *Indira Gandhi, the "Emergency," and Indian Democracy*. New Delhi: Oxford University Press, 2000.

Downs, A. "An Economic Theory of Political Action in a Democracy." *The Journal of Political Economy* 65, no. 2 (1957): 135–50.

Drèze, Jean. "Distribution Matters in Cost–Benefit Analysis." *Journal of Public Economics* 70, no. 3 (1998): 485–88.

———. "Economic Development, Public Action, and Social Progress." *Canadian Journal of Development Studies* 15, no. 3 (December 1994): 329–46.

Drèze, Jean, and Amartya Sen. *An Uncertain Glory: India and Its Contradictions*. Princeton: Princeton University Press, 2013.

———. *Hunger and Public Action*. Oxford: Oxford University Press, 1989.

———. *India: Development and Participation*. New Delhi: Oxford University Press, 2002.

Dunning, Thad. *Crude Democracy: Natural Resource Wealth and Political Regimes*. Cambridge: Cambridge University Press, 2008.

Duverger, Maurice. *Political Parties, Their Organization and Activity in the Modern State*. Translated by Barbara and Robert North. New York: John Wiley & Sons, Inc., 1954.

Economic Advisory Council to the Prime Minister. *Economic Outlook 2011/12*. New Delhi: Government of India, July 2011. https://bit.ly/2Ydu2Vr (accessed January 17, 2021).

Elster, Jon. "Rational Choice History: A Case of Excessive Ambition." *American Political Science Review* 94, no. 3 (2000): 685–95.

Eyal, Gil. "For a Sociology of Expertise: The Social Origins of the Autism Epidemic." *American Journal of Sociology* 118, no. 4 (January 2013): 863–907.

Faraz, Naseem, and Marc Rockmore. "Election Cycles in Public Credit: Credit Provision and Default Rates in Pakistan." *Journal of Development Economics* 147 (2020).

Farooqui, Adnan. "Political Representation of a Minority: Muslim Representation in Contemporary India." *India Review* 19, no. 2 (2020): 153–75.

Fearon, James. "Why Ethnic Politics and 'Pork' Tend to Go Together." Presented at the SSRC-MacArthur sponsored conference on "Ethnic Politics and Democratic Stability," University of Chicago, 1999.

Fehr, E. and C. F. Camerer, "Social Neuroeconomics: The Neural Circuitry of Social Preferences." *Trends in Cognitive Sciences* 11, no. 10 (2007): 419–27.

Fehr, Ernst, Holger Herz, and Tom Wilkening. "The Lure of Authority: Motivation and Incentive Effects of Power." *American Economic Review* 103, no. 4 (2013): 1325–59.

Fella, Stefano, and Carlo Ruzza. "Populism and the Fall of the Centre-Right in Italy: The End of the Berlusconi Model or a New Beginning?" *Journal of Contemporary European Studies* 21, no. 1 (2013): 38–52.

Feyerabend, Paul. *Against Method*. London: Verso, 2010.

Fossen, T. "Constructivism and the Logic of Political Representation." *American Political Science Review* 113, no 3 (2019): 824–37.

Franck, R., and I. Rainer. "Does the Leader's Ethnicity Matter? Ethnic Favoritism, Education, and Health in Sub-Saharan Africa." *American Political Science Review* 106, no. 2 (2012): 294–325.

Frankel, Francine. *India's Political Economy, 1947–2004*. New York: Oxford University Press, 2005.

Fukuyama, Francis. "America in Decay." *Foreign Affairs* 93, no. 5 (September 2014): 5–26.

———. *Identity: The Demand for Dignity and Politics of Resentment*. New York: Farrar, Straus and Giroux, 2018.

Galinsky, Adam D., Joe C. Magee, M. Ena Inesi, and Deborah H. Gruenfeld. "Power and Perspectives Not Taken." *Psychological Science* 17, no. 12 (2006): 1068–74.

Galinsky, Adam, and J. Magee. "Social Hierarchy: The Self-Reinforcing Nature of Power and Status." *The Academy of Management Annals* 2, no. 1 (2008): 351–98.

Gandhi, Aditi, and Michael Walton. "Where Do India's Billionaires Get Their Wealth?" *Economic and Political Weekly* 47, no. 40 (October 6, 2012): 10–14.

Gandhi, Indira. *Democracy and Discipline: Speeches of Shrimati Indira Gandhi*. New Delhi: Indraprashta Press, 1975.

———. *My Truth*. New Delhi: Orient Paperbacks, 2013.

———. *Selected Speeches and Writings of Indira Gandhi*. Vol. 2 (August 1969–August 1972). New Delhi: Publications Division, Ministry of Information and Broadcasting, Government of India, 1975.

———. *Selected Speeches and Writings of Indira Gandhi*. Vol. 3 (September 1972–March 1977). New Delhi: Publications Division, Ministry of Information and Broadcasting, Government of India, 1984.

———. *Speeches and Writings*. New York: Harper & Row, 1975.

Gandhi, Indira, and Dorothy Norman. *Indira Gandhi: Letters to an American Friend, 1950–1984*. San Diego: Harcourt Brace Jovanovich Publishers, 1985.

Gandhi, Jennifer. *Political Institutions under Dictatorship*. New York: Cambridge University Press, 2008.

Geertz, Clifford. "Thick Description: Toward an Interpretive Theory of Culture." In *The Interpretation of Cultures: Selected Essays*, 3–30. New York: Basic Books, 1973.

Gehlbach, Scott, and Edmund Malesky. "The Contribution of Veto Players to Economic Reform." *The Journal of Politics* 72, no. 4 (2010): 957–75.

Gehlbach, Scott, and Philip Keefer. "Investment without Democracy: Ruling-Party Institutionalization and Credible Commitment in Autocracies." *Journal of Comparative Economics* 39, no. 2 (2011): 123–39.

George, Alexander, and Andrew Bennett. *Case Studies and Theory Development in the Social Sciences*. Cambridge, MA: The MIT Press, 2005.

Gerring, John. *Case Study Research: Principles and Practices*. New York: Cambridge University Press, 2006.

Geuss, Raymond. *The Idea of a Critical Theory*. Cambridge: Cambridge University Press, 1981.

Giugni, M., D. McAdam, and C. Tilly, eds. *How Movements Matter: Theoretical and Comparative Studies in the Consequences of Social Movements*. Minneapolis: University of Minnesota Press, 1999.

Golwalkar, M. S. *We or Our Nationhood Defined*. New Delhi: K. Prakshan, 1947 [1939].

Goodwin, Doris Kearns. *Team of Rivals: The Political Genius of Abraham Lincoln*. New York: Simon and Schuster, 2005.

Green, Duncan. *From Poverty to Power: How Active Citizens and Effective States Can Change the World*. Oxford: Oxfam International, 2008.

Grewal, Sharan. "Military Defection during Localized Protests: The Case of Tataouine." *International Studies Quarterly* 63, no. 2 (2019): 259–69.

Grimshaw, Damian, and Jill Rubery. "The End of the UK's Liberal Collectivist Model? The Implications of the Coalition Government's Policy during the Austerity Crisis." *Cambridge Journal of Economics* 36, no. 1 (2012): 105–26.

Guha, Ramachandra. *India After Gandhi: The History of the World's Largest Democracy*. New York: Harper Perennial, 2008.

———. *Patriots and Partisans*. New Delhi: Penguin Books, 2013.

Gumuscu, Sebnem. "The Clash of Islamists: The Crisis of the Turkish State and Democracy." Contemporary Turkish Politics Workshop, Baker Institute, Rice University, 2016.

Gupta, Akhil. *Red Tape: Bureaucracy, Structural Violence, and Poverty in India.* New Delhi: Orient Blackswan, 2012.

Hafez, Mohammed. "Fratricidal Rebels: Ideological Extremity and Warring Factionalism in Civil Wars." *Terrorism and Political Violence* 32, no. 3 (2017): 604–29.

Haksar, P. N. *Premonitions.* Bombay: Interpress, 1979.

Hall, Peter. "Policy Paradigms, Social Learning, and the State: The Case for Economic Policymaking in Britain." *Comparative Politics* 25, no. 3 (1993): 275–96.

———. "The Economics and Politics of the Euro Crisis." *German Politics* 21, no. 4 (2012): 355–71.

Hall, Peter, and Rosemary Taylor. "Political Science and the Three New Institutionalisms." *Political Studies* 44, no. 5 (December 1996): 936–57.

Hallerberg, Mark. "The Role of Parliamentary Committees in the Budgetary Process within Europe." In *Institutions, Politics, and Fiscal Policy*, edited by R.R. Strauch and J. von Hagen, 87–106. Boston: Kluwer, 2000.

Hamilton, Alexander, John Jay, and James Madison. *The Federalist Papers.* Springville, UT: Sweetwater Press, 2010.

Harris-White, Barbara, and Anushree Sinha, eds. *Trade Liberalization and India's Informal Economy.* New Delhi: Oxford University Press, 2007.

Hasan, Zoya. *Congress after Indira: Policy, Power, Political Change (1984–2009).* New Delhi: Oxford University Press, 2012.

Hawkins, Kirk, Madeleine Read, and Teun Pauwels. "Populism and Its Causes." In *The Oxford Handbook of Populism*, edited by C. R. Kaltwasser, Paul Taggart, Cristóbal Rovira Kaltwasser, Paul Taggart, Paulina Ochoa Espejo, and Pierre Ostiguy, 267–86. Oxford: Oxford University Press, 2017.

Held, D., and A. McGrew, eds. *The Global Transformation Reader.* Cambridge: Polity Press, 2000.

Herrera, Yoshiko. *Imagined Economies: The Sources of Russian Regionalism.* New York: Cambridge University Press, 2005.

Hirschman, Alberto O. "The Search for Paradigms of a Hindrance to Understanding." *World Politics* 22, no. 3 (1970): 329–43.

Hobbes, Thomas. *Leviathan.* New York: Penguin Books, 1982.

Homans, George Caspar. *Social Behavior: Its Elementary Forms.* London: Routledge Press, 1974.

Human Rights Watch (HRW). "'Shoot the Traitors': Discrimination against Muslims under India's New Citizenship Policy." HRW report, April 9, 2020. https://bit.ly/3mChYHw (accessed October 1, 2020).

Iyer, Lakshmi, and Anandi Mani. "Traveling Agents: Political Change and Bureaucratic Turnover in India." *Review of Economics and Statistics* 94, no. 3 (2012): 723–39.

Jabko, N. *Playing the Market: Political Strategy for Uniting Europe, 1985–2005*. Ithaca: Cornell University Press, 2007.

Jacobs, Alan. *Governing for the Long Term: Democracy and the Politics of Investment*. New York: Cambridge University Press, 2011.

———. "Process Tracing the Effects of Ideas." In *Process Tracing: From Metaphor to Analytic Tool*, edited by Andrew Bennett and Jeffrey T. Checkel, 41–73. New York: Cambridge University Press, 2015.

Jaffrelot, Christophe. "Refining the Moderation Thesis: Two Religious Parties and Indian Democracy—The Jana Sangh and the BJP between Hindutva Radicalism and Coalition Politics." *Democratization* 20, no. 5 (2013): 876–94.

———. "The First Reign of Indira Gandhi: Socialism, Populism, and Authoritarianism." In *India Since 1950: Society, Politics, Economy and Culture*, edited by Christophe Jaffrelot, 24–40. New Delhi: Yatra Books, 2012.

———. *The Hindu Nationalist Movement in India*. New York: Columbia University Press, 1998.

———. "The Political Guru: The Guru as Eminence Grise." In *The Guru in South Asia: New Interdisciplinary Perspectives*, edited by Jacob Copeman and Aya Ikegame, 80–96. New York: Routledge Press, 2012.

Jaffrelot, Christophe and Louise Tillin, "Populism in India." In *The Oxford Handbook of Populism*, edited by Cristóbal Rovira Kaltwasser, Paul Taggart, Paulina Ochoa Espejo, and Pierre Ostiguy, 179–94. Oxford: Oxford University Press, 2017.

Jaffrelot, Christophe and Pratinav Anil. *India's First Dictatorship: The Emergency, 1975–77*. London: Hurst & Co., 2020.

Jalal, Ayesha. *Democracy and Authoritarianism in South Asia: Comparative and Historical Perspective*. Cambridge: Cambridge University Press, 1995.

Jayakar, Pupul. *Indira Gandhi: A Biography*. New Delhi: Penguin Books, 1992.

Jha, Prashant. *How the BJP Wins: Inside India's Greatest Election Machine*. New Delhi: Juggernaut, 2017.

Jha, Rajani Ranjan. *Lokayukta: The Indian Ombudsman*. Varanasi: Rishi Publications, 1990.

Johnson, Chalmers. *MITI and the Japanese Miracle: The Growth of Industrial Policy, 1925–1975*. Stanford: Stanford University Press, 1982.

Kagan, Robert. "The Weight of Geopolitics." *Journal of Democracy* 26, no. 1 (January 2015): 21–31.

Kahneman, Daniel, and Amos Tversky, *Thinking Fast and Slow*. New York: Farrar, Straus and Giroux, 2011.

Kalaycioglu, Ersin. "Justice and Development Party at the Helm: Resurgence of Islam or Restitution of the Right-of-Center Predominant Party." *Turkish Studies* 11, no. 1 (2010): 29–44.

Kapoor, Coomi. *The Emergency: A Personal History.* New Delhi: Penguin Books, 2015.

Kapur, Devesh, Milan Vaishnav, and Neelanjan Sircar. "The Importance of Being Middle Class in India." 2017.https://carnegieendowment.org/2017/11/03/importance-of-being-middle-class-in-india-pub-74615 (accessed October 1, 2020).

Kapur, Devesh. *Diaspora, Development, and Democracy: The Domestic Impact of International Migration from India.* Princeton: Princeton University Press, 2010.

———. "Explaining Democratic Durability and Economic Performance: The Role of India's Institutions." In *Public Institutions in India: Performance and Design*, edited by Devesh Kapur and Pratap Bhanu Mehta, 28–76. New Delhi: Oxford University Press, 2005.

Karanjia, Rustom Khurshedji. *Indira–J.P. Confrontation: The Great Debate.* New Delhi: Chetana Publications, 1975.

Katzenstein, Peter, and Rudra Sil. *Beyond Paradigms: Analytic Eclecticism in World Politics.* New York: Palgrave Macmillan, 2010.

Kaushik, Arun, and Rupayan Pal. "Political Strongholds and Budget Allocation for Developmental Expenditure: Evidence from Indian States, 1971–2005." Mimeo, Indira Gandhi Institute of Development Research, 2012.

Keats, John. *The Letters of John Keats.* Edited by H. E. Rollins. Cambridge: Cambridge University Press, 1958 [1817].

Keefer, P., and D. Stasavage. "The Limits of Delegation: Veto Players, Central Bank Independence, and the Credibility of Monetary Policy." *American Political Science Review* 97, no. 3 (2003): 407–23.

Kejriwal, Arvind. *Swaraj.* New Delhi: Harper Collins India, 2012.

Kessler, Clive. "Malaysia's GE13: What Happened, What Now?" *Aliran Monthly* 33, no. 4 (2013): 9–14.

Khatkhate, Deena. "Looking Back in Anger." *Economic and Political Weekly* 38, nos. 51–52 (December 27, 2003): 5350–53.

Khemani, S. "Political Cycles in a Developing Economy: Effect of Elections in the Indian States." *Journal of Development Economics* 73, no. 1 (2004): 125–54.

Kim, D., and G. Loewenberg. "The Role of Parliamentary Committees in Coalition Governments: Keeping Tabs on Coalition Partners in the German Bundestag." *Comparative Political Studies* 38, no. 1 (2005): 104–29.

Kincaid, Harold. *Philosophical Foundations of the Social Sciences: Analyzing Controversies in Social Research.* Cambridge: Cambridge University Press, 1996.

Kissinger, Henry. *Diplomacy.* New York: Simon and Schuster, 1994.

Kitschelt, Herbert, and Steven Wilkinson, eds. *Patrons, Clients, and Policies: Patterns of Democratic Accountability and Political Competition.* Cambridge: Cambridge University Press, 2009.

Kjaer, P., and O. Pedersen. "Translating Liberalization: Neoliberalism in the Danish Negotiated Economy." In *The Rise of Neoliberalism and Institutional Analysis*, edited by J. L. Campbell and O. Pedersen, 219–48. Princeton: Princeton University Press, 2001.

Knight, Frank. *Risk, Uncertainty, and Profit.* Eastford: Martino Fine Books, 2014 [1921].

Knight, Kathleen. "Transformations of the Concept of Ideology in the Twentieth Century." *American Political Science Review* 100, no. 4 (2006): 619–26.

Kochanek, Stanley. "Briefcase Politics in India: The Congress Party and the Business Elite." *Far Eastern Survey* 27, no. 12 (1987): 1278–301.

Kohli, Atul. *Democracy and Development in India: From Socialism to Pro-Business.* New Delhi: Oxford University Press, 2010.

———. *State-Directed Development: Political Power and Industrialization in the Global Periphery.* Cambridge: Cambridge University Press, 2004.

———. *The Success of India's Democracy.* New York: Cambridge University Press, 2001.

Kothari, Rajni. *Politics in India.* New Delhi: Orient Blackswan, 1970.

———. "The Congress 'System' in India." *Asian Survey* 4, no. 12 (1964): 1161–73.

Krishna, Ananth. *India since Independence: Making Sense of Indian Politics.* New Delhi: Pearson, 2011.

Krishna, Anirudh. "Continuity and Change: The Indian Administrative Service 30 Years Ago and Today." *Commonwealth and Comparative Politics* 48, no. 4 (2010): 433–44.

Krueger, Anne O. "Trade Policy and Economic Development: How We Learn." *The American Economic Review* 87, no. 1 (1997): 1–22.

Kwak, James. *Economism: Bad Economics and the Rise of Inequality.* New York: Penguin Random House, 2017.

Kyle, Jordan, and Limor Gultchin. "Populists in Power around the World." Tony Blair Institute for Global Change, November 2018.

Lakatos, Imre. "The Methodology of Scientific Research Programmes." Edited by John Worrall and G. Currie. Cambridge: Cambridge University Press, 1978.

Lake, David. "Why 'Isms' Are Evil: Theory, Epistemology, and Academics Sects as Impediments for the Iraq War." *International Studies Quarterly* 55, no. 2 (2011): 7–52.

Lansford, Tom, ed. *Political Handbook of the World 2014.* Thousand Oaks: CQ Press, 2014.

Laver, Michael, and Kenneth Shepsle, eds. *Cabinet Minister and Parliamentary Government.* Cambridge: Cambridge University Press, 1994.

Laver, Michael, and Norman Schofield. *Multiparty Government: The Politics of Coalition in Europe.* Oxford: Oxford University Press, 1990.

Lavigne, R. "The Political and Institutional Determinants of Fiscal Adjustment: Entering and Exiting Fiscal Distress." *European Journal of Political Economy* 27, no. 1 (2011): 17–31.

Lawson, Letitia. "The Politics of Anti-Corruption Reform in Africa." *The Journal of Modern African Studies* 47, no. 1 (2009): 73–100.

Lee, Poh Ping. "Malaysia in 2015: A Denouement of Sorts for the Prime Minister." *Asian Survey* 56, no. 1 (2016): 101–07.

Leighton, Wayne, and Edward Lopez. *Madmen, Intellectuals, and Academic Scribblers: The Economic Engine of Political Change*. Stanford: Stanford University Press, 2012.

Levitsky, Steven, and Lucan Way. "The Myth of Democratic Recession." *Journal of Democracy* 26, no. 1 (January 2015): 45–58.

Lieberman, Evan. *Race and Regionalism in the Politics of Taxation in Brazil and South Africa*. Cambridge: Cambridge University Press, 2003.

Lijphart, Arend. "Consociational Theory: Problems and Prospects. A Reply." *Comparative Politics* 13, no. 3 (1981): 355–60.

———. *Patterns of Democracy: Government Forms and Performance in Thirty-Six Countries*. New Haven: Yale University Press, 1999.

Linz, Juan, and Alfred Stepan, eds. *The Breakdown of Democratic Regimes*. Baltimore: Johns Hopkins University Press, 1978.

Lipset, Seymour M., and Stein Rokkan. *Party Systems and Voter Alignments: Cross-National Perspectives*. New York: Free Press, 1967.

Little, I. M. D. *A Critique of Welfare Economics*. Oxford: Oxford University Press, 2003.

Lockwood, David. *The Communist Party of India and the Indian Emergency*. New Delhi: SAGE Publications, 2016.

Luce, Edward. *In Spite of Gods: The Strange Rise of Modern India*. London: Little, Brown, 2006.

Luebbert, Gregory. *Comparative Democracy: Policymaking and Governing Coalitions in Europe and Israel*. New York: Columbia University Press, 1986.

Lukes, Steven. *Power: A Radical View*. Basingstoke: Palgrave, 2005.

Mahoney, James, and Kathleen Thelen, eds. *Explaining Institutional Change: Ambiguity, Agency, and Power*. Cambridge: Cambridge University Press, 2010.

Malhotra, Inder. *Indira Gandhi: A Personal and Political Biography*. London: Coronet Books, 1991.

Manor, James. "Did the Central Government's Poverty Initiatives Help to Re-Elect It?" In *New Dimensions of Politics in India: The United Progressive Alliance in Power*, edited by Lawrence Saez and Gurharpal Singh, 13–25. London: Routledge Press, 2011.

———. "The Congress Party and the Great Transformation." In *Understanding India's New Political Economy*, edited by Sanjay Ruparelia, Sanjay Reddy, John Harriss, and Stuart Corbridge, 204–20. London: Routledge Press, 2011.

Marian, C., and R. F. King. "A War of Two Palaces: Semi-Presidential Government and Strategic Conflict." In *Romania under Basescu: Aspirations, Achievements, and Frustrations during His First Presidential Term*, edited by R.F. King and Paul Sum, 107–34. Lanham: Lexington Books, 2011.

———. "Perceiving the Line: The Relevance of the Left–Right Ideological Dimension for Voter Preferences in Romania." *Expert Electoral* 2 (2014): 3–18.

Martin, L. W., and G. Vanberg. "Coalition Policymaking and Legislative Review." *American Political Science Review* 99, no. 1 (2005): 93–106.

Masani, Minocheher Rustom. *Is J.P. the Answer?* Delhi: Macmillan Co. of India, 1975.

Matthijs, Matthias. *Ideas and Economic Crises in Britain from Attlee to Blair (1945–2005)*. London: Routledge, 2011.

McDonnell, Duncan, and Marco Valbruzzi. "Defining and Classifying Technocrat-Led and Technocrat Governments." *European Journal of Political Research* 53, no. 4 (2014): 654–71.

McGibbon, Rodd. "Indonesian Politics in 2006: Stability, Compromise, and Shifting Contests over Ideology." *Bulletin of Indonesian Economic Studies* 42, no. 3 (2006): 321–40.

McMillan, Alistair. "Deviant Democratization in India." *Democratization* 15, no. 4 (August 2008): 733–49.

McNamara, Kathleen and Matthias Matthijs. "The Euro Crisis' Theory Effect: Northern Saints, Southern Sinners, and the Demise of the Eurobond" *Journal of European Integration* 37, no. 2 (2015): 229–45.

Mehta, Jai. "The Varied Roles of Ideas in Politics." In *Ideas and Politics in Social Science Research*, edited by Daniel Béland and Robert Henry Cox, 25–36. New York: Oxford University Press, 2010.

Mehta, P. B., and M. Walton. "India's Political Settlement and Development Path." Mimeo, Centre for Policy Research and Harvard Kennedy School, 2012.

Mehta, Pratap Bhanu, and Michael Walton. "Ideas, Interests and the Politics of Development Change in India: Capitalism, Inclusion and the State." September 30, 2014, ESID Working Paper No. 36.

Melo, M., and C. Pereira. *Making Brazil Work: Checking the President in a Multiparty System*. London: Palgrave Macmillan, 2013.

Mill, John Stuart. *A System of Logic, Ratiocinative, and Inductive*. Vol. 1. Cambridge: Cambridge University Press, 2011.

Misra, Biswa Swarup. *Revisiting Regional Growth Dynamics in India in the Post Economic Reforms Period*. London: Palgrave Macmillan, 2013.

Mitra, Subrata K. "Desecularising the State: Religion and Politics in India after Independence." *Comparative Studies in Society and History* 33, no. 4 (October 1991): 755–77.

Mitropolitski, Simeon. "Balkan Politicians, Mostly Immune to the Influence of EU Integration." *Romanian Political Science Review* 14, no. 4 (2014): 367–84.

Monteiro, John. *Corruption: India's Painful Crawl to Lokpal.* Houston: Strategic Book Publishing and Rights Co., 2013 [1966].

Moraes, Dom. *Mrs. Gandhi.* London: Jonathan Cape, 1980.

Mudde, Cas. "The Populist Zeitgeist." *Government and Opposition* 39, no. 4 (2004): 541–63.

Mukherjee, Pranab. *The Dramatic Decade: The Indira Gandhi Years.* New Delhi: Rupa Publications, 2015.

Mukherji, Rahul. *Globalization and Deregulation: Ideas, Interests, and Institutional Change in India.* New Delhi: Oxford University Press, 2014.

Mungiu-Pippidi, Alina, Masa Loncaric, Bianca Vaz Mundo, Ana Carolina Braga, Michael Weinhardt, Angelica Solares, et al. "Contextual Choices for Results in Fighting Corruption." Commissioned by NORAD. Hertie School of Government, Berlin, 2011.

Murphy, R. O., and K. A. Ackermann. "Social Value Orientation: Theoretical and Measurement Issues in the Study of Social Preferences." *Personality and Social Psychology Review* 18, no. 1 (2014): 13–41.

Musil, Pelin A. "Emergence of a Dominant Party System after Multipartyism: Theoretical Implications from the Case of the AKP in Turkey." *South European Society and Politics* 20, no. 1 (2015): 71–92.

Naqvi, Saba. *Capital Conquest: How the AAP's Incredible Victory Has Redefined Indian Elections.* New Delhi: Hachette India, 2015.

Narayan, Jayaprakash. *Nation Building in India.* Ulan Press, 2012.

———. *Prison Diary 1975.* Edited by Amritlal Shah. Seattle: University of Washington Press, 1979.

———. "Total Revolution." In *Towards Total Revolution*, Vol. 4. Bombay: Popular Prakashan, 1978.

———. *Towards Total Revolution.* Bombay: Popular Prakashan, 1978.

Nayak, Pulin B. "Planning and Social Transformation: Remembering D.P. Dhar as a Social Planner." *Indian Economic Review*, New Series 50, no. 2 (July–December 2015).

Nayar, Kuldip. *The Judgment: Inside Story of the Emergency in India.* New Delhi: Vikas Publishing House, 1977.

Nehru, B. K. *Nice Guys Finish Second: Memoirs.* New Delhi: Viking, 1997.

Nooruddin, Irfan. *Coalition Politics and Economic Development: Credibility and the Strength of Weak Governments.* New York: Cambridge University Press, 2011.

North, Douglass C. *Institutions, Institutional Change, and Economic Performance.* Cambridge: Cambridge University Press, 1990.

Nurkse, Ragnar. *Equilibrium and Growth in the World Economy: Essays by Ragnar Nurske.* Edited by Gottfried Haberler and Robert M. Stern. Cambridge, MA: Harvard University Press, 1961.

O'Donnell, Madelene. "Post-Conflict Corruption: A Rule of Law Agenda?" In *Civil War and the Rule of Law*, edited by Agnes Hurwitz and Reyko Huang, 225–61. Boulder: Lynne Rienner, 2006.

Olken, Ben, and Rohini Pande. "Corruption in Developing Countries." *Annual Review of Economics* 4, no. 1 (2012): 479–509.

Oren, Karen and Stephen Skowronek. *The Search for American Political Development*. Cambridge: Cambridge University Press, 2004.

Orenstein, Mitchell. *Privatizing Pensions: The Transnational Campaign for Social Security Reform*. Princeton: Princeton University Press, 2008.

Orwell, George. *Notes on Nationalism*. London: Penguin Classics, 2018 [1945].

Ostergaard, Geoffrey. *Nonviolent Revolution in India*. New Delhi: Gandhi Peace Foundation, 1985.

Ozbudun, Ergun. "AKP at the Crossroads: Erdogan's Majoritarian Drift." *South European Society and Politics* 19, no. 2 (2014): 155–67.

Paige, J. T. "Indonesia Seven Years after Soeharto: Party System Institutionalization in a New Democracy." *Contemporary Southeast Asia* 28, no. 1 (2006): 88–114.

Palmier, L. *The Control of Bureaucratic Corruption: Case Studies in Asia*. New Delhi: Allied Publishers, 1985.

Parakh, P. C. *Crusader or Conspirator: Coalgate and Other Truths*. New Delhi: Manas Publications, 2014.

Persson, Anna, Bo Rothstein, and Jan Teorell. "A Failure of Anti-Corruption Policies: A Theoretical Mischaracterization of the Problem." The Quality of Government Paper Series. University of Gothenburg, Gothenburg, June 2010.

Persson, Torsten, Gerard Roland, and Guido Tabellini. "Separation of Powers and Political Accountability." *The Quarterly Journal of Economics* 112, no. 4 (1997): 1163–202.

Petit, P. "Why and How Philosophy Matters to Politics." In *Oxford Handbook of Contextual Political Studies*, edited by R. E. Goodin and C. Tilly, 35–57. Oxford: Oxford University Press, 2006.

Pilkington, Philip. *The Reformation in Economics: A Deconstruction and Reconstruction of Economic Theory*. London: Palgrave, 2016.

Pinto-Duschinsky, Michael. "Financing Politics: A Global View." *Journal of Democracy* 13, no. 4 (2002): 69–86.

Polsky, Andrew. "When Business Speaks: Political Entrepreneurship, Discourse, and Mobilization in American Partisan Regimes." *Journal of Theoretical Politics* 12, no. 4 (2000): 455–76.

Popper, Karl. *Conjectures and Refutations: The Growth of Scientific Knowledge*. London: Routledge Press, 1963.

Pouliot, Vincent. "Practice Tracing." In *Process Tracing: From Metaphor to Analytic Tool*, edited by Andrew Bennett and Jeffrey T. Checkel, 237–59. New York: Cambridge University Press, 2015.

Powell, Melchior, Dina Wafa, and Tim A. Mau, eds. *Corruption in a Global Context: Restoring Public Trust, Integrity, and Accountability.* London: Routledge, 2019.

Power, Timothy. "Continuity in a Changing Brazil: The Transition from Lula to Dilma." In *Brazil under the Workers' Party: Continuity and Change from Lula to Dilma*, edited by Fabio de Castro, Kees Koonings, and Marianne Wiesebron, 10–35. London: Palgrave, 2014.

Power, Timothy, and Matthew Taylor, eds. *Corruption and Democracy in Brazil: The Struggle for Accountability.* Notre Dame: University of Notre Dame Press, 2011.

Praino, Rodrigo, Daniel Stockemer, and Vincent G. Moscardelli. "The Lingering Effect of Scandals in Congressional Elections: Incumbents, Challengers, and Voters." *Social Science Quarterly* 94, no. 4 (2013): 1045–61.

Prakash, Gyan. *Emergency Chronicles: Indira Gandhi and Democracy's Turning Point.* Princeton: Princeton University Press, 2019.

Price, R. W. "The Political Economy of Fiscal Consolidation." OECD Economics Department Working Papers No. 776 (2010).

Pritchett, Lant. "Is India a Flailing State? Detours on the Four Lane Highway to Modernization." Working Paper Series RWP09-013, John F. Kennedy School of Government, Harvard University, Camnbridge, MA, 2009.

Pritchett, Lant, Kunal Sen, and Eric Werker, eds. *Deals and Development: The Political Dynamics of Growth Episodes.* Oxford: Oxford University Press, 2018.

Przeworski, Adam. *Crises of Democracy.* Cambridge: Cambridge University Press, 2019.

Przeworski, Adam, Michael Alvarez, Jose Cheibub, and Fernando Limongi. *Democracy and Development: Political Institutions and Well-Being in the World, 1950–1990.* Cambridge: Cambridge University Press, 2000.

Puri, Balraj. *Revolution, Counter-Revolution.* New Delhi: Newman Group of Publishers, 1978.

Qiu, H., Y. Zhang, G. Hou, and Z. Wang. "The Integrative Effects of Leading by Example and Follower Traits in Public Goods Game: A Multilevel Study." *Frontiers in Psychology* 9 (2018): 1687.

Raina, Ajay. "Why There Are No Partisan Turnovers in Malaysia: A Perspective." *Asian Survey* 56, no. 5 (2016): 833–58.

Ramesh, Jairam. *Intertwined Lives: P.N. Haksar and Indira Gandhi.* New Delhi: Simon and Schuster, 2018.

Reif, Linda. *The Ombudsman, Good Governance, and the International Human Rights System.* Leidan: Martinus Nijhoff, 2004.

Rodrik, Dani. "When Ideas Trump Interests: Preferences, Worldviews, and Policy Innovations." *Journal of Economic Perspectives* 28, no. 1 (Winter 2014): 189–208.

Rodrik, Dani, and Arvind Subramanian. "From 'Hindu Growth' to Productivity Surge: The Mystery of the Indian Growth Transition." *IMF Staff Papers* 52, no. 2 (2005): 193–228.

Roett, Riordan. *Brazil: What Everyone Needs to Know.* Oxford: Oxford University Press, 2016.

Rogoff, K. "Equilibrium Political Budget Cycles." *American Economic Review* 80, no. 1 (1990): 21–36.

Rom, S. C. and P. Conway, "The Strategic Moral Self: Self-Presentation Shapes Moral Dilemma Judgments." *Journal of Experimental Social Psychology*, 74 (2018): 24–37.

Rothstein, B. *Social Traps and the Problem of Trust.* Cambridge: Cambridge University Press, 2005.

Rudolph, Lloyd I., and Susanne Hoeber Rudolph. *In Pursuit of Lakshmi: The Political Economy of the Indian State.* Chicago: University of Chicago Press, 1987.

———. *The Modernity of Tradition: Political Development in India.* Chicago: University of Chicago Press, 1967.

Rudorf, Sarah, Katrin Schmelz, Thomas Baumgartner, Roland Wiest, Urs Fischbacher, and Daria Knoch. "Neural Mechanisms Underlying Individual Differences in Control-averse Behavior." *The Journal of Neuroscience* 38, no. 22 (2018): 5196–208.

Runciman, W. G. *Sociology in Its Place and Other Essays.* Cambridge: Cambridge University Press, 2010.

Ruparelia, Sanjay. *Divided We Govern: Coalition Politics in India.* New Delhi: Oxford University Press, 2015.

Saalfeld, T. "Institutions, Chance, and Choices: The Dynamics of Cabinet Survival." In *Cabinets and Coalition Bargaining: The Democratic Life Cycle in Western Europe*, edited by K. Strom, W. C. Muller, and T. Bergman, 327–68. Oxford: Oxford University Press, 2008.

Sahai, Shashi. *Lokpal Bill: Anna's Movement That Shook the World.* New Delhi: Kalpaz Publications, 2014.

Sahasrabuddhe, P. G. and M. C. Vajpayee. *The People versus Emergency: A Saga of Struggle.* New Delhi: Suruchi Prakashan, 1991.

Sahgal, Nayantara. *Indira Gandhi: Tryst with Power.* New Delhi: Penguin Books, 2012.

Sahin, Engin. "From the Declaration of the Republic to Present Presidential Election Methods in Turkey." *Turkish Journal of Politics* 4, no. 2 (Winter, 2013): 87–105.

Samaddar, Ranabir. *Crisis of 1974: Railway Strike and the Rank and File.* New Delhi: Primus Books, 2017.

Sandholtz, Wayne, and Mark M. Gray. "International Integration and National Corruption." *International Organization* 57, no. 4 (2003): 761–800.

Sardesai, Rajdeep. *2014: The Election That Changed India.* New Delhi: Penguin Books, 2014.

Sastry, Trolochan. "Towards Decriminalisation of Elections and Politics." *Economic and Political Weekly* 49, no. 1 (2014): 34–41.

Saurugger, Sabine. "Constructivism and Public Policy Approaches in the EU: From Ideas to Power Games." *Journal of European Public Policy* 20, no. 6 (2013): 888–906.

Savarkar, V. D. *Hindutva.* New Delhi: V. S. Prakashan, 1989 [1923].

Scarfe, Allan, and Wendy Scarfe. *J.P.: His Biography.* New Delhi: Orient Blackswan, 2014 [1975].

Schmidt, Vivien. *Democracy in Europe.* Oxford: Oxford University Press, 2006.

———. "Taking Ideas and Discourse Seriously: Explaining Change through Discursive Institutionalism as the Fourth 'New Institutionalism.'" *European Political Science Review* 2, no. 1 (2010): 1–25.

Sen, Amartya. *Choice, Welfare, and Measurement.* Oxford: Basil Blackwell, 1982.

———. *Identity and Violence.* New York: Norton & Co., 2006.

———. *Poverty and Famines: An Essay on Entitlement and Deprivation.* Oxford: Clarendon Press, 1981.

———. "Public Action for Social Security." In *Social Security in Developing Countries,* edited by E. Ahmad, 3–32. Oxford: Clarendon Press, 1990.

———. *Resources, Values, and Development.* Oxford: Basil Blackwell, 1984.

Sen, Amartya, and Jean Drèze. *India Economic Development and Social Opportunity.* Oxford: Oxford University Press, 1995.

Sen, Kunal. "Why Did the Elephant Start to Trot? India's Growth Acceleration Re-Examined." *Economic and Political Weekly* 42, no. 43 (2007): 37–47.

Sending, Ole Jacob. *The Politics of Expertise: Competing for Authority in Global Governance.* Ann Arbor: University of Michigan Press, 2015.

Sengupta, Arjun. "Financial Sector and Economic Reforms in India." *Economic and Political Weekly* 30, no. 1 (January 1995): 39–44.

Sezhiyan, Era, ed. *Shah Commission Report: Lost and Regained.* Chennai: Aazhi Publishers, 2010. (Copy available at the London School of Economics.)

Shah, Ghanshyam. *Protest Movements in Two Indian States: A Study of the Gujarat and Bihar Movements.* New Delhi: Ajanta Publications, 1977.

Shah, J. C. *Interim (and Final) Report(s).* Delhi, 1978. https://librarysearch.lse.ac.uk/primo-explore/fulldisplay/44LSE_ALMA_DS21124190800002021/44LSE_VU1. (Copy available at the London School of Economics.)

Shankar, Promila. *Gods of Corruption.* New Delhi: Manas Publications, 2015.

Sharada Prasad, H. Y. *The Book I Won't Be Writing and Other Essay.* New Delhi: Chronicle Books, 2003

Sharma, Mihir. *Restart: The Last Chance for the Indian Economy.* New Delhi: Random House India, 2015.

Sharma, Ruchir. *The Rise and Fall of Nations: Forces of Change in the Post-Crisis World.* New York: W. W. Norton & Co., 2016.

Shelef, Nadav G. *Evolving Nationalism: Homeland, Identity, and Religion in Israel, 1925–2005*. Ithaca: Cornell University Press, 2010.

Sherlock, Stephen. "The Parliament in Indonesia's Decade of Democracy: People's Forum or Chamber of Cronies." In *Problems of Democratisation in Indonesia: Elections, Institutions and Society*, edited by E. Aspinall and M. Mietzner, 160–78. Singapore: Institute of Southeast Asian Studies, 2010.

Sinclair, Betsy. *The Social Citizen*. Chicago: University of Chicago Press, 2012.

Singh, Daman. *Strictly Personal: Manmohan and Gursharan*. New Delhi: Harper Collins India, 2014.

Singh, Khushwant. *Indira Gandhi Returns*. New Delhi: Vision Books, 1979.

Singh, Manmohan. "Book Review: Jagdish Bhagwati and Padma Desai, India: Planning for Industrialization; Industrialization and Trade Policies since 1951 (Oxford University Press, 1970)." *The Indian Economic and Social History Review* 9, no. 4 (December 1972): 413–17.

———. *India's Export Trends and the Prospects for Self-Sustained Growth*. Oxford: Clarendon Press, 1964.

Sircar, Neelanjan. "The Politics of Vishwas: Political Mobilization in the 2019 National Election." *Contemporary South Asia*, 28, 2 (May 2020): 178–94.

Sitapati, Vinay. "What Anna Hazare and the Indian Middle-Class Say about Each Other." *Economic and Political Weekly* 46, no. 30 (2011).

Skocpol, Theda. *Protecting Soldiers and Mothers: The Political Origins of Social Policy in the United States*. Cambridge, MA: The Belknap Press of HUP, 1992.

Slaughter, Anne-Marie. *A New World Order*. Princeton: Princeton University Press, 2005.

Spiliopoulos, L., A. Ortmann, and L. Zhang. "Complexity, Attention, and Choice in Games under Time Constraints: A Process Analysis." *Journal of Experimental Psychology: Learning, Memory, and Cognition* 44, no. 10 (2018): 1609–40.

Sridharan, E., ed. *Coalition Politics in India: Selected Issues at the Centre and the States*. New Delhi: Academic Foundation, 2014.

———. "Principles, Power, and Coalition Politics in India: Lessons from Theory, Comparison, and Recent History." In *Principles, Power, and Politics*, edited by D. D. Khanna and Gert W. Kueck, 270–91. New Delhi: Macmillan Press, 1999.

Srivastava, C. P. *Corruption: India's Enemy Within*. New Delhi: Macmillan Press, 2001.

Stoiciu, Victoria. "Austerity and Structural Reforms in Romania: Severe Measures, Questionable Economic Results, and Negative Social Consequences." International Policy Analysis. Friedrich Ebert Stiftung, August, 2012. https://library.fes.de/pdf-files/id-moe/09310.pdf (accessed January 27, 2021).

Stokes, Susan. "Perverse Accountability: A Formal Model of Machine Politics with Evidence from Argentina." *The American Political Science Review* 99, no. 3 (August 2005): 315–25.

Streeck, Wolfgang, and K. Thelen, eds. *Beyond Continuity: Institutional Change in Advanced Political Economies.* Oxford: Oxford University Press, 2005.

Strøm, Kaare, Wolfgang C. Müller, and Daniel Markham Smith. "Parliamentary Control of Coalition Governments." *Annual Review of Political Science* 13, no. 1 (2010): 517–35.

Styczynska, Natasza. "Non-existence of Bulgarian Party-Based Euroscepticism: Why Should We Care?" *Politeja* 12, no. 33 (January 2015): 201–14.

Sukhtankar, Sandip. "The Impact of Corruption on Consumer Markets: Evidence from the Allocation of 2G Wireless Spectrum in India." *Journal of Law and Economics* 58, no. 1 (February 2015): 75–108.

Sukma, Rizal. "Indonesian Politics in 2009: Defective Elections, Resilient Democracy." *Bulletin of Indonesian Economic Studies* 45, no. 3 (2009): 317–36.

Suryadinata, L. "The Decline of the Hegemonic Party System in Indonesia: Golkar after the Fall of Soeharto." *Contemporary Southeast Asia* 29, no. 2 (2007): 333–58.

Suryadinata, Leo. "Pancasila and the Challenge of Political Islam: Past and Present." *Trends in Southeast Asia* 14 (2018): 1–20.

Swidler, Ann, and Susan Cotts Watkins. "Working Misunderstandings: Donors, Brokers, and Villagers in Africa's AIDS Industry." *Population and Development Review* 38, no. 1 (2013): 197–218.

Tandon, B. N. *PMO Diary-I: Prelude to the Emergency.* New Delhi: Konark Publishers, 2003.

Tansey, Oisin. "Process Tracing and Elite Interviewing: A Case for Non-Probability Sampling." *PS: Political Science and Politics* 40, no. 4 (October 2007): 765–72.

Tarlo, Emma. *Unsettling Memories: Narratives of the Emergency in Delhi.* Berkeley: University of California Press, 2003.

Tarrow, S. *Power in Movement: Social Movements and Contentious Politics.* New York: Cambridge University Press, 1998.

Tarrow, Sidney G. *Power in Movement.* 3rd edition (rev. and updated). Cambridge; New York: Cambridge University Press, 2011.

Tavares, J. "Does Right or Left Matter? Cabinets, Credibility, and Fiscal Adjustments." *Journal of Public Economics* 88, no. 12 (2004): 2447–68.

Tett, Gillian. *The Silo Effect: The Peril of Expertise and the Promise of Breaking Down Barriers.* New York: Simon and Schuster, 2016.

Thachil, Tariq. *Elite Parties, Poor Votes.* Cambridge: Cambridge University Press, 2014.

Thaler, Richard, and Cass Sunstein. *Nudge: Improving Decisions about Health, Wealth, and Happiness*. New Haven: Yale University Press, 2008.

Thaper, Raj. *All These Years: A Memoir*. New Delhi: Penguin Books, 1991.

The Forum for Human Rights in Jammu and Kashmir. "The Impact of the Lockdowns on Human Rights in Jammu and Kashmir, August 2019–July 2020." Report Co-Chairs: Justice Madan Lokur and Radha Kumar. https://bit.ly/3nm8dOZ (accessed October 1, 2020).

Tilly, Charles. *Social Movements, 1768–2004*. Boulder: Paradigm Publishers, 2004.

Transparency International, "Corruption Perceptions Index 2013." 2013.https://bit.ly/2pPOka8 (accessed October 1, 2020).

Tsebelis, George. *Veto Players: How Political Institutions Work*. Princeton: Princeton University Press, 2002.

Tsebelis, George, and Eunyoung Ha. "Coalition Theory: A Veto Players' Approach." *European Political Science Review* 6, no. 3 (2014): 331–57.

Tsingou, Eleni. "Power Elites and Club-Model Governance in Global Finance." *International Political Sociology* 8, no. 3 (September 2014): 340–42.

Tudor, Maya. *The Promise of Power: The Origins of Democracy in India and Autocracy in Pakistan*. Cambridge: Cambridge University Press, 2013.

Vaishnav, Milan, ed. *The BJP in Power: Indian Democracy and Religious Nationalism*. Washington, D.C.: Carnegie Endowment for International Peace, 2019.

———. *When Crime Pays: Money and Muscle in Indian Politics*. New Haven: Yale University Press, 2017.

Vaishnav, Milan, and Saksham Khosla. "The Indian Administrative Service Meets Big Data." Carnegie Endowment for International Peace, September 2016.

Valdés, Juan Gabriel. *Pinochet's Economists: The Chicago School of Economics in Chile*. New York: Cambridge University Press, 1995.

Van Evera, Stephen. *Guide to Methods for Students of Political Science*. Ithaca: Cornell University Press, 1997.

Varshney, Ashutosh. "Contested Meanings: India's National Identity, Hindu Nationalism, and the Politics of Anxiety." *Daedalus* 122, no. 3 (Summer 1993): 227–61.

———. *Ethnic Conflict and Civic Life: Hindus and Muslims in India*. Connecticut: Yale University Press, 2003.

———. "The Emergence of Right-Wing Populism in India." In *Re-Forming India: The Nation Today*, edited by Niraja Gopal Jayal, 327–45. New Delhi: Penguin Viking, 2019.

Venkataraman, Ramaswamy. *My Presidential Years*. New Delhi: South Asia Books, 1994.

Waldner, David, and Ellen Lust. "Unwelcome Change: Coming to Terms with Democratic Backsliding." *Annual Review of Political Science* 21 (2018): 93–113.

Walker, Lydia. "Jayaprakash Narayan and the Politics of Reconciliation for the Postcolonial State and Its Imperial Fragments." *The Indian Economic and Social History Review* 56, no. 2 (2019): 147–69.

Wapshott, Nicholas. *Keynes, Hayek: The Clash That Defined Modern Economics.* London and New York: W. W. Norton & Co., 2012.

Weiss, Meredith. "Malaysia's 13th General Elections: Same Result, Different Outcome." *Asian Survey* 53, no. 6 (2013): 1135–58.

Welch, Susan, and John Hibbing. "The Effects of Charges of Corruption on Voting Behavior in Congressional Elections, 1982–1990." *Journal of Politics* 59, no. 1 (1997): 226–39.

Wendt, Alexander. "The Agent-Structure Problem in International Relations Theory." *International Organization* 41, no. 3 (1987): 335–70.

Wilkinson, Steven. *Votes and Violence: Electoral Competition and Ethnic Riots in India.* New York: Cambridge University Press, 2004.

Woll, C. *Firm Interests.* Ithaca: Cornell University Press, 2008.

World Bank. "Reforming Public Services in India: Drawing Lessons From Success." Washington, DC: World Bank, 2006.

Wright, Joseph. "Do Authoritarian Institutions Constrain? How Legislatures Affect Economic Growth and Investment." *American Journal of Political Science* 52, no. 2 (2008): 322–43.

Yadav, Vineeta. *Political Parties, Business Groups, and Corruption in Developing Countries.* New York: Oxford University Press, 2011.

Yadav, Yogendra. "The Third Electoral System." *Seminar*, no. 480 (1999): 14–20.

Yadav, Yogendra, Suhas Palshikar, and K. C. Suri, eds. *Party Competition in Indian States: Electoral Politics in Post-Congress Polity.* New Delhi: Oxford University Press, 2014.

Yokoyama, R., Takayuki Nozawa, Motoaki Sugiura, Yukihito Yomogida, Hikaru Takeuchi, and Yoritaka Akimoto. "The Neural Bases Underlying Social Risk Perception in Purchase Decisions." *NeuroImage* 91 (2014): 120–28.

Yuda, Hanta. "Portrait of the Institutionalization of the Presidential System." *Indonesia 2006.* Jakarta: Indonesian Institute, 2007.

Zaidi, Moin, ed. *The Encyclopedia of the Indian National Congress.* Vol. 20, *1968–69: Facing the City Bosses.* New Delhi: Chand and Company Ltd., 1983.

Zakaria, Fareed. *The Future of Freedom: Illiberal Democracy at Home and Abroad.* New York: W. W. Norton & Co., 2007.

Zhang, Xiangyi, Xiyou Chen, Yue Gao, Yingjie Liu, and Yongfang Liu. "Self-Promotion Hypothesis: The Impact of Self-esteem on Self-other Discrepancies in Decision Making under Risk." *Personality and Individual Differences* 127 (2018): 26–30.

Ziblatt, Daniel. *Structuring the State: The Formation of Italy and Germany and the Puzzle of Federalism*. Princeton: Princeton University Press, 2006.

Ziblatt, Daniel, and Steven Levitsky. *How Democracies Die: What History Reveals about Our Future*. New York: Crown Press, 2018.

Ziblatt, Daniel, and Giovanni Capoccia. "The Historical Turn in Democratization Studies." *Comparative Political Studies* 43, nos. 8–9 (2010): 931–68.

Ziegfeld, Adam. "A New Dominant Party in India? Putting the 2019 BJP Victory into Comparative and Historical Perspective." *India Review* 19, no. 2 (2020): 136–52.

———. "Coalition Government and Party System Change: Explaining the Rise of Regional Political Parties in India." *Comparative Politics* 45, no. 1 (2012): 69–87.

Index